Seeing Fans

Seeing Fans

Representations of Fandom in Media and Popular Culture

Edited by

Lucy Bennett and Paul Booth

Bloomsbury Academic
An imprint of Bloomsbury Publishing Inc

B L O O M S B U R Y
NEW YORK · LONDON · OXFORD · NEW DELHI · SYDNEY

Bloomsbury Academic

An imprint of Bloomsbury Publishing Inc

1385 Broadway	50 Bedford Square
New York	London
NY 10018	WC1B 3DP
USA	UK

www.bloomsbury.com

BLOOMSBURY and the Diana logo are trademarks of Bloomsbury Publishing Plc

First published 2016
Paperback edition first published 2018

© Lucy Bennett and Paul Booth, 2016

Library of Congress Cataloging-in-Publication Data
A catalog record for this book is available from the Library of Congress.

ISBN: HB: 978-1-5013-1845-0
PB: 978-1-5013-3954-7
epub: 978-1-5013-1846-7
epdf: 978-1-5013-1847-4

Cover image : Photo by John Lamparski/Getty Images

Typeset by Integra Software Services Pvt. Ltd.

*Paul and Lucy dedicate this book to the amazing
community of fan scholars across the world,
who make reading and researching such a pleasure.*

Contents

List of Figures

List of Tables

Foreword
Orlando the Fangirl

It was Friday May 27th. The year was 1977. I was a latchkey kid on a mission.

After school, I returned home to an empty house. Both my parents worked. I wasn't allowed to play outside until an adult got home. I'd recently gotten a canary yellow skateboard for my birthday in April and I could not wait to rocket down the steep hill at the end of the block before the sun disappeared behind the trees. Nearly every kid on my street had suffered a broken arm or wrist trying to dismount the death ride while the wheels wobbled out of control from pure speed. If I could successfully tame the mountain without breaking my neck, neighborhood bragging rights would be mine forever. The only thing standing in my way was my mother.

After work she wanted me to go see a film called *Star Wars*. This wasn't the first time my mom had abused her parental powers and forced me to be her movie date. My dad had patently refused to watch a giant ape fall in love with a teeny tiny white lady in the jungle and be transported in the belly of a ship to America only to be hunted and killed by every able-bodied New Yorker. While my mother cried over the *King Kong* love story, I surreptitiously slid deeper into my seat hoping none of my friends saw me. To a nerdy basketball loving skater kid who listened to *Kraftwerk* and regularly referred to *REO Speedwagon* as Oreo Speedwagon without a hint of irony, *Star Wars* was the lamest sounding movie ever. I didn't know any of the actors and to make matters worse, one of the main characters looked like a runt from King Kong's litter. Not even CinemaScope 4-track stereo could save this picture. And yes, I knew what that was as a kid. I wasn't allowed to touch my Dad's Marantz 4300 Quadrophonic receiver but I knew way more about it than he did. Even then, my nerd game was on point. I remember walking as slowly as humanly possible into the theatre on North Pleasantburg Drive in Greenville, South Carolina, running my hand along the maroon colored walls as my mother chided, "You better put a pep in your step before I smack the black off you. We're going to miss the previews." The previews? When would this nightmare end?

Two hours and five minutes later it was over. Before Mrs. Jones could ask my critique, I stood on the tips of my toes to make myself taller and used all the bass my pre-pubescent voice could muster. "**I need a light saber RIGHT NOW!!!** The force is strong with me Mom, I swear it is." That's the moment I became a fan.

A few years later, the next entry in the *Star Wars* saga would represent yet another significant milestone in my understanding of the role that media plays in shaping our views of ourselves and the world around us. In *The Empire Strikes Back*, I saw a representation of myself in the form of Billy Dee Williams' Lando Calrissian, the smuggler who became a hero. It was transcendent. I never forgot the feeling of self-worth that I experienced as a young person when I saw faces of color in movies and television as inventors, leaders, and heroes rather than the more common tropes that minority actors were regularly subjected to.

A decade later, I was working in the entertainment business, first as a writer and producer on shows like *A Different World, Martin, Roc Live,* and others and then launching News Corp's fledgling cable network FX as one of its first hosts alongside Jeff Probst, Phil Keoghan, and Tom Bergeron. Once my career as a performer began taking off, I was asked by Quincy Jones to join the original cast members on *MadTV.* I became acutely aware that I had a responsibility to do for the current generation of young people what Billy Dee Williams had done for me.

My career continued to evolve in exciting and unexpected ways; as the spokesperson for 7-Up in a series of commercial spots that are still ranked on various advertising industry websites as one of the "Top 100 Most Recognizable Ad Campaigns of All Time," and then as the costar in a number of fan-favorite feature films that continue to play in a seemingly endless rotation on cable television, including *Drumline, The Replacements, Evolution, The Time Machine,* and many more. Like any working professional, I had my share of missteps along the way; jobs I took for the money, or because I followed someone else's advice against my better judgment. Since my goal was never to be famous, I found a consistent groove as a working actor, producer, and entrepreneur; winning awards for my work on stage, launching my own talk show, creating a successful fashion line. Each of these career pivots represented a larger canvas through which to tell stories and build experiences that would connect, promote, and inspire creative and intellectual curiosity in myself and others.

Even as I continued to pursue my passions and achieve my dreams, I never lost sight of being a fan: geeking out on the latest sci-fi/fantasy film or television show, eagerly waiting for the release of my favorite video game, trying to use my connections to get an advance copy of a new comic book or graphic novel. I devoured content that titillated and inspired my creative muse wherever I could find it. I lurked in the digital shadows of fan forums and online communities to read fan fiction (and maybe try my hand at writing some which I can neither confirm nor deny) and scroll through galleries of fan art. I always kept a respectful distance however, careful to honor the theoretical integrity of the imaginary fourth wall, which protected audiences and creators from the vicissitudes of fandom.

By the time I joined the cast of Fox's *Sleepy Hollow* as Captain Frank Irving in 2013, the mainstream media landscape had changed considerably. YouTube, Vine, Instagram, Tumblr, and Snapchat competed and won for the hearts and minds of millennials who rejected the conventions and constrains of "traditional media" en masse. For those still watching TV in real time, audiences now had numerous platforms through which to engage with creators more directly than they ever had before. This allowed for a steady stream of both adulation and derision. It also meant that historically marginalized groups that still weren't seeing multifaceted representations of themselves in media with any regularity had a platform by which to demand accountability and change.

Sleepy Hollow's creative team running the show took great pride in our status as one of the most multicultural shows on television with three African American leads (star Nicole Beharie, me, and costar Lyndie Greenwood), and recurring characters who were Asian and Latino. I felt both a sense of pride and responsibility by being a part of this unique and special ensemble and gleefully (and some might say foolishly) took on the role of social media provocateur by interacting directly with the fans. As I made clear to those who questioned my motives and expressed discomfort at my methods of engagement, I would have been a fan of the show even if I were not one of its lead actors. Admittedly, I was not fully prepared for the level of intimacy and expectation that my activities would garner. Taking on the moniker of "Trollando," I trolled the show and attempted to playfully mock both the show itself as well as some of its more ardent fans. In the vernacular of social media, a troll is usually an individual with malicious intent but the response I was seeking out was laughter, but humor is subjective. Despite no ill intent, I often caused considerable offense and experienced considerable backlash. Those reactions would have likely driven a sane person to hit the pause button but it actually emboldened me to stay the course and develop the navigational tools to communicate with the audience on their terms.

Eventually, my consistency and candor earned considerable goodwill and I was accepted as a genuine fan who was, in the words of the fandom, "one of us." It also gave me substantial insights into the essential importance of intersectional diversity and representation. As I sought to understand this further, I discovered the work of Henry Jenkins (2006a), author of the seminal book *Convergence Culture*, about participatory fan practices and their role in transforming the media ecosystem. I quickly devoured more books; Anne Jamison's (2013) *Fic: Why Fan Fiction Is Taking Over the World*, Jenkins' *Textual Poachers* (1992), *Understanding Fandom* by Mark Duffett (2013), and many more. I befriended "Aca-Fans" on Twitter and spoke to Fan Studies students at various universities across the country and overseas. I befriended actor Misha Collins, one of the stars of the hugely successful series *Supernatural*, who himself had been recognized in academic circles as a pioneering innovator in the realm of fan/creator interaction. Most importantly, I forged an identity that reflected the arc of my lived experiences thus far; from being that pre-teen boy watching *Star Wars* for the first time to creating stories that would entertain current and future generations. I was Trollando; actor, writer, producer, troll, fan.

So, here I stand before you, an unabashed and unafraid fangirl. I tried being a fanboy, but it was too limiting. Fanboys are exclusionary. Fanboys are guarded. They don't scream loud and refuse to have *all the feels*. And although I've had female fans express concern with my co-opting of this chosen fan persona and the implication that I am contributing to gender stereotypes, the exact opposite is true. I understand that I don't fit the commonly understood description of a fangirl and that's OK. It's a role I will continue to embrace as I passionately interact in a community that explores and challenges the role that media plays in all facets of our connected lives and pursues a version of what the world can be. It's an adventure as exciting today as it was for my nine-year-old self to ride my skateboard down that steep hill at the end of my block.

The authors of the chapters you're about to read explore fandom in great depth and with a range of unique perspectives. They shine a light on the dynamics of fan communities and the ways in which they can represent the best and worst of our human nature. From *Star Trek* to *One Direction*, from pro wrestling to anime and so much in-between, these Aca-Fans help us better understand how fandom is changing the world and what it all means. I'm fangirling over this book already. I hope you'll join me.

Orlando Jones
July 2015

Figure 1 Orlando Jones. ©Elizabeth Reynolds Photography - All Rights Reserved

Acknowledgments

Putting together a book like this takes coordinated effort from so many people, it would be nearly impossible to thank them all! First and foremost, Lucy and Paul thank all the contributors—your thoughtfulness, insight, and patience are to be commended. Our grateful thanks also to Matt Hills for writing the afterword, and to Orlando Jones for the amazing foreword. We are also appreciative to all our interviewees: Robert Burnett, Jeanie Finlay, Luminosity, Laurent Malaquais, Roger Nygard, and Emily Perkins. Special thanks to Lynn Zubernis and Katherine Larsen for putting us in touch with Perkins. Thanks also to Katie Gallof and Mary Al-Sayed at Bloomsbury for the care and attention before, during, and after the production process.

Paul wishes to thank all the fan classes he has taught, and the hundreds of students who have helped shape his ideas and perceptions about fans and the increasing popularization of fan studies. Thanks also to the furry ones (Slinky, Rosie, Gizmo, and Black Kitty) who are really good at listening to the day's ups and downs. And thanks as always to Katie, who is lovely beyond belief.

Lucy would like to thank first and foremost her parents and Jimmy for their incredible and constant support through everything. Huge gratitude also to her friends: Iñaki Garcia-Blanco and his very wonderful kindness, encouragement, and belief in me; Cheryl Jones, Claire Howard, Ellen Kirkpatrick, Janet Harris, and Rebecca Williams for their very lovely and extremely valued support toward me and this book; and to Bertha Chin and Bethan Jones for being there always, with hugs, enthusiasm, and ball pits.

Introduction: Seeing Fans

Paul Booth and Lucy Bennett

Who are fans? To many of the people reading this book—the fans and scholars who have more than a passing interest in fandom—media fans have been analyzed, discussed, debated, and defined for over thirty years within scholarly literature. A fan may be creative, productive, transformative, influential, affirmational, antagonistic, or any other of the hundreds of ways that media fans have been described since the first scholarship on them was written. Although scholars and fans themselves may disagree about the specifics of what constitutes a fan, and the types of meanings that fans can and do generate, the general image of a fan as central to the media environment has held constant for decades.

To many others, however—including media creators, general audiences, and popular press writers—fandom remains a pathologized and stereotyped identity: the geek, the nerd, the dweeb, the loser. Such characterizations are often inaccurate but still common in popular culture. As the chapters in this collection point out, the stigma of fandom has yet to disappear—and, in fact, for some (female/non-white/non-cis-gendered) fans, the stigma of fandom compounds with the antipathy toward other nonnormative identities as a complex nexus of pathologization. For many in popular culture, the stereotyping of fans comes across not as a problem to solve or an issue to address, but as yet another cliché that can garner laughs or sympathy. Both scholars and fans focus on representations of fans as a way of encompassing multiple issues within studies of fans and understanding fan cultures. As Mel Stanfill (2013) notes:

> if representations of fans by non-fans in popular and news media have typically framed fandom as a practice of uncontrolled, socially unacceptable desire, scholarship has equally tended to understand fans as empowered through their fandom to have more control over their media experience, either by fighting the media industry or by being courted by it. What the two have in common is a tendency to consider fans as subjects with no history—both assume from the outset that these individuals or communities are already fully formed. (p. 118)

This book seeks to explore where these identities and communities come from, and what they mean to the contemporary media environment.

Fans are a compelling, ever-changing audience with multiple layers that are often more dimensional than the overarching and limited ways they have been historically represented in media and popular culture. This book is intended as an endeavor to

initiate a reflection on how these individuals and their practices have been portrayed—
an important factor when considering how media and popular culture can both
critically shape and reflect societal and cultural values. As Roger Silverstone (1999)
has argued, media operate at the center of human experience and understanding, since
they exist "at the heart of our capacity or incapacity to make sense of the world in
which we live" (p. ix). This book, then, works toward unraveling the range and breadth
of these representations, and how these representations may inform understandings,
and "making sense of" fandom, by fans and nonfans. It seeks to question and trace,
through chapters from academics and interviews with industry practitioners, how we
understand the current landscape. Ultimately, these contributions articulate that fans
are multifaceted, complex, and sometimes contradictory—prospects which have not
always been visible in the representations they have received in the media and popular
culture—but are beginning to evolve in tandem with the burgeoning growth of their
visibility to the wider public and industry producers. We hope that this book will
beckon future scholarship and tease the way for a broader vista of seeing fans.

To date, there has not been a book-length study of how media fans have been
depicted in mass media.[1] This is particularly unusual considering how common
references to depictions of fans are in scholarly literature. Henry Jenkins's influential
Textual Poachers (1992) starts with a description of William Shatner's "Get a Life" skit
on *Saturday Night Live* as the quintessential interpretation of stereotypical fandom,
and this particular depiction has become a *sine qua non* for fan studies, having been
mentioned in scores of articles and books. More recently, representation of *Twilight*
fans has become a focus of scholarly analysis, perhaps motivated by the boon in
professionalized fan fiction heralded by the publication of *Fifty Shades of Grey* (Hills
2012c). The centrality of fannish media audiences in the media environment and
the prominence of fans as a key demographic for both marketing and advertising,
however, would seem to indicate a need for the study of fans' representations. *Seeing
Fans: Representations of Fandom in Media and Popular Culture* sets out to form a new
reference for the field of fan studies by connecting the mass mediated representation
of fans with the burgeoning "fandom industry" of the mass media.

As fandom becomes a more mainstream identity, representations of fans are
becoming more visible in the mass media (see Duffett 2013). The power and influence
of the mass media to impact the interpretation of representation has been a major
concern of media studies more generally, especially as this interpretation relates
to subcultural groups like fans. In this edited book, we bring together over twenty
international fan scholars to discuss how both fannish and mass media representations
of fandom can have both empowering and disciplinary functions. Fans often participate
in their own disciplinary activity, either specifically identifying and drawing out what
they perceive as "negative" stereotypical traits or highlighting what they see as the
more positive. This edited book connects fan representation to the economic, cultural,
and ideological practices of fan culture, looking through the lens of scholarship, media
creation, and fan work.

The popularity of fandom has exploded. It is no longer considered "weird" to be a fan.
Hundreds of thousands of people descend on San Diego, CA, each year for Comic-Con;

millions tune in to "cult" programs on television; billions of dollars are made on comic book movies. Yet fandom sits in an uneasy position in the media industries. Both courted and held at arms' length, fans are still seen as deviant and pathological, even as their enthusiasm is channeled into more "authorized" avenues. From popular television series like *The Big Bang Theory* to cult ones like *Supernatural*, from the thousands of *Twilight* fans at Comic-Con to scores of *Harry Potter* fans at LeakyCon, fandom is more than just a particular subculture: it has become a major economic force in its own right. In an effort to connect the academic study of fans to the larger world of fandom itself, this book also includes interviews with media producers and fans who have created works about fans or representations of fans in their own work. It is our hope that the variety of topics in the book will speak to the variety of representations— and *interpretations* of representations—in both fan culture and academic culture.

In terms of fandom, the parodic representation of fans has a relatively well-established history. As mentioned, William Shatner's famous "Get a Life!" *Saturday Night Live* sketch becomes a concrete representation of the prejudice and antipathy surrounding fans and fan cultures in the 1980s and 1990s (Jenkins 1992). In her chapter for *The Adoring Audience*, which many of the contributors to this volume cite, Joli Jensen (1992) notes that two common representations of fans in the media are "the obsessed individual and the hysterical crowd" (p. 9). Although representations of fans are becoming more normalized in the media, there are still hints of this familiar pathologization. Take, for example, *The Big Bang Theory* (2007–), one of the most popular television series in the United States. In what Booth (2015b) has called a "hyperfan" representation, the show illustrates multiple types of fans at the same time in order to develop a greater fluency with modern audiences. That is, the representation of Sheldon Cooper as an exponentially more "geeky" fan than the others essentially hides the pathologization of the other fans within the show. As Jenkins (2012d) notes in an interview with Suzanne Scott for the reprint of *Textual Poachers*, however, *The Big Bang Theory* is more complicated than that initially appears. The show "starts with the same core clichés," but audiences are also encouraged "to see the world from the fan characters' perspectives ... [who] value their friendship and intellectual mastery," and ultimately see them as "more complex than the stereotypes upon which they were based" (p. xvi). Yet, the hyperfandom of the representation within *The Big Bang Theory*, as Scott (2012a) argues, "seems to perfectly encapsulate the industry's conflicted desire to acknowledge fans' growing culture influence, while still containing them through sitcom conventions" (p. xvii). Ultimately, as Kristina Busse (2013a) describes, "the show isn't certain whether it is 'laughing with or at the geeks'" (p. 81, citing Heather Hendershot).

Beyond individual portrayals of fans, however, whole fan groups have been subject to media interpretation and representation. The classic fan film *Galaxy Quest* (1999) features a parody of *Star Trek*, complete with a group of "Questarians"—fans of this fictional show. Both Matt Hills (2003) and Lincoln Geraghty (2007) have written about Questerian fandom and its analogue to contemporary fan audiences. More recently, one of the editors of this volume (Booth 2013b; 2015b) has written about *Fanboys* (2009) and the comparison between *Star Wars* and *Star Trek* fan audiences in that film.

By overly emphasizing the traditionally pathologized characteristics of *Star Trek* fans, the film makes the *Star Wars* fans seem more "normal."

Using all of these characteristics, today's media industries are representing fans that more "normal" (re: more disciplined) audiences can safely mock. For Matt Hills (2012c), writing about *Twilight* fans, this type of representation occurs at two levels: the intertextual and the intratextual. On the one hand, representations of fandom on extra material, like official DVDs, can discipline "proper" fan behaviors by highlighting particular fan practices and identities as more valid than others. This type of "fandom as pedagogy" teaches "proper" fandom. On the other hand, the stereotyping of *Twilight* fans by other fan groups, such as *Buffy the Vampire Slayer* fans, can create its own disciplinary functions for fandom. By creating their own stereotypes of *Twilight* fans, these other fan groups attempt to pathologize *Twilight* fans into particular images, what Hills calls "fandom as stereotyping" (p. 114). As Booth (2015b) notes, "both types of fan disciplining regulate audience activity, creating particular interpretations of fan identities" (p. 80). This same type of stereotyping within fan groups has been discussed by Mel Stanfill (2013) as well, regarding *Xena: The Warrior Princess* (1995–2001) fandom and the stereotypes some fans of the series make regarding other fans of the series; and an intertextual fan stereotyping has been documented by Rebecca Williams (2013) in her exploration of how interconnected *Twilight* fans and Muse fans became, given the use of the band's music in the films.

This collection intends to expand the range of texts and fandoms analyzed in terms of their representation. Rather than focus on the most popular types of fan representations—the Trekkies, the Whovians, or the Twi-hards—this volume proposes to look deeper at some of the more underexplored fandoms, such as wrestling fans, international fan audiences, and Otaku fans, to name just a few. In short, this collection will expand the range of fan scholarship by turning an analytical lens onto the media itself to develop new ways of seeing the disciplinary and self-disciplinary mechanisms surrounding fan texts, the media industries, and fans themselves.

Chapter summaries

This book is split into four main sections, with some shorter sections interspersed throughout. We hope that this organization of the book—and the special "Spotlight on" sections in particular—will be of use for instructors hoping to explore key concepts in fan studies in the classroom. Each full-length section includes chapters by fan scholars and at least one interview with a media creator or professional whose work has focused on fandom and has used representations of fandom in that work. We open the book with four chapters about documenting fans in nonfiction and real-world events. Mark Duffett's chapter "Beyond Exploitation Cinema" opens the book, exploring the connections between disability and fandom in the documentary *Mission to Lars* (2012). He argues that the film draws on some notions of exploitation cinema to frame its subject matter and that while the film reflects a genuine attempt to please the fans within the film, it also utilizes markers of the exploitation genre to reconsider both disability and music fandom as interrelated subject matters. Rebecca Williams follows up in Chapter 2 with her analysis of the fans represented in the music documentary *Pulp: A Film About Life, Death & Supermarkets* (2014). Although a documentary ostensibly about a band, Williams argues that the film represents both fans and forms of celebrity and considers how these portrayals of fans and local characters have much to tell us about the contemporary mediation of both. Documenting fandom presents a range of fan identities which offer more progressive and positive portrayals than have often been present, and in depicting different types of fan, *Pulp: The Film* offers a space for fan voices and for a diversity of representation across gender, age, and class. Sam Ford's Chapter 3, in a discussion of the representation of fans within pro wrestling story worlds, shows how the realism of fandom is concomitant with how much belief goes into fandom's construction of the self. By examining how mainstream media accounts of wrestling fan behavior have traditionally demonstrated a strong lack of understanding and a concern about the performative nature of participating in an immersive story world, Ford discusses both the motivations, pleasures, and creativity involved in performing the role of wrestling fan and the "always on stage" and traditional lack of separation between actor and character in the world of pro wrestling. We conclude this section with an interview with Roger Nygard, the director of the documentaries *Trekkies* (1997) and *Trekkies 2* (2004). Both films depict *Star Trek* fan communities, and in this interview we ask Nygard about his responsibility to the communities he depicts in the films.

Our first "Spotlight On" section focuses, in particular, on the documentary *Crazy About One Direction*, which aired in 2013 on the British Channel Four television station. *Crazy About One Direction* explored fandom surrounding the band One Direction and was controversial within fan communities for its depiction both of the "extreme" fan audiences as well as for its focus on "*Larry* shippers" (or "Stylinson")—those fans who posited a homosexual relationship between Harry Styles and Louis Tomlinson, two members of the band. Chapter 5, the first chapter of this "Spotlight On" section, is by Bethan Jones, who describes the controversy and contextualizes its place within the history of fan representations in documentaries, including *Wacko about Jacko* (2005) and *Bronies* (2012). Jones examines the depiction of Stylinson and fandom responses to this following the film's airing, drawing on discussions of interfandom hate, as well as discussions around the ethics of real person fiction. Following this, Chapter 6 is from William Proctor, who delves more deeply into the role that social media played in the development of the *Larry* shippers as well as the antagonism experienced by those in the documentary. We conclude this first "Spotlight On" section with a piece by the director of *Crazy About One Direction*, Daisy Asquith, who explores the reaction of One Direction fandom to the release of her film in more depth. Asquith further analyzes the factions that divide the fandom and fan the flames of rage when there is a contested representation of either the band or their fans. She explores the ethics of television documentary and the representation of teenage girls in particular.

Our next section explores what is probably the most common type of fan representation—that seen in fictional programs. Fans have been present within media texts for decades; today, however, the representation has shifted to take into account newer fan practices and the way that fandom has been mainstreamed. We open the section with our interview with Robert Burnett, the writer and director of the film *Free Enterprise* (1998), a film that takes a humorous look at the lives of two grown-up *Star Trek* friends who encounter their hero, William Shatner. In this interview, we ask him about his fandom of *Star Trek* and how he balanced his fandom with his directives as a filmmaker. We then move to Lincoln Geraghty's exploration of "Fans on Primetime"—a historical analysis of fan representations on American primetime television since the infamous *Saturday Night Live* "Get a Life" sketch to examine to what extent fans have been stereotyped and how far those stereotypes go in perpetuating myths surrounding fandom and the affective relationship with media texts. Geraghty charts a history of network drama and sitcom series that were not specifically about fans but would often use fandom as the basis for stories in certain episodes. He argues that television series that play up and focus on the multiple practices that make being a fan so attractive are instructive in the processes that fans go through to create, build, and maintain their fan identity. In Chapter 10, Karen Hellekson examines an underdiscussed television series, *Stargate SG-1* (1997–2007). While known as being friendly to fans, with fans granted access to the set, early breaking information, walk-ons, and interviews, *Stargate* displaces the fan onto characters with fannish markers, including detailed canonical knowledge and obsession. Through these humorous characters, SG-1 portrays the fan as an ultimately lovable nut whose obsessions end up being vindicated and validated. Moving to more contemporary media texts, Melissa A. Click and Nettie Brock's Chapter 11 explores the liminal line between producers and fans in *Doctor Who* (1963–1989, 1996, 2005–) and *Sherlock* (2010–). Both British series have featured depictions of fans within episodes, and although these representations are brief when set within their larger stories, Click and Brock use them to explore the producers' conceptualizations of the series' real-life fans through producers' public comments about the *Doctor Who* and *Sherlock* fandoms. Chapter 12, by Ellen Kirkpatrick, explores representations of superheroes and comic book fans within comics themselves. The superhero genre, the comic book medium, and their fans and scholars all have a complicated relationship with representation. Fans are represented within long-established cultural and social categories and stereotypes, now subsumed under the often pejorative *fanboy* and *fangirl* monikers. Kirkpatrick analyzes these cultural codes about comic book fans within the superhero genre and illuminates the ways in which these representations do not speak to the nature of their fandoms, or to the diverse and ranging actuality of their fans. The final two chapters of this section focus on the US television series *Supernatural* (2005–) specifically—*Supernatural* has been much discussed in scholarship on fandom for its continual in-text depiction of its fan audiences. Chapter 13, by Katherine Larsen and Lynn Zubernis, unpacks the multiple representations of fandom within *Supernatural* to chart a history of the show's understanding of, and interaction with, its own fan audience. We follow this, and conclude this section with an interview with Emily Perkins, the actress who plays super-fan Becky Rosen in *Supernatural*. Perkins describes her time on the show and how she prepared for her role, as well as her views on being and playing a fan.

We follow our discussion of representations of fictional fans with another special "Spotlight On" section; this one focusing on representations of fandom within fan works. Fans are not immune to representational and disciplinary mechanisms, and within texts, like fan fiction, fan videos, and transmedia franchises, fandom itself can become stereotyped by fans themselves. We open this section with Chapter 15 by Kristina Busse, who explores and revalues the infamous "Mary Sue" genre of fanfic writing. In Mary Sue fic, fan authors (who are mostly women) write themselves into contemporary media by creating alter egos they insert into their expanded fan worlds or by creating characters with fannish perspectives. Such stories allow the fans to project self-inserts into the show universes to experience its characters and worlds. Fan writers effectively feminize hypermasculine characters, give them geeky interests and writerly preoccupations, and, in so doing revert the voyeuristic gaze while projecting their actions and emotions onto the characters. Busse suggests that fan fiction not only offers particular modes of interpreting the source texts but also ways to discuss and analyze theories of audience reception, especially as they relate to gender and the insufficient representation of women. Following this analysis, Louisa Stein's Chapter 16 examines transmedia web series like *The Lizzie Bennet Diaries* (2012–13) as both the product and representation of fan audiences. These web series transforms iconic female characters into fangirls, lending verisimilitude and relatability to the characters and the series' narratives. Moreover, by casting these characters as fans, these web series take female figures who were limited to private sphere, and recast them as public figures speaking in and for a culture that insistently undermines long-standing divides between intimate and public, individual and collective. Finally, we conclude this special "Spotlight On" section with an interview with noted fan vidder Luminosity, who discusses her role as a fan and the ways in which fandom itself can represent fan audiences in work as diverse as fan videos.

The next section opens up our discussion of fan representations to take into account a greater variety of cultural issues. Fandom is of course not free of larger cultural issues of diversity and privilege, and in Chapter 18, Mel Stanfill explores how the proliferation and diversification of representations of fans in the age of the Internet continues to be constructed as involving failed masculinity and whiteness through failed adulthood and heterosexuality. What is new in the contemporary era is that this narrative of failure now comes along with a path to redemption for white male fan bodies. Through an analysis of fictional and nonfictional representations of fans in television, film, and news, and statements made by industry workers, Stanfill considers the ongoing equation of fandom to normatively inadequate masculinity, maturity, heterosexuality, and whiteness. Ruth A Deller's analysis of newspaper narratives of music fans in Chapter 19 explores newspaper coverage of mature female fans of male singers such as Tom Jones, Barry Manilow, and Daniel O'Donnell. A recurring series of narratives of mature female fandom (50+) is constructed across national and local English language newspapers that position these women as excessive, immature curiosities, while also often offering a "feel-good" account of fan practices that allow readers to "humor" the fans. These accounts, all position the fans as "other" to the author and reader, yet unthreateningly so—they may be a neighbor, an aunt, or parent—a seemingly "ordinary" person whose "unusual" devotion to a star allows for a humorous human interest narrative to be constructed around their curious fandom. Rukmini Pande's

Chapter 20 focuses on racial, cultural, and ethnic identity in fan communities and fan studies. Fan communities are increasingly being theorized as functioning as a highly dynamic interlinked interpretative matrix, constantly reforming internal conventions in response to newer theorization about norms and practices produced by participants. These theories often concern depiction of minority groups (LGBTQ communities in the case of slash fandom). However, only very recently has scholarship acknowledged that the community has significant demographic representation of fans from racial and ethnic backgrounds other than white and middle-class Americans. Pande explores these engagements and the possibility of resistance and containment they display through fan interviews and case studies. We conclude this section with an interview with Laurent Malaquais, the director of the documentary *Bronies: The Extremely Unexpected Adult Fans of* My Little Pony (2012). *Bronies* explores cultural issues in the representation of fans, including gender, ethnic, and national identities. We spoke with Malaquais about his responsibility in representing Bronies with care and the result of focusing on cross-cultural fandom.

Our final section of *Seeing Fans* opens up the focus of the book onto global fan audiences. In Chapter 22, Darlene Hampton explores transcultural representation of *Sherlock* slash fans and the politics of pathologization within Chinese audiences. She argues that the body of the fangirl has become a discursive site for the enactment of not only cultural but also geopolitical anxieties—deployed alternately to police the "unruly" fangirl and promote national interests. Lori Morimoto extends this argument in Chapter 23 by exploring representations of Hong Kong star fans in Japanese cinema and the discursive construction of the female fan audience in two Japanese-Hong Kong film coproductions, *Moonlight Express* (1999) and *Moumantai* (1999), as well as the Japanese made-for-television film, *Hong Kong Star Fans* (2002). She situates these films' depictions of female fans against a historical backdrop of Japanese female fan pathologization within mass media in order to foreground their uses of fans to sociopolitical and economic ends. Nicolle Lamerichs, in Chapter 24, turns the analytic lens toward Japanese popular culture to examine how particular anime and manga include the figure of the otaku. Otaku are often stereotyped as obsessive adult fans who are unable to connect with reality. She provides a close reading of several exemplary manga and anime in order to illustrate multiple meanings of "otaku" culture. Finally, we conclude this section with a short interview with Jeanie Finlay, director of the British documentary *Sound It Out* (2011). We ask Jeanie about music fan culture and the particularly unique elements that make it different from, but also similar to, other types of fan audiences. We conclude the book with an afterword by noted fan scholar Matt Hills, who explores the future of fan representations.

Ultimately, it is our hope that readers of this volume will not find *one* particular representation of fandom as dominant, but rather that representations of fandom become a multilayered portrait of an ever-changing audience. Fandom is constantly evolving, and to stay beholden to any particular image is limiting for the fan and fan scholar. Seeing fans involves more than just observation; it is a constant process of critique and comparison. The authors in this volume illustrate that fandom is not just an image, but a prism.

Notes

1   We use the term "media fans" here largely to differentiate our study from those
     of sports fans—a related field of study, but one that reflects a different set of
     methodologies, research questions, and analyses. Sports fandom is understudied
     in what has come to be a body of literature called "fan studies," and far too little
     crossover research has occurred. That being said, the chapter from Sam Ford on
     depictions of wrestling fandom within and outside of wrestling proper is an example
     of how sports and media fandom can be analyzed together.

Part One

Documenting Fans:
Shades of Reality

1

Beyond Exploitation Cinema: Music Fandom, Disability, and *Mission to Lars*

Mark Duffett

Mission to Lars (Moore and Spicer 2012) is a feature documentary in which Kate and William Spicer help their brother Tom make his dream come true. Tom wishes to meet drummer Lars Ulrich from the heavy metal band Metallica. He also has Fragile X syndrome, which Kate calls, "a sort of autism with bells on." *Mission to Lars* is therefore a film about disability and popular music fandom. Its marketing and reviews suggest a warm and sympathetic portrait of family life in which two siblings help a third to achieve his ambition. On the aggregator site RottenTomatoes.com, an audience member called Damian O takes a very different position, arguing, "Anyone with any emotional intelligence can see that Tom genuinely does not like his sister and can probably tell that she is using him for the specific means of making a film."[1] Although such claims can be debated, no documentary innocently captures its subject.[2] *Mission to Lars* explores issues of disability awareness. Raising the possibility that Kate and Will Spicer may not have been motivated by altruism, it deliberately contrasts able-bodied and disabled cast members by using fan stereotypes. The film is therefore an unusual *fansploitation* picture, depicting fandom both as a training ground for employment and as a compensation for the disabled.

Drawing on arguments developed by Pointon and Davies (1997), media scholar Karen Ross (2001) notes that the term "disabled people" is preferable to *people with disabilities* because "*society* disables people, rather than an individual's particular impairment" (p. 433).[3] Narrative representations of the disabled do not, therefore, simply matter as reflections of disability; they are also active constructions. Waltz (2005) considers autism as a category constructed by medical case studies: "The issue of voice in these narratives seems to be the most crucial: people with autism are denied primacy, and even agency, in all but the least-mediated personal texts" (p. 432). This tendency to speak for others in medical investigations has had significant consequences. "In the field of autism research," Waltz reasons, "the text has so frequently and uncritically been mistaken for the subject that uncovering the ideologies within these narratives is of crucial importance" (p. 434). Medical case study notes are not the only form of representation that help to circulate constructions of disability, however. Media representations also play a role.

In 1992, after consulting its eighty-two member organizations and a further twenty-five broadcasters and advertisers, the British Council of Organizations of Disabled People produced an extensive and influential report called *Disabling Imagery and the Media: An Exploration of the Principles for Media Representations* (Barnes 1992). Although two decades have elapsed since the report's publication, the set of commonly recurring stereotypes it describes remain relevant. The *Disabling Imagery* stereotypes include portrayals of disabled people as pitiable and pathetic; as subjected to ridicule; as objects of violence (victims); as sinister and evil; as their own worst enemies; as incapable of fully participating in community life; for atmosphere or curio; as "super cripples" successfully triumphing over extreme odds; and, finally, as (emphatically) *normal(ized)*.[4] While it might be hard to offer any character entirely divorced from the *Disabling Imagery* stereotypes, the list forms a useful set of starting points from which to analyze cinematic portrayals of disability.

Exploitation films are cheaply made pictures, each built around a simple and shocking central concept that is easily grasped by viewers. Such films have been "continuously dismissed as cheap or irrelevant rubbish" (Mathijs and Mendik 2004, 4). Both fandom and disability have been the subject matter of such films in the past. Exploitation films about disabled people have often associated them with abnormality, social rejection, and violent retribution. A range of films such as *Freaks* (Browning 1932) and *Basket Case* (Henenlotter 1982) have interpreted the deformed body as something hideous and excluded from ordinary social life.

Films about music fandom have regularly stereotyped the phenomenon. Henry Jenkins (1992) listed a series of stereotypes propagated in mainstream media representations of fans. These include the notions that fans are framed as "brainless consumers" or "social misfits," who place inappropriate importance on devalued cultural material and are unable to separate fantasy from reality (p. 10). The two terms correspond to Theodor Adorno's (1938/2001, 52) much older descriptions of hypothetical faddists ("beetles whirring around in fascination") and socially inadequate individuals ("shy and inhibited"). In turn, they roughly suggest gendered positions: at worst, female fans are supposed to be gregarious but stupid, while male fans are clever but socially isolated (see Jensen 1992). Fansploitation films like *Groupie Girl* (Ford 1970) and *The Fan* (Bianchi 1981) present fannish activity as a slippery slope, a temptation either "entrapping" vulnerable females or "turning" sociopathic males. In such representations, media fandom is cast as a pretext for marginalized, inadequate, isolated, and resentful males to vent their fury on the social world. The portrayals suggest that fandom is the result of commercial betrayal and/or a refuge for Oedipally arrested, male killers. Even documentaries about dedicated music audiences have tended to interpret their subject matter by focusing on fandom as a mass "phenomenon" (exploring communities of like-minded followers or the travails of celebrities on tour), or by dwelling on the lives of smaller cohorts of "extreme" fans.[5] Recent documentary portrayals have developed in ways that can accommodate a range of readings. Analyzing the television documentary *Wacko About Jacko* (Leveugle 2005), for instance, fandom scholar Matt Hills (2007) argues that it is too simple to frame contemporary representations as either wholly positive or wholly negative. Mainstream audience members increasingly participate in fannish activities like performing their passions on social media. Fandom has become normalized as a mode of media consumption. Features like *Wacko About Jacko*, therefore, attempt to both grapple with the pervasive legacy of mass culture thinking and present fan practices in a more positive light. The stereotypes have not entirely disappeared, but rather have been re-imagined as shared *conditions* in need of knowing commentary. The polysemy of some contemporary media representations allows fan participants to celebrate their time in the spotlight, while still acknowledging that derogatory readings remain acceptable.

Unlike typical exploitation films, *Mission to Lars* is not a "descent" movie, but rather an "ascent" one, offering something different to the formulaic plots of traditional commercial exploitation fare. It avoids many of the classic stereotypes that associate fandom and disability with monstrosity and revenge, and departs significantly from "trash" films in that respect. Insofar as the film uncritically draws on stereotypes about music fandom and associates it with clinical disorder and social rejection, *Mission to Lars* is a fansploitation movie. It portrays fandom and disability not on their own terms, but in relation to common assumptions about them.

On common ground? United by fannish desire

Celebrities exude what Walter Benjamin (1936/2007) calls the "spell of personality" (231). They are understood as having ascended to a separate, privileged, and glamorous realm. As the media studies writer Nick Couldry (2007) puts it, "It is 'common sense' that the 'media world' is somehow better, more intense, than 'ordinary life,' and that 'media people' are somehow special" (p. 353). The idea of famous people as stellar beings ("stars") emphasizes the distance between them and their audiences (Williams 2012). Stratospheric descriptions of performers suggest that electronic media (which include sound recording) bring performers and audiences together, but do so in an inevitably distanced and alienated way. Titles of exploitation films reflect their high concepts and make them easy to market. The name of the Spicers' documentary is an obvious pun on "mission to Mars," a reference to real space exploration and the scientific imperative to reach the red planet. In the context of the film's title, the idea of Mars as an inaccessible destination reinforces our interpretation of celebrities as distant people: individuals located way out in the firmament of the cosmos.[6] *Mission to Lars* extends its stellar theme by marking different segments of the narrative with titles such as *6 Days to Launch*. The feature-length documentary contrasts rainy, green, English countryside with the idea of "this trip to America." The film recycles a familiar phrase to promote the stereotypical idea that music fandom is a form of personal obsession imbued with relentless momentum. It reminds us that able-bodied viewers and disabled people share the same desires.

Most people are fans of somebody or something, and many are thrilled by the thought of meeting their heroes. Fans frequently have urges to get closer to the objects of their interest. The practice of celebrity following—which has largely been neglected by the last two decades of fan studies—can be analyzed from a range of perspectives. Psychologists such as Gayle Stever (2013), for example, understand celebrity pursuit as a form of "proximity-seeking" behavior. On the other hand, Kerry Ferris and Scott Harris (2011) have approached it purely as a specific kind of micro-sociological practice. In my own work (Duffett 2013), I have used Durkheim's notions of totemism and effervescence as explanatory frameworks. There is also an emergent literature on the role of celebrity in non-Western fandom (see Lee et al. 2008; Yang 2009; Zhou 2013).

In *Mission to Lars*, Tom's fannish desire helps to shift his representation beyond that of a disabled other (an anonymous medical subject who has inherited Fragile X). His fascination is specifically with Lars Ulrich, not anyone else; it indicates something specific about his personality. Tom's fannish motivation for the "mission" is a point of association with the spectator; at one point, he and his sister met Metallica's tour manager, who explains, "Everyone who goes to the show wants to meet Lars if they could," adding that Tom needs a "contact on the inside…a triple A: access all areas pass. To get that you need to go right up the pole, right to the top."

Having established fandom as a point of audience identification, *Mission to Lars* uses further fan stereotypes to explore Tom's condition. Henry Jenkins (1992) has noted that media representations negatively portray fans as needing to "get a life" (p. 11). Tom is a manual laborer who recycles newspapers to make animal bedding. The film begins with him repeatedly saying "Meet Lars!" We find that Tom was previously obsessed by Arnold Schwarzenegger. The implication is that his fannish passions are compensations for a lack of growth in his personal life, whether in terms of social mobility or establishing intimate relations. In *Mission to Lars*, the phrase "get a life" therefore takes on an unusual hue, as it is related to the social stigmatization that the disabled can face. Because of Tom's impairment and the way that Fragile X sufferers are treated socially, he has not had access to the social opportunities shared by his siblings and faces greater challenges than most in his bid to "get a life."

Another stereotypical idea about fandom is that it takes the form of a clinical compulsion. For Jenkins (1992), this is reflected in portrayals that cast fans as "social misfits who have become so obsessed with the [television] show that it forecloses other types of social experience" (p. 10). Kate Spicer raises this issue when she interviews various experts as part of the documentary and its DVD supplement. For instance, Dr. Randi Hagerman - a Fragile X specialist from UC Davis - is given a sagacious, helper role in the Spicer's quest:

> Kate Spicer: Is Tom genuinely "crazy mad" to meet him, or is it just a kind of behavioral tick?
> Dr. Hagerman: No—he is "crazy mad" to meet Lars, because individuals with Fragile X can oftentimes have very intense interest areas. Very intense. And that's the really exciting aspect of how they get enthused with life.

The term "crazy mad" is passed across like a verbal baton. It creates a conceptual space in which meaningless obsession ("a behavioral tick") is separated from a "genuine" impulse to meet Lars, something which itself is therefore considered both insane ("crazy mad") and fannish (a genuine need to connect). When Kate Spicer interviewed Lars Ulrich for a *Mission to Lars* DVD extra, she further focused on this question of fan stereotyping and obsession. Their encounter revealed that Ulrich himself flew from Los Angeles to London to see the metal band Diamondhead and ended up staying with them for six weeks, learning how to be in a band. The famous drummer's personal fandom is framed as *professionally productive*. It raises a broader question: How should music fandom be seen? Kate's perception seemed to be that fandom was acceptable as a step toward something else (such as employment), but unacceptable ("crazy mad") as a goal in itself. She therefore asked, "Do you think that fandom is a kind of pathological, obsessional type behavior, or—?" Lars replied:

> Err, I'm not sure what the clinical term is, but maybe—I don't know—it's "obsessed."
> When I'm into something, I'm just really into it. So "obsessive behavior"? Sure,
> why not? I'll go along with that sound bite.

In other words, fan obsession is positioned as something that is *both* a little insane (a clinically labeled disorder) and also familiar. In that dual sense, it is a source of mirth. The shared predicament of having a fan object of one's own aligns those who have autism with able-bodied spectators. Disabled fans are dreamers, just like us.

Although *Mission to Lars* assumes that desiring to meet one's hero is a normal, and therefore a *normalizing* form of behavior, it still frames fandom as a clinical disorder. While Tom is evidently a Metallica fan—he wears the t-shirt—in the film his obsession to "meet Lars" is understood outside of any other fan practices or forms of sociability. At one point, Kate asks Tom, "If you meet Lars, will you stop saying you want to meet Lars all the time?" Tom appears unable to drop persistent thoughts. He therefore expresses a fannish desire *through* a clinical compulsion. This association adds to the drama of the narrative, because it helps us question the extent to which Tom's expression of interest in meeting Lars reflect his fandom, his mental condition, or, perhaps, later on, a way of expressing his identity in relation to family members. The film interprets Tom's fascination with Metallica as a form of social compensation (his life lacks "adventure") but sees his *expression of it* as a compulsive disorder stemming from his medical condition.

Passive fandom and the danger of speaking for the disabled

Between 1977 and 1998, BBC Radio 4 broadcast a program called *Does He Take Sugar?* As its title implied, unless the able-bodied are challenged to review their assumptions, they can easily place disabled individuals in an infantile role, framing them as people unable to do things for themselves, display any initiative, or even respond at all. The widespread assumption that the disabled must be spoken for can mean, however, that they do not have a say. *Mission to Lars* confronts this issue of patronizing the disabled head on. It explores the potential folly of viewing a disabled person as an object who has to be managed for his own good.

If the wish to meet a celebrity is a relatively common one, the degree to which any individual actually pursues it can, of course, vary greatly, depending on his or her values, motivations, peer network, agency, and dedication. It is significant that Tom does not actually create his mission. Instead it is planned as a kind of gift from his siblings. In other words, *Mission to Lars* initially portrays Tom's fandom as pure desire: something despite which he remains isolated, inactive, and able to act only when assisted. While Tom has said hundreds of times that he wishes to "meet Lars," the mission becomes proper only when Kate and Will have decided that they will dedicate their professional skills to making Tom's dream come true.[7] As Kate explains in the film, "As much as about meeting Lars, it's also about giving Tom that one big adventure in his life." Tom is portrayed as having limited agency; in order to make things happen he must be assisted, but the achievement of the mission will also increase his personal sense of confidence and capability to do other things. The film therefore asks how much the roles of disabled people are shaped by the projections and assumptions of their able-bodied carers.

Much of Mission to Lars explores Kate Spicer's motivations. Tom's sister is a journalist and their brother, Will, a filmmaker. Kate explains that as the siblings have grown up, they have drifted apart. She and Will have moved to London to lead middle-class, professional lives. Kate starts the film by explaining that part of the reason for the mission is her guilt in not doing more to help Tom. As the main narrator in the documentary, she expresses her regret about not helping enough by saying, "I've never earned that mug with 'Best Sister in the World' on it." Dilemmas about helping Tom on his mission seem to stem, in part, from the conflicted inner worlds of his siblings. Their mission is, arguably, a form of patronage: not only in its assumption that Tom cannot meet Lars by himself—which may be accurate - but, more significantly, the imposed assumption that he wants his family to help him do so. After all, so far, except saying that he wants to "meet Lars," Tom has taken no steps.

The Spicers' film is much less about meeting Lars than obstacles faced on the journey. At one point in the film, upon recognizing the difficulties involved, Kate explains that she feels obligated to help Tom on his mission, in part, to save her own image. For that reason, as much as any other, she cannot give up. From this perspective, Tom's apparent reluctance to fulfill his dream could be seen as part of his own bid to become enfranchised in "his" mission and assert some personal autonomy. As the Spicers visit America, a quote from Lars Ulrich is taped to the window of the Winnebago: "What's the message from Metallica? ... Look within yourself for the answers." Although the film leads us to believe that Fragile X people often get more introspective as they get older, Tom himself is portrayed as having minimal capacity for rational self-interrogation. Although he says he wants to meet Lars, the film asks us to consider whether Tom may eventually have been responding to his siblings trying to organize something that he did not actually want to happen. Furthermore, the narrative places us in the same role as Tom's assistants. If he has trouble finding and expressing his interior thoughts, how can we tell which of the explanations is correct? While the "mission" encourages us to take Tom's place (as fellow music fans), its documentary unfolding does not come from his perspective, but from the perspective of the able-bodied helpers around him.

Mission to Lars plays upon the idea that individuals with autism or related conditions are their own worst enemies. As a highly sensitive person with a specific impairment, Tom apparently has a much smaller zone of capability and comfort than an individual without Fragile X Syndrome. His parents think that the mission will be a challenge because it will be a change from Tom's routine; he is known to be stubborn and unlikely to listen to some of those around him. Will says he feels that his brother is "really unpredictable and we would have to second guess him." Tom is therefore positioned as a character who needs to be handled in the right way, and, in effect, to be *managed*. The possibility of Tom's fears sabotaging the mission is prominent in the film's narrative. Early on, Kate explains, "He's in borderline freakout mode. We've just left him alone and he's gone to work." The Spicers' directorial approach is to use a handheld camera and follow the key agents. With two days "to launch," sister Kate uses her journalistic skills to further investigate. She tells the camera, "To be honest with you, just getting Tom to meet Lars for five minutes will be a miracle." Once the mission proper begins, the Spicers say, "Well, we always knew we would have to call [Tom's step mother] Jane in, didn't we?" The narrative reveals, however, that Tom has a rational reason for his reluctance to meet Lars at a concert arena. Along with a big list of other constraints, his mother explains, "He's nervous or unwilling to join big crowds." If Tom is frightened about something—just like anyone else—he may well refuse to do it.

Dr. Randi Hagerman explains that Tom hears concert music ten times louder than someone without Fragile X, and suggests he might take anti-anxiety medication and wear earplugs to counter "the chaos of the crowd." In this sense, *Mission to Lars* assumes that Tom will only further develop as a capable individual if he can reach the edge of his physical and mental comfort zone and begin to confront his fears. When they actually get to Las Vegas, to visit Lars at a Metallica show, Tom does not want his party to park their van near the concert; his willful refusal to see Metallica seems to sabotage the mission. His sister feels "It's us imposing our bit of misery on him. We had all these plans to do lovely things for our brother, but actually it's a bit of a nightmare for him." They show Tom at the sound check, but he says that he won't stay for the show, as it will be too loud. By means of montage, the volatile, collective scene of the gig—with fans making devil hand signs and shouting "Metallica!"—is contrasted to Tom's hum-drum visit to the laundromat. Kate laments, "They're making things easy for us, but Tom doesn't want to go to the show." After the Las Vegas visit fails, she adds, "They're waiting for us with open arms. Metallica are sitting there saying, 'Come on in, the Spicer Family.'" The Spicers then visit Sacramento via the "chill space" of Yosemite national park. Kate says, "There's no doubt in my mind that Tom wants to see Lars. It's just breaking through fear. It's like jumping out of an airplane." Having failed to meet up with Metallica twice, the Spicers further follow the band on tour to California. At their next opportunity, in Anaheim, Kate explains to Tom that Metallica have promised they will see him in their exclusive tuning room. At the film's climax, Kate suggests that Tom thinks Lars might be "too busy" to meet him. It is hard to tell whether Tom actually does want to meet Lars, or whether, perhaps, he instead feels beaten down by the enormity of the task, unworthy or anxious because of his hero's social status, or afraid to lose his fantasy through its fulfillment. Despite the film's use of fan stereotypes, it suggests that fandom is the vehicle through which Tom can find the social support necessary to achieve his personal breakthrough.

Achieving the mission

In face-to-face meetings with celebrities, fans can feel intimate, if only momentarily, with an individual who is important in their lives. In such moments, the celebrity can give his or her fans an immense thrill by gracing them with their presence alone. Documentaries and television shows occasionally feature examples of such moments.[8] They provide the emotionally resonant drama—the "dream coming true"—and may associate it with the celebrity doing a good deed, sometimes in the name of charity. The problem with such tropes, of course, is that for those who pursue it, fandom is *already* thrilling—and in that sense "empowering"—to the extent that it can get people through hard times. With less than ten minutes of the documentary left to go, Lars Ulrich arrives in a light beige jacket. When this happens, Kate says, "Who's the most famous drummer in the world?" Tom answers "Lars." Backstage in the tuning room, Lars plays the intro of "Enter Sandman" especially for Tom and asks him to play too. His sister encourages him, and he has a go; he gets given a set of drum sticks. Sometimes dreams come true. Backstage, Lars explains to a member of Slayer, "This is Tom. He came all the way from England to see Metallica." Lars treats Tom as an equal person. Especially given that Lars's dress sense is *unlike* his black-clad heavy metal peers, he also emerges as a surprisingly *unspectacular* and ordinary person. The narrative therefore positions Lars Ulrich as someone who occupies a magical *role*: a figure at the end of the fannish rainbow who can, through his public endorsement of Tom in front of the live audience, confer celebrated status upon him.

While this experience is the same for privileged and less-privileged fans alike, the narrative arc of stories about such encounters is that marginalized and vulnerable people are more deserving of celebrity attention. The segments also work for the celebrity, meanwhile, who receives kudos by "giving back" some of his or her privilege and helping those in need. As collaborator in the stellar project commissioned by the Spicers, Ulrich is portrayed as a place-holder in one fan's dream. His duty is to take Tom to the summit of his aspiration. When they meet, the Metallica drummer asks Tom, "What's your favorite Metallica song? How about if when I walk out on stage, you can walk with us? We'll all walk out on stage." Kate explains that Tom has refused to go out on stage, but finally he says yes. His love for his hero has overtaken his fears.

The film climaxes with Tom and Metallica walking out on stage in front of a vast crowd of excited fans, before Metallica perform "Enter Sandman." Tom has met his hero and conquered his fear of crowds. With Lars's help, his "mission" has finally been achieved; he has become socially accepted as a focus of attention in his own right. At the climax of the film, Tom is not rejected, managed, or treated as an infantile individual, but accepted as an ordinary person. His very "normality" is, however, premised on the same assisted mission that has framed him as an impaired individual and documentary subject.

Across the documentary's final credits we hear a Skype conversation back in the Spicers' Winnebago as Tom's parents discover that he has, in fact, finally met Lars. Other Fragile X sufferers are asked who they would go on a mission to see. Their answers include Iron Maiden, Bryan Adams, and Cliff Richard. Dreaming of meeting pop stars, it seems, is an ordinary practice that might give the socially marginalized some hope. What the feature documentary film does not give is any sense that William and Kate Spicer might also have had desires of their own as fans of popular culture. Implicit in such *nonrepresentation* is the assumption that since Tom's siblings had achieved superior social status—with their middle-class metropolitan lives and professional roles— they do not need to express any fan dreams. If they need assistance with anything, it is with the social project of helping their brother achieve his dream, not with any "mission" of their own. The implication, again, is that while fandom matters as a form of compensation for the disabled, it is less required by those who are socially successful.

In this chapter, I have suggested that the feature documentary *Mission to Lars* is an unusual film, one that draws on stereotypes of music fandom to explore issues of disability. Any claim that Tom's siblings have simply exploited his impairment does not fully hold up; the film works by broaching stereotypes of both fandom and disability in order to interrogate the role of able-bodied carers in helping those with autism and other conditions to achieve their desires. While its assumption that fandom can be a route through which "social misfits" find acceptance is something of a stereotype, *Mission to Lars* uses it to say that the disabled can be treated as normal human beings. The Spicers' documentary assumes that once Tom has faced his fears, he will begin to become a different person, but it cannot hope to demonstrate how far that is true. What it can say is that although it would be foolish to ignore their impairments, the disabled are, in part, socially *normalized* only with the help of their able-bodied peers. As part of that process, Tom momentarily achieves a level of endorsement to which many able-bodied fans can only aspire. Once his desire to meet the "most famous drummer in the world" is satisfied, it is what he might find on the other side of the mission that will make his life fulfilling. His story is a reminder that all of us—both disabled and able-bodied—get by better with a little help from our friends.

Notes

1   See: http://www.rottentomatoes.com/m/mission_to_lars/reviews/#type=user&page=2 (accessed October 2, 2015).

2   Although the proceeds from *Mission to Lars* went to the mental health charity MENCAP, Kate Spicer had already appeared as a celebrity on the BBC series *Masterchef*.

3   Emphasis in original.

4   "Normalized" characters are marginal to the main plotline so not used to reflect upon the varied experiences of disabled people (Barnes 1992, 18).

5   The former category includes documentaries such as *Britney Spears Saved My Life* (Jayanti 2009) and *Abba: Bang a Boomerang* (McElroy 2013); the latter, *Mondo Elvis* (Corboy 1984) and *Wacko About Jacko* (Leveugle 2005).

6   Given that a feature film was being made about the Spicers' project, it may have
     damaged Metallica's reputation if Ulrich had not greeted his disabled admirer on
     camera. After a demo of the song "I Disappear" was shared online in 2000 without the
     group's authorization, its legal representatives filed a suit that successfully removed
     300,000 Napster users from the service. In effect, Metallica had dismissed a section of
     its fanbase as pirates.
7   It is debatable if Metallica would have responded if Kate and William had not used
     their professional approach and resources. The meeting might never have happened if
     no film was being made, or, perhaps more importantly, if Tom had been able-bodied.
8   I am thinking here of shows like the BBC television series *Jim'll Fix It* (1974–1995) or
     ABC's *Jimmy Kimmel Live* (see Garrison 2010).

2

"We Live Round Here Too": Representing Fandom and Local Celebrity in *Pulp: A Film About Life, Death & Supermarkets*

Rebecca Williams

On Saturday June 7, 2014, the documentary *Pulp: A Film About Life, Death & Supermarkets* opened the twenty-first annual Sheffield Documentary Film Festival. The film focuses on the British indie band Pulp, combining footage of the band's preparations for the final live show of a 2012 tour in their home town of Sheffield with interviews with their fans and residents of the city. Screened in Sheffield's City Hall, the film's debut was followed by a question and answer session with the director Florian Habicht and band members Jarvis Cocker, Candida Doyle, Mark Webber, Steve Mackay, and Nick Banks. The film was generally well received, described by film critic Mark Kermode (2014) as an "affectionate documentary [that] tells the story of the band from the streets of Sheffield with the help of friends, family and fans, aged and youthful alike." This chapter analyzes the diverse representations of fandom in *Pulp: A Film About Life, Death & Supermarkets* (hereafter *Pulp: The Film*). While the film does feature young female fans who express desire and attraction toward Pulp's lead singer Jarvis Cocker, fans from a broader generational spread are also represented. *Pulp: The Film* thus presents a space for fan voices and a diversity of fan representation. Secondly, the chapter explores the presentation of local figures from Sheffield in the film, arguing that these "localebrities" (McElroy and Williams 2011) perform crucial functions in representing similar ideas about class and place and location as both the band themselves and their fans.

Pulp and the music documentary

Pulp formed in 1978, released their first album *It* in 1984, and continued to produce albums, none of which made any impact until 1994s Mercury Music Prize nominated *His 'n' Hers*. It was their follow-up album, *Different Class*—released in 1995—which propelled the band to fame, largely as part of the mid-nineties music scene Britpop, which also included bands such as Blur, Oasis, and Suede. However, while the media of the time established a clear rivalry between Blur and Oasis—which played on existing divides between the South of England and the North, and between being middle class and working class—Pulp, and their fans, were largely exempt from these media-constructed conflicts. As the biography on the official website for the documentary notes:

> In July [1995], Pulp accepted a last-minute headlining slot at Glastonbury Festival when The Stone Roses had to cancel. Pulp's set was rapturously received, launching the band into superstar status in England and conveniently setting the stage for their forthcoming album, *Different Class*. (*Pulp: The Film* 2014)[1]

After two subsequent albums—1998s *This Is Hardcore* and *We Love Life* in 2001—the band went on indefinite hiatus. Following this, lead singer Jarvis Cocker released two solo albums, recorded with a new band Relaxed Muscle, became a DJ for the digital music station 6Music, and maintained a visible media presence. Keyboardist Candida Doyle performed live on Jarvis's solo tours while guitarist Steve Mackay produced songs for artists including Florence + The Machine and The Long Blondes. In contrast, the rest of Pulp returned to their pre-fame lives. In September 2006, three of the band's CD's (*His 'n' Hers, Different Class,* and *This Is Hardcore*) received deluxe re-issues, each featuring extra discs of rarities, B-sides, and cover versions, while a live album *The Peel Sessions* was released in October of 2006. The band thus continued to have some presence in their dormant years until the announcement in 2011 that they were reforming for two summer festival gigs in the United Kingdom, which were followed by a subsequent tour. It is the final concert of this tour that is the focus of *Pulp: The Film*.

There is a long tradition of music documentary as a genre, and visible in many of these films is the figure of the fan—whether seen as homogenous crowds during gig footage or as individuals with different interests in a band. However, there has been relatively little work conducted on how music fans are represented in documentary. One exception is Matt Hills's (2007) analysis of the Michael Jackson documentary *Wacko About Jacko* (screened in 2005 on Channel 4 in the United Kingdom), which explores how fan's emotional connections to the artist are represented as odd and as almost entirely negative. Fan responses to the 2013 Channel 4 documentary about boy band One Direction—entitled *Crazy About One Direction*—also indicate that fan practices are often constructed and represented negatively in popular culture (see Chapters 4, 5, and 6). Indeed, the titles of both these films—*Wacko About Jacko* and *Crazy About One Direction*—connote madness, emotionality, and obsession, often linked to female fandom (see Jensen 1992). However, documentaries about fans continue to offer "an opportunity to consider how fans are represented when the media zeroes in on them, making them the sole focal point of documentary footage" (Hills 2007, 460–1).

"I love you Jarvis Cocker:" Female fandom, attraction, and waning celebrity

In many ways, the fans featured in *Pulp: The Film* are privileged. Everybody who is interviewed on film is listed in the end credits by their full names under the heading of "Co-starring." Equally, fans seen waiting outside the Sheffield Motorpoint Arena before the band's gig are listed somewhat approvingly as "The hardcore fans in the cold" and listed by their first names only (this reveals a total of twenty fans; four male and sixteen female). However, the representations of fandom on display here also map onto, and complicate, existing fan representations regarding gender, age, and fan "subcultural capital" (Thornton 1995). These on-screen fans fall into two main types: a group of dedicated fans who are waiting outside of Sheffield's Motorpoint arena before Pulp's concert, and two older fans, Terry and Josephine, who are interviewed in the film. Across these two groups, issues of gender, generational identity, and celebrity intersect to represent the complexities of fandom through the lens of documentary. *Pulp: The Film* depicts a group of primarily female fans who are waiting outside the Motorpoint Arena in Sheffield before the start of Pulp's final gig. These fans are there early, presumably to ensure a place at the front of the gig for close proximity to the band; this is supported by later shots of the crowd showing some of these female fans on the barriers in front of the stage. Short interviews with some of these waiting fans offer insight into their connections to the band and information about their journeys to see this final concert. These predominantly female fans express a range of views about the band including their attraction to Jarvis Cocker, despite the obvious age gap. One fan notes, "I told people I was going to see Pulp and they were like 'Shouldn't they be on Zimmer frames by now?'" Her image is then accompanied by the caption "Lowri, Pulp Fan" as she continues, "And I was like 'don't say that!' He's, Jarvis Cocker like what is he? Fifty? An icon and he's probably gonna put on a show better than people half his age and it's gonna be ahh I can't even think about how good it's gonna be. He's going to be there thrusting on stage and dancing." The notion of Jarvis as a sex symbol had already been derided by his own bandmates during the height of their fame in the mid-1990s. For example, drummer Nick Banks noted that "The idea of Jarvis being a sex symbol was utterly, utterly hilarious […] 'cos [British music magazine] *Smash Hits* were starting to pick up on Pulp and starting to go on about sexy Jarvis, and people were just in fits of laughter'" (Sturdy 2003, 223). However, in *Pulp: The Film*, the notion that Pulp (and, in particular, Jarvis) are too "old" to be worthy objects of fandom is linked here to the notion that they are "past it" and that their fame has waned. Indeed, the fleeting notion of fame is seen elsewhere in the film in relation to the band members who enjoy relative levels of anonymity. With the exception of lead singer Jarvis Cocker, the members of the band are most commonly seen in "normal" circumstances. Guitarist Mark Webber, for instance, admits that he is rarely recognized: "I'm just a regular guy. I catch the bus all the time. […] I go to the shops. I mean fortunately, not being the center of attention in the group." Similarly, drummer Nick Banks is seen coaching his daughter's football team and stating "My daughter plays football and all the team like to have a team sponsor so I asked the chaps if they'd like to throw a few quid in and have Pulp on the shirts […] It was very funny the first game they put them on and all the girls were going 'Pulp? Who's that?' and she had to say 'Yeah, it's my dad's crap band.'" The apparent ignorance about the band's success and history displayed by this younger generation of girls highlights both the fleeting and tangential nature of fame, as well as suggesting the generational disconnect between those who were fans of the band and those who have "never heard of them." The potential for people to be dismissive of fans' ongoing devotion to the band is thus clearly linked to the fact that they took a hiatus from performing and their celebrity positions have shifted.

Usually there is a clear imbalance of power between the celebrity and the "ordinary" members of the public since there are "major status differentials as the famous rub shoulders with the obscure and the extraordinary and ordinary collide" (Ferris and Harris 2011, 34). However, *Pulp: The Film* constructs Sheffield as an environment where such established dichotomies between the ordinary (citizen/fan) and the extraordinary (star) break down, facilitated by the resolutely commonplace geography and inhabitants of the city. According to their representation in *Pulp: The Film*, band members operate at the level of local fame or "localebrity," (McElroy and Williams 2011) recognized only by those within a specific geographic area, or as examples of "subcultural celebrity" who are "mediated figures who are treated as famous only by and for their fan audiences" (Hills 2003, 61). Although still recognizable by fans across geographical locations, most of the members of Pulp no longer have ubiquitous cultural recognition or "constitute a mass-mediated and shared currency within contemporary consumer cultures" (Hills 2003, 59). Despite this, fans such as Lowri continue to value the band members both as embodiments of their ongoing dedication to the group and as celebrities who retain currency as appropriate and—in the case of Jarvis Cocker—desirable objects of fandom.

Attraction to Jarvis Cocker is also articulated in a sequence where a female fan is interviewed in a swimming pool in her swimsuit after an aqua aerobics session. Identified as "Cherie, Pulp fan," she comments, "My husband thinks I'm quite mental. He's not that really into Pulp and he just accepts that Jarvis is probably the third person in our relationship even though Jarvis doesn't actually know that. But he is. We do get a bit obsessed you know. Um, I have Pulp underwear you know. […] I made it myself actually. It says Pulp on the front and Jarvis on my bum. I'd like Jarvis on my bum." Such female fans echo the figure of Anika, the only female fan who appears in the Michael Jackson documentary *Wacko About Jacko* and who "is immediately linked to the stereotype of the 'desiring' or besotted female fan" (Hills 2007, 465). In *Pulp: The Film*, Lowri and Cherie appear as stereotypical female fans who are attracted to the object of fandom and driven by libidinal desires. This is further highlighted by an unnamed female fan who is waiting outside of the Motorpoint area and declares "Jarvis Cocker, I love you" while making a heart shape with her fingers and walking forward to kiss the documentary makers' camera. While the documentary presents these fans without judgment, such images clearly recall cultural associations of "hysterical" female fandom, typified in music fandom "by 'Beatlemania' in the 1960s and continued in perceptions of the crowds of screaming girl fans for boy bands such as Take That or N*Sync in the 1990s" (Williams 2013, 338). What is different about the fans seen in *Pulp: The Film* is the more unlikely status of Jarvis Cocker as a "heart-throb," given his position as an aging celebrity. The object of affection may change but, in this instance, the representation of female fandom does not.

The female fan granted the most screen time, however, does not state any overt physical attraction to Jarvis. The young woman, identified as "Melina, Pulp fan," is interviewed at some length in the following exchange:

Q: Where do you come from?
A: Georgia in the USA
Q: For a concert?
A: For a concert?
Q: [Admiringly] You came here for the concert?
A: Exactly. First time in the UK. All the way to see Pulp in their home town. Cos I've loved them since I was sixteen. [Cut] I was just so happy that they got back together because I have no words. I can't travel to see them, they didn't come to Atlanta where I live and so, except '94 but I didn't go. I didn't go. I didn't know about them.
Q: What do you do in Atlanta?
A: I'm a nurse. Yeah. I'm a nurse and a single mom. And Jarvis sings about single moms so [laughs].

Melina features again after the gig has finished, waiting outside the venue for a glimpse of the band as they leave. As she confirms that she is flying back to the United States the following morning, she is asked, "And the dream is over?" She replies, "it was nice. It was a nice dream." While fans such as Lowri and Cherie invoke the stereotype of "female fans, as mentally unstable, deviant, and somehow dangerous members of society" (Pinkowitz 2011, 3.3), via their attraction to fan objects, Melina's fandom is established as dedicated via its longevity and her decision to travel a great distance to see Pulp's final gig. Melina thus embodies how fandom can "prompt our self-reflexivity, encourage us to discuss shared values and ethics, and supply us with a significant source of meaning that extends into our daily lives" (Duffett 2013, 18). As with Bomar's story discussed below, Melina is allowed to author the story of her own fandom, narrativizing and making sense of her attachment to the band as being long-standing (since she was sixteen) and her own personal history and situation as a single parent, a trope often featured in Pulp's songs.

'I'm a man': Representing male fandom in *Pulp: The Film*

While female fans are often represented as excessive and hysterical, male fans have also suffered from a variety of stereotypes and, with the exception of sports fans, are often characterized as being "awkward around women, sarcastic, intelligent, obsessive and protective of [their] collection [of merchandise]" (Geraghty 2014, 24). In *Pulp: The Film*, male fans subvert some of these categories but, unlike many of the female fans, are not constructed in relation to their sexual attraction to Jarvis Cocker. Instead, they are allowed space to offer their own stories and claim their own fan identities. Indeed, it is not just female fans that gather outside the venue. Two male fans are interviewed on-screen in this location, although both remain unnamed. The first is seen as part of a heterosexual romantic couple and he outlines how they met: "Funnily enough we met at a Jarvis concert. Yeah in 2008 he was playing in Manchester Academy." This unnamed male fan appears only once and is positioned both as appropriately displaying his heteronormative masculinity and drawing on subcultural capital that is relevant to the couple's fandom of Pulp, having met at one of Jarvis Cocker's solo gigs. Their fandom works to represent appropriate and sanctified forms of fan identity through longevity and dedication, following Cocker's career even when it had become less commercially successful and less "mainstream."

The second male fan we see on-screen is interviewed and his words are presented via subtitle and translated from the original German. This fan is, again, unnamed and seen only once in the film. He comments, "I think that what makes Pulp so interesting is that they're moments from real life. And they're beautifully expressed. That's why it works so well. You can relate to it because it's real life." His fandom is articulated as an appreciation of Pulp's songs from an artistic perspective (their songs are "beautifully expressed") but this fan also works to narrativize the experience of fandom, intertwining moments of real life with an appreciation for how the band captures these in songs. As Harrington and Bielby (2010) note, "media fans' life narratives might thus be said to comprise complex interactions between our 'real' life (our biography), our autobiography (our storying of our life), and the media texts which help construct, give meaning to and guide the relationship between the two" (p. 444). This fan shares some similarities with another key figure from the documentary, a male called Bomar. Bomar isn't explicitly identified as a Pulp fan on-screen but, nevertheless, discusses the impact of both the group and his experiences of living in Sheffield. Bomar is labeled as a musician and is an eccentric figure with bleached blonde hair, makeup, and a fur leopard print coat. He discusses his relationship with Pulp and the city of Sheffield:

> I accidentally moved to London for about six months once and it was pretty chaotic. I got mugged twice in one night [...] so straight away I got the Megabus back up to Sheffield and had quite a rough time of it. [Bomar goes onto explain how his friend took him to a local pub] He says "you know what to do" to the barman and he put a Pulp CD on and I just sat in the pub all day, listening to Pulp and gradually I felt my strength coming back [...] I felt better. I always feel much more at ease in Sheffield [...] I'm not saying you don't get mugged but it's usually funny. You'd usually know the person who is mugging you or something.

Later, Bomar discusses his favorite Pulp song, noting, "I think 'Babies' because there's a chord in it—a D major 7—and it sums up that kind of not-quite-right feeling, you know [...] not quite happy, its nearly happy and that for me like makes it seem homely. I'm comfortable in that kind of mess." Although Bomar isn't explicitly labeled on-screen as a fan of the band (constructed instead as a musician), his fandom of Pulp is clear (see Finlay's interview at the end of this book). The intertwining of the band's music with his own return home to Sheffield shows a sense of self-narrativization, reflecting how individuals often utilize media texts and objects to develop self-identity

(Williams 2015). As with the unnamed German fan interviewed outside the concert venue, Bomar is permitted a level of self-reflection and logical distance that many of the female fans are not allowed. His discussion of his favorite Pulp song is both rational (the discussion of specific musical chords) and personal (via his admission that he is happy living in chaos and "mess"), while his story of return to Sheffield is an example of the intertwining between self-identity, narrative, and fandom that characterizes a range of different media fan cultures.

"Help the aged": The aging pulp fan and/as local celebrity

In addition to the younger male and female fans seen in *Pulp: The Film*, the documentary also explores issues around aging and generational identity via the second type of fans depicted in the film. These are local people from Sheffield who fall outside of the demographic we might usually expect to see in mediated texts about fandom. These consist of two older people, Terry and Josephine, who are identified on-screen by their names and the title of "Pulp fan." Whereas the predominantly female fans discussed above tended to discuss their love for the band, and the figure of Jarvis Cocker, both Terry and Josephine offer broader thoughts on Pulp as well as wider issues such as life, and living in the city of Sheffield. The inclusion of these figures echoes the film's emphasis on aging, as well as offering a counterpoint to the aging, "sexy" celebrity represented by Jarvis Cocker.

Josephine is a grey-haired woman with walking sticks who is interviewed on a bench in the center of Sheffield. Her knowledge of Pulp, and contemporary music in general, is fairly detailed and she comments that "I know [Jarvis has] been based in France over the last few years and now Pulp have reformed so they're going on a national tour. When they first started out, listen to music them and Blur and of the two, I prefer Pulp […] More melody, and better words actually. He says, it makes you think what they're saying and I like music that makes you think." Later in the film she notes that "It might be nice to look into his background and find out what motivates him. Because if you're not motivated you can't do well and he's done very well for himself. But you have to be motivated." Here Josephine displays common knowledge and subcultural capital—knowing for example, that Jarvis has recently lived in France—as well as expresses a desire for further knowledge about the object of fandom in learning about Jarvis's background and history. In contrast, the figure of Terry displays no such intimate knowledge. First seen working in a newspaper kiosk outside Sheffield's indoor Castle Market (where a teenage Jarvis Cocker famously worked), Terry offers little insight into his status as a fan, even though he is identified as one on-screen. His comments are brief and include his declaration that his favorite song is Queen's "We Are the Champions" and the following:

Q: Are you going to the big concert tonight? The Pulp concert?
A: Yes. Yes I am. I enjoy it.
Q: You like Jarvis?
A: He's alright, yeah.

The presence of these older "fans" speaks to one of the film's broader concerns around aging and the ongoing march of time. As Jarvis Cocker notes about the Pulp song "Help the Aged," "getting old is what happens" and "nothing lasts forever. I tried to imagine what it would be like when my generation were pensioners [...] There's only one way that road is leading. I accept that it's inevitable." Seeing figures from an older generation on-screen as fans clearly poses a visual challenge to commonsense ideas around who fans are and what they do, echoing the findings of prior studies of aging, and older fans who have drawn attention to the role of fandom across one's life course. For example, Harrington and Bielby (2010) consider the importance of considering the impact of "the aging *body* on fan identities and practices" and "the aging *mind*" (436), while the aging of groups such as Goths (Hodkinson 2011) and punks (Bennett 2006) have also been analyzed. However, despite positioning the fandom of Terry and Josephine as equally legitimate as that of the younger fans outside the concert venue, there are some moments in the film where the fandom of older people seems out of place or somehow odd. This is perhaps clearest in a shot of younger gig-goers alongside the older Terry; given our commonplace understanding of what fans *should* look like and who they *should* be, Terry's presence at the gig is jarring and incongruous. *Pulp: The Film* thus presents Terry as an unconventional fan who is treated both affectionately and also as a slightly absurd figure when placed amongst more typical types of fan.

Despite the limited representation of his fandom, Terry performs a more complex role regarding the film's depiction of fandom as celebrity. The links between fandom and celebrity have been discussed in prior work; for example, Matt Hills (2006) questions "how—and to what degree—fan and celebrity cultural identities can overlap and interact rather than belonging to wholly separable domains" (p. 103), and suggests challenging "the otherwise 'restrictive categories' of pure celebrity and fan, where media production and consumption are neatly carved apart" (p. 103). The figure of *Pulp: The Film*'s Terry is both constructed as a fan (albeit an unusual one) and as a local celebrity. Indeed, it is the local aspect to Terry's recognition that is most crucial here since, although other participants in the film (primarily Bomar) are discussed in reviews and publicity materials, it is Terry who functions as a local character and, via the film's promotion and distribution, a form of subcultural star or "localebrity" (McElroy and Williams 2011).

Before the film debuted at Sheffield Doc/Fest, an appeal was made on social media to locate Terry so that he could be invited to attend the event. Director Florian Habicht claimed that Terry was a "star of the film" (No author 2014) and he was eventually tracked down via resolutely local networks involving the local Sheffield newspaper *The Star*. The paper detailed how "We asked for help and dozens of you told us where to find him in Boynton Road, Shirecliffe" and outlined how, at the premiere, "Pulp fan Terry Hunter wasn't one of the Common People at the band's European film premiere—he got The Star VIP treatment" (No author 2014). Terry himself notes, "'I'm going to be as famous as them [laughs]'" (No author 2014). Terry is thus "known within [the] very specific bounded locale" of Sheffield and even after his mediation via the film "carr[ied] some of these elements with [him], remaining resolutely local and with status based on such intimate recognition and renown" (McElroy and Williams 2011, 11–12). Indeed, the movement of Terry, and all of the attendees at the film's screening, into the realm of the celebrity is necessarily fleeting. They cross the threshold of the media—the "boundary between 'ordinary person' and 'media person'" (Couldry 2004, 60)—only temporarily before moving back into everyday life; Terry will not, despite his joke, become "as famous as" Pulp and, if his recognition does continue, it will be in the pages of the local newspaper rather than in the global media circuits on which *Pulp: The Film* plays. As Ferris and Harris (2011) rightly note, certain places are more likely than others to facilitate celebrity encounters, such as Los Angeles and New York, "where entertainment is a dominant industry and ordinary citizens may see celebrities sitting in a restaurant or in line at a movie theater" (p. 34). However, the "alternative geography of celebrity" (Couldry 2001, 147) displayed in *Pulp: The Film* does draw attention to nonnormative forms of celebrity through the local character (and, in Terry's case, the nonnormative fan) to offer more marginal representations of the geography of celebrity and the types of locally recognizable figure who live there. It also suggests the possibility of types of local fandom which could be usefully explored further within fan studies.

Conclusion

Despite claims that fandom is "everywhere and all the time, a central part of the everyday lives of consumers operating within a networked society" (Jenkins 2007a, 361), cultural stereotypes still surround certain forms of fandom and fan practice. Fan cultures, especially those involving young females, are often still linked to established "pop cultural representations of fan audiences," which pathologizes fans as "cultural 'Others'—as obsessive, freakish, hysterical, infantile and regressive social subjects" (Hills 2007, 459–60). In this discussion of *Pulp: The Film*, I have considered contradictory and complex mediated representations of both fandom and forms of local celebrity. *Pulp: The Film* represents a variety of fandoms, from desiring female fans to older, less-common forms of fan who are linked very much to local identities and a sense of place. The fans we see on-screen are varied, although there are still aspects of their portrayal that mark some of them as "odd," whether this is the seemingly incongruous figure of a fan of Terry's age attending a Pulp concert or Lowri's declarations of desire for a man old enough to be her grandfather. Similarly, the film presents a range of celebrity representations, from the nationally recognizable and enduring stardom of Jarvis Cocker and the more residual fame of other Pulp band members to the geographically rooted and limited recognition of those figures who appear in the documentary itself. Similarly, the links and overlaps between celebrities and fans—or celebrities who position themselves as fans—begin to open up avenues for further discussion of how established oppositions between the everyday and extraordinary or producers and consumers of celebrity and stardom may be blurred within local and subcultural contexts.

The film largely avoids any attempt at an authoritative voice to guide the viewer. The only instance of this occurs when the names of participants and their status (as "Pulp fan" or "dance troupe" and so on) are labeled on-screen. By avoiding visual or aural cues such as a voice-over to guide the viewing of the film, viewers are largely left to make their own minds up about the different types of fan that they see on screen, even if certain stereotypes of fans—such as the adoring female fan—are sometimes invoked. As Hills (2007) notes in his discussion of the Michael Jackson documentary *Wacko About Jacko*, representations of media fans can seldom be divided into a simple positive/negative binary. To attempt to fit representations into these oppositions risks missing "the contradictory, even oxymoronic, way in which contemporary media fans can be portrayed" (p. 460). *Pulp: The Film* thus offers a variety of representations of fan and celebrity and, in its apparent leveling out and equalizing of both fan identity and forms of local celebrity, asks us to formulate our own views of the characters we see before us. While some "types of media fandom are still far from entirely 'normalized' within contemporary culture" (Hills 2007, 463), *Pulp: A Film About Life, Death & Supermarkets* presents some challenges to what is presented as "normalized" and how a range of fan and/or local celebrity identities can be represented on screen.

Note

1   Despite this statement, the band was actually propelled to fame across the United Kingdom, including Northern Ireland, Wales, and Scotland alongside England.

3

"I Was Stabbed 21 Times by Crazy Fans": Pro Wrestling and Popular Concerns with Immersive Story Worlds

Sam Ford

Barnum had a saying: 'The most thankless thing in the world is wising up a sucker.' I was reminded recently ... of the astonishing renaissance of professional wrestling. Vaudeville might die, fashion might change, man might go to the moon—but the ranks of the gullible in our society never thin, the capacity for self-deception never seems to diminish. —Jim Murray, *The Los Angeles Times*, 1985

The old 'it's fake but it hurts!' defense, the one wrestling fans have clung to ever since the ruse was blown in the 90s. Are you sure that's the Thames I can see over there, because it feels like you're in denial. —Judas Hardwood, VICE, 2012

Time may pass, but cultural critics' fascination with the "real/fake" construct for discussing professional wrestling—and its fans—never loses favor. Since before wrestling became an early TV staple, commentators have marveled at those who immerse themselves in the matches. US pro wrestling's roots are entangled with societal concerns about the impact entertainment can have on one's moral character. From its glorification of individualistic competition and emphasis on the human body to popular narratives about the effects it can have on spectators' aggression levels and fans' mental stability, critics routinely rank wrestling among the most dangerous toxins in our pop culture environment.

The perception that wrestling is especially "lowbrow," and its viewers are less able to defend themselves against pop culture's dangers, is pervasive. While their study was often empathetic to the complex ways fans engage with wrestling, this quote from sociologists Gregory Stone and Ramon Oldenberg (1967) is illustrative:

Lower-status persons seldom question the concrete world around them. Consequently, they are more susceptible to staging than persons on higher status levels ... We can deduce that wrestling spectators, and especially wrestling fans, believe the wrestling hero is *really* good and that the villain is *really* bad. (pp. 526–7, emphasis in original).

Meanwhile, Murray's 1985 piece quoted earlier emphasizes a concern that those "lower" people cannot ultimately be rescued: "(W)restling is like sex. You can rail against it, legislate against it, condemn it, threaten it with punishment and campaign against it. But you'll never make it unpopular with the masses."

Concerns about wrestling's negative effects extend beyond issues of class. Chad Dell's research (2006) into mainstream press accounts of 1950s female fans highlights how moral handwringing centered on protecting the virtues of girls, grandmothers, "maiden aunts," and housewives. And, looking at the late 1990s and early 2000s, when a sexist "concern for the fairer sex" had gone out of style for moral panic, Nicholas Sammond (2005) highlights how the fear of what wrestling might "do" to fans turned to (white/middle-class) adolescents, who risked immersion while "slumming it" in this spandex-clad world. In short, wrestling fans—whether simpletons, women, or children—need cultural critics' protection while also are deserving their scorn.

This chapter explores why outside representations of wrestling fan behavior often fail to grasp the performative environment of professional wrestling in representing wrestling fans either as victims or as monsters. In particular, it argues that cultural critics writing "from the outside" often misrepresent the motivations, pleasures, and creativity of the wrestling fan because their analysis misses one or more of three crucial points of context—the concept of *kayfabe* that pro wrestling adapted from its carnival roots; the exaggerated tradition of storytelling among those in the wrestling industry; and the degree and nature of performativity among wrestling fans.

The "fanatic" stereotype

Concerns about media accounts stereotyping fans are at the heart of fan studies' origins. Responding to the "Get a Life" mentality aimed against *Star Trek* fans, Henry Jenkins (1992) writes of one account of *Star Trek* fandom, "Details (of fan activities)...are selective, offering a distorted picture of their community, shaping the reality of its culture to conform to stereotypes already held by *Newsweek*'s writers and readers" (p. 11). The pathologizing of wrestling fans goes well beyond a general fear of fandom and encompasses as well a fear of what especially immersive stories might do to people. The volume of wrestling texts mimics the season of a "real" sports league, meaning that wrestling narratives are always "to be continued." However, wrestling has no "off-season." Almost every week, World Wrestling Entertainment alone airs at least five hours of new cable network programming, multiple hours of new programs on its WWE Network, and a steady stream of material in myriad media forms. That volume helps drive the concern that wrestling fans don't occasionally dip into the fiction but rather reside there.

Pro wrestling shares this hyperserialized storytelling style—and a designation near the bottom of the cultural "value" hierarchy—with the US soap opera, a genre whose fanbase has long been similarly pathologized. Perhaps it's no surprise that C. Lee Harrington and Denise D. Bielby's (1995) attempts to debunk the stereotypes of fans as "either losers ... or lunatics who pose serious threats to celebrities' physical safety" in the early years of fan studies centered on soap opera fans (1). Beginning with soaps' origins in radio, critics have voiced concerns of what immersion in soaps might do to fans—a sentiment best illustrated by the work of psychologist Louis Berg, who spoke out regularly about the various mental illnesses housewives risked from listening to radio serials (see, for instance, Berg 1942).

While soap fans have suffered continuous ridicule, wrestling fandom has surely fared worse. Perhaps it's in part because so-called "fanatical" behavior has long been more condoned in response to the "real" world of sports—and, thus, pro wrestling is particularly troubling because it distorts all the trappings of sacred "authentic" competition. But wrestling is also scorned because of attributes hard to grasp from the outside. To understand why wrestling fandom has been severely misunderstood—and why both wrestlers and fans willingly perpetuate some of these myths—again, we must examine:

- how the carnival roots of professional wrestling led to a traditional wrestling code called *kayfabe*;
- how *kayfabe* and the hyperbolic nature of wrestling performers often confuse the outside world (and, occasionally, those within pro wrestling as well);
- and how the performative nature of fans shapes what outsiders see.

To better understand why pro wrestling and its fans are so often the target of public concern/derision, we must examine each of these aspects of wrestling culture in detail.

Wrestling's carnival roots

Jim Murray's evocation of P.T. Barnum highlighted earlier is apropos, considering that carnivals played a significant role in shaping modern professional wrestling. As Gerald Morton and George O'Brien (1985) note, wrestlers looking to professionalize their skills in the 1880s and 1890s did so at fairs and circuses "in that day long before radio and television when all Americans came 'to see the elephant'" (p. 31). The marriage of wrestling and carnival shaped both wrestling's showmanship and its focus on "fleecing the betting public" through fixing contests.

Pro wrestling's rise via the carnival circuit led to a carny mentality within the wrestling industry, which still persists. As George Kerrick (1980) explains, the language used in wrestling draws from a combination of the circus, the business world, performance arts, horse operas, and melodrama. In particular, the use of jargon as argot to shield the wrestling business from outsiders particularly evoked carny culture. Most relevant to this analysis, wrestlers have long used the term "mark" to describe the wrestling spectator. Perhaps Freddie Blassie (with Greenberg 2003), writing about his days wrestling in carnivals, put it best: "The whole point of any carnival is keeping the 'marks' in the dark about the techniques being used to separate them from their money" (p. 14). And wrestlers have used business terms like *work* and *selling* to talk of their own efforts. *Work* refers to "any rehearsed or preestablished plan or movement" in wrestling (Kerrick 1980), while "convincing his audience that he is … in great pain or incensed" is called *selling* … as "the wrestler must *sell* the spectator, just as a vacuum-cleaner salesman would convince a homeowner" (pp. 142–3). In other words, *workers* must *sell* if they are going to convince the *marks*.

Wrestlers' desire to ensure "the business" wasn't exposed to "the marks" is encapsulated by the idea of *kayfabe*. Sharon Mazer (1998) writes that *kayfabe* is borrowed from the carnivals, medicine shows, and sideshows of the 1800s and "simply refers to a con or deception": "most wrestlers are proud to be called kayfabians because it means they're in on the (con) game" (pp. 22–3).

Wrestling's "business" was built on the idea that fans were being duped into believing the show was real. And, while wrestling now typically admits "the con" outside the narrative, this language of "fooling the marks" persists. So do instances of "maintaining kayfabe" and concerns about "exposing the business," meaning many wrestlers still stay somewhat in character offstage. For instance, one performer with regional league New England Championship Wrestling told my 2007 MIT class on pro wrestling about being recognized by a waiter who was a fan. He explained that he stiffed the waiter on the tip because he wanted the waiter to tell fellow fans, "I met him in real life, and he's an even bigger asshole than his character is."

The hyperbole of wrestling performance

Stories of fans who lose sight of the line between reality and fiction is a staple of wrestling lore and a favorite for performers who played heels (villains) to share when addressing a wider audience. Examining the memoirs of famous wrestling heels, in the words of wrestler Ole Anderson, "(t)he stories are endless" (Anderson and Teal 2003, 112):

- Ric Flair (with Greenberg 2004, 44–5) describes fans throwing penknives, hitting wrestlers with pennies from slingshots, throwing a rattlesnake into the ring, and biting a wrestler's finger off, after the wrestler challenged the fan to come into the ring.
- Jimmy Hart (2004, 87) writes about being hit with a dart from a homemade blowgun, among other stories.
- Ole Anderson (with Teal 2003, 112–16) writes of being hit by a motorcycle helmet, attacked with seat belts, and "stabbed several times in my career" before giving detailed account of an incident that received mainstream attention—having his chest sliced open by a 79-year-old man, requiring 100 stitches.
- Terry Funk (with Williams 2005, 84) writes that "Puerto Rican fans were nuts. They hated me with a passion," before describing how those fans threw rocks and bricks at him and how he had to fight them to his car each night by throwing full, open beer cans at them.

- Jesse Ventura (1999, 96–8) describes working fans "into such frenzies that they really believed you were what you were in the ring" and shares stories of a mob tearing down his dressing room door, death threats, and a fan cornering him with a 10 inch hunting knife.
- Bobby Heenan (with Anderson 2002, 153–60) describes fans throwing chairs, rocks, nails, hardboiled eggs, a trumpet, and lighters; shooting him with a pellet gun in the arena; and hitting him in the head with a ballpeen hammer. He also talks of being in the ring when a fan stabbed a wrestler with a stiletto knife dipped in pig fat, so the wound would become infected, and fans destroying wrestlers' cars (although, he claims, the wise wrestlers would make it look like another car in the lot was theirs so the damage would come to the property of some poor spectator rather than them).

Perhaps no one was better at spinning a yarn about crazed fans than "Classy" Freddie Blassie. His memoir is filled with stories of being attacked by fans and even arena security guards. And, while describing his character's acrimonious relationship with those fans, Blassie begins hurling the same sorts of barbs he was known for on stage within the memoir itself—continuing that performance "against" the fans while he looks back on his career:

> People swung sticks, clubs, anything they could get their hands on … In the ring, I'd have to keep one eye on my opponent, and the other on all the debris that was being tossed my direction. I'd get hit with beer bottles, rotten apples, oranges, even bags of shit … I like to think that these birdbrains scooped up dog shit before they came to the arena. But when you got a look at some of these half-wits, you had to wonder. (Blassie with Greenberg 2003, 53)

Blassie brags that, while his *drawing heat* (wrestling terminology for riling up the crowd) sold the tickets, other performers didn't want to be seen with him, for the fear that fans might come after them, too (pp. 56–7).

There's likely more than a kernel of truth in most of their stories, as these wrestlers' penchant for drawing intense heat from thousands of people several nights a week for decades got them in many compromising situations. But it's equally important to understand their own motivations for choosing stories that best demonstrate their narrative of how much they were hated. Such stories are—for wrestlers who primarily worked as heels—the clearest marker of being a great performer, proving they are masters at maintaining kayfabe and inciting emotions. Terry Funk (with Williams 2005) described this pride directly, writing about the two pocket knives on the wall of his office, which came out of his body after being stabbed by fans: "In a strange way, I took being stabbed as a badge of honor … Those people were really giving me an award, even though they didn't realize it. They were telling me I had done my job, as a heel, and done it pretty well" (p. 84).[1]

Beyond the heel performer's particular motivation, it's important to keep in mind the sensationalistic nature of most wrestling stories. Sharon Mazer (1998) writes that *kayfabe* also refers "to participants' self-promotional, rhetorically inflated, and somewhat truth-obfuscating patter that resembles that of the talkers at the traditional sideshow" (p. 22)—"the hyperbole that is at the heart of the wrestling experience" (p. 9). Wrestling promoters exaggerate attendance figures, add inches and pounds to wrestlers' descriptions, and create "big fish tales" about characters' backstories. Such descriptions have the same flare for exaggeration as the in-ring performance does for demonstrating anger, suffering, humiliation, and other core human emotions—all prime examples of Roland Barthes's description of wrestling as a "spectacle of excess" (1957; trans. 1972, 15).

For example, in the early days of television, when a Japanese wrestling show included a close-up of Freddie Blassie biting wrestler Rikidozan, local reports indicated that six elderly men across the country had heart attacks (Meltzer 2004, 23). However, Blassie took typical wrestling "liberties" with the story over time. He says to Andy Kaufman in the 1983 mockumentary *My Breakfast with Blassie*: "In that four-week tour, about twenty people dropped dead of heart attacks from me biting. I was the one that introduced the first biting in wrestling."

It's no surprise, then, that descriptions of fanatical audience behavior become wrestling lore, as it is crucial not only for performers' self-mythologization but also for promoters' "legend-making" processes. One of Blassie's most repeated lines was that he had been cut and stabbed repeatedly. In *My Breakfast with Blassie*, it was eleven times. Murray's 1985 piece quoted earlier claims he was stabbed "about twenty times leaving the ring." By Blassie's induction into WWE Hall of Fame in 1994, the number had expanded to twenty-one, according to a *Baltimore Sun* interview (Kaltenbach 1994).

Wrestling's lack of separation between actor and character—in the narrative and in performers' minds—has contributed to a significant lack of understanding from cultural commentators encountering wrestlers' stories of fan attacks. When media producers cover wrestling from the outside, these stories often make it through without the hyperbole inherent in pro wrestling acknowledged—or perhaps because wrestling's carny-inspired love of sensationalizing is a welcome sound to the ear media outlets have for "not letting the truth get in the way of a good story," as the adage goes.

Role-playing in the stands

Wrestlers aren't the only ones performing, however. The ways wrestling fans engage with the narrative are likewise often misunderstood—a fact once wonderfully parodied by *The Onion*'s 2010 story, "Wrestling Fan's Comments Alternate between Admitting It's Fake, Forgetting It's Fake" (*The Onion* 2010). Many fan studies scholars have been fascinated with the oscillation between critical engagement and "the willing suspension of disbelief" (Coleridge 1817)—a mode of dual engagement Cassandra Amesley (1989) calls "double viewing." However, this paradox—the fan who knows it's "not real" yet engages as if it is—has been especially a focus when discussing wrestling fans, particularly since the text itself is predicated on blurring the lines between reality and fiction. For instance, Stone and Oldenberg (1967) write that the origins of their study referenced earlier came after hearing a fan yell at the TV in a bar, "I don't give a damn if it is a fake! Kill the son-of-a-bitch!" (p. 503).

Gerald Craven and Richard Moseley (1972) assert that the experience of the wrestling fan must be understood "as pure theater" (p. 327). However, most existing academic research into wrestling performance has still framed fans as spectators. Thus, most studies of wrestling fans have not contextualized fans' actions within a performance studies perspective—looking not just at how fans suspend disbelief but also how they become active players in the show.

Nick Trujillo et al.'s 2000 ethnography of wrestling fans at live events is one exception. Trujillo et al. acknowledge that "many audience members stage their own performances as spectators to fully enjoy and participate in the event" and write that observing the wrestling fan in the element of the live event led to their research team "reevaluat(ing) our own initial classist, sexist, and racist assumptions about the (wrestling) audience and … critiquing what we thought were the classist, sexist, and racist tendencies of some of the researchers who have written about wrestling audiences" (pp. 538–9).

I first encountered fan studies through my work on wrestling fandom a little more than a decade ago, while completing an honor's thesis at Western Kentucky University. At the time, I was performing in local wrestling shows, as a heel (nonathletic) character. These shows were a "double performance"—local (mostly) boys who weren't trained as professional wrestlers organizing unsanctioned shows in which we put on a full night's performance as if we were the characters of WWE.[2] I typically played the role of WWE owner Vince McMahon. In the process, I became intrigued by the relationship between the audience and our "on-stage" performers in a small-town setting, where several of us in the show knew a good portion of those in attendance.

One particular moment drove my initial curiosity. I was standing in line for the portable toilet that wrestlers and fans alike used during intermission. A boy—perhaps eight or nine—had been arguing with my character throughout the night. While we were standing in line, he smiled and said, "You're doing a good job out there." I thought to myself, "You, too," but probably didn't say it aloud—after all, there was kayfabe to maintain. That young fan's performance illustrates well what Shane Toepfer (2011) describes in his dissertation on wrestling fan engagement at live events as "playful audience" practices—imagining the wrestling arena as a space for identity experimentation and performativity.

Yet, there were also moments where I thought I was going to get punched by a fan—for instance, while lecturing a father whose son yelled at me about how children today aren't taught basic respect. The collective performance was made all the more complicated when we later obtained a wrestling promoter's license and used legitimate pro wrestling performers on the card, and I began playing an evil version of myself— Sam Ford, owner of Universal Championship Wrestling (a grandiose name for an organization headquartered in Hartford, Ky.—home of "2,000 happy people and a few soreheads," according to the town sign).

I did what I could to draw heat. During one of my trips home from graduate school, I tried to incite fans while talking about my affluent private school East Coast lifestyle while they struggled to pull together the funds to buy a ticket to our show. In the process, I drew on my "real" identity—and the fans'—to further blur that designation between "real" and "fake." During my time in graduate school, I was also a contributor to the local *Ohio County Times-News*, writing a column called "From Beaver Dam to Boston." My character indicated to wrestling fans that the affable columnist the general public read was the façade. Meanwhile, those who attended the UCW shows knew the "real" Sam Ford—who couldn't wait to leave Kentucky and felt nothing but contempt for having to come back to "The Bluegrass State"—only doing so to ensure the profits kept flowing in from the pockets of the fans whose poverty he mocked.

In February 2004, while working on my WKU honors thesis, I completed an ethnographic project, interviewing wrestling fans during and after five live events in Indiana, Kentucky, and Tennessee. These ranged from one of our own small-town "costume" shows (before we "went legit," if there's such a thing in the wrestling world) to televised events and a stop on WWE's national tour (Ford 2007). I found that those in attendance engaged with the live event in five ways—as spectators, as critics, as theorists, as community members, and as performers—often moving fluidly among those modes of engagement throughout the show. (In comparison to Amesley's "double viewing," we might suppose these fans were engaged in "quintuple viewing.")

In particular, I estimated that about half of the fifty fans I spoke with seemed, themselves, engaged at times in performing as "sports fan"—despite the fact that all fifty adults I interviewed openly acknowledged understanding that wrestling was scripted entertainment. Most of the fans I interviewed knew they were expected to not just watch but also provide the "heat" that wrestlers were looking to achieve. And several of the fans acknowledged that the show was scripted in a way that expected a certain response from them in order to achieve the story's full effects. As I wrote (Ford 2007, 23–4):

> For these fans, the price of admission was the chance to pay to become part of an acting experience, not as a spectator but as an active and vital part of the show ... Some of these fans seemed to explicitly believe that ... they could change the outcome of the event through their performances, by taking their performance in a way different than they were scripted to.

Some fans explicitly felt a call to action to perform. One said, "The people are up in the ring doing their thing, and they need our help and support to keep in character. Basically, that's why I cheer and go on." Another said, "The screaming and hollering makes the show. If the crowd is quiet, the show is boring" (pp. 28–9).

I was fascinated with how a few of the fans I interviewed at these events justified their active engagement. They wanted to ensure I was aware that, while they realized the show was staged, many of the others who attended wrestling matches didn't (even though my interviews indicated that must be an extreme minority). Thus, they saw their performance as a way of preserving the illusion for those who hadn't been "smartened up." One person told me, "Some people actually believe this. I participate in the show to help make it seem more real to them. If I get into it, then I can make it feel more real." And another said that her not participating in the show as a believing fan would be akin to revealing the truth about Santa Claus to a child (p. 26).

To put it in wrestler parlance, these fans justified their own acting as a way to maintain kayfabe for the marks. Just as wrestlers have traditionally relied on empowering their performance through depicting fans as gullible believers, so do fans distinguish "the marks" from their more enlightened positions as smarts. *Smarts* refers to those fans who keep up with what's happening backstage in the wrestling industry and was once used to warn carnies about fans wise to the con. As Lawrence McBride and S. Elizabeth Bird (2007) write, "Smarts see (Marks) as the stereotypical 'dupes' imagined by wrestling's critics" (p. 169). However, while McBride and Bird are somewhat correct when they say that "Smarts view Marks with scorn" (p. 169), they also envy them. As Mazer (1998) and others have explored, smarts constantly strive to so lose themselves in their performance that they momentarily forget they're playing a role—a process wrestling fans call *marking out*—and critically praise those storylines and in-ring performances that still *sell* them, no matter how *smart* they are.[3]

Conclusion: Wrestling performance as collective con

At the 2015 WWE Hall of Fame ceremony, veteran wrestler Larry Zbyszko engaged in a direct address to his fans that simultaneously encapsulates the kayfabe hyperbole of the pro wrestler, acknowledges the performance of fans, and engages in the framing of the "dangerous fan" stereotype:

> There's something I've been wanting to say about the professional wrestling fans for a long, long time. You know, without each other to share the power of our imaginations with, there would be no dreams at all. And what I'm going to say about the professional wrestling fan…I want logged forever in cyberspace. I want it written on the pages of Wikipedia. I want it shouted out on every forecast, broadcast, podcast. I want it archived by every secret government agency and foreign country spying on this transmission, for this is the truth. I have felt the love of standing in the ring with millions and millions of people chanting my name… And I have felt the wrath of fighting my way out of riots, night after night, whiskey bottles and chairs crashing and smashing from the balconies above. I ran out to my car to escape the mob; it was set on fire. Others were smashing rocks and bricks. I was overturned in a cab behind the Boston Garden, shot at leaving an arena in Albany, New York. And stabbed in the ass by the greatest fans of all! WWE UNIVERSE… you are what's awesome.

Here, Zbyszko seemingly brags about the fact that the marks' belief is what made his career possible. Yet, he opens the address by acknowledging wrestling as "a dream" that comes out of having "each other to share the power of our imaginations with." And he closes, perhaps, with giving a nod to the fans' own performance over the years as being equally "Hall of Fame" worthy. In short, his career is a collective con that is only possible in the combined imagination of in-ring performer and fans.

Wrestling performers and fans aren't the only ones who rely on the carny mentality of imagining the audience as marks, though. Cultural critics who are either naïve in their belief that wrestling fans are unable to parse reality from fiction or else engage in their own "willing suspension of disbelief" and pretend that wrestling fans are overly gullible to fit their own hyperbolic purposes engage in a process of performance perhaps not that far removed from the kayfabe engaged in by the wrestling industry and fandom. (I mean to echo here the theme of wrestler Mick Foley's 2001 book *Foley Is Good...and the Real World Is Faker than Wrestling*—that the deceptions of the wrestling world pale in comparison to the less expected fakery in journalism, media effects research, and other "more legitimized" communication forms.) The treatment of wrestling fans as marks by cultural critics has often led to the victimization of wrestling fandom, on the one hand, and a fear of it, on the other.

Writing in response to Sut Jhally and Jackson Katz's 2002 film *Wrestling with Manhood*, Henry Jenkins (2005) says their "literal-mindedness" in watching the performance of wrestling fans at the live event on camera "depicts wrestling spectators as moral monsters" (p. 300). Jenkins writes that the film lacks an acknowledgment "that these fans, who come to ringside in costume, mimic the catchphrases, waving signs they hope will get on camera, might see themselves as part of the performance, enacting, spoofing, taking pleasure in the imaginary roles and fantasy values on offer" (p. 300). Also writing in response to *Wrestling with Manhood*, McBride and Bird (2007) point out that "[t]his 'cultural dope' theory of the audience has been effectively dismantled when it comes to most media-reception situations, yet wrestling fans as critical readers seem hard for critics to grasp" (p. 175). This is particularly true because the performative nature of wrestling fandom and fans' engagement in some logics of kayfabe mask what McBride and Bird call an "elaborate criticism of wrestling" (p. 175) that many fans engage in.

Analyzing wrestling fandom from the outside remains particularly difficult without understanding that wrestlers are rarely, if ever, out of character. For on-stage wrestling performers, the stage isn't confined by the ring. In other words, many wrestling performers rarely attempt to appear "extratextually."[4]

But, even more vital to understanding wrestling is acknowledging that it is a 360-degree performance between on-stage talent and "in-the-stands" talent. Wrestling fans play a vital role in the fictional story world of WWE and in maintaining kayfabe, in the arena and elsewhere. (Note that WWE itself calls both its narrative world and its fandom the "WWE Universe"—indicating that fans are, themselves, part of this fictional world. Perhaps, then, pro wrestling can best be understood as a continuous alternate reality game.) If the wrestling industry's hyperbole is built around pretending that fans are being deceived and fans are dedicated to performing being deceived, we can ultimately see both the wrestling industry and wrestling fandom engaged together in maintaining this "con" on the rest of the world. And this collective performance often continues to provide just the exaggerations and examples that cultural critics seek when describing their disdain for pro wrestling.

We are at a moment in which fan studies is necessarily deepening its use of performance studies as a lens through which to understand fans and their relationships to media producers and texts (see, for instance, Bennett and Booth 2015). The fandom engaged with story worlds like those provided by pro wrestling, soap operas, and comic book narrative universes provide particularly productive locations for understanding the nature of fan performance. In particular, the active role wrestling must grant to fan performance within the text itself makes it an especially crucial venue for exploring fandom as performance. Only by understanding the fans' engagement as a performance can cultural critics and academics really examine what draws people to immersive texts and provide proper context to the role fandom plays in the lives of those who participate.

Notes

1   While wrestling heels have a particular penchant, motivation, and culture that encourages sharing such "crazed fan" stories, these stories are by no means particular to wrestlers' memoirs. For instance, with the similar modes of immersive storytelling between pro wrestling and soap opera noted in this essay, it's perhaps not surprising to find soap opera actors using fan stories to praise their own performances in similar ways. Soap opera star Eileen Fulton—who played *As the World Turns'* Lisa Miller (Hughes Eldgridge Shea Colman McColl Mitchell Chedwyn Grimaldi, to fit in all her married last names throughout the course of the show) from 1960 until the show's ending in 2010—echoes pro wrestling heels when talking about the "defining moment" of her career in her memoir: "If … your sights were set on becoming the first deliciously wicked, scheming vixen on daytime television, what could possibly be a more definitive measure of success than having total strangers call you a 'bitch' and a 'whore' or having your ears boxed in the streets of New York" (Fulton with Atholl and Cherkinian 1995, ix).

2   For more on my history with wrestling fandom, see Ford (2014).

3   It's worth pointing out that the notion that most of the wrestling audience—or even carnival audiences in general—were ever completely duped by the con game deserves a strong dose of skepticism. In his analysis of Barnum and the culture of nineteenth-century hoaxes more broadly, Neil Harris (1973, 77) writes, "Experiencing a complicated hoax was pleasurable because of the competition between victim and hoaxer, each seeking to outmaneuver the other, to catch him off-balance and detect the critical weakness." This is quite an apt description for the wrestling fan's competing pleasures as spectator, as performer, and as critic … and the desire to be "sold," despite their critical examination.

4   For a particularly poignant look at the difficulties this lack of distinction between performer and character can cause, see Tom Phillips's 2015 essay on fans' negotiations around understanding WWE performer Chris Benoit—whose wrestling persona was likewise Chris Benoit—in the years after Benoit killed himself, his wife, and his child in a murder-suicide.

4

Interview with Roger Nygard,
Director of *Trekkies* (1997)

Lucy Bennett and Paul Booth

Roger Nygard is the director of the influential documentary about *Star Trek* fans, *Trekkies* (1997), which was one of the first widely released films to document the everyday stories of fans. The film features extensive interviews with these individuals, discussing how their fandom impacts on their daily lives. Most notably featured within was Barbara Adams, a juror who attended court in her Starfleet uniform, and Gabriel Köerner, who eventually became a visual effects artist for *Star Trek: Enterprise*.

In 2003 *Trekkies 2* was released, revisiting the memorable fans from the original film, and broadening the scope to include European fans and conventions. We interviewed Roger Nygard via email, questioning how *Trekkies* originated, and asking him to ruminate on the processes and challenges he found surrounding the representation of fans in documentary film.

Q: How did you get the idea for these films, and how did they come to fruition?
A: I am an accidental documentarian. *Trekkies* was [*Star Trek* actor] Denise Crosby's idea. I cast her in my first film, *High Strung*, and a few years later she pitched the *Star Trek* fan documentary idea to me. I said, "I can't believe nobody has done this yet. It seems so obvious." Neither of us had made a documentary before. To prepare, we rented a pile of documentaries, then watched and studied them; films like *My Brother's Keeper*, *Crumb*, *Hoop Dreams*, *Roger & Me*, and anything by Les Blanc. Then we started shooting. After our first weekend, I was hooked on documentaries. Unlike a narrative project, where it's a challenge to come as close to the script as possible, shooting a doc is a journey, it's exciting not knowing what's around the next corner, exactly how the story will end.

Q: How did you select what fans to include in the films?
A: I have a process that evolved during filming, which in hindsight I call the Three R's: Research, Referral, and Random chance. First we do research on the Internet or through word-of-mouth, looking for the most interesting people. Once we find and interview them, we ask them to refer us to others they think would be interesting. And finally, we just show up at conventions and see who we bump into. When you go to a

Star Trek convention, the people are so colorful, just about anybody you pull aside for an interview makes a great subject.

Q: In *Trekkies 2* you revisited some of the fans that you featured in the first film— was there anything that surprised you when encountering these subjects again, years later?
A: Checking in seven years later on some of our favorite fans from the first film was an homage to Michael Apted's brilliant *Up* series of documentaries. I was surprised by something in almost every interview. I never know what to expect—that's part of the beauty of the documentary journey. I had one of my favorite surprises when I did a follow up interview with Barbara Adams, arguably the most famous *Star Trek* fan in the world at that time, due to her notoriety from being on the Whitewater jury where President Clinton was on the list of potential people to testify. One of the members of Barbara's ship (i.e., club) was her neighbor, an elderly woman named Jean Whitehead. During the interview with both of them, Jean talked of having met somebody who met an alien and drew a portrait of the alien. During the interview, Barbara Adams glanced at Jean with a look like Jean was going a little bit overboard. It's such a fun moment to see the person who you might say is one of the most extreme *Star Trek* fans raising her eyebrows it someone who she thinks is more out there than she is.

Q: Did you face any struggles when representing these fans? For example, was there anything that your film subjects did not want on camera?
A: I try not to include anything that an interviewee would feel bad about. I want everybody to be proud to be included in the film. But sometimes people change their minds about what they have said. There is no foolproof rule. I go by instinct.

Q: As you filmed these fans, did you feel any sense of accountability, in terms of representing individuals, and the wider fan culture?
A: My only goal is to provide the most evenhanded and entertaining product possible. The fan culture will fend for itself. If my film is not entertaining, nobody will see it. One of the criticisms I've gotten from fans is, "you don't show enough normal fans." But who gets to decide what's normal? That's one reason I made the focus of *Trekkies 2* that very question; the subtitle of the film is: how much is too much? I asked people to explain what is normal for a *Star Trek* fan. Guess what? Nobody could agree. Everybody seemed to think that whatever amount of fandom he or she chose for himself or herself, that was the correct amount, and anything else beyond that was too much.

Q: The end credits of *Trekkies 2* shows us some varied reactions from fan subjects to the actions of fans in first film. Can you tell us a bit more about the general response from the Trekkie communities afterwards to both *Trekkie* films? And the media in general?
A: There is often a lot of laughter from viewers watching *Trekkies*. My feeling is that as a documentarian, you provide a soapbox for people who can choose to get on it and speak their mind, or not. Some make a great point and some don't. It is up to them.

I've been at many screenings of *Trekkies* for both *Star Trek* fan audiences and civilian audiences. Guess who laughs harder? The *Trek* fans. They get it; they have a great sense of humor about themselves. Most do, anyway. Perhaps the few that don't, feel like they are looking into a mirror, and they don't like what they see; they have not accepted the geek in themselves. So they may accuse those who point it out as being condescending, blaming the messenger. But I don't see why being a geek can't be a badge of honor.

I think the *Trekkies* doc is like a Rorschach test. Because we had no narration, because we don't overtly comment on the fans and their lifestyles, because we present the fans and allow the viewer to judge, people tend to project motives onto the filmmakers that coincide with attitudes within themselves. If viewers are intolerant of alternate lifestyles such as those presented, they may see the film as an indictment. If they are open-minded about how other people choose to live their lives, they may see the film's presentation as sympathetic.

Q: *Trekkies 2* delves a bit more into the complicated judgments of fans by other fans, and notions of engagement such as "extreme" and "normal" fans. By doing this, it shows the different shades and kinds of fans within one fan culture, and that they are not all uniform in their acts and devotions. How important do you think this was to show in the film, and why?
A: I don't consider the people that I have included in the films to be weird or strange. I see them as exceptional. If I made a documentary about baseball players, and I only put the most average or normal people in the movie, nobody would want to see it—it would be too pedestrian. Audiences want to see portraits of the exceptional people. The most exceptional, colorful, interesting, dynamic, and charismatic people are the ones who make it into the documentaries.

Q: Is being a Trekkie a unique identity, or do you think aspects of *Star Trek* fandom apply to other elements of fan life?
A: There is a lot of overlap in the various fandoms and the lives of fans. *Star Wars* fans, Twihards, Ringers, Trekkies... many persons belong to all these fandoms. But what sets *Trekkies* apart from the others are the philosophies: infinite diversity in infinite combinations, the prime directive, Live long and prosper... *Star Trek* portrays a positive future, where everybody is equal, men and women and the disabled all have opportunities, and humanity is going forth exploring the Universe in a positive, brighter future. Most science-fiction portrays a darker, decaying, more decrepit future. *Star Trek* fans are attracted to the positive energy of *Star Trek* fiction.

Q: One of the criticisms of the films is that the interview subjects "played up" their fandom for the camera. Did you get a sense of that while filming?
A: There is something called the observer effect, or the Hawthorne effect, that says when you observe somebody, their behavior changes. This is a natural aspect of documentary filmmaking. Everybody acts differently when there's a camera in the room. The only true documentary form would be candid camera, where an observer is not aware that

he is being filmed. With respect to the *Trekkies* films, it didn't matter whether it was a 100 percent accurate portrayal. My goal was to find the most interesting people and showcase them. Interestingly, *Star Trek* fans are already so expressive and enthusiastic, there isn't a need to play things up

Q: Have you kept up with any of the fans after the two films?

A: I have stayed in touch with many of the fans that I interviewed. I have friends around the world now. That's one of the perks of being a documentary filmmaker; your friend list increases dramatically in quantity and uniqueness. This is partly related to why the tone of my films is affectionate and nonjudgmental. I like my subjects. I like getting to know them, I get something out of the process. So it's in that regard a symbiotic relationship.

Q: How do you think fan conventions, or fan culture, has changed in the almost twenty years since *Trekkies* first came out?

A: *Star Trek* fandom only grows larger. Nobody really leaves once they are in; once a *Star Trek* fan, always a *Star Trek* fan—until you die. The new series and the new movies all brought new fans on board. The documentaries have had a fan-recruitment effect as well.

Q: Whenever I screen *Trekkies* in my classes, I find that students have a mixed reaction—some find it very funny while others find it touching and some excessive. Have you noticed audiences reacting in particular ways?

A: The way *Trekkies* is designed, the first half of the film showcases the more unusual fans. So the initial reaction is, "these people are strange." But once the audience is hooked, and drawn in, the second half of the film switches gears and features the more humanistic aspects of fandom. By the end of the film, even if you started out thinking *Star Trek* fans are weird, you will probably have changed your opinion in the direction of: "Well they're not so bad. They may be a little odd but they seem like nice people. There are certainly worse things to be obsessed with then *Star Trek*." Part of the satisfaction of making a documentary is changing people's perceptions.

Q: During the filming of the films, you spoke with a lot of behind-the-scenes people. How have you seen their reaction to fans and fandom change over the years?

A: Some of the Enterprise actors said that the moment they were cast on the show, they watched *Trekkies* to see just what they had gotten themselves into. Over the last two decades, sci-fi and fantasy has made a transition from geeky subculture to mainstream. When I was in high school, the perception of a *Star Trek* convention was that it was for the fringe dwellers; now going to Comic-Con is cool, and it is heavily promoted as such.

Q: How did *Trekkies 2* get made?

A: We sent a letter to Paramount announcing that we planned to do a follow-up—and they shocked us by saying yes!

Q: There is a bigger emphasis on cosplay, filking, and fan filmmaking in the second film—what other changes in fan representations did you focus on in the intervening seven years?

A: *Star Trek* is a huge international phenomenon. I felt that we never quite got to show the whole picture in the first documentary. So we broke *Trekkies 2* down into three aspects:

1. Check in on our favorite fans seven years later.
2. Probe the questions that the first film brought up, that we didn't cover in *Trekkies*.
3. Meet the international fans, because the first film only covered US and Canadian fans.

Trekkies 3 still has open to it many parts of the world with unique aspects of fandom that we have not yet explored, as well as the new fandom created by the rebooted franchise. In fact, I'd recommend interesting fans stay in touch with us and send their stories to: trekdoc@aol.com. Stay tuned.

Spotlight On: *Crazy About One Direction*

5

"I Will Throw You off Your Ship and You Will Drown and Die": Death Threats, Intra-Fandom Hate, and the Performance of Fangirling

Bethan Jones

In recent years fandom—and particularly female fandom—seems to have come under the media spotlight. Documentaries like *Bronies: The Extremely Unexpected Adult Fans of My Little Pony* (see Chapter 21) and *Fan Armies* have been produced and aired in the United Kingdom on terrestrial television, Sky, radio, or streaming services, for example, Netflix. The publication and subsequent film adaptation of *Fifty Shades of Grey* led to articles discussing fan fiction and female sexuality, and the #gamergate controversy had writers and critics on Twitter, blogs, and newspapers debating the treatment of women in video game fandom. Among these various discussions, it is easy to ignore the position of One Direction and their fans. The group is one of the largest, and most successful, boy bands, and routinely trends on Twitter, given its massive fanbase. But they are "just" a boy band, and their fans "just" teenage girls. In debates about the need to create inclusive spaces within fandom and discussions about the ethics of fan labor, what is the point in studying a boy band and their female fans?

Sarah Baker (2013) notes how the "trivialization of 'teenbop' relates to long-standing assumptions regarding girls' engagement with popular music" (p. 15). Girls have typically been seen as passive consumers who were duped (much as fans more broadly were) into buying lightweight, vapid commodities: "In popular music discourse, this is where the word 'mainstream' operates in its most negative mode" (Baker 2013, 15). There are thus several ways in which the portrayal of One Direction fans mirrors other ways in which female fans are represented in the media, particularly in relation to franchises such as *Twilight*. Dan Haggard (2010) has noted that "The *Twilight* fan is interesting because of reports […] of a degree of extremism that goes beyond what is acceptable […] The point here is not so much whether *Twilight* fans are any more extreme than standard fans, but that there is a perception that they are so." Substitute *Twilight* with One Direction and media representation of Directioners is easy to see reflected in Haggard's statement. And this criticism of extremism is a discourse presented time and again in media responses to One Direction fans. When

Harry Styles and Taylor Swift began dating the press, detailed death threats were sent to the US star (Westbrook 2012), while the *Mirror* reported that Gabriel Agbonlahor was the subject of abuse from Directioners after injuring Louis in a charity football match (Malyon 2013). Similarly, when Zayn left the band in the spring of 2015, media reports commented on the extreme reaction of fans (Fahy and Crossley 2015; Sanghani 2015).

Negativity toward One Direction fans is not uncommon, and indeed negativity toward others within similar fandoms has been a part of fan practices for a long time. Jonathan Gray (2010) notes that fandom often involves anti-fandom: "think of the *Star Wars* fan who hates *Trek*, since his galaxy isn't big enough for both franchises, or of X-Philes who hated the addition of the Terminator in the final seasons." Anti-fandom in popular music can be seen as early as the 1950s, as Liz Guiffre (2014) points out: "Elvis Presley's manager Colonel Tom Parker sold both 'I love Elvis' and 'I hate Elvis' badges at his concerts, a masterful piece of 'if you can't beat 'em, join 'em' marketing" (p. 55) and the Rolling Stones/Beatles dichotomy played out in the public press, with newspapers pitting both bands against each other.[1] During the boy band era of the early 1990s, divisions between Take That and Boyzone fans were common, and anti-fandom is often produced in sports where one of the central meanings is competition between teams (Theodoropoulou 2007, 318).

Of course, these are all examples of broader fandoms: sports, music, pop, rock, television; One Direction fans can be subject to hatred from both within and outside the community.[2] This chapter examines two such examples: the July 2013 British *GQ* interview with One Direction; and the response of One Direction fans to the *Crazy About One Direction* documentary (see Chapters 6 and 7). With regard to the former, I suggest that by embodying a specific performance of One Direction fandom on Twitter, fans cement their place in the fandom while defending the object of fandom. This performance is, however, mistaken for irrationality by "distant" anti-fans (Gray 2003). I position this as a recoding, adopting Stuart Hall's encoding/decoding model,[3] and suggest that journalists confuse nonfandom and fannish discourses while simultaneously claiming "rational," educated cultural capital for themselves. In the latter, I analyze the distinctions between the media's response to *Larry Stylinson*[4] shippers[5] and fan responses, drawing on Matt Hills's notion of inter-fandom antagonism. Hills (2012c) argues that this is "not quite 'anti-fandom' in the sense defined in existing literature, but is rather a kind of fan protectionism, and boundary-maintenance" existing between different media fandoms, such as *Buffy the Vampire Slayer* and *Twilight* (p. 115). I argue that similar practices are at work *intra-fandom*, and that fan responses to *Larry* shippers following *Crazy About One Direction*'s premiere raise questions about the versions and roles of fan performativity. I argue that both anti-fan discourses ("those fans are crazy") and intra-fandom antagonism ("those fans aren't real fans") are grounded in debates about subcultural capital and specific fan cultural performativity. I suggest that nonfan readings of certain behaviors demonstrate a disconnection between fan culture and fan performativity, while intra-fan hate functions as an embodied version of fan capital specific to that culture.

"Harry Styles is a cupcake, not a whore": Fan responses to *GQ*

The September 2013 issue of British *GQ* men's magazine featured an interview with One Direction along with five separate covers featuring photographs of each of the band members. The covers were released days before the issue went on sale and generated thousands of tweets from Directioners aimed at *GQ*, most of which were angry with the depiction of Harry on one of the covers, and containing what the magazine called threats of violence:

> "I'LL FUCK YOU UP GQ, I SWEAR YOU'VE MESSED WITH THE WRONG PEOPLE"
> "@BritishGQ I'M GONNA BOMB YOUR HEADQUARTERS! DIRECTIONERS ARE THE WORST FANDOM TO MESS WITH! FUCK YOU GUYS!"
> (Tweets aimed at *GQ* magazine following their September 2013 issue).

The interview—as its author explains—was conducted in "two fifteen-minute slots, with the five band members split into two separate groups—Liam and Niall, followed by Louis, Zayn and Harry" (Heaf 2013). The first interview took place with Liam and Niall, while the second began with Harry, before Louis and Zayn arrived after being held up by traffic. The interview with Harry was the one most fans took umbrage with, along with his cover featuring the tagline "up all night to get lucky." Heaf questioned Styles on his sexuality as well as pushing him to provide the number of people he had sex with, and fans argued that this was salacious and unfair:

> "HARRYS COVER SAYS HE UP ALL NIGHT TO GET LUCKY. @BritishGQ YOU'RE MAKING HIM SOUND LIKE A WHORE. HES NOT A FUCKING WHORE YOU STUPID CUNTS".
> "'He's up all night to get lucky' GQ kindly shut the fuck up before I chop your head off".
> "the interviewer from GQ who interviewed harry can go shove a butcher knife up her ass for all I care #SorryNotSorry".
> (Tweets referring to Harry Styles's *GQ* interview)

Nate Erickson, *GQ*'s social media editor, received many of these tweets, which he subsequently reposted. *GQ*'s publishers also posted an article online in which they spoke of "the most terrifying responses" to the covers:

when we unveiled One Direction as the cover stars of our September issue last
night, we weren't quite prepared for how many tweets we would receive in such
a short space of time. (In fact, the response was so large that GQ.co.uk briefly
crashed under the strain.) While most were positive, and some less so, a few
frankly had us fearing for our lives. (GQ 2013)

It is, of course, doubtful that *GQ* staff actually feared for their safety following these
tweets, but their response to them—both the shaming of Directioners by retweeting
their messages and in the several articles *GQ* has since published about the issue—
speaks to the way in which young female fans are viewed by the media. The article
regarding fans' responses contained the warning: "the following article contains serious
abuses of Caps Lock" (GQ 2013), while the Huffington Post's interview with Nately
referred to fans as "enraged children" (Makarechi 2013). Writing in the *Guardian*,
Peter Robinson (2013) suggests that this shaming of Directioners sends out the wrong
message, arguing that "Like most trolling, this is scattergun fury from a generation that
should understand the social impact of technology better than any other, yet somehow
views the world inside its handset as 'not real.'" In his attempt to critique the portrayal
of fans by *GQ*, however, Robinson ultimately utilizes the same discourse: the idea that
fans are behaving irrationally and are unable to separate reality from fiction. I argue,
however, that fans are neither behaving irrationally nor failing to separate reality from
fiction. Rather they are performing a specific set of fannish practices, but doing so
in an environment which collapses the context (boyd 2008) of the public/private fan
performance.

Papacharissi (2012), writing about Twitter, argues that "performances of sociality
[on always-on platforms lack] the situational definition inherently suggested by public
and private boundaries" (1992)—in other words, expressions of "I'm going to kill *GQ*"
in a private fan forum take on a substantially different meaning to the same utterances
on public social media platforms. Fan forums operate through the production and
circulation of specific codes or modes of address, in which words or phrases specific
to that fan culture abound and are decoded within the context of that culture. Posts
about killing *GQ* staff in a fan community (be that public or private) are thus highly
performative. They express anger—in this case at how One Direction were depicted by
GQ—but are not threats of actual violence. For fans, threats against *GQ* on both private
fan forums and public Twitter accounts are expressions of fan capital—the more
extreme the response to a threat against the object of fandom, the more subcultural
capital (Thornton 1995) the fan has—but on Twitter these performances are misread
by the press as irrational responses by irrational fans. Hall (1980) posits that "the
degrees of 'understanding' and 'misunderstanding' in the communicative exchange
[…] depend on the degrees of symmetry/asymmetry (relations of equivalence)
established between the positions of the 'personifications,' encoder-producer and
decoder-receiver" (p. 131). *GQ* staff recognized that fans were angry, but believed this
anger to be irrational. This asymmetry between the ("emotional") fangirl encoder and
("rational") journalist decoder thus led to a recoding of the fannish message, aligned
with the "superior" rational capital of the press.

Press discourse, then, performs a distant reading of One Direction fans' behavior. In particular, when Directioners are viewed by adult men, "a textuality is born into existence in large part separate of what might be 'in' the text as produced" (Gray 2003, 71)—or "in" the fandom as performed. Journalists writing about fans as irrational, hormonal teenage girls have a very clear idea of the "text" of One Direction fandom even though they have never been a part of that fandom. Furthermore, press discourse around Directioners "overloads" expectations of the fandom (Barker et al. 2001, 28), "predetermining and often limiting the frames through which many [readers] could make sense of it" (Gray 2005, 844). When confronted with tweets threatening violence then, anti-fans view these as irrational responses, blaming the excess of teenage hormones and the corruption of young girls' sexuality. Directioners, however, are constructing polysemic messages, "encoded with meanings that are decoded differently by each potential audience member" (Papacharissi 2012, 1994). "Performing" as One Direction fans, these tweets cement the fan's place in the fandom while defending the object of fandom and, by extension, fans themselves. Similar processes are at work in the documentary *Crazy About One Direction* and media and fan responses to the film. Whereas the producer presents fans performing their fandom, anti-fan discourse conducts a distant reading, drawing the conclusion that Directioners are hysterical fangirls and claiming rational, educated cultural capital for themselves. Nick Couldry (2005), drawing on Bourdieu, states that just as the state's meta-capital "is not confined to specific fields but radiates outward into social space generally, so the media's meta-capital may impact on social space through the general circulation of media representations" (p. 180). Grace Dent (2013), in her review of *Crazy About One Direction*, writes:

> Oh, ladies, please note, gorgeous boys do NOT tend to have sex with each other as they haven't met the right girl yet. [...] These girls have all this, and much more, to learn. If they ever left their bedrooms, aside from standing outside concert venues screaming at coaches that might, but don't, contain Zane [sic] Malik, they would possibly learn it all the more quickly.

The emphasis on what these "girls" have to learn privileges Dent's age and education— she has learnt these lessons herself and that wisdom will, in time, be imparted to Directioners as well—and this discourse is utilized in other journalists' responses. Media representations of fangirls thus draw on their hyper-emotive behavior in opposition to the rational, educated cultural capital displayed by members of the press.

Crazy About One Direction and re-presentations of directioners

Crazy About One Direction is a 45-minute documentary which aired on Channel 4 on 15 August 2013. The film was made by Daisy Asquith, a BAFTA-award-winning documentary maker, and produced by Mentorn Media (see Chapter 7). The documentary follows fans on One Directions' 2013 UK tour and focuses on twenty-two girls in particular. Their ages range from thirteen to nineteen (Becky, at nineteen, is the oldest fan in the documentary). Interviews are conducted with these fans, predominantly in their bedrooms although footage of the girls waiting for the boys at concerts and their hotels is also included. The documentary opens with an introduction from the narrator, who outlines the three areas the documentary will examine: fans' use of Twitter; Directioners' loyalty to the band; and *Larry Stylinson*. The introduction ends with the question "What drives their obsession and why do so many girls love One Direction?" The premise for the documentary, at least for the production company, is the extreme end of fandom:

> Meet the Directioners: They're young, they're in love, and they're obsessed!
>
> One Direction have become the biggest global pop phenomenon since The Beatles. Their army of young fans (over 10 million followers on twitter) love them obsessively, and even dangerously.
>
> But the way young people use technology to interact with each other and the stars makes the "Directioners" a very different breed of fan from those that have come before.
>
> In this documentary, we get under the skin of this strange 21st century army of young girls and find out what it means to be a true "Directioner"—meeting some of the most intensely obsessed young fans in the world. (Passion Distribution 2013)

The words "obsession," "strange," and "dangerous" pepper the synopsis, and the focus on the age of these fans (i.e., young girls) is very much foregrounded. In this way, Passion Distribution typifies "concerns" about young, female fans and their vulnerabilities—to manipulation, to commodification, and to (inappropriate) sexual desire.

The documentary itself, however, focuses on the performative aspect of fan behavior. All of the fans interviewed featured One Direction posters prominently on their bedroom walls along with fan-made collages, and the girls often wore One Direction clothing. The performative aspect of fandom was further underscored through the documentary's focus on One Direction dolls—many of the girls interviewed had dolls of the boys and these featured in several sets of interviews—and a video of fourteen-year-old Sandra in Harry's hometown. The video was set to, and interspersed with, the band's hit "One Way or Another," and featured Sandra and a friend, wearing a cardboard Harry mask, visiting Harry's former school and workplace. In the video, Sandra and "Harry" kiss, and stage a proposal, and it is clearly positioned as a performance. Jim Shelley (2013), in *The Daily Mail* alludes to this, writing:

> Not lacking in a talent for the melodramatic and smart enough to make the most of her time in front of Channel 4's camera, Sandra gazed in to the window of Harry's local bakery and sighed: "I've never been jealous of some bread. I can literally smell Harry when I'm here. It just feels like I'm more connected to him. He was on this concrete!"

Others, however, took the documentary at face value, and as many responses to *Crazy About One Direction* demonstrated, "extreme" fans are seen as the norm, and fan behavior such as "'stalking," writing erotic fan fiction, becoming emotionally invested in the band, is something female fans should be criticized for.

This criticism came from both outside of, and within, the One Direction fandom, but the approaches each set of criticisms took were very different. Critics of the band and their fans argued that Directioners were creepy, hormone-riddled teenagers (Diaz Dennis 2013; Pauley 2013) and that *Larry Stylinson* fans in particular are unable to differentiate between fantasy and reality (Watson 2013), reiterating discourses already used in the *GQ* instance. Mike Ward (2013), in his review of the documentary, pointed out that the filmmakers had a clear agenda in creating the documentary: "The title alone was a clue as to the producers' agenda: *Crazy About One Direction.* As opposed to Reasonably Keen On One Direction, or One Direction Are One Of Several Bands We Quite Like At The Moment." Commenting on Ward's review, one fan wrote:

> [Asquith] asked me some simple questions about my love for the band and even asked if I had loads of posters on my wall (I don't have any). She asked if I'd ever met them or tried to meet them (I tried to meet them once but wasn't successful). She was basically asking questions that would show how "crazy" I am about the band, I obviously wasn't crazy enough for her documentary because she even said she was looking for fans to interview who we [sic] maybe a bit more dedicated, extravagant and passionate with basically every piece of 1D merchandise ever to exist!

The documentary thus, for these fans, acted as what Matt Hills (2007) calls a "failed re-embedding," that is, a mediation of their self-understandings and self-identities, relying to a considerable extent on negative fan stereotypes that did not match up with fans' own experiences. I would argue, however, that some fans responding to the documentary by critiquing its depiction of fans are viewing fans' performances through frames already predetermined by anti-fan discourse of Directioners as irrational and emotional.

Fans criticized the girls depicted in the documentary for not being "true" Directioners, and as the program aired, took to Twitter to convey their disappointment at the way they were being portrayed. The hashtags #thisisnotus and #channel4thisisnotus were created in response to the documentary, playing on the title of the One Direction film *This Is Us,* which was two weeks from opening at the time the documentary aired. Fans highlighted the extreme behavior depicted in the documentary in their responses to it, pointing out that 90 percent of the fandom did not harass the boys or their families and had not issued death threats to the bands' girlfriends:

> "Dear Channel 4: The majority of us have
> -never sent death threats
> -never sent hate to their girlfriends
> -never mobbed them

#ThisIsNotUs".
"'Fans' mob 1D.
Directioners don't.
'Fans' send death threats.
Directioners don't.
There's a difference between the two".
(Tweets regarding *Crazy About One Direction* sent
after the documentary aired).

Implicit in these tweets was what Kristina Busse (2013a) describes as border-policing; that is, where fans dictate the image they do and do not want to present to the world. Busse argues that fans "border police on two fronts, excluding both those not enough and those too much invested in the fannish object or practices" (p. 84). In the case of *Crazy About One Direction*, fans attempted to distance themselves from those too invested in the band. As Busse notes, "what underlies much of this border policing is a clear sense of protecting one's own sense of fan community and ascribing positive values to it while trying to exclude others" (p. 75). Those sharing the #thisisnotus hashtag thus outlined the examples of good and bad fan practice, and positioned themselves on the side of the good. What Busse does not take into account, however, is the performative aspect of this fannish policing. As I suggested earlier, the kind of distant anti-fandom enacted by much of the media mistakes fan performativity for irrationality. At first glance the fans tweeting about "real" fans appear to do the same. However, these fans are members of the One Direction fandom and therefore do not misread the fandom as anti-fans do. Rather, they enact their own intra-fan hatred through a similar version of this performativity.[6] Perhaps the most striking example of this intra-fandom antagonism comes in responses to *Larry* shippers.

Larry Stylinson and intra-fandom hate

The reading and writing of real person fiction has long been contested in fandom, and is the source of much intra-fandom conflict and shaming. Bronwen Thomas (2014) notes that "The strength of feeling expressed against RPF is also perhaps indicative of fans' sensitivity to enduring stereotypes and clichés about their behavior as immature, obsessive, or extreme" (p. 174). Although *Crazy About One Direction* prefaces the section on *Larry* with the rejoinder that some fans have a "funny way" of expressing themselves, the girls interviewed actually presented a far more nuanced view of *Larry* than was subsequently suggested on social media sites. Discussions ranged from shipping the boys as a bromance versus a romance, demonstrating a complex understanding of different kinds of relationships, to *Larry*'s status as "part of the band," there from the beginning and (arguably) encouraged by the band's management. As Mark Simpson (2013) writes, "You could argue that the *Larry* shippers are only joining the dots that have already been drawn—very close together—by 1D's management and the whole history of boy bands. As one girl put it, 'I think the management secretly love *Larry*.'" The inclusion of two of the girls reading an extract from a *Larry* fic further cemented the performative element of shipping, not least given the embodied aspect of the story itself, with its focus on the boys' sexual pleasures.

Helena Louise Dare-Edwards (2014a) notes that real person slash fandoms have traditionally maintained a distance from the celebrities they ship, but *Larry* fans "publicly support the 'romance' with such fervor that their hashtags frequently top the list of worldwide trends" (p. 521). The inclusion of *Larry* in the documentary brought further attention to the practice from those outside fandom. This was the cause of one criticism from anti-*Larry* fans, who accused *Larry* shippers of making the fandom look bad by recirculating notions of (young, female) fans as crazy. Hills (2012c) notes that negative stereotyping is not simply done to fans by those outside fandom, but is also "enacted by and between fan groups" (p. 121). Hills argues that "Inter-fandom uses devaluing discourses of 'creepy' fandom [...], or sexualized 'crazies' [...] to elevate one popcultural fandom by devaluing an othered text and its audiences" but One Direction fans use the same discourses *intra*-fandom, particularly in discussing *Larry* shippers (126). In many ways *Larry* anti-fans position themselves along the same lines as One Direction anti-fans. They pathologize and stereotype *Larry* shippers, arguing that they are unable to differentiate reality from fiction, bring the fandom into disrepute and are not true fans. Unlike inter-fandom, or anti-fandom, however, intra-fandom antagonists do not misread One Direction fandom; rather they perform their hatred through another version of fan performativity.

Responses by Directioners to both *GQ* and Channel 4 on Twitter often included the organizations' handles. Fans were thus speaking to the producers, even if they were doing so performatively, rather than expecting to be listened to. In writing about *Larry* shippers following *Crazy About One Direction*, however, fans were rarely tweeting organizations: they were either speaking to their own followers or to other Directioners (by means of hashtags). The discourses evident in *Larry* anti-fan speech were thus specific to the fandom and drew on hierarchies and fannish capital, rather than on distant readings of the fandom. In addition, these discourses relied on the fan's imagined audience (Marwick and boyd 2010) to make sense of them. This audience could be fellow Directioners or fellow *Larry* anti-fans who would understand the complexities of *Larry* within the context of One Direction fandom as well as the fan culture surrounding *Larry*. The audience would not be the media, picking up on hate tweets as a result of *Crazy About One Direction* and the rumors of fan suicide that followed it. The context of the fan performance once circulated in the mainstream press was thus lost, and hate tweets directed at *Larry* shippers viewed as literal, if extreme, responses by fans.

In discussing the performative nature of fan fiction, Francesca Coppa (2006b) writes "fan fiction is itself a textual enterprise, made of letters and words and sentences written on a page (or, more likely these days, a screen), and it therefore seems sensible to treat it as a literary rather than an essentially dramatic form [but] I submit [fan fiction] is more a kind of theatre than a kind of prose" (p. 226). Coppa's view of fan fiction can also be considered here. Like fan fic, hate tweets are a textual enterprise, comprised of words on a screen and taken as literary (and literally) by the media. Coppa further argues, however, that "A live audience has always been a precondition for fandom [...] Fan fiction, too, is a cultural performance that requires a live audience; fan fiction is not merely a text, it's an event [...] there's a kind of simultaneity to the reception of fan fiction, a story everyone is reading, more or less at the same time, more or less together" (pp. 238–9). Responses to *Crazy About One Direction* echoed this idea of liveness: SecondSync, who analyze the relationship between Twitter and television, recorded 368,000 tweets about the documentary, peaking at 6,141 tweets per minute as the program ended. The hashtags #thisisnotus and #channel4thisisnotus also generated 176,000 tweets within SecondSync's monitoring window. Tweets continued to come in after the program ended, when the documentary was moved to Channel 4's on demand website, but echoing Coppa, tweets about the documentary and hate tweets aimed at *Larry* shippers were stories that everyone was reading, more or less together and more or less at the same time. Those in fandom, however, took a different meaning from these stories than those outside fandom. boyd (2010) suggests that teens online use "social steganography" to hide information in plain sight: "creating a message that can be read in one way by those who aren't in the know and read differently by those who are [...] communicating to different audiences simultaneously, relying on specific cultural awareness to provide the right interpretive lens" (online). boyd uses the example of a teen using song lyrics in a Facebook post to alert friends that she had broken up with her boyfriend while simultaneously pretending to her mother that everything was alright. Fan cultural performativity functions in a similar way, although the meaning is misunderstood by those without the fannish cultural awareness, rather than hidden by fans.

Larry hate tweets thus function as a form of embodied subcultural capital, and the meaning decoded by fans is either one of subcultural superiority (for *Larry* haters) or subcultural inferiority (for *Larry* shippers). Bourdieu (1986) writes, "The accumulation of cultural capital in the embodied state, i.e., in the form of what is called culture, cultivation, *Bildung*, presupposes a process of embodiment [...] which, insofar as it implies a labor of inculcation and assimilation, costs time, time which must be invested personally by the investor" (p. 244). *Larry* anti-fans consciously acquire "the basic elements of the legitimate [fan] culture" (Bourdieu 1984, 70–1) through assimilation into fandom and induction into fannish norms, and perpetuate those norms through displaying their own subcultural capital. *Larry* shippers, for example, are seen as engaging in "tinhatting"—a term which describes the behavior of fans who, according to other fans, are unable to recognize the difference between fictional stories about real people and their actual lives. Tinhatting exists across a myriad of fandoms and seems to be universally reviled by those fans who do not believe that a real life relationship exists between the actors or band mates in question. Fans tweeting that they wished *Larry* shippers would die and calling them pathetic and psychopathic were positioning themselves as superior to *Larry* shippers:

> "'Larry shippers' I will throw you off your 'ship' and you will drown and die".
> "I think larry shippers are mentally and psichologic ill".
> "and still larry shippers can't see how pathetic they look oh dear".
>
> (Collection of tweets aimed at *Larry* shippers).

Furthermore, Dare-Edwards (2014b) notes that there is little tolerance for *Larry* shippers, partly because "*Larry* supporters are discounting or questioning official PR-driven narratives about the boys' relationship" (p. 6) and partly because some *Larry* shippers sent questions, sexually explicit theories, or fan art to the band, thus breaking the fourth wall, which deconstructs the boundaries between fans, creators, and the objects of fandom. Lynn Zubernis and Kathy Larsen (2012) have pointed out that "Fans who bring certain fan activities to the attention of actors, writers and showrunners are sanctioned within fandom" (p. 144), and the response of *Larry* anti-fans to *Crazy About One Direction* certainly seems to corroborate this. It also demonstrates, however, that there are two fractured modes of subcultural capital that are in conflict.

Conclusion

It is apparent, then, that the discourses surrounding *Larry* shippers in the media and in fandom are markedly different, even though both may evidence similar anti-fan attitudes. Lucy Bennett argues a similar case in discussing "droolers": R.E.M fans who focus on the physical aspects of the band members and their personal lives. Bennett (2013a) suggests that "Droolers are targeted as 'matter out of place,' a pollutant within Murmurs, due to their noncompliance with normative discourse" (p. 218) and notes the strategies that fans developed to prevent droolers discussing R.E.M's private life. The emphasis placed on the star's right to privacy here mirrors the debates taking place in One Direction fandom about the way in which *Larry*, particularly the overt performances of shipping *Larry*, negatively impact the boys' right to privacy. These attempts to police Directioners' behavior also become attempts to repress the "fangirling" aspect of the fandom. Typically used in a derogatory way, "[a]s a noun 'fangirl' names a form of cultural consumption that is excessive and associated with girls [and can] also be used as a verb, describing a (hyper) feminine performative act of consumption" (Cann 2015, 166). Intrinsic to that performative act of consumption is the language used by fan(girl)s, particularly—in regard to Directioners—the language developed on Tumblr, which transitions to other platforms. Tumblr has become a key site for fan-related content and its community of users, as Kimberley Hernandez (2013) notes, "employs a special set of terminology to describe various actions and features on the site, common memes, and community members. Tumblr speak is often hyperbolic in nature and usually associated with fandoms [...] learning the language of Tumblr is essential in order to navigate the platform and have fun."

One Direction fans have adopted Tumblr as a key site for their fandom and along with the platform have adopted its hyper performative language and behaviors. Rhiannon Bury (2005) writes that "[p]erformance and articulation are critical to understanding an online media fan culture that defines itself and is defined by others through the female body" (p. 10); Directioners—defining themselves as fangirls and defined by others as emotional teenage girls—thus understand performative expressions such as "I can haz all the feels" and "OMG his face I cannot even!" as existing in a specific, bounded community where the meaning is understood and shared amongst others in the fandom. Moving this performative language where "caps lock is de rigueur and telling someone you want to stab her in the uterus is an expression of mild annoyance" (Romano 2013a) to another platform, and moreover a platform which scrutinizes fans in a more literal way, further cements the recoding of what fans recognize as performativity and anti-fans understand as irrationality.

Hills (2002a) suggests that fandom is "always performative; by which I mean that it is an identity which is (dis-)claimed, and which performs cultural work" (p. xi). This performative aspect of fandom can be seen in *Crazy About One Direction*, where fans are presented as performing (be that performing for the camera as Sandra does, or performing a reading of *Larry* fan fic) as well as in responses to *GQ* where specific forms and types of language are used. Anti-fans outside One Direction fandom misread this performance, however, as irrational behavior by a group of emotional teenage girls, unable to tell fantasy from reality. Their distant reading of the fandom, through societal norms rather than fannish norms, thus creates a disconnect between what the fans are doing and what others believe they are. Similar discourses appear to be at work intra-fandom, but Directioners (*Larry* and non-*Larry* shippers) are keenly aware of the cultural norms and hierarchies within fandom. Anti-fan behavior intra-fandom, then, is markedly different to that enacted by the media and complicates discourses around the representation and re-presentation of fans, as well as our understanding of anti-fandom itself.

Notes

1   Some fans of The Beatles also romanticized relationships between band members, most noticeably John and Paul. The activity which One Direction fans undertake, both textual (fan fiction) and physical (attending concerts, chasing the band), is not new (Scodari 2007).

2   The term "community" to describe a fandom can be misleading. As Bertha Chin (2010) argues, micro-communities exist which subscribe to different interpretations of a text, and disagreements between those communities can become both public and highly divisive. My use of community here, then, is an analytical construct and should not be read as endorsing a homogenous view of fandom.

3   Hall's encoding/decoding model examined reception contexts of media messages, primarily in news production, but I suggest that it can equally be applied to other contexts, particularly in relation to fan practices and fannish discourse.

4   Derived from the names of Harry Styles and Louis Tomlinson. *Stylinson* fans imagine the boys to be in a gay relationship, kept under wraps by the band's management. These shippers are often reviled in One Direction fandom and are the subject of bullying on various social media networks, including Twitter and Tumblr.

5   A shortened form of the word "relationshipper," shippers are fans who wish to see a relationship develop between people or characters.

6   In using the words "performance" and "performativity" throughout this chapter, I do not intend to minimize the actual hurt than bullying and policing can cause within fandom.

6

A New Breed of Fan?: Regimes of Truth, One Direction Fans, and Representations of Enfreakment

William Proctor

One hardly needs to be reminded that fan audiences have historically been viewed as "obsessive, freakish, hysterical, infantile and regressive social subjects" (Hills 2007, 459). The body of scholarly work that we now describe as fan studies has sought to rescue the figure of the fan, so often a figure of fun, from discourses that have diagnosed fandom "as a psychological symptom of a presumed social dysfunction" (Jensen 1992, 9). Such meanings are often given life through the oxygen of discourse, by "the media, fans themselves and academics that have sought to study their practices" (Geraghty 2014, 5).

But there has been a significant turning point, we are told: "none of the high-profile fan cultures in recent years—from X-Philes via Eminem fans to *Sex and the City* enthusiasts—had to endure the derogative treatment of *Star Trek* fans…Rather than ridiculed, fans are courted and wooed by cultural industries" (Gray et al. 2007, 4–5). Likewise, as McArthur (2009) claims, the pejorative term "'geek' has now become an endearing term of affection (and perhaps jealousy) and label for those who demonstrate expertise in a particular field […] what was once geek is now chic" (p. 61).

Now that fans "have moved from the margins to the mainstream within convergence culture" (Scott 2012a, xv), and that "the digital landscape makes fandom more visible and more approachable than at any other time in the past" (Bennett and Booth 2015, 1), is it time, then, that we move on, having redressed and resolved the aporia of representation? Unfortunately, I think not.

To be sure, there has been a marked shift, but this so-called mainstreaming has also been paralleled by a continuation of traditional "regimes of truth" (Foucault 1975), discourses within which female fans are denounced as "fake geek girls" who dare to trespass on masculine territories, such as the comic convention circuit. Sadly, this has led to a rallying cry from the fangirl community who report on the way in which they have been sexually harassed at such events, which range from "cat calling to groping to taking underskirt shots at the world's biggest convention," Comic-Con (Dockterman 2014). That female fans are "negatively feminized" (Busse 2013a), both within and outside fandom, indicates that fan cultures remain heavily gendered. Such negative feminizations continue to construct female fans as part of "the hysterical crowd" (Jensen 1992, 9) and "predicated on unruly sexuality" (Busse 2013a, 73).

Fans may actively partake in policing, but media reportage and representation also collaborate in the construction of a (gendered) regime of truth. Such a discursive politics splinters into a binary or, following Hills (2002a), a moral dualism, which is "created and sustained by systems of cultural value, of binary camps between 'good' and 'bad'" (p. 21). In this case, the moral dualism dichotomizes "good," masculine fandom—"intellectual, aggressive and objective" (Busse 2013a, 74)—as distinct from "bad" feminine idolatry—"passive, emotional, sensitive and subjective" (2013a). Thus, if fandom has traditionally been viewed as a psychological symptom, and that "[o]nline fandom has made fandom as a whole more visible" (Booth and Kelly 2013, 57), such exposure has become double-binding. This "mainstreaming" opens up previously hidden ideologies for media outlets to mine as evidence of homogeneity and "freakishness," especially in relation to female fans of *Twilight* or *Fifty Shades of Grey*, for instance. In many accounts, these women and girls are often fans of popular music, boy bands such as Duran Duran, Take That, Back Street Boys, N*Sync, and One Direction, the latter of which is the focus of this chapter.

In the Channel 4 documentary *Crazy About One Direction* (*CAOD*), a selection of teenage fangirls are represented in ways that converge with commonsense stereotypes of the kind traditionally associated with fan cultures historically. However, *CAOD* not only negatively stereotypes Directioners as "non-normative" fans but also functions as "an entertainment spectacle" within which teenage girls are "peered at by the predatory camera" (Richardson 2010, 1). In so doing, *CAOD* promotes an exploitative narrative of "enfreakment" (Richardson 2010) wherein Directioners are embroiled within a representational display of otherness that rehabilitates the boundaries of "normalcy."

McArthurs' (2009) contention that the "transition from geek-as-sideshow-freak to geek-as-intelligent-expert has moved the term from one of insult to one of endearment" 61) undervalues the way in which *CAOD* operates as a political/ideological representational space, "a space within which judgments are made, judgments of inclusion and exclusion" (Silverstone 2007, 54).

In this chapter, I argue that representation constructs a negative feminization and, by extension, a narrative of enfreakment around female fans of One Direction. Despite Channel 4's contention that the One Direction community is "a new breed of fan," and that the behaviors they enact to "worship their idols" is a new phenomenon, I show that these behaviors are nothing of the sort.

Channel 4: Merchant of enfreakment

In many ways, One Direction[1] is the ultimate "bad" fan-object; a band which began their career performing on the reality TV series, *X-Factor* and managed to launch a successful career after signing with Simon Cowell's Syco Records. In media discourse, One Direction fans are often reported as "crazy," "obsessed," "delusional," and, in many cases, with a propensity toward threatening, even violent behaviors. Spurred on by new media, especially Twitter, avid Directioners perform their fandom by tweeting Niall, Harry, Liam, and Louis directly, often begging the band to "follow them" on social media.

In *Transgressive Bodies: Representations in Film and Popular Culture*, Richardson (2010) examines Channel 4's reputation as merchant of "enfreakment" and argues that many documentaries and/or reality TV programs "demonstrate an explicit, and unashamed freakshow style," especially in relation to "the non-normative body" (p. 1). These programs—for example, *The 15-Stone Babies* (2012) and *Embarrassing Bodies* (2007)—are exploitative for sure, but other texts on the broadcaster's agenda are equally exploitative and promote an enfreakment of social subjects in series such as: *Benefit Street* (2014), *The Undateables* (2012–), and *My Self-Harm Nightmare* (2015). Although theories of enfreakment have traditionally been adopted to examine regimes of truth about disability, nonnormative physicality (Richardson 2010), and the grotesque body (Garland-Thompson 1996), this range of selective examples highlights that it is not only "the body" which is "othered" in these texts, but also lived experiences, the majority of which engage with the process of culturally constructing freakish behaviors for the purpose of exhibition.

Channel 4 is readily exploiting such "freakishness," not as proclamations or celebrations, but by pointing "an intrusive camera at the fringes of society, so that 'us' normal people can have a quiet chuckle or an ill-informed rant at our TV screens" (Thomas 2014). As Richardson (2010) states, "the archaic spectacle of the freakshow is gradually creeping back into popular culture—if, indeed, it ever left" (p. 2). *CAOD* narrativizes and represents Directioners as enfreaked examples of feminized, nonnormative fandom.

Whether or not one considers *CAOD* as documentary, infotainment, or reality TV, "representations—especially popular culture representations which are widely consumed—should never be underestimated" (Richardson 2010, 1). In *CAOD*, "only certain types of fan voices are heard" (Hills 2007, 462) and this judgment of inclusion/exclusion functions to construct a representational space brimming with stereotypes and judgments. In so doing, *CAOD* "cherry picks" a limited selection of fans and passes them off as homogenous, something which fan studies has been challenging for over two decades. Yet, what is remarkable about the program is how *un*remarkable these fan behaviors and performances actually are when contextualized.

Contexts of performance

CAOD begins with narrator, Julia Davis, explaining that Directioners are "simply crazy" about the band, and that the fan culture is nothing less than a "new breed of fan" who use social media to "worship their idols," and "go to extreme lengths to get noticed by the boys." This narration is juxtaposed with images of screaming teenage girls waving concert tickets in front of the camera; shots of fan art that depict band members Harry Styles and Louis Tomlinson as homosexual; and interjections from the Directioners themselves edited in a montage. Comments include: "I've met them sixty-four times"; "they say I'm a stalker but I don't care"; "I am part of a fandom that could literally kill you if they want." Directioners, we are told, "are fearlessly loyal and not to be crossed … what drives their obsession?"

Multiple stereotypes are distilled into this brief sequence without contextualizing the way in which performativity operates in the community. Indeed, many of these exclamations are just that: performances (the camera certainly encourages such "actings out"). The way that producers select, edit, and arrange the discourse narrativizes a fear of the fanatical fan insofar as performances are taken literally rather than as figurative displays of emotion and affect. As Nichols (2010) argues, a person:

> does not present in exactly the same way to a companion on a date, a doctor in a hospital, his or her children at home, and a filmmaker in an interview. Nor do people continue to present the same way as an interaction develops; they modify their behaviors as the situation evolves. (p. 9)

So while screaming loudly in a doctor's surgery or using threatening behaviors toward other people is certainly unacceptable, screaming collectively outside of a hotel or at a press conference is a sine qua non for One Direction fans and, by extension, other "teenyboppers" (Andrews and Whorlow 2000).

There are multiple ways in which performativity is enacted both within and across fan cultures, so much so, that there is no such singular thing as "fan performance," but a wide-range of pluralist performances which shift in relation to the fan-object, whatever that may be. Also, different modes of performativity may also exist within this-or-that fandom, so that it becomes impossible to align a particular fan culture with a general, overarching theory (with the proviso that patterns also emerge). So, if one identifies as a Trekker, then, this does not necessarily mean that she or he attends conventions sporting Spock ears nor does it mean that she or he writes fan fiction, slash or otherwise (even though this may be the norm for other fans).

Not wanting to condone threats of violence, some Directioners demonstrate the seriousness of their fandom by posting invective on the Internet, usually in response to negative criticism. In *CAOD*, one fan ostensibly loses control when she sees a blog post titled "KILL HARRY STYLES."

> What the fuck is this? I would like to see Harry Styles dead?! Oh my fucking god, is this a joke? Bitch, I will pour bleach down your fucking throat if you don't shut the fuck up! I'm cleaning your mouth out, bitch, so why don't you, you, go and get some help in a mental institution—SHUT UP!

At a basic level, this seems to be an affirmation of fan mania, and a sense of ownership/possession about Harry Styles, who should be protected from outside criticism. Such emotional intensity and cathected investment is a significant component of fan identity, and outbursts such as this are used to safeguard that identity. Directioners often perform a kind of ownership by seeking to erect a paratextual force-field around the band by attacking such negativity via "vocabularies of involvement and pleasure"

(Barker and Petley 1998, 8). (The possibility exists that such overt emotionality is a tongue-in-cheek performance.)

Such overt displays of aggression are stereotypically associated with masculine fan cultures, such as football or other sports. Football fans that perform "emotionally charged behaviors," often have "intense reactions, shout obscenities, get extremely upset and passionate, and sometimes become aggressive" (Theodoropoulou 2007, 324). Sports fans "enjoy participating in a 'game,' as they call it, of exchanging witty lines with their 'rivals' and take up a contest of *who will defend and prove that his/her fan object is better*" (p. 323, my italics).

Whether or not Directioners' aggressive and threatening behaviors can be viewed as a "game" given the general nastiness of the invective represented in *CAOD*, one could hypothesize that lambasting negative discourses about the band are cathartic and affective "mechanisms to safeguard one's fan identity but also ways to gain a great deal of 'identity boost' and self-esteem" (Theodoropoulou 2007, 325). From this perspective, negative discourses "act as a counterforce to an object of admiration," an object that is to be fiercely protected and defended if one is to be viewed as a "real" fan (p. 316). Such a context is excluded from the Channel 4 documentary. Football rivalry, even hooliganism and physical violence, are expected from masculine men; what one should be anxious about, and fearful of, is that these are *teenage girls*, not adult men, and that such behaviors ought to be corrected or censored. In other words, One Direction fandom is dangerous, even harmful, and the documentary illustrates just how lost, "freakish," and misbehaved these poor girls are (which is discursively constructed). It is not the teenagers that are at fault, but One Direction themselves who, like other boy bands and teen idols, have the power to corrupt: "there is a ready truism that enthusiasm for typically male fan objects, such as sports and [certain kinds of] music, are generally accepted whereas female fan interests are much more readily mocked" (Busse 2013a, 75).

Not only do some of the fans represented in *CAOD* perform their affective involvement through discourses of violence toward those who threaten the fan-object, but also toward themselves, often using signifiers of suicide or self-harm, even murder, to proclaim their dedication. "What would you do if you get to meet them today," asks the narrator. One girl states that "she would die," while another claims she would "jump off that cliff over there." Other proclamations include: "I wouldn't kill a puppy but I'd probably kill a cat" which is challenged by a friend—"Oh that's so horrible"—so she revises her statement to, "Okay, I'd kill a goldfish." Another believes that "people would kill each other, I reckon. Definitely."

There is a "clear link between identity and object of fandom—one reflects the other" (Geraghty 2014, 4). A threat to the fan-object, then, becomes a threat to one's identity and narrative of the self (Williams 2015). Also, a fan's sense of ontological security can present itself when "the idealized fan object is potentially threatened" (Hills 2012a, 114). It is not that Directioners are

> somehow neurotic or pathological, but rather because these fans' sense of self-
> identity are so firmly enmeshed with narratives of [their favorite band]. Threats to
> [the fan-object] can thus be felt as threats to these fans' self narratives. (Hills 2012a)

Thus, these performative behaviors "can be read as a desire for ontological security" (p. 116). One of the ways fans deal with this challenge to self-narrative is by turning to social media to "sustain ontological security" (p. 115).

Directioners in cyberspace

The narrative about Directioners as "a new breed of fan" is principally about computer-mediated communication—in particular, the rise of social media, and especially Twitter. As one fan remarks, "Twitter is obviously a big part of it … can't really be in a fandom if you don't have Twitter." Other comments—"I'm always on it," "I'm on it all-day," "you can't not check Twitter"—and one fan's claim that she tweeted the band 182 times in one day strengthens the self-narrative of the "real" fan—demonstrating the importance of social media in affirming and maintaining the fan identity. Twitter is "like a prayer place. When you go to a prayer place you feel like you're connected to God. When you're on Twitter, it's like you're connected to One Direction," explains one fan.

To be sure, there has been a general and marked shift: the proliferation of new media technologies, especially the Internet, has led to the so-called mainstreaming of fandom precisely because it renders previously marginalized voices visible and accessible. But this has also had a detrimental effect on the way fandom is represented in the media as commentators frequently mine available and accessible information—which they see as extreme—without acknowledging, or understanding, how such behaviors are not reflections of psychologically unhinged individuals, but cathected modes of communication and performance. Interactive modes certainly broaden and diversify opportunities for fan cultures (Scodari 2007), but also allows for moral judgment and scorn of such behaviors from those on the "outside" peering in from different social and cultural contexts.

New media technologies do not necessarily replace old ways of being a fan, but enhance and accentuate offline performances, such as gatherings outside hotel rooms, concert attendance, and "symbolic pilgrimages" (Brooker 2007), such as visiting Harry Styles's hometown and finding out where he lives. The fact that Directioner Sonja claims she found out Styles's address from Twitter and then visits his home symbolizes how off- and online identities comingle in significant ways as a dialectical process rather than siphoned off into binary compartments. "It has become clear that the separation between the online and the offline cannot be sustained, rather that online and offline contexts inform and enable each other" (Orgad 2009, 37–8). Hills (2002a) argues that "the mediation of 'new media' must be addressed rather than treated as an invisible term within the romanticized 'new'" (p. 172), but at the same time, this is hardly an exclusive component of One Direction fandom. As Booth and Kelly (2013) state, "many aspects of fan identity have remained relatively unchanged, despite the rapid diffusion of new technology into fans' lives" (p. 57).

In *CAOD*, Twitter is shown as a platform for affective proclamations. This may take the form of aggressively protecting and valorizing the band, as discussed above, but also to appeal to, and even beg them to "follow them" on Twitter. As one fan pleads in the documentary: "please please follow me I love so much please please on my knees I'm going to die if you don't follow me. Arrrrr, please follow me, I love you." A shot of a mobile phone is shown in close-up displaying a fan's tweet: "why wont u follow me?! Shall I kill myself?"

In these examples, these fans seek One Direction's attention by invoking narratives of self-harm as a bargaining chip, going so far as emotionally blackmailing the band ("Shall I kill myself?"). Online comments and blog posts can work as a quest for recognition—"notice me!" (Hills 2012a, 117)—but consideration should also be given to the exchange value offered when a member of One Direction chooses to follow a fan as a form of subcultural capital. "I want to be more than a fan," states one girl, "I want to be noticed and remembered."

In many ways, this shares an affinity with those fans represented in *CAOD* who congregate outside hotels and "stalk" the band in the hope that they can get a photograph taken with their idols. In a rather telling scene, one fan demonstrates the power of such capital when she displays photographs of herself with each band member which clearly has an effect on another girl as she is visibly pained by the images. "How do these pictures make you feel?" asks the invisible narrator. "Jealous," she responds.

In an important scene, we are shown how one fan actually meets the band and adapts her behaviors—her *performance*—accordingly. No longer "crazy," "neurotic," or "freakish," she is restrained and calm. Here, we get an intimate glimpse into the way in which fans—or at least, this particular fan—are in control and less "crazy" than the discourse permits.

Fans also use social media to "act out," and further deal with threats to self-narratives by lashing out against negative criticism. But in what ways do such aggressive performances shift when fan performance occurs online? Suler (2004) conceptualizes such performances as part of an "online disinhibition effect." Such disinhibition can be benign and commenters "reveal secrets, emotions, wishes" and also "show unusual acts of kindness and generosity" (p. 321). But the disinhibition "is not always so salutary ... we witness rude language, harsh criticisms, anger, hatred, even threats." Directioners may "say and do things in cyberspace that they wouldn't ordinarily do in the face-to-face world. They loosen up, feel less restrained, and express themselves more openly" (Suler 2004).

Online activity, then, supplements and accentuates fandom but does not replace traditional modes: "with little exception, much of what was written about fans twenty-five years ago applies just as well today" (Booth and Kelly 2013, 57). That the documentary states that "the new breed of fan turns to Twitter where they can track their every move," is hardly atypical—indeed, it is a cornerstone of contemporary convergence culture—but is represented as a narrative of enfreakment in *CAOD*. Some fans may endorse multiple modes of communication to "get the boy's attention," but are these behaviors truly "extraordinary" when contextualized and compared with other fan cultures? Do Directioners really "have some funny ways of showing their love"?

Fantasy online and offline: Libidinal voltage?

Directioners, we are told, "turn to a fantasy world online where they can share their wildest dreams about [the band]." Fans engage in the act of "shipping," that is, composing narratives about One Direction that articulates a homosexual relationship. Through fan art and fan fiction, Directioners are said to "ship" Styles and Tomlinson as lovers, which is, according to *CAOD*, a "funny way of showing their love."

Other music fans also ship their favorite idols, and "one such faction of Beatles fans tends to [...] homoeroticize relationships among the Beatles, especially between songwriting partners, Lennon and McCartney [and] compose slash stories envisioning such dalliances" (Scodari 2007, 54). But what is potentially worrying for the *CAOD* filmmakers is that, once again, these social subjects are *teenagers*, and recognizing them as sexual beings is unacceptable. That fan fiction of this kind may "offer insights into female sexual fantasy" (Scott 2012a, 192) or proudly proclaimed as "pornography by and for women" (Russ 1985), such fantasies should certainly be *verboten* for teenage girls who require protection from the onset of potent, sexual awakenings which need to be curbed (Jensen 1992).

Anxieties about teenage sexuality have a historical precedent, most notably in accounts of "the hysterical crowd," those who scream, weep, and lose control of their bodily functions in the presence of their idols. During the twentieth century, fans of Elvis Presley screamed and swooned to his gyrating hips and trademark sneer; and Frank Sinatra was a source of female adulation during the 1940s (Duffett 2013). It was the arrival of The Beatles, however, that not only rivaled but also "surpassed all previous outbreaks of star-centered hysteria [...] in its intensity as well as its scale" (Ehrenreich et al. 1992, 86). During a period marked by "a genuinely political movement for women's liberation," Ehrenreich et al. view Beatlemania as:

> the first and most dramatic uprising of *women's* sexual revolution [...] To abandon control—to scream, faint, dash about in mobs—was, in form if not conscious intent, to protest the sexual repressiveness, the rigid double standard of female teen culture [...] Shy subdued girls could go berserk. "Perky" ponytailed girls ... could dissolve in histrionics ... Girls peed in their pants, fainted, or collapsed from the emotional strain. (pp. 87–9)

Although difficult for adults to acknowledge, "at least part of the fans' energy was sexual" and a genuine mode of expression (p. 89). To assert "an active, powerful sexuality by the tens of thousands and to do so in a way calculated to attract maximum attention was more than rebellious. It was, in its own unformulated, dizzy way, revolutionary" (p. 89). The regime of truth discursively circulating around the figure of the female teen, both historically and in *CAOD*, enforces the belief that girls are expected to be not only "good" and "pure" but also to be the enforcers of purity within their teen society (p. 85). Indeed, "most Americans did not like to believe that twelve-year old girls had any sexual feelings to repress," nor have the "libidinal voltage required for three hours of screaming, sobbing, incontinent, acute-phase Beatlemania" (p. 90). Such unbridled energy—of feminine, *sexual* energy—is coded as unruly, promiscuous, and unacceptable. As Anderson (2012) argues, "this bias derives from a persistent denigration of women's media, which in itself originates from a deep-seated historical fear and pathologization of anything associated with feminine sexuality" (p. 241).

In *CAOD*, fans express emotions through phenomenological language, intense physical reactions that are automatic: "I start shrieking," "I had a panic attack," "I had an asthma attack," "I burst into hysterical tears." Is this, then, really about sexuality, and teenage libido? In what ways do fans "express sexual yearnings that would normally be... simply repressed" (Enrenreich et al. 1992, 97)? Or are these behaviors also performative? In the documentary, one fan comments on Harry's body—"his sexy abs, oh my god!"—and we see disembodied text displayed—"#they are so hot"—but another states:

> I could not believe they were in front of me. I had like a panic attack. I got carried out by a bouncer. Basically, we thought that if we did that, we'd have more of a chance to be getting put over the barriers and on the stage with them.

In this statement, we are told that this fan had a panic attack, but then this is explained as a method of persuasion to influence the bouncers to rescue her, which would somehow culminate with a visit to the band's performance space. Rather than "a panic attack," then, this fan *performed having a panic attack* to get closer to the band.

I have no doubt that some fans are sexually attracted to teen idols and boy bands and engage in fantasies that may be sexual or romantic. As Anderson (2012) argues in her ethnography of adult Duran Duran fans, "many of these women claim that their first teen idols stirred their first sexual desires" (p. 24). Perhaps, however, sex is not the only marker of Directioner fandom. Indeed, in *CAOD*, some fans have not yet experienced a "real" relationship. Vicky informs us that she does not have a boyfriend of her own to which Channel 4 asks, "what do you think of 'real' boys?" Vicky responds: "I don't really, like, speak to them. I like focusing on One Direction." Interestingly, this marks out the figure of the fan through the convergence of traditional stereotypes usually associated with the Trekker and used to explain the nonnormative behaviors of fanboys—that is, asexual and lonely, obsessed with the object of fandom that privileges a fantasy world over "the real."

Sue Wise's (1990) account of her Elvis fandom mandated, should the regime of truth be accepted, that "the ideological impurity of Elvis" (p. 394) was so manifest that this is certainly not the kind of thing a feminist be fascinated with, so much so that, being a fan "[of Elvis] was to collude in one's own oppression" (p. 394). For Wise, Elvis's narrative as "butch god," equipped and endowed with phallic weaponry, and "a masturbation fantasy-object for adolescent girls," is endorsed and written by male archivists of popular culture. Linking Elvis with the moral panic surrounding the behaviors of women and girls constructs a regime of truth about "negative femininity," stricken by "the force of an ungovernable, if somewhat, disembodied lust" (Ehrenreich et al. 1992, 90). "What better way," exclaims Wise (1997), "to explain the frightening spectacle of hordes of uncontrollable females than by 'discovering' that they were being sexually stimulated and manipulated by a man—literally man-ipulated" (p. 397).

That Elvis was primarily about "rampant male sexuality" discredits those fans who, like Wise (1997), "did not experience him in this way," and the ways in which such an account gained the currency as a regime of truth is a crucial question for fan and audience scholars (p. 396). "What women thought then and now is largely unknown because, quite simply, no one bothered to ask or even thought our views were worth anything" (p. 397). As with One Direction fandom, the media might find it disturbing, and a cause for moral concern, but they also love it, fuel it, and foster it (p. 397). In so doing, various media cherry pick from the litany of materials circulating in cyberspace to simplify the complexity of fan cultures; to report in newspapers that something is rotten in the world; to continue discriminating through the anthologizing lens of the "predatory camera," as Richardson (2010) describes it (1), and parading social subjects in a contemporary adaptation of the Victorian freakshow. As scholars, we need to recognize that the movement from the margins to the mainstream has not yet redressed the gender politics at work in the representational spaces of the media, fan communities, and academia.

Conclusion: This is NOT Us

Following the documentary's broadcast, many fans took to Twitter to express their rage. These were fans that had been featured in *CAOD* and, also, those who believed that Channel 4 had misrepresented the community. One tweet, for example, reads: "Dear Channel Four, the majority of us have—never sent death threats—never sent hate to their girlfriends—never mobbed them #ThisisNOTus" (Klompus 2013). The Twitter hashtag is an inversion of the One Direction film, *This Is Us* (2013), and demonstrates that the fan community is anything but homogenous.

The final sequence of the documentary is arguably the most poignant as a section of fans are angered as the band ignores them and drive away from the scene. What this shows is that fans are aware of their position as "ideal consumers" (Hills 2002a) and that this economic commitment should be rewarded: "we're the ones that buy all their albums, we're the ones that voted for them on The X Factor, without us they wouldn't even be here … they could at least try and meet us … this is one of the worst things they could do." This is given strength by showing us those fans who could not get tickets for the most recent tour, many of whom are visibly upset and emotional. One of the reasons they could not get tickets was due to the economic realities of being a teenager and positions of class. "Everything's about money and fame," states one fan, and the lowest ticket price of £42.50 (about $65) is simply too much for some families' income brackets. Concert attendance is a form of fan cultural capital, and one fan comments upon the way her peers ask, "how can you not go if you're a big fan?" Her response crystallizes the economic situation: "couldn't afford that."

CAOD endorses a regime of truth about teenage female fans, but representation constructs moral dualisms between "good," and "bad" forms of fan performances. By using a fan studies perspective, I have been able to deconstruct the representation of the figure of the teenage One Direction fan as neither freakish nor outlandish. Yet we must take account of the fact that this exegesis is a scholarly one and that for people unfamiliar with the fan studies tradition, the Channel 4 documentary's narrative of enfreakment is charged with ideological and political regimes of truth. Although this goes some way to conceptualize performance in the Directioner community, a more rigorous, ethnographic study is called for.

Acknowledgments

I would like to express my sincere gratitude to Professor Clarissa Smith for her insights in relation to the topic and for recommending Niall Richardson's work.

Note

1   One Direction has over ten million followers on Twitter but this pales in comparison to other figures such as Katie Perry (66.85 m), Justin Bieber (61.48 m), and Barack Obama (66.51 m). Statistics show that One Direction's Twitter fandom does not even warrant an appearance in the top ten.

7

Crazy About One Direction:
Whose Shame Is It Anyway?

Daisy Asquith

On August 13, 2013, a disturbing hashtag began to trend worldwide on Twitter. *#RIPLarryShippers* appeared to be reporting and mourning the tragic deaths of 42 *Larry* shippers—the One Direction fans that celebrate, fantasize, and sometimes believe in the idea that Harry Styles and his bandmate Louis Tomlinson are in a secret gay relationship. Thousands of fans on Twitter were claiming that the shippers had killed themselves as a direct result of the inclusion of some of their homoerotic *Larry* fan art in a documentary I had made for Channel 4, *Crazy About One Direction* (Asquith 2013). Although the program was only officially available on British television, the tech-savvy fandom had copied and shared it globally overnight with astonishing speed. The fandom were furious that I had included *Larry* in my representation of them, and sent hundreds of death and bomb threats to my Twitter account. *#RIPLarryShippers* trended worldwide for 48 hours.

In this chapter, I conduct a reflexive postmortem on this fandom crisis of my own causing. I happily extend my immersion in the creative, subversive, and globally networked fans of One Direction, uncover the queer erotic meanings in their *Larry* fan art, and investigate the subcultural codes that dictate who can enjoy it and share it. I also examine the ethical challenges of television documentary and look at the wider media context in which my documentary was made. The hierarchies, taste policing, and internalized shame within the fandom (see Zubernis and Larsen 2012) collide awkwardly with the projected shame and derision that is applied from outside. While my extensive research at the time of broadcast quickly established that the *Larry shipper suicides* were in fact just a rumor, the fans' reasons for starting the rumor are important. I will argue that in moving *Larry* from Tumblr to television, my film may have decontextualized it, but the fears and fury of fans result from their understanding of the total unacceptability of teenage female desire in patriarchal society. Analysis of the fan response to *Crazy About One Direction* must be situated and understood within this climate of shame. It is important to recognize that a fandom that is repeatedly pathologized and derided by the media will have low expectations of any representation. Fan identities are riddled with internalized shame, which is consistently reinforced by the performance of distaste, even disgust, that largely male critics and detractors display to them. Schoolboys, their brothers, their fathers, the music press, tabloid journalists, even teachers: all would like to tell girls what music they *should* like, and how they *should* behave around it. This encourages secrecy and the anonymity they are afforded online allows for both free expression and a global audience of like-minds, for the first time in fandom. This is a story that deserves to be told, albeit with careful attention to ethical documentary practice, which foregrounds the needs of the filmed and recognizes the subjectivity of the filmmaker. Documentary theory has dispensed with the idea of objectivity and a single authoritative truth in recent years, and it may be most accurate to say that *Crazy About One Direction* is simply a documentary about what happens when you make a documentary about Directioners. Representing the identity of an entire fandom to their satisfaction may be impossible, but the One Direction fandom is a story of creative female sexuality and international networking that has given 20 million teenage girls a voice, and to ignore it would do them a great disservice.

The One Direction fandom and me

I was delighted when Channel 4 asked me to make a documentary about One Direction fans. Fandom has fascinated me since the late 1980s when I first tippexed *Siouxsie and the Banshees* on the back of my leather jacket. Perhaps my decision to wear that Siouxsie uniform (despite a secretive musical preference for pop) indicated a desire for subcultural capital: a "cultishness" that pop music didn't offer me (see Hills 2002a). So it seems I was born to be a *Larry* shipper—a rare deviant space of queer rebellion within a fandom that couldn't be more mainstream in its musical taste. Professionally, as a documentary maker, I saw a gap that needed filling between what I knew of fandom and the way it has been represented ever since screaming Beatles fans were derided by the media in the 1960s. This simplification of young women's emotional and cerebral response to an artist or production takes the threat out of the phenomenon, infantilizes them, and belittles their emotional experience and impressive skill—networking and coordinating large groups in common purpose, producing and distributing creative fan material and gathering intelligence on their chosen subject. Fandoms have always been "stereotyped and pathologized as cultural 'others'—as obsessive, freakish, hysterical, infantile and regressive social subjects" writes Hills (2007, 463), marked by "danger, abnormality and stillness" (Jensen 1992, in Hellekson and Busse 2015) and thought to engage in "secret lives ... without much purpose" (Harris 1998, 5). There is no doubt that *Crazy About One Direction* was commissioned in the wake of yet another fuss about the fandom's behavior in the tabloids, and it is undeniable that television commissioners desire their audiences to be both compelled and appalled by the most extreme stories possible. But it is also true that the commissioning editor on this occasion was a One Direction fan herself, and that she and I shared huge admiration for the fandom and an explicitly feminist mission to celebrate this unashamed display of teenage girls' desire. In the twenty years of my making television documentaries, I have learned the value of working in this seemingly fickle medium. Television has the least self-selecting audience in the world—it is possible to bring a story you are proud of into the living room of someone who would never otherwise come across it. The opportunity to celebrate fandom in public was irresistible.

If, as Hills (2002a) says, fans and academics have an uneasy relationship, fans and the media have a completely dysfunctional one (p. 3). Perhaps being a documentary maker I don't suffer from the type of *imagined rationality* that an academic might project in fan representations (Hills 2002a, 11). Instead I suffer from an imagined *media-type untrustworthiness*, or conversely, an imagined *journalistic objectivity*, depending on your perspective. In fact my representation of fans was an entirely subjective one, as I will argue all documentaries are, and I had no dark motive other than to understand what drives the immersed and passionate fan. The reflexivity that Hills employs in his theoretical work acknowledges that his "theories are also stories" (p. 70). Our gender, class, age, sexuality, politics, and sense of self are all players in the stories we tell. This chimes with much recent work in documentary theory on the impossibility of objectivity (see Morris 2002; Bruzzi 2006; Pearce 2007). Neither the academy nor the documentary industry benefit from the invisible or detached researcher. My practice was characterized by a personal, experiential, authored, and immersive approach.

Filming fans

When I arrived at the Manchester Arena in April 2013, there were around 500 teenage girl members of the One Direction fandom waiting outside. Sandra and Becky had been there since 8 a.m. and bounced over to my camera and me. They were singing and dancing in the street, not so much waiting for "the boys," as partying, being together, and belonging. Sandra and Becky were extremely keen to be part of the film—as were almost every one of the hundreds of fans I met.

Of course, having your identity represented on television is a powerful form of recognition and establishes belonging. The performance of the self that occurs when a camera is pointed at someone is a powerful way of working through identity. The camera seems to say *I see you and hear you and you exist and matter* (Piotrowska 2013). The performance of the self that occurs when a camera is pointed at someone is a powerful way of working through identity. Two and a half decades after Butler's *Gender Trouble* (1990), the social media generation is accustomed to performing their own identities online and constantly thinking through the way they represent themselves. Every selfie posted on Facebook, every invitation to "ask me anything" on Tumblr, every Instagram photo and tweet invites recognition or offers it to someone else, or both. If love is returned, then all the better, but if criticism, or "hate" is the result, then at least the initial poster has received attention, and has a chance to learn something more about who they are, who they might become, and what their impact and position might be in the world, or, in other words, "instigate a transformation" (Butler 2004, 44). In the case of *Crazy About One Direction*, the "becoming" they may have wished to solicit was the elevation of self into uniqueness, from "just another fan" into a significant fan, so significant in fact that the band were bound to notice them, and to see oneself projected onto the future, immortalized and made special, making the ordinary extraordinary (see Piotrowska 2013, 268). My job in this context was to make sure I found fans who were emotionally capable of managing this extraordinariness and to prepare them psychologically for the impact of broadcast. Their parents were also engaged in this process.

Unsurprisingly, there was some pressure from Channel 4 to include the most angry and hysterical fans, the crazy fans. I resisted this stereotype from the start, but I am also obliged to accept the commercial demands that ultimately fund my programs. The pre-title sequence and trailers therefore privilege the most extreme moments in order to attract an audience, but as all makers of television documentaries understand, this does not negate or obstruct the documentary itself being subtle, thoughtful, and even warm. However, when it came to the title, it is significant that I was not allowed to keep my preferred choice: *I Heart One Direction* was changed by Channel 4 on the very last day of the edit to *Crazy About One Direction*. This news required me to speak personally to all the fans in the film and explain that it wasn't me calling them crazy, and it wasn't the intended message of the program. They took the news well, at that moment accepting more readily than I did that this was their dramatic reputation and therefore inevitably the selling point of the documentary.

The Michael Jackson fan documentary *Wacko About Jacko* (Leveugle 2005) was another victim of Channel 4's trick of re-titling its programs at a late stage, with or without the approval of the filmmaker. The problem is, Hills (2007) writes, that *Wacko About Jacko* "undermines fans' moral narratives by linking them to emotivism" but actually *Wacko About Jacko* appears to have been made with genuine affection and respect for the fans. The process of editorial selection, narration, use of slow motion, and soundtrack are all mediation on the part of filmmaker Leveugle, but they are not utilized in such a way as to make fun of, or exoticize, Jackson fans. The fans are not *wacko* at all, but likable, passionate people who are willing to be led by fantasy rather than behaving in a self-consciously sensible fashion. It would be counter-productive to suggest that a focus on the affective or embodied response should be considered less important, valid, or interesting than a response driven by rationality or cognitive critique. Hills (2007) rightly argues that the film does nothing to *normalize* fandom (p. 468), but many fans that I met with did not wish to be *normalized*, preferring that their extraordinary passion and creativity be celebrated. The words *Wacko* and *Crazy* are clearly what are considered necessary to draw an audience to a slot. *Wacko* can be seen as a judgment call offered to the audience. Unfortunately, as in the case of *Crazy About One Direction*, the title's impact has the potential to reach far beyond the program's attentive audience, and taken at face value, it can have a stigmatizing effect.

Ethical documentary practice can be an elusive and imprecise target. There are clear ethical guidelines in television that take care of the audience with regard to the truth claims of a documentary (exemplified by the BBC's Safeguarding Trust course to be taken by every producer after 2008). But what about ethical practice with regard to the care of participants in television documentaries? Winston (2013, 1) has claimed it is our relationships with the people we film that are the most important measures of ethical production. In general terms, I will argue that ethical documentary is made when the filmed person is treated as a collaborator rather than a resource, and fully informed of the intentions of the filmmaker and the ambitions of the film; if attention is not abruptly withdrawn at the end of filming but a meaningful relationship pursued throughout the edit, broadcast and beyond; if participants are shown the rough cut, genuinely consulted on its veracity (not necessarily on editorial decisions); and if they are held in equal regard by the filmmaker as the ratings-hungry executive. In these ideal circumstances, a documentary can be a truly rewarding and satisfying experience for those filmed—the film about their life, a rare and therapeutic reflection to be treasured. At the opposite extreme, if those filmed are treated as a commodity by a team of researchers as inexperienced as they are eager to please, lazily commodified as "contribs" (contributors), sweet-talked, flannelled, made to sign release forms within five seconds of the camera rolling, abandoned instantly the camera returns to its bag, ill-informed, misunderstood, then re-fashioned in the edit to fit whatever the broadcaster has been promised, being filmed can be a disastrously disturbing experience of powerlessness and misplaced trust. The reality can fall anywhere between these extremes.

If my filming of Directioners was to be ethical, it was necessary that I try to make the film in the language of the fans so that they became active collaborators rather than defensive subjects. As Heinich writes, "in matters of admiration and celebration every request for justification produces a backlash" (in Hills 2002a, 65). By asking a fan to explain their fandom, a filmmaker (or academic) immediately invites defensiveness. I attempted to get around this by participating in fan activities alongside the fans I filmed and allowing their voices to overtake mine. I waited outside the back gates of arenas for hours, spent days on YouTube and Twitter, following One Direction themed hashtags, even spent a night on a Dublin pavement with them in pursuit of concert tickets. I also included, with specific permissions, their YouTube videos, filmed before and during my filming period, and not originally intended for my film. These captured a performance of fandom that was intended for other fans, but they translate well to an outsider audience. The "stalking" of Zayn and Niall in the corridors outside their hotel room is here represented by the fan as tongue-in-cheek comedy as well as evidence of the courage required to get close to the band, an important status booster within the fandom. In the filming period I allowed a space for fans to perform the identities they wanted. Bruzzi (2006) argues that all documentaries are "performative acts, inherently fluid and unstable and informed by issues of performance and performativity" (p. 154). There are many subtle forces at play in their fan performance. It must be sufficiently true to the self that they inhabit, and sufficiently close to the self they wish to project. Documentary maker Errol Morris describes this territory as "a strange limbo land between fantasy and reality" (Vice 2013), and both realms should be welcomed when filming. The self projected must also be the self that they are comfortable offering in the presence of filmmaker and camera. The camera creates a space for feelings to be verbalized, enacted, and shared, and in a complex exchange "a documentary only comes into being as it is performed" (Bruzzi 2006).

There is also an element of performing the behaviors that are expected by the rest of the fandom, and by the wider society. Derrida, in the reflexive documentary about him by the same name, comments "when one improvises in front of a camera one ventriloquizes." He says he felt obliged while being filmed to "reproduce the stereotypical discourse" (*Derrida*, Ziering-Koffman and Dick 2002). I found that One Direction fans did this to a point, particularly before they felt confident enough to present a more subtle version of themselves. They were more complex in their performed identities when in the familiar safe space of their own bedrooms, whereas outside in the street, in large groups, they performed more stereotypical fan identities. It may be most accurate to say that *Crazy About One Direction* is a documentary about what happens when you make a documentary about Directioners. What is recorded is the space between the filmer and filmed, an ever-evolving negotiation resulting in a complex, compromised truth (Bruzzi 2006, 9). Nash (2010) describes a "flow of power" that happens in an ethical documentary relationship; "a contested relationship in which each is acting with the goal of influencing the other" (p. 27). And furthermore, by virtue of their subjectivity, any other filmmaker would have made a different film. As Derrida (2002) says, "the reflector interrupts the reflection."

There is no doubt that my subjectivity was in play when making this film. It was *my* story about the One Direction fandom. Consequently, it is not a definitive version of all fans everywhere. I do not make overt truth claims in my films, but hope instead that the reflexive and interactive aspects of what I do communicate an experiential integrity. As the filmmaker Chris Terrill says, "Our stock in trade has to be honesty; not necessarily truth, whatever truth is—truth is a construct" (in Lee-Wright 2010, 103). Making a documentary involves "endless choices" (Barnouw in Bruzzi 2006, 6) and *Crazy About One Direction* was no exception—the choices of who to film; where to film; what questions to ask; what cuts to make; what music to add; and what meanings to convey; were all mine. In addition to the title, some choices were made by Channel 4, such as how long to allow me to make it (six weeks filming and seven weeks editing), how extreme the trailer should be (very), and who should record the voice over (not me, it was decided eventually, but the comedian Julia Davis). These choices all result in signifying certain meanings and render the notion of one truth an impossibility.

Watching fans

On broadcast of *Crazy About One Direction*, it was significantly not the fans I had filmed that objected to my representation of the fandom. By taking care of all the stages of research and production myself, I had been able to be consistent with my participants, keep my promises, and keep them informed and consulted during and after filming. Apart from being ethically sound, the sense of increased power this gives subjects during filming tends to make for a better, more intimate film, which in turn increases the likelihood that they will approve of the final cut. Relationships also affect the reception of a documentary because "the assumptions which the viewer makes about this relationship, on the basis of signals intended or unintended, will inform his [sic] perception of the film" (Vaughn in Austin 2007, 104). My relationships with the fans I filmed were strong enough for them to have positive expectations of the film and understand its affectionate humorous tone. For reasons I will explore in this section, their confidence and appreciation was not shared by the majority of the fandom.

Within minutes of the broadcast of *Crazy About One Direction* on August 15, 2013, it was being ripped on Tumblr, viewed (in part at least) and criticized passionately by fans all around the world. One link I found the following day had over a quarter of a million views. There were 368,139 tweets during the hour of transmission, ten times more than *Big Brother* initiated that evening. Twitter was dominated by related hashtags for the next 48 hours, including *#RIPLarryShippers*, *#ThisIsNotUs*, *#1DWereNotLikeTheseGirlsontheDocumentary*, and *#BeliebersareHereforDirectioners*, touchingly uniting the normally antagonistic Justin Bieber fandom in rare sympathy with the One Direction fandom. Twitter has been used by One Direction fans since the band's first *X Factor* appearance to gather and share intelligence on the boys. Fans use it to collectively protest management decisions, share fantasies, police each others' fan behavior, provide tactical false information and rumors, vote in competitions, and form factions and hierarchies within the fandom. Ultimately, each fan covets a tweet or follows from a band member, a high-value chip of cultural capital in the fandom, which gives an instant boost to fan status. In the days after the broadcast, tweets were split between hate for *Larry* shippers, who had supposedly embarrassed the fandom by sharing their fantasy, and hate for the producers of the documentary for broadcasting it. There were thousands of bomb threats to Channel 4, death threats to me, and invitations to *Larry* shippers to *Go kill yourself.* Following *#RIPLarryShippers* in real time, I watched the number of reported *Larry* "suicides" creep up from 4 to 12, then to 19, to 28, and then 42 in a few hours. It was a huge relief to me to discover the concept "pseuicide," in which an online avatar dies when a Twitter or Tumblr account is deleted, often in protest. Why and how teenagers use suicide as a cultural bargaining tool, or an emotional weapon, is beyond the scope of this chapter, but an analysis of the YouTube rants that were tagged #ThisIsNotUs provides some understanding of the fans' issues with my film.

In the months after the broadcast, I took a sample of forty YouTube videos with the intention of analyzing the arguments made in them. Of these, thirty-six are made by US teenagers, two are British, one German, and one Danish. Their apparent ethnicities are as follows: twenty-five white, six Hispanic, five black, and four Asian. There are thirty-eight girls and two boys, both boys identifying as gay within their channels. Their ages appear to range from 12 to 20. The videos last between three and nine minutes and have many features in common. They are all filmed on either a computer webcam or a mobile phone and they all feature one teenager addressing the camera directly, almost always from their bedroom. The videos share content as well, sometimes seeming to chime together, occasionally using almost the same words to make the same arguments. My current practice involves the purposefully minimal editing of this material to create a new film, which is intended to allow the fandom to contest my representation of them while simultaneously questioning the shame that they have internalized (*This Is Not Us*, Asquith 2016).

Twenty-one fans were critical of the girls who were filmed and said the documentary should have been about "normal fans who have never met the boys and have boring lives" (justalyssa). Eleven of the videos expressed the idea that *Larry shipping* and fan art should not be on television—"that stuff doesn't go on television!" (alanagrace). Nine said they were ashamed of the fandom "Right now I'm ashamed to show my face!" (6directionerxo) and eight said they were afraid of what the band would think: "The boys are gonna see that! Aaargh!" (iwannabeaunicorn). Seven YouTubers worried that *Larry* shippers may commit suicide and five admitted that fans are "sometimes crazy." Five of the videos were extremely critical of Channel 4, but three admitted they had not seen the documentary yet. Interestingly, it was considered acceptable to join the protest against the documentary, in fandom solidarity, without having actually seen it. The actual sequences in the program, which are joyful, proud, creative, often performed in a knowing and comedic fashion, do not get specific mention. The *Larry* section is one of these, but in the fandom response, the noisy fact of its simple existence overwhelms and drowns out the actual content.

What I am arguing here is that the shame these fans describe does not necessarily originate in *Crazy About One Direction*. The meanings carried by a documentary are the result of a complex negotiation between text and context. The reception of a film by its audience is a player in the making of those meanings, arguably as important an influence as the intentions of the filmmaker and the cultural moment it is born into. In this light, the defensive reaction of the fandom was unsurprising and even justified in the context of three years of negative and patronizing media representations of Directioners. Just as tabloid journalists might assume that the documentary is about the mass hysteria of silly teenage girls; just as fan sympathizers might connect with the positive aspects portrayed about fandom; Directioners will receive the message they expect, which is one of derision, criticism, and humiliation. They have adopted a generalized sense of shame about their fandom, taught to them by a patriarchal society that looks down on expressions of extreme emotion, teenage passion, mainstream pop, and female sexuality. *Larry* in private fan spaces is fun, clever, and naughty, but seen through the public eye, it suddenly feels embarrassing and stupid to fans, not because it is, but because everyone keeps telling them it is.

The *Larry ship* is the biggest and most hotly contended division in the One Direction fandom. Approximately half the fandom *ship Larry*, the other half preferring *Elounor* (the heterosexual relationship between Louis and his girlfriend Eleanor). *Elounor shippers* are deemed homophobic, and in opposition to Louis and Harry's human right to be gay together in public. *Larry* shippers are often accused of invading the band members' privacy and of being pornographic and morally vacuous. *Larry is* an erotic space in which fans can play out their sexual fantasies unhampered by the dull and limiting sexual identities offered to them as teenage girls. The boys in their artwork are often rendered so androgynous that gender is transcended. They have queered and given emotional and erotic depth to what is on offer to them by the band's corporate producers making something less blandly fixed in gender roles, and far more desirable and limitless in potential (see Doty 1993; Rand 1995). One of the most intriguing arguments made by the YouTubers in my sample is that including *Larry* meant I had trespassed on their "private" fan spaces. But although the majority of fans use aliases online, they do not prevent outsiders from seeing their productions, which are readily available on Tumblr, Twitter, and YouTube. Although all the fan art I included was cleared with individual artists, the fandom assumed they must have been stolen. They consider Tumblr to be an almost sacred space, in which the *Larry* fandom can be private, and this false sense of obscurity may have prevailed for a few years because outsiders did not know what to look for. As Zubernis and Larsen (2012) write, "The twin cultural biases against overt displays of emotion and (for women) displays of inappropriate sexuality combine to keep fans in the closet" (p. 45). *Larry* is in the closet and the closet is Tumblr.

So *Crazy About One Direction* outed the *Larry* ship. Jenkins (2012d) describes being asked by fans not to write about real person slash (RPS) for the first edition of his landmark fan studies book *Textual Poachers*, as it was seen as "fandom's dirty little secret" (p. xxxiv). But he acknowledges that these secrets are not as easy to keep in digital fandom, raising important questions as yet unanswered about the etiquette of online cultural spaces and the way meanings are altered by context. "What happens when materials produced within a subculture get decontextualized, when slash videos circulate to people who do not have slash reading practices?" (p. xxxvi). He cites the example of the *Closer* video—a Kirk/Spock slash cut to a *Nine Inch Nails* song, which broke out of the fandom and now has 1.7 million views on YouTube. Jenkins says it received titillated laughter from outsiders, despite being originally intended to make people think about sexual violence. The conclusion that moral codes of slash can only be understood by *insiders* seems rather old-fashioned and unworkable—a parochial approach to a cultural practice that is defined by its open-minded, open-source sensibilities. Striking a balance between the invisibility of texts that express female desire and the kind of mainstreaming of subcultural information that causes it to lose its value (Thornton in Hills 2002a) is a challenge. But agreeing not to document some forms of slash at all carries a judgment and only helps perpetuate the perception of *wrongness*.

Conclusion

It is of course impossible to represent all fans at once. They are "not an amorphous mass of hysterical bed-wetters" as Robinson (2014) rightly points out. But neither are they all sensible thoughtful citizens. Fans vary wildly and it is the interaction between them that constitutes fandom. The One Direction fandom are perpetually writing their communal rulebook and trying to pin down the territory and own it, and my documentary trespasses on and meddles with that delicate process. Fans are of course a problematic source on themselves and not a source of "pristine knowledge" (Hills 2002a, 68). As Hills (2002a) writes, "personalized, individual and subjective moments of fan attachment interact with communal constructions and justifications without either moment over-writing or surmounting the other" (p. xiii). In representing them we should not treat "the ways in which fan identities are legitimated as authentic 'expressions' of a group commitment" (p. xii), but explicitly allow each fan to perform their personal individuality simultaneously alongside their communal fan identity. The individual and the communal are both important parts of Hill's definition of fandom as a "cultural struggle over meaning and affect" of which contested descriptions, identities, and representations are a large part (p. xi).

Perhaps it was difficult for fandom to accept the individuality of the performances in *Crazy About One Direction*. When Natasha says she got braces because Niall got braces and that Zayn being from a Muslim family has helped her deal with her own identity issues, she is not speaking for the whole fandom. When Pip cries because she can't afford tickets to the stadium tour, or gasps in comedy performance at the hotness of Harry tweeting Louis, she is not speaking for every fan. But because the fandom have committed themselves to the label(s) that outsiders use to identify them, that is, *Directioner(s)*, they feel as if they are being universally represented, and sadly their expectations of representation are dominated by internalized shame. Moving *Larry* from Tumblr to television decontextualized it and had a destabilizing effect on the fandom, who were already arguing about its significance. The mainstreaming of *Larry* may have destroyed some of its subcultural authenticity for some fans, who wanted to keep it their little secret. But the various negative responses to its inclusion also importantly highlight the taboo around expressions of teenage female sexuality and the shame that is projected onto One Direction fans. Girls making porn for girls is something they only want each other to know about, aware as they are that the idea is unacceptable in a patriarchal society.

I have argued that a fandom that is repeatedly shamed and derided by the media will have low expectations of any representation and therefore respond defensively regardless of the content. I have also shown the necessity of embracing the subjectivities and performances of both filmmaker and fans if the production of a documentary is to be ethical. *Crazy About One Direction* should only really be seen as a film about what happens when a certain filmmaker makes a film about certain fans. Any documentary is a subjective project that records the space between filmer and filmed. The seemingly small changes made in service of the commercial pressures of a broadcaster, such as the change of title, should be handled with care as these little details matter and can lead to re-stigmatization. Television shows, and titles in particular, have the power to redefine communities, either challenging stereotypes or re-stigmatizing. But they don't have the power to control the way those messages are received by different audiences, who may project their own shame onto the subject. Despite the drama that my documentary caused, even stretching to a commemorative event on the one year anniversary of broadcast, termed "15/8" by fans (it should be noted that fans have a rather blasé attitude toward death threats, and so on, and many describe it as *just entertainment*), it was worth giving the *Larry ship* its place in history and not letting it go unrecorded as a cultural practice. In May 2014, the verb *to ship* was entered in the Oxford English dictionary and it is tempting to think *Crazy About One Direction* may have had a hand in that. *Crazy About One Direction* suggests *Larry* is not a source of shame, but something to be celebrated, and deserves a wider audience, just as Barry Manilow fantasies are immortalized by Vermorels' classic study *Starlust* (1985). That audience, however, must take a close look at their own response—whose shame is it they are feeling? Shame is in the eye of the beholder.

Part Two

Fictional Fans:
Reading between the Lines

8

Interview with Robert Burnett, Writer and Director of *Free Enterprise* (1998)

Paul Booth and Lucy Bennett

Robert Burnett is the director, co-writer, and editor of the film *Free Enterprise* (1999), a romantic comedy about being a *Star Trek* fan and meeting your celebrity idol. In the film, Mark and Robert (fictionalized version of Burnett and his writing partner Mark Altman) meet actor William Shatner (Captain Kirk from *Star Trek*), who convinces them to invest in his one-man rap musical based on Shakespeare's *Julius Caesar*. The film relies on the cinematic representation of a specific type of fan, and pokes fun at both the fan attitude and society's attitude about fans. Burnett has worked in Hollywood for twenty-five years, and is currently developing *Living in Infamy*, a television series version of his self-published comic book. We spoke with Robert over email and social media to find out about how his own fandom played into the creation of *Free Enterprise*, and how fans are represented in contemporary Hollywood.

Q: You were the director, co-writer, and editor of *Free Enterprise*—why did you want to make this film, and how did it come to fruition?
A: One evening, Mark calls me up and reads me a scene he'd written. He'd scripted a story I'd told him about December 7th, 1979, the day *Star Trek: The Motion Picture* opened in US theaters. I'd been in the seventh grade and gone to school wearing a *Star Trek* uniform to celebrate the film's release. As soon as I'd arrived, I'd been taken into a girl's bathroom and beaten up by an upperclassman, who obviously didn't see the charm in wearing a *Trek* uniform to school. But in Mark's scripted account of this very real moment from my own life, after getting knocked out, the character of Rob has a vision of the real William Shatner materializing and offering advice. Rob awakens and turns the tables on the bully. The scene was so good, we both immediately decided to […] work exclusively on the script we were then calling *Trekkers*, inspired by the recent success of *Swingers*, and carrying on the idea we were the serious and cool *Star Trek* fans. Using both *Swingers* and Woody Allen's *Play It Again Sam* as inspiration, we embarked on writing a semi-autobiographical story about ourselves, our friends, Los Angeles, and our ultimate wish fulfillment, having Captain James T. Kirk as our good friend. Mark and I would both write the script, I'd direct and he'd produce. It seemed like the greatest idea we'd ever come up with.

Q: How much of the dialogue and scenes were based on your own personal experiences as a fan?

A: Most of the scenes in *Free Enterprise* were direct lifts from our own lives as not only fans, but hopeful future movers and shakers in the entertainment industry. Los Angeles of the late 80s and early 90s was like Devil's Tower in *Close Encounters*. A cadre of Geeks, influenced by not only George Lucas and Steven Spielberg, but all kinds of filmmakers—Francis Ford Coppola, John Carpenter, Francois Truffaut, David Cronenberg, Michelangelo Antonioni, Mario Bava, Wim Wenders, David Lynch, Dario Argento, and many others—heard the call of the industry and migrated to the city. Through film school, revival screenings, conventions, comic book stores, and other genre-related events, we all sort of found one another.

Many of my core group of friends found their way into the *Free Enterprise* script, simply because after we'd decided to write about ourselves, writing about our real friends seemed the obvious way to go. Our conversations were peppered with references, quotes, and catchphrases from hundreds of sources and it was sort of our own way of not only constantly testing each other's arcane knowledge, but also speaking in a new metaphoric language only we'd understand. When I saw the *Star Trek: The Next Generation* episode "Darmok," with the Tamarian race's use of their own metaphor, I completely understood where they were coming from.

Ultimately, we wanted to show ourselves and our friends as the antithesis of the fan stereotype made famous by Shatner's famous *Saturday Night Live* "Get a Life" sketch. We thought of ourselves as the exact opposite of them, spending our nights drinking in bars, meeting women and having active sex lives, all the while quoting lines from *Rollerball* to one another and getting away with it. In all honesty, the truth was somewhere in the middle. But if nothing else, I wanted *Free Enterprise* to be a celebration of my friends.

Q: As you filmed these characters, and being a fan yourself, did you feel any sense of accountability, in terms of representing wider fan culture?

A: I felt no accountability to wider fan culture. As someone who'd been going to conventions and comic book stores since I was very young, I actively hated what I saw fandom becoming. Shatner's "Get a Life" sketch, and later *The Simpson's* Jeff Albertson, Comic Book Guy, became self-fulfilling prophecies. Perhaps it was only me getting older, but the "Boldly Going" aspect of *Trek* didn't mean cosplaying a Mugatu and hitting the local Holiday Inn, but instead learning some French, getting a passport, travelling to Paris, and meeting hot French babes. We might not be able to go to alien planets and meet Orion Slave Girls, but we can hop on a plane and go where we'd never gone before! That said, I did still enjoy literary-based or fan-run conventions, like WorldCon or CONvergence.

Q: What was the response from the *Star Trek* fan communities afterwards? And the media in general?

A: The positive reaction to the film actually surprised me. For years I'd been reading about the Sitges Film Festival, or the *Festival Internacional de Cinema Fantàstic de Catalunya*. Specializing exclusively in Science Fiction, Fantasy, and Horror films, I'd wanted to attend the festival most of my life, so it was the first place I submitted *Free Enterprise*. The festival hosted the world premiere of the film in October of 98 and I made my very first trip to Europe to attend. It was a magical two weeks. We'd sent the script in advance, so they could subtitle the film in both Spanish and Catalan. Initially, I was worried the jokes were so inside, so Los Angeles, it might not play, but the film went over like gangbusters. It was shown in the main festival auditorium to a sold out crowd of 1500. Just amazing.

The fan community was decidedly mixed. The "Get a Lifers" were uncomfortable with the R-Rated lifestyles and sexuality portrayed in the film, claiming the characters were the height of Mary Sue wish fulfillment. [Some] "cool geeks" embraced the film, and I still get emails, texts, and tweets from fans who passionately adore it, which is nice.

Q: Did you find representing fan characters any different to representing people in your other films?
A: Not at all. You still try to create believable characters no matter what they might be interested in. In fact, another film I developed and produced, *The Hills Run Red*, also has uber-fans as central protagonists, but this time they're diehard fans of horror cinema searching for a notorious lost film.

Q: What are your views on the ways fans have been represented in films? Had you watched any prior to making this film?
A: Aside from my own films, fans always get the short shrift in cinema. The default position has always been that of the nerdy outcast, whether it's Jamie Kennedy's character in *Scream*, or the characters in *Detroit Rock City* or *Fanboys*. But if a film comes out with a fan character in it, I'll absolutely see it.

Q: Were you aware of fan studies as an academic field and did you do any research before beginning the film?
A: I wasn't aware of fan studies as an academic field. The only book I'd ever really read about fandom was Joan Winston's *The Making of the Trek Conventions*. But I was just about the biggest fan I knew, so I didn't have to do any research. I was on the cutting edge of that blade!

Q: Is being a Trekker a unique identity, or do you think aspects of *Trek* fandom apply to other elements of fan life?
A: Obviously, identifying with a television show as strongly as others identify with their own deity puts you on some kind of crazy ground! But for me, *Star Trek* was always about applying the concepts of the show to daily life. Make great friends. Go on adventures together. Love interesting women. Learn as much as you can. But most of all, seek out the wonders life has to offer.

Q: While on set, did the actors/producers/creators discuss different ways of representing fans? What was that conversation like?
A: We really didn't. All of those discussions took place during script readings or in conversations before we got around to shooting the film. Since none of the actors really

knew anything about fandom, we made them a two-hour reference tape with all of the quotes and scenes referenced in the script. That way, we hoped they would bring an authenticity to their line delivery.

Q: If you were to make *Free Enterprise* today, how would it be different from what you made in 1999?
A: I wouldn't make the film today. *Free Enterprise* remains a prophetic film, absolutely a product of its time, at least as far as fandom is concerned. The characters in the film represent a very small segment of fandom, the high-functioning geek. The Internet was just beginning to become a cultural force, we still loved our Laserdiscs and the idea you'd ever see an expensive, retro-hipster *Star Trek* feature with a new Kirk and Spock was simply unthinkable. But now, we live in a world where Marvel Comics movies are huge box office draws, two *Avengers* films even exist, and *Batman vs. Superman* is coming out next year. If you'd told me this back in 1998, I'd never have believed you. Back then, I couldn't imagine a world where *Avatar* became the highest grossing film in history, *Walking Dead* was the biggest show on television, *Big Bang Theory* is the most successful sitcom, and Chris Hardwick runs a multi-media empire called, of all things, Nerdist. Everything I grew up loving, all those niche interests I had for the first four decades of my life, have gone completely mainstream. We've got robots roaming freely around Mars, I'm carrying a supercomputer in my pocket which allows me to instantly communicate with anyone on the planet and soon Americans will be going back to Cuba on vacation. The world went and became a science fiction movie.

Q: There are aspects of *Star Trek* culture that are not touched on in this film—slash fandom, crossover fans, vid makers—why focus on just one type of fan representation?
A: The characters in *Free Enterprise* are absolutely aware of all types of fandom. I can tell you the character of Robert owns a lot of slash fiction, if only because he collects all kinds of *Trek* literature and he's a very open-minded guy! If we had more time we could've dealt with these things…but there's only so much time you have to tell your story.

9

Fans on Primetime: Representations of Fandom in Mainstream American Network Television, 1986–2014

Lincoln Geraghty

In this chapter, I discuss the varying representations and stereotypes of fans presented on primetime American network television. Many would argue that William Shatner's "Get a life" sketch on *Saturday Night Live* from 1986 cemented the stereotype of the nerdy, basement dwelling *Star Trek* fan—unable to discern real life from what appears on the television screen. Not only has this image permeated popular culture, but it has also become the ultimate stereotype from which fan scholarship post-Jenkins has tried to distance itself. Subsequently, any and all recent media texts that have depicted fans and fan practices have been viewed by academics with, at best, suspicion, and, at worst, as negative and harmful. These discussions try to correct the stereotype rather than understand the necessary actions and production decisions on behalf of creators and writers that brought about those representations in the first place. So, for example, in Suzanne Scott's (2012a) interview with Henry Jenkins (see Jenkins 2012d), there is a connection made between the "Get a life" fan stereotype from 1986 and more recent films and television shows that depict fans such as *The 40-Year-Old Virgin* (2005) and *The Big Bang Theory* (2007–present). Similarly, David Scott Diffrient's (2010) work on what he calls "the cult imaginary" (p. 463) contends representations of fans and cult religions on screen have drawn on existing stereotypes that depict loners and losers getting caught up in the more controlled life of being in a cult. Mentioning fans but concentrating entirely on cult members, his work serves to stereotype fans as cultists rather than objectively analyze depictions of fans on screen.

However, in my previous work I have argued that contemporary representations of fans should not be dismissed as exclusionary and nerdy but rather should be seen as celebratory of what it means to be a fan in a networked and socially connected community. In a film like *Galaxy Quest* (1999), a parody of the *Star Trek* franchise, fans are portrayed as strong and competent individuals who are part of a supportive and culturally integrated group (see Geraghty 2007). Similarly, in his analysis of the fictional show within a show *Inspector Spacetime* from NBC's *Community* (2009–present), Paul Booth (2013a) argues that "being a fan" is a practice "imbued with symbolic and mythological meaning" (p. 147) and "can be a powerful and important identity in and of itself" (p. 158). Indeed, films and television that play up and focus on the multiple practices that make being a fan so attractive, such as collecting memorabilia and attending conventions, are instructive in the processes that fans go through to create, build, and maintain their fan identity (see Geraghty 2014).

Thus, in this chapter, I want to provide a historical analysis of fan representations on American primetime television since the *SNL* sketch and examine to what extent fans have been stereotyped and how far those stereotypes go in perpetuating myths surrounding fandom and the affective relationship with media texts. Instead of focusing on those obvious and popular series like *Big Bang*, I want to chart a more complex history of network sitcom and reality documentary series that are not necessarily about fans but often use fandom and recognized fan practices as the basis for stories in certain episodes. It is in the comedy genre where we see fans being stereotyped most often (e.g., *Big Bang* and *SNL*) and in the reality documentary format we see how fans and fan communities are often used as catalysts for discussions surrounding practices such as collecting, and selling items of popular culture and related fan ephemera (e.g., the sort lampooned in films such as *The 40-Year-Old Virgin*). While previous scholarship looked at both film and television examples, in my following analysis of specific American primetime television series I assert that the processes which fans go through to create, build, and maintain their fan identity are celebrated (switching from being laughed at to being laughed with); thus, also bringing to light important changes in television production and network strategies intended to attract new and knowing audiences in an increasingly competitive market.

Such recent and mainstream attention paid to fans and fandom on US screens is perhaps suggestive of an overarching fascination for the popular and is an important clue as to where fans might lie in the wider contexts of society and the power relation between fan groups and the media industry. Television series that play up and focus on the multiple practices that make being a fan so attractive and culturally valuable are instructive in the processes that fans go through to create, build, and maintain their fan identity. Furthermore, representations of fans and the objects of fan affection on primetime television highlight important changes in programming production practices and network marketing strategies. Within this, niche audiences, like fans, are targeted as highly desirable in an increasingly competitive and fragmented broadcasting environment. Indeed, where networks are able to connect "must see" primetime shows to their preexisting fan favorite franchises through intertextual references and special appearances by popular cast members we see evidence of a complex television culture where producers and fan audiences are continually negotiating notions of identity and cultural capital.

The following case studies of the sitcom and reality documentary genres highlight the changing representation of fandom and, I would argue, suggest that fans and fan practices are moving from the periphery to the center of mainstream television programming. Such a shift is noted by Booth (2013a) who states that "there has been a rise in visibility of fans" on film and television and "fandom of media has become a norm of viewership" (p. 147). While one could argue that fans have been a regular part of mainstream television in the form of the stereotypical nerd/geek character, as discussed in the scholarly work I have already mentioned and shall summarize further in the next section, the intention of this chapter is to suggest that the movement from outsider to insider no longer positions fans or their behavior as bizarre or inappropriate in contemporary culture. Indeed, different genre series that appear on various US networks narrate a story of fandom that many fans have previously struggled to promote in contrast to that which was lampooned on *SNL*. With this in mind, the two case studies I will be using to analyze fan stereotypes on primetime are the sitcom *Frasier* (1993–2004) and the reality documentary *Toy Hunter* (2012–present).

Fans and their stereotypes

In keeping with its comic book roots, the most famous and long-standing representation of the fan on primetime television is Comic Book Guy from *The Simpsons* (1989–present). Encompassing all the stereotypes of the middle-age male fan—awkward around women, sarcastic, intelligent, obsessive, and protective of his collection—he is an iconic representation of the comic book fanboy. As seen in numerous episodes, his shop, The Android's Dungeon, is home to a vast array of comics, toys, and other media merchandise. In the 1999, "Treehouse of Horror X" story "Desperately Xeeking Xena" Comic Book Guy plays the role of super villain, The Collector. He raids a *Xena: Warrior Princess* (1995–2001) convention attended by various "nerd" characters, including Professor Frink, to kidnap Lucy Lawless and add her to his collection of favorite cult television characters. In "Worst Episode Ever" (2001), Comic Book Guy takes a break from running his store, due to a heart attack, and falls for Agnes Skinner—without the distractions of the store he is seen to be able to have a romantic relationship with a woman. The popularity of *The Simpsons* and those episodes that focus on the fanboy practices of Comic Book Guy threaten to pathologize fan behavior on primetime television. As other chapters in this book have noted as well, Joli Jensen (1992) describes how excessive fandom has been seen "as a form of psychological compensation, an attempt to make up for all that modern life lacks" (p. 16), and Comic Book Guy is a key example of that archetype. Yet, Comic Book Guy is but one character in an ensemble cast of bizarre and excessive personalities that correspond to various stereotypes circulated in popular culture. Singling him out as representative of a typical fan would be as problematic as suggesting Waylon Smithers typifies all gay men or, indeed, Homer Simpson is the archetypal American male.

However, the example of *The Simpsons* reminds us not to forget that popularity does not equate to positivity. Comic Book Guy is indeed a fan favorite and the stories in which the character appears lampoon fan practices such as collecting and conventions, but at the same time he is reflective of writers' subcultural capital since they clearly understand the intense emotion and devotion expressed by media fans. Such is the impact and longevity of *The Simpsons* that one could argue it has helped to normalize the representation of fandom at least to the extent that television audiences now understand the importance of popular media texts to fans and that the demonstration of their affection is very much part of the contemporary media landscape. In this way, Comic Book Guy and *The Simpsons* correspond to Cornel Sandvoss's (2005) statement that,

> with the proliferation of multi-channel television and the arrival of new information technologies such as the internet, fandom seems to have become a common and ordinary aspect of everyday life in the industrialized world. (p. 3)

Nonetheless, recent studies of fan representations argue Sandvoss has been too quick to suggest fans are now culturally accepted and their practices no longer stigmatized. While Mel Stanfill (2013) agrees that "fans are central to how contemporary American culture understand media audiences," in her study of how *Xena* fans view and reject perceived extreme behavior within their own community, she argues that "not all fans or fan practices have been equivalent to the mainstream, even as it has been persuasively shown by previous scholars that fandom is mainstream in some respects" (p. 130). And, in his analysis of the UK documentary *Wacko About Jacko* (2005)—which focuses on the reactions of Michael Jackson fans after his trial in 2005—Matt Hills (2007) maintains that fan stereotypes are still commonplace on television. The documentary worked to symbolically equate fandom and emotivism, upholding "significant ideological cultural norms by suggesting that nonfans ('us') *are* able to rationally evaluate the innocence of guilt of alleged abusers, unlike fans ('them') blinkered by their powerful devotion" (p. 475). So, despite the assertion that fans are part of mainstream media, recent work still highlights the fact that extreme stereotypes serve to counter any steps made toward a sympathetic and informed representation of fandom and fan-related practices.

Fans on the couch

Frasier, the *Cheers* (1982–1993) spinoff, was broadcast on NBC and was a huge hit for the network, appealing to a diverse and mainstream audience. Interestingly, several episodes include fan characters whose behavior attracted the attention of the eponymous radio psychiatrist. Initially, critical of the fan practices he observes, pathologizing fandom as obsessive, harmful, and antisocial, Frasier is invariably proved wrong in his diagnosis—even shown to be ignorant or indeed just as much a fan as those he criticizes. Indeed, NBC's *Frasier* was part of what Amanda Lotz (2007) describes as the second wave of success the network had in the primetime schedules of the 1990s (p. 269). Like contemporary sitcoms such as *Friends* (1994–2004) and *Will & Grace* (1998–2006), the series was a success in its own right and formed part of a cycle that propelled the network to the top of the ratings. Series that built up a regular and loyal audience did so through their concentration on high production values (highly paid stars), compact narrative, and intense use of marketing and hype to produce a sense of "essential viewing" or "must see TV" (see San Martín 2003) that ensured people would tune in over a set period of time: "These programmes have also been referred to as 'date' or 'appointment' television, and they are distinguished by the compulsive viewing practices of dedicated audiences who organize their schedules around these shows" (Jancovich and Lyons 2003, 2).

Frasier contained positive representations of fans and fandom but it also spoke to fans through a succession of intertextual references, including certain actors making special appearances from other cult shows. This suggests that the network and producers were trying to appeal to a specific fan audience—rather than stereotyping, they were promoting a kind of cultural capital that makes the series and important fan text in its own right. It also had a pre-established audience since it was a spin-off of the hugely popular *Cheers*, and in its main character/star—Frasier Crane/Kelsey Grammer—it had a compelling lead around which the writers could build storylines and scenarios. The ensemble cast was also crucial to the series' success, with a character like Dr. Niles Crane (David Hyde Pierce) drawing audiences to the show. Indeed, it is through the relationship between Frasier and his brother Niles that we see how *Frasier* tackles issues relating to fans and fan obsession.

In "The Show Must Go Off" (2001) and "The Two Hundredth Episode" (2001), the practices of conventions and collecting are cast into the spotlight. In the former episode, while attending a science fiction convention to secure an autograph for his son, Frasier runs into Jackson Hedley (Derek Jacobi) and is surprised to learn that the actor he once adored for introducing him to Shakespeare is now more famous for playing android Tobor on the cult TV show *Space Patrol*. Sharing with Niles the distress he felt after seeing Hedley at the convention (supposedly stuck doing something he felt was beneath him), Frasier decides to offer Hedley the chance to put on a one man show so new generations could experience Shakespeare just as the brothers did when they were children. Niles and Frasier book a theater and sell out the performance; however, after they see Hedley rehearse, they come to realize that he was never the great actor they thought he was. Going to great lengths to try and cancel the show so they are not embarrassed in front of their social set, the brothers' own fandom of Hedley is challenged, yet it also serves to highlight the intertextual nature of *Frasier* and the humor many fans experience when actors crossover between popular series.

In a reversal of how thespian Jacobi played Hedley, once a stage actor known for Shakespeare, now playing the popular science fiction character Tobor (itself a reference to how Shakespearean actor Patrick Stewart moved from stage to screen in playing Jean-Luc Picard [see Pearson 2004]), Grammer, known for playing Frasier on *Cheers*, moved onto *Frasier* in 1993 after appearing as Captain Morgan Bateson in the *Star Trek: The Next Generation* episode "Cause and Effect" (1992). The one-off role was minor and could only be fulfilled as Grammer's shooting schedule for *Cheers* allowed him the time to cross sound stages on the Paramount lot to film his scenes without any interaction with the *TNG* cast. However, Captain Bateson quickly became a fan favorite because of Grammer's star appeal and went on to appear in various fan fictions and the popular official spin-off novel *Ship of the Line* by Diane Carey in 1997. The bringing together of two concomitant Paramount-made series, *Star Trek* and *Frasier*, may not have been a promotional stunt (more the result of clever casting and the availability of actor); it was indicative of what Kevin S. Sandler (2007) calls "cross-promotion and cross-pollination," which drove media activity on channels like NBC at the turn of the century (294). The link between both shows was cemented for fans when Kate Mulgrew (Captain Janeway) joined the ensemble cast from *Frasier* playing her crew on board *Voyager* for the television special *Star Trek: Thirty Years and Beyond* in 1996. These examples suggest that fan parody stems from its "dual address"; speaking to fans and depicting what it means to be one while also playing on stereotypes for the mainstream audience (see Brooker 2002). Drawing on the star appeal of Grammer, *Frasier* and the episode from *TNG*, in which he appears, offers an alternative reading to those dedicated fans who are able to recognize the intertextual references within the storyline—an actor known for playing two roles—and empathy with Frasier and Niles, who feel let down by Hedley's poor performance.

In "The Two Hundredth Episode," Frasier is seen celebrating the two thousandth episode of his radio show. We see that upon returning home with the tape of its recording, he adds it to a vast collection of all his radio shows made at KACL, kept in a large cupboard in his bedroom. Just as he slots the most recent tape into its assigned place, he notices that one of the other tape boxes has been put in upside down; on correcting the position of the box, it is observed that the tape inside this box is actually the wrong one. A brief and comical investigation exposes Daphne as the one who accidently destroyed Frasier's tape and sets him on a mission to find a replacement so that his collection no longer remains imperfect. After much soul searching and a debilitating feeling of lack, Frasier is overjoyed to hear that a listener had made a recording of the show he is missing, so he travels to the fan's house to obtain a copy. On arrival, Frasier and Niles encounter a stereotypical fan that has clearly devoted too much of his time and money into collecting everything related to Frasier's radio show; even quitting his job, so he could record it and having a wall of pictures and memorabilia where his apartment window should be. Feeling guilty for supposedly ruining the fan's life, Frasier attempts to give the fan a short counseling session before leaving without the missing tape recording—taking it would signal that he is as obsessive and "sick" as the fan he just visited. While this episode might overtly suggest that being a fan who earnestly collects means they are somehow lacking something more important and wholesome, it also stresses the significance of the collection and processes of collecting in the formation of fan identity. The B story of the episode sees Martin trying to make Daphne feel better for breaking the tape by showing her all of Frasier's antique statues he has broken and repaired without being caught since living with him. As a follow-up to this, the end credit sequence shows Frasier spotting his father's handiwork and again getting irate—so, despite supposedly realizing his obsession for a complete tape collection was problematic he is still portrayed as a collector because he values the condition of his artifacts even though others clearly do not. *Frasier* ridicules and then promotes what it means to be a fan and thus again speaks to a fan audience well aware of the importance of objects in the celebration and preservation of favorite media texts. This in many ways reflects Roberta Pearson's argument that cultural distinction within fandom is more complex than a juxtaposition between high and low culture; rather that the varying hierarchies of fandom can be identified in how people perceive themselves: as "fans," "enthusiasts," "aficionados," "devotees," and "connoisseurs," among other labels (Pearson 2007, 99).

In *The System of Objects*, Jean Baudrillard (2005) proposes that the collection is personal and "what you really collect is always yourself" (p. 97). As in fan studies, there is a clear link between identity and object of fandom—one reflects the other. In that respect, Sandvoss (2005) argues that fandom is "a symbolic resource in the formation of identity and in the positioning of one's self in the modern world… and the integration of the self into the dominant economic, social and cultural conditions of industrial modernity… it is, in every sense, a mirror of consumption" (p. 165). In Frasier's collecting, then, we see personalized depictions of history—mirrors to the self. Objects therefore embody memories of things past and inform activities and what you do with the collection in the present. There are necessary components of life as it is defined by the historical trajectory from birth to death. Baudrillard (2005) continues, "It is in this sense that the environment of private objects and their possession (collecting being the most extreme instance) is a dimension of our life which, though imaginary, is absolutely essential. Just as essential as dreams" (p. 103). That *Frasier* is playing with notions of fandom and the importance of media texts in the construction of identity might not be so surprising considering that television networks use primetime shows as a way of addressing issues of identity and thus attract more diverse and smaller audiences to the channel. As Jason Mittell (2010) points out about the period in which *Frasier* became one of NBC's "must see" sitcoms,

> In the multi-channel era, the question of *who* has become more prominent, as cable channels and networks have focused on reaching smaller, more concentrated audience segments as defined by demographic and psychographic characteristics. Thus the concept of the television audience had become more fragmented, with specific segments such as the eighteen-to-thirty-four-year-old male audience, the urban professional audience, or the working woman audience emerging as the key categories used within the industry. (p. 75)

In the following discussion of *Toy Hunter*, the network strategies described by Mittell used to locate and attract new primetime audiences are further explored. One of many examples from the increasingly popular reality documentary genre, the series again turns attention to the routinely stereotyped practices of fandom.

Fans on the road

The reality documentary *Toy Hunter* (2012–present) uses fan cultural capital as its central premise. Following the travels of a toy dealer across America, searching for rare and valuable collectibles, *Toy Hunter* emphasizes the importance of authenticity and history to fans that place great value on the physical objects of popular culture (toys, merchandise, etc.) typically considered mere commodities or even throw away trash. While the popularity of a reality series that focuses on fans and the financial value of their collections might suggest that fans are only represented as part of the mainstream because they own something of worth, thus serving to legitimate fandom only through economic capital, I would argue the opposite. Only those toys deemed culturally valuable to the fan collector in *Toy Hunter* are seen as financially lucrative, and cultural value is given greater importance than profit as all the toys shown are either bought for preservation in a museum or fan collection or prove too sentimental to part with no matter the potential financial reward. Fans and their collections represent important components in America's cultural history and thus fan practices such as collecting, displaying, and attending conventions are depicted as typical, necessary and regular activities for not just those in the show but also those television audiences watching at home.

The prevalence of primetime reality series like *Hollywood Treasure* (2010–2012), *Pawn Stars* (2009–present), and *Toy Hunter* on cable networks such as SyFy, History Channel, and Travel Channel suggests that fandom, particularly fans who participate in the collecting and preserving of rare and vintage objects, is about the pursuit of authenticity. Not only do the fan collectors continually search for authentic pieces of social and cultural history in these series but also the audience enjoys watching the integral processes of collecting such as the hunt and acquisition. Gaining access to previously lost or forgotten periods of pop culture history is, I would argue, their primary appeal for the participants and viewers. All three shows give fans the opportunity to legitimize their fandom and have an expert affirm not just the financial worth of their fan objects and antique collections but also their cultural and historical value. For Jerome de Groot (2009), antiques "demonstrate a complex commodification of the past—the fetishization of the object due in main to its age and historical context as well as any innate value or craftsmanship" (p. 67). Thus, antiques are representative of both the owner's economic and cultural capital, they are worth a sum of money or cost something to buy and they enhance the owner's sense of worth and establish their position in a hierarchy of collectors. Like fandom, the collecting community is built on hierarchies of taste defined by cultural capital, however, economic capital plays an important part in the distinction between individuals as objects are bought and sold and rarity increases both financial value and esteem. Primetime reality series about the acquisition and preservation of fan objects make popular history appear worthy and highlight the significance of collectibles to the fan collector and viewers at home:

> They communicate to the viewer that the past might be valuable, that the expert can guide you, and that anyone can undertake it… [S]uch shows contribute to a democratization of the historical, with knowledge and ability moving from the elite—as represented by antique experts, connoisseurship and collectors perhaps— and an emphasis on the intervention of "ordinary" people into previously fenced off arenas. (de Groot 2009, 71–2)

The fencing off of what's valuable and worthy of preservation is exemplified in a series like *Toy Hunter*, aired on the Travel Channel. Jordan Hembrough, fan, presenter, toy dealer, and owner of the Hollywood Heroes toy and collectible store in Westwood, New Jersey, travels the United States to pick collectible toy items for auction, to sell in his store, and market at Comic-Cons around the globe, including San Diego, New York, and Birmingham in the United Kingdom. Literally rummaging through boxes in attics, garages, abandoned storage lock ups, and even other dealers' stores, Hembrough is on a mission to uncover lost items that people think are worthless. The fact that he assigns value to throwaway items subverts the typical scale of taste promoted in other reality shows like BBC's *Antiques Roadshow* (1979–present) and redraws the line between high and low culture. Items from film and television, toys and games, become the contemporary antiques of popular culture. The hunt for that rare and valuable piece of popular culture is important for him as a dealer but also for the fan who wants to make a profit. The setup for the series on the show's website reads like a film plot, almost promoting the hunt for vintage toys as a matter of life or death for him and fan collectors:

> In this season of the Travel Channel's *Toy Hunter*, Jordan finds the picks of a lifetime for struggling businesses owners, annual toy events and even a few celebrity collectors. He's out of his comfort zone, so he has to set his search into high gear. The stakes are higher, the haggles are tougher and the payoffs are much greater than before, because he's hunting for more than just himself—this time, people's livelihoods are on the line if he doesn't deliver! It's a high stakes toy game with demanding players that could potentially set him up for life!

Toy Hunter is pitched like a movie; with Hembrough described more like Indiana Jones than a toy dealer or fan. Old toys, collectibles, and pieces of pop culture are thus portrayed as authentic objects of historical significance—worthy of the hunt. The dealer may make a profit from their sale but ordinary fans will also benefit, either financially or culturally. Objects of popular culture are reclaimed and extolled as valuable—in need of preservation. As Dr. Jones might say, they "belong in a museum!" The Indy metaphor is most obviously played out in a recent episode from 2014 where Hembrough is charged by super fan and curator of The Hall of Heroes in Elkhart Indiana, the only museum of comics and superheroes in the world, with finding a rare and stellar piece to be preserved in his collection for comic book fans to come and see. Hembrough takes his mission seriously and sets out on a road trip from his store to Indiana via Ohio to search for the perfect item. Following a lead he arrives in the suburbs of Cleveland to visit a Superman fan collector who has amassed a collection of 40,000 pieces. Unwilling to part with some of the oldest and most interesting items in his attic, the fan frustrates Hembrough until a non-Superman object catches his eye. A 1946 Captain Marvel plastic statuette, mint-in-box, proves to be the "holy grail" Hembrough was longing for. Agreeing a deal for $1,000, Hembrough sets off with this prized purchase and hopes that it will prove highly valuable to the museum in Indiana. At the end of the episode, the curator agrees to buy the statuette and stresses it will be a welcome addition to the collection, to be preserved for future visitors. Hembrough is relieved and emphasizes to the audience that this was a difficult task but he now knows how to source items for a museum and that he is thrilled to find another toy loving client.

In *Toy Hunter*, we see how collections can come to define a fan collector, often leading to those stereotypes repeated in the media, yet we can also recognize how collectors are able to redefine the meaning of physical objects depending on their cultural value and financial worth. The preservation of toys like the one found by Hembrough to go in the superhero museum and valued by fans as legitimate cultural artifacts suggests that fans are bound up in the constant struggle to validate and prove their fandom is authentic, worthy of recognition. For Walter Benjamin (1936/2007), the aura of authenticity is bound up with originality and is therefore "jeopardized by modern reproductive technologies" that turn an original into just one of many (Appadurai 1986, 45). However, in the case of *Toy Hunter*, where a once mass produced toy—for example, the Captain Marvel plastic statuette—has become the only remaining example of its kind originality is of the utmost importance. The fact that the toy still comes in its original box, no damage or wear, means that the once commonly owned becomes the "one in a million" rare item that requires preservation as "the last of its kind" inside a museum's glass cabinet. As Fiske (1992) argues, authenticity "is a criterion of discrimination normally used to accumulate official cultural capital but which is readily appropriated by fans in their moonlighting cultural economy" (p. 36). Thus, *Toy Hunter* represents fans and the objects they collect as both authentic and culturally important. Fans are historians, archivists, curators, who actively engage in a cultural economy that doesn't just appear on primetime television as entertainment but is represented as an essential part of the history of popular culture in America.

Conclusion

Over the course of this chapter, I have argued that fan stereotypes increased in circulation on American primetime television at the same time that fandom has become more prevalent and its practices more familiar in mainstream media (see also Sandvoss 2005; Booth 2013a). For some fan scholars (e.g., Hills 2007; Jenkins 2012c; Stanfill 2013), this serves to obscure the problematic representation of fans as emotional and unable to discern reality from fiction. Taking this further, Paul Booth (2015b), in his recent *Playing Fans*, describes the new stereotype of the "hyperfan," which he argues has been created by media corporations to discipline fans by showing them how they should and shouldn't behave (p. 22). Twinned representations of "bad" and "good" fans, the former "excessive, transformative, feminine" and the latter "appreciative, supportive, commercial," work to "generate more fandom" for networks and "attract non-fan audiences" (p. 75). However, through my analysis of two types of network series, sitcom *Frasier* and reality documentary *Toy Hunter*, I have maintained that through the depictions of fans and fandom, these shows work to expose the intertextual nature of primetime programming on NBC (where series writers display their own cultural capital) and emphasize the search for authenticity (through the collecting of popular Americana), which sits at the heart of what it means to be a fan. So, using stereotypes to go beyond what audiences have typically assumed about media fandom, primetime television serves to complicate rather simplify fan behavior.

Above all, perhaps what this short chapter has highlighted the most is that with the increasing array of primetime television that seemingly speaks to and about fans, there needs to be a much more open discussion within fans studies about how representations of fandom effect and contribute to the field. Whether in fact or fiction, series that play with fan stereotypes are actively engaged with the processes of meaning making and are essential components in the creation of a fan identity. The varying degrees to which fans and fan practices are parodied in the media are indicative of an industry that is itself caught up in a form of identity crisis: who are they making television for, who is watching, how and for how long? With the multiplicity of platforms through which audiences engage, combined with the competitive nature of multichannel television, American networks are keener than ever to court fans. And even if, as many scholars have argued, some shows continue to represent some fans as obsessive and excessive, there are a selection of primetime examples like those discussed in this chapter that articulate a more authentic understanding of what it means to be a fan.

10

The Image of the Fan in *Stargate SG-1*

Karen Hellekson

In today's era of self-aware, in-the-know, self-reflexive televisual media, the image of the fan can be represented directly instead of hiding the fan under cover of metaphor. Gone are the days of *Star Trek: The Next Generation* (1987–1994), whose adolescent Wesley Crusher was a stand-in for the fan, brought into the text as a supersmart geek and Gene Roddenberry stand-in.[1] *Supernatural* (2005–), to cite possibly the best-known example, is famed for its depiction of fans as recognizable current-day media fans (see also Chapters 13 and 14). *Supernatural* not only acknowledges the existence of fans but also shows them engaging in recognizable and stereotypical behavior— wearing costumes, writing erotic fan fiction, and attending conventions. The character of Becky, in particular, presents the fan directly, steeped in the source text and maybe a little scary in her focus on her fan object (Tosenberger 2010b). Particularly in earlier-era texts, however, this direct mode of fan representation is not common, likely because the idea of the fan, much less their modes of engagement and activity, had not yet percolated into popular consciousness, and likely because the sort of metadiscourse implied by the existence of such fans was not something these popular narratives chose to engage in, preferring to stay within the boundaries of their chosen genre. Instead, these texts present a coded fan, someone recognizably as a fan only because he or she exhibits fanlike behaviors. These texts, which are often played for laughs, feature a character who exhibits extensive knowledge of the object of fandom, who simultaneously desires and fears interaction with the fandom's principals, and who longs for validation by the object of devotion.

The long-running science fiction TV (SFTV) show *Stargate SG-1* (1997–2007) has an active fanbase and has long been known to be sympathetic to fans. As Cherry (2005) notes, "The producers of *Stargate* have played a significant part in the encouragement of active fan participation.... The official *Stargate* websites have encouraged active participation by the fans" (p. 68).[2] During its ten seasons, *Stargate SG-1*, an SFTV program about alien gates that permit almost instantaneous travel between far distant planets and the US Air Force–affiliated team, SG-1, that traverses these gates, aired several episodes that feature the figure of the coded fan. These episodes, which I examine in detail here, present the fan as a knowledgeable outsider who needs something from the object of desire. In 4.11 "Point of No Return," the fan is coded as a conspiracy theorist (a kind of fan) who thinks he is an alien—and who discovers he is right. In 6.08 "The

Other Guys," two fan-coded guys find themselves embroiled in an actual adventure—one they are engaging in instead of watching from afar. Finally, in 8.15 "Citizen Joe," the titular character, Joe, discovers that his fannish stories are not stories but reality. *Stargate SG-1* ultimately validates the fan: the fannish object is not fiction but reality.

Previous *Stargate SG-1* scholarship has touched on fan reaction to these episodes (as fans clearly saw themselves in these characters—and were not always happy about it) but not within the context of what *Stargate SG-1* ultimately does with the image of the fan: approve of and validate fans and fannish behavior. I argue that in the episodes I analyze fannish activity is both tacitly acknowledged and affirmed, thus foregrounding, even valorizing, fandom as well as its affective nature.

4.11 "Point of No Return"

In 4.11 "Point of No Return," a conspiracy theorist, Martin Lloyd (Willie Garson), phones and leaves a message that displays disturbing knowledge of the secret Stargate program.[3] Martin is convinced he is an alien, whereas the SG-1 team is convinced he's crazy—a notion bolstered by finding large quantities of psychiatric drugs in Martin's house. However, Martin is proved right: he is an alien. He and several of his fellows deserted from a war they were losing, abandoned their ship, and came down to Earth in a pod. Martin felt guilty about deserting and wanted to return home, but his compatriots did not, so they drugged him so he would lose his memory, with one of the aliens posing as Martin's psychiatrist to ensure Martin kept taking the memory-blocking drugs. After Martin's memory returns, he is taken through the Stargate to his home world, only to find it abandoned, devastated by the evil alien Goa'uld. If he had returned, he would be dead.

Although a conspiracy theorist may not be perceived as a fan on the face of it, the narrative clearly codes him as a fan: he has extensive knowledge of arcane facts. He is a fan of the obscure, the hidden, the deliberately concealed. Martin embodies the pervasive popular cultural image of the fan as a pathologic other, which here gains resonance in the person of conspiracy theorist Martin. Jensen (1992) remarks, "The literature on fandom is haunted by images of deviance. The fan is consistently characterized (referencing the term's origins) as a potential fanatic. This means that fandom is seen as excessive, bordering on deranged, behavior." Jensen's essay "explores how and why the concept of the fan involves images of social and psychological pathology" (p. 9). In the character of Martin, the idea of the fan is expressed by Martin's pathologic conspiracy theories—extreme, irrational beliefs, coupled with a lack of trust in big institutions like the military and the belief that he is being constantly monitored, along with fannish markers like extensive knowledge of the subject at hand. In short, Martin is a fan. Martin's initial rambling phone call brought him to Stargate Command's attention:

> I know this call is being monitored but don't bother to set up a trace. I'm at a phone booth in Butte, Montana, but I'll be long gone before your black ops teams can get here. You're not dealing with an amateur.... I know all about Roswell, and the

Kennedy cover-ups and the [tape is fast-forwarded, so we know he is listing more than what is provided here]... CIA-sanctioned microwave harassment and the... lizard people. But the point is none of these compare to your secret, Colonel. I'm talking about a large circular object discovered in Egypt and currently residing in the bottom of a missile silo under Cheyenne Mountain. I believe you call it the Stargate.[4]

This initial phone call sums up Martin's character: he's a mess, but ultimately, he's right. Mixed in with the bizarre cover-ups and lizard people is the truth: knowledge of the Stargate. Martin has some awareness of this himself: "The word Stargate stuck in my head. It triggered what I later realized was a suppressed memory. You see, Colonel O'Neill, the truth is I'm not just interested in outer space. I'm from outer space!"

Further, Martin lives like someone's idea of a fan might: in a dark house cluttered with sci-fi toys and odd, complex computers and machinery. While Jack O'Neill (Richard Dean Anderson) talks to Martin, the other members of SG-1 ransack his house, mocking his toy collection and taking note of the plethora of drugs in his cabinets: "Tranquilizers, antidepressants, antipsychotics. Looks like our friend here has been treated for a number of different psychiatric problems," Samantha Carter (Amanda Tapping) says. Daniel Jackson (Michael Shanks) replies ironically, "Yeah, why doesn't that surprise me?"

The metaphorical pathologic nature of the fan has thus become literal: the drugs imply that Martin is crazy in a way that his spewing conspiracies do not. When SG-1 visits the prescribing psychiatrist (and, unbeknownst to SG-1, fellow alien) Dr. Peter Tanner (Robert Lewis), Tanner's response further emphasizes the perceived pathology: "People like Martin sometimes compensate for their feelings of insignificance by creating elaborate fantasies in which they are the center and focus of all the attention. These people are usually harmless, although they may try and draw others into their illusions." This remark may just have well been made about fans: harmless fantasists who seek attention and who seek to draw others in.

Yet, the more SG-1 delves into Martin, the more things don't add up. Chemical analysis of the drugs reveals that they are not what they seem to be. Martin writes alien symbols that SG-1 team members recognize as glyphs that appear on Stargates, thus implying that Martin has seen an actual Stargate. Suspiciously, Tanner abandons his office after another interview with SG-1 about the tampered-with drugs. And most importantly, a now drug-free Martin leads SG-1 to the crashed remains of his extraterrestrial pod, and he is able to explain why he is on Earth and why people seem to be after him.

With the drugs cleared from his system, Martin is able to rationally explain what has happened. His conspiracy theory fandom transmutes from pathology to sublimated memory: he thought there was a conspiracy against him because there really was a conspiracy against him. However, it wasn't CIA-sanctioned microwave harassment or lizard people; it was his own people, determined to stay in hiding. Martin experiences the ultimate vindication: not only has he been right the whole time (at least about his being under surveillance, if not the lizard people) but also his fraught decision to desert a war his people were losing proves to be the correct decision: he is alive when everyone from his planet is dead or scattered. The fan is therefore presented as being, in all the ways that count, ultimately right. *Stargate SG-1* here presents a pathologically coded fan—just as its own superfans might be coded—but redeems the fan in the end, thus tacitly acknowledging the importance of fan interest and focus.

6.08 "The Other Guys"

The episode 6.08 "The Other Guys" presents the characters of two scientists who are also fans: Jay Felger (Patrick McKenna), a fan of the SG-1 team and their reports, and Simon Coombs (John Billingsley), a fan of classic *Star Trek* (1966–1969).[5] The two play off each other: Felger doesn't understand Coombs's *Star Trek* references to Vulcans and people wearing red shirts, and Coombs mocks Felger's unseemly interest in the SG-1 team members. Felger and Coombs are on an off-world scientific mission, guarded by SG-1, when they are attacked by enemy alien ships. They see the members of SG-1 captured, and, determined to save them, they follow, despite explicit orders to the contrary, by boarding a spaceship. First they learn that the entire capture was a setup; SG-1 let themselves be taken so that they could have a secret meeting with an informant. Then, when the secret meeting is revealed to their captors and the informant executed, the scientists have to save SG-1 for real. Thanks to their technical know-how, they manage to free the members of SG-1 and save the day. Storm (2005) calls the episode "a giant rollicking good time that every sci-fi nut wishes would happen to them" (p. 375).

Rather than being presented as a pathologic Other, in 6.08 "The Other Guys," fans are presented as nerds with inappropriate obsessions that lead to trouble. Felger, in the presence of SG-1, tries to stay cool, particularly in the presence of his idol, Samantha Carter, but completely fails—behavior Coombs characterizes as "butt-snorkeling." Coombs mocks Felger: "So tell me how you finally defeated Apophis, Colonel O'Neill. Oh, Major Carter, I based my doctoral thesis on your amazing wormhole stability theories." Felger mocks right back: "Bite me, Coombs! At least my heroes exist. If this was a *Trek* convention you'd be all dressed up like a Klingon."

Once aboard the alien spacecraft, Felger and Coombs reveal themselves to be supremely ill-equipped to deal with being members of an away team. Felger fires wildly the moment they are brought up to the ship (Coombs's sarcastic response: "Nicely done. We were alone, but that'll probably change now"), and both are terrible at being stealthy as they lurk in stereotypically confusing corridors, trying to stay out of sight while tracking down the SG-1 team's whereabouts. In fact, their entire experience aboard an alien vessel parodies conventional SFTV representations, including confusing corridors and ultimate evil bad guys; as Ndalianis (2010, 242) remarks, "During their adventures [Felger and Coombs] manage to parody the conventions of small-screen science fiction." Also implied here is what fans would be like if faced with an actual SG-1 mission: despite detailed knowledge, they are ultimately unprepared for the reality of an away mission. The bad guys are not only bad but will also shoot at you.

Within the narrative, Felger and Coombs are brilliant scientists, with Felger a lecturer at MIT and Coombs an applied math teacher at Yale. This is metaphorically extended to the detailed knowledge of a fan, thus granting them a useful level of expertise. Felger has detailed knowledge of the ship's layout, thanks to his fannishly compulsive study of SG-1's reports; and Coombs masterfully works a computer interface within the ship, which enables him to remotely help SG-1 escape even as the bad guys pin him down. In the right context, this information is useful. But in the wrong context—planning covert ops, for example—their expertise is not remotely helpful. Their specialized knowledge, which is related to their role as scientists, is extended to fans as general: all are knowledgeable but ultimately outsiders. They are out of their element when presented with a life-or-death situation. In such cases, knowledge ultimately takes a back seat to the practicality of staying alive.

Felger and Coombs's scientific knowledge, and by extension fannish knowledge, bears fruit: they do save the day, and not only that, no one is left behind—Stargate's central tenet. Their reward: a well-attended ceremony in the gate room where Stargate Command's general honors them with the Air Force Civilian Award for Valor.[6] O'Neill pins the medals onto the scientists, saying, "Despite the fact that you gentlemen disobeyed my orders, which, in my little world, constitutes screwing up... twice, the truth is, we wouldn't be here without you. You are true heroes." This public declaration is followed by Carter's planting a long kiss on Felger's mouth—whereupon the entire scene is revealed to be in Felger's imagination as Coombs pokes him awake. The episode ends with Coombs saying to Felger, "Geek," and Felger responding, "Nerd"—acknowledgment of their interests and thus their related (fannish) outsider status. Although their validation is a dream, they—and fans—experience validation nonetheless. Within the context of fannish expertise and knowledge, the fans win. *Stargate SG-1* thus presents fans that, despite their lack of mission-specific qualifications, by just being themselves, have skills that helped them save the day. The kiss (even if revealed to be wish fulfillment) serves as the ultimate reward: it implies emotional engagement, not just engagement via action—an important point that touches on affect in fans and fandom that acknowledges their emotional investment.

8.15 "Citizen Joe"

In 8.15 "Citizen Joe," barber Joe Spencer (Dan Castellaneta) has a years-long obsession with telling and writing stories about the exploits of SG-1 and the Stargate program. Joe's son provides a baseline for how much time has passed: he starts out as a little kid who enjoys hearing about SG-1's exploits as bedtime stories and ends up a disaffected teen. When Joe's obsession costs him his wife and his job, he breaks into O'Neill's house to confront him. Joe and O'Neill learn that their minds have been linked, thanks to an alien artifact that Joe purchased at a garage sale years earlier. Everything that Joe's loved ones thought was fiction is actually fact. Two things about this episode stand out. First, it is a clip show. Joe's stories, told in loving detail to his increasingly irritated family and customers, are presented as clip flashbacks, suggesting that he has been privy not just to SG-1's exploits but also to the show itself, as aired. This places Joe in the position of a fan of the SG-1 team and of the *Stargate SG-1* program itself, emphasizing the connection between fans and Joe, the fan proxy. Second, the show has a level of metatextual interest: O'Neill is famously a fan of *The Simpsons* (1989–), as is Anderson himself, and Castellaneta voices character Homer Simpson—a layer of subtext that in-the-know fans would enjoy and that is a nice nod to the fans.[7]

"Citizen Joe" presents Joe as having detailed, special—that is, fannish—knowledge. However, more than that, Joe also engages in stereotypical fannish behavior: writing. Although he is actually channeling O'Neil's mind and transcribing O'Neil's SG-1 mission reports, albeit with narrative flourishes, the behavior is presented as writing fan fiction, with detailed back stories, mythology, and interconnected plots. Further, this behavior is presented as pathologic: he stays up late at night, desperately typing, as his wife, Charlene (Deborah Theaker), pleads with him to come to bed. Eventually she leaves him because he cannot stop his compulsive behavior; nor can he discard the artifact that grants him access to the images he sees. Part of the fun of the episode lies in its self-referentiality, as it turns back upon and comments on *Stargate SG-1* itself. For example, when Joe asks his wife what she didn't like about a plot he describes at the dinner table, she says, "It's just that personally, I like stories that are more about interpersonal relations, and a little less to do with things blowing up." When a customer comments on the intricacies of the alien Goa'uld life cycle, Joe snaps, "It's not confusing, it's complex!"

Joe's narrative abilities are presented as failures. Early in the episode, as he cuts a customer's hair, he tells a joke, but the pacing is off and the terms confused. "It's a good thing you can cut hair," his customer responds to the failed quip. Further, Joe is terrible at creating a coherent narrative. When he tells stories to his wife and son, he can't construct a satisfying story arc. The details are too overwhelming and thus confusing. When Joe asks Charlene for feedback after he tells his first SG-1 story, she responds, trying to be nice, "Well, you know I'm not the biggest science fiction fan. But no, no, it was… it was just so… detailed." Further, closure is elusive. As his son, Andy (Alex Ferris), notes, "Well, you gotta finish it, Dad. You can't just end a story in the middle." Joe, however, can't finish the narrative because he doesn't know what happens next. He can't construct a fiction; he can only record fact. He is too literal, unable to use the special knowledge granted to him by the alien device to construct satisfying stories.

At Charlene's urging, Joe writes down his stories and sends the manuscripts off for consideration for publication; Charlene hopes that if he writes them down, Joe will stop annoying everybody with his storytelling. Although his stories are rejected, his coworkers prove supportive while simultaneously providing an implicit critique of the *Stargate SG-1* episodes sourced: "See, I'm not sure you should have sent in this one about Seth. It wasn't one of your best," says one; another, in an ironic nod to what is acknowledged by fans as possibly the worst episode ever, says, "They rejected Hathor?! Oh, but it was gold!"[8] His customers grow increasingly annoyed and stop coming in, which only gives Joe more time to write. His barbershop employees gradually lose their goodwill, and one accepts a job elsewhere. When Charlene confronts him and asks him to stop writing, he has accrued 326 rejection letters.

Worse, he can't stop writing. "I think they're real, Charlene. I'm not making them up. They're happening. Somewhere. I can see them," he tells her, which only convinces her that he is unhinged.

Validation is at hand, however. After a desperate Joe breaks into O'Neill's house, SG-1 discovers the alien artifact linking Joe and O'Neill. In fact, the link went both ways. O'Neill had been seeing Joe's life for the past seven years, while he was on the base writing mission reports, but he characterizes the experience as "quite relaxing." With the mystery solved, the only thing that remains is for Joe and Charlene to reconcile. The episode ends with the couple meeting in a park. Just as Charlene asks for a divorce, O'Neill, in full uniform, pulls up in an official-looking black SUV. "It's a pleasure to meet you, ma'am. I think we have some things to talk about," he tells her. Then come the words that all fans wish for: "It's all true."[9]

As Hipple (2006) remarks, this episode points to fan activity outside the narrative frame the program itself:

> We might also recognise that [Joe's] engagement with SG-1's activities reflects that of *Stargate SG-1*'s fans, most evidently in his devastation over the death of Daniel Jackson… and delight at his reappearance…. This recognizes the furore among fans when Michael Shanks (Jackson) left the series…. Joe's sentiments in this episode constitute the makers' direct, non-judgemental acknowledgment of fans' role in the presence and standing of their series. (pp. 41–2)

Joe thus stands in for fans of *Stargate SG-1*. Yet fan reaction to the episode was not uniformly positive: Storm (2005) notes that some fans saw the coded fan referentiality as "a slap in the face" that "made some fans feel that their interest in the show was a laughing matter to the writers…. Was it an homage or a parody" of "fan rabidity"? (pp. 495–6).[10]

Joe, instead of using what he sees as inspiration, as a fan fic—writing fan of *Stargate SG-1* might do, simply describes what he sees, literally and in incredible detail. Joe, as an embodiment of the fan, is presented as someone with detailed knowledge but no way to act on that knowledge, and, like Felger and Coombs, without the training, expertise, or disposition to fully engage with the fannish desired object. Like Martin, he is presented as possibly pathologic in his interest, unwilling to set aside the alien artifact that grants him the visions and unable to stop his compulsive writing, even as his relationships and his livelihood dissolve. As a storyteller and writer of fiction, Joe is perhaps the most recognizably fannish of all the coded fan characters. He engages with his fannish object through narrative, imperfect as it is. Like fans, he finds affective pleasure in his fandom, finding it increasingly seductive.

Conclusion

The coded fan characters all suffer from a pathologically intense connection to what might be called their fandom: Martin to his conspiracy theories and his desire to learn about the Stargate, which link to his being an alien from another world, and Felger and Joe to the SG-1 team. Fans are presented as outsiders with special knowledge—knowledge of the supersecret SG-1 program and knowledge of his home planet's Stargate address (Martin), knowledge of science and computers (Felger and Coombs), and detailed knowledge of SG-1's classified exploits (Joe). Yet within the confines of the program, *Stargate SG-1* ultimately validates fans and their experience. In every case, in the end, they are proven to be right: Martin is really an alien; Felger and Coombs prove that they have what it takes to save the day despite SG-1's skepticism; and Joe isn't making up stories but rather transcribing true events. Their intense focus is explicable, even valuable, within the context of the narrative.

Analysis of the coded fan is of interest because it permits nuanced analysis through a metafannish lens of texts that do not blatantly address fans or fan experience. Such coding naturally extends from the image of the fan to the production itself: *Stargate SG-1* is commenting on itself and its fans. This sort of coding could be interestingly applied to other early media texts; it may be interesting to watch the development of the fan through early (that is, before the recognizable image of the fan, as in *Supernatural*) media fandoms such as *The Man from U.N.C.L.E.* (1964–1968) or *The X-Files* (1993–2002). By validating fans and their experiences, *Stargate SG-1* builds on its fan-friendly ethos. The coded fan characters are played for laughs, but in my reading (and that of Storm 2005), each episode's tone manages to remain inoffensive. Pathologic fan activity is presented and even mocked, particularly in 4.11 "Point of No Return," but the episodes draw out the thorn by validating the coded fan experience. Telotte (2014), in his analysis of SFTV, notes,

> Media SF… increasingly serves an important cultural function. For in that reflexive tendency, one driven by those ubiquitous images of technological imaging and construction, it not only helps us better see a world that always seems to be disappearing into the technological landscape of modern life, but it also enables another, and ultimately more important envisioning: letting us see ourselves as inhabitants of increasingly strange… landscapes, and thus better understand our needs in this "brave new world." (p. 20)

The coded fan episodes of *Stargate SG-1* ask viewers, some of whom are fans, to make an affective link with the fans displayed on the screen. These episodes reflect back onto the fans: we see what Telotte calls "inhabitants of increasingly strange… landscapes," but with affective doubling. We see the coded fan on screen, and in addition to the possibilities inherent in this technological otherworld, we see ourselves, now, in the present. The image of the fan permits us to cross that boundary.

As I've argued here, the coded fan in *Stargate SG-1* permits SFTV conventions to be foregrounded, which in turn causes them to lose their power—one reason why the episodes are played for laughs. The metatextuality of this stepping out "[lays] bare the conventions of science fiction and [subverts] its transparent language of mimesis and believability" (Ebert 1980, 93). Ultimately, as the coded-fan episodes described here demonstrate, *Stargate SG-1* pays homage to both fans and the genre of SFTV.

Notes

1   Gene Roddenberry, whose middle name is Wesley, noted that the character was a bit like himself at age fourteen; see the "Wesley Crusher" entry at Memory Alpha (http://en.memory-alpha.wikia.com/wiki/Wesley_Crusher) (accessed February 2, 2016).

2   Perhaps the franchise's biggest valentine to fans was the "Get in the Gate" sweepstakes, which permitted a fan to win a trip to Vancouver (where the show was shot) and a studio tour, with a walk-on role on *Stargate SG-1* or its spin-off, *Stargate Atlantis* (2004–2009). Winners were announced starting in 2003; see Sumner (2006). In addition, the producers supported the Gateworld fan website (http://www.gateworld.net/) (accessed February 2, 2016), providing it with news tidbits, images, and interviews.

3   The episode 4.11 "Point of No Return" has two sequels, 5.12 "Wormhole X-Treme!," the 100th *SG-1* episode, and its sequel, 10.06 "200," the 200th *SG-1* episode. Both also feature Martin, and both are tremendously self-referential. The episode 5.12 "Wormhole X-Treme!" goes on the set of a new SFTV show, *Wormhole X-Treme!*, headed by an again amnesiac Martin—the details of which exactly correspond with SG-1 and their off-world missions. This episode features actual *Stargate SG-1* crew members playing crew members on its fictional counterpart (see Stargate Wiki, http://stargate.wikia.com/wiki/Wormhole_X-Treme!_%28episode%29, for a list of who plays whom) (accessed February 2, 2016). *Wormhole X-Treme!* is also referenced in 8.15 "Citizen Joe," where we learn that it was quickly canceled. The episode 10.06 "200" romps through various pitches and scenarios in a hilarious, touching homage to SFTV in general (see "200," Stargate Wiki, http://stargate.wikia.com/wiki/200, for a list) (accessed February 2, 2016). These episodes are interesting because they posit the fan as influence-wielding producer, in contrast to Jenkins's (1992) classic assertion that fans are powerless, poaching creators in opposition to producers. The notion of fans as a powerless elite is discussed by Tulloch (1995), which analyzes power dynamics between "the industry that makes the show" and "the general public on whose 'votes' its future depends" (144).

4   All quotations from episodes are taken from their respective transcripts at Stargate SG-1 Solutions (http://www.stargate-sg1-solutions.com/) (accessed February 2, 2016).

5   Actor John Billingsley played the alien Doctor Phlox on *Star Trek: Enterprise* (2001–2005), which was airing when 6.08 "The Other Guys" was broadcast in 2002, thus adding a layer of metaintertextual interest.

6   The Air Force Civilian Award for Valor is a real award, not one made up for the program; see US Department of the Air Force, "Air Force Guidance Memorandum for Air Force Instruction (AFI) 36-2803, The Air Force Military Awards and Decorations Program," http://static.e-publishing.af.mil/production/1/af_a1/publication/afi36-2803/afi36-2803.pdf (accessed February 2, 2016).

7   For more details, see "Stargate SG-1," Simpsons Wiki, http://simpsons.wikia.com/wiki/Stargate_SG-1 (accessed February 2, 2016); and "Richard Dean Anderson," Simpsons Wiki, http://simpsons.wikia.com/wiki/Richard_Dean_Anderson (accessed February 2, 2016).

8   For fan reaction, see "Hathor (episode)," Stargate Wiki, http://stargate.wikia.com/wiki/Hathor_%28episode%29 (accessed February 2, 2016). Regarding "metanarrative discussions and critiques of various episodes of *Stargate SG-1*" surrounding Joe's rejected stories, see Beeler (2008, 278).

9   See also *Supernatural* and *Galaxy Quest* (1999)—the latter another text that directly (and humorously) validates fan experience.
10   See also fan reaction to the character of Becky in *Supernatural*.

11

Marking the Line between Producers and Fans: Representations of Fannish-ness in *Doctor Who* and *Sherlock*

Melissa A. Click and Nettie Brock

Reviewing a number of changes evident in "Television's Golden Age (2.0)," *The New York Observer* (Grant 2014) focuses on one specific change—the increased engagement between a show's writers and fans—and attributes it almost entirely to social media. Today the web hosts endless fan creations and communities, and also facilitates seemingly direct communication between fans and television production teams. Because social media gives producers easier access to fans' thoughts and desires, it has become more common for series to court and reward fans by planting "Easter eggs" in primary texts and by creating transmedia stories that extend narratives outside the television. Despite such indications that producers have become more interested in acknowledging fans and fulfilling their desires, the article asserts that "new formats and new ways of delivering story are actually taking power out of fans' hands" (Grant 2014, para. 4). To explain this, the article asserts that fans' diminished power is tied to television's increasing cultural status, meaning that it is "no longer the bastard cousin of cinema" (Grant 2014, para. 5). Taking a firm hold of this new cultural power, many television showrunners have assumed the disengaged, elitist personas of film auteurs, and have found that distinguishing themselves from fans is a useful strategy for convincingly creating the aura and authority for which auteurs are known.

Although the relationship between industry and fans has been an enduring concern in fan studies, two recent studies have approached this topic in the context of digital media culture. Felschow (2010) explores producers' direct address to fans in the *Supernatural* episode "The Monster at the End of this Book," finding that the series' representation of fans serves as a playful power grab. Felschow concludes that fans remain relatively powerless to producers because the writers' room, the showrunner's territory, continues to be a site where the battle between producers and audiences is waged. Similarly, Suzanne Scott (2013a) uses the career of Zack Snyder to examine the "fanboy auteur," an archetype that unites the masculine creative authority long expressed by auteurs and the feminized reverence of the devoted fanboy. Scott's examination of the DVD commentaries that accompany Snyder's films demonstrates a persistent push and pull between the two halves of the fanboy auteur, and reveals that while the auteur's fannish investments allow him to connect with fans and demonstrate his worthiness to remake a beloved text, his work ultimately upholds media industry goals through his assertion of his vision and interpretive power.

Uniting and extending Felschow's and Scott's work, we argue that fanboy auteurs must carefully balance their public comments about their fandom with expressions of their mastery over their respective series, and that similar pressures prevail when representing fans. To explore specific manifestations of the changing dynamics between producers and fans in the contemporary digital media environment, we examine two cases in which producers have actively worked to distinguish themselves from their fans. The first analyzes Russell T Davies and his representations of fans in *Doctor Who*, and the second analyzes Steven Moffat and Mark Gatiss and their representations of fans in *Sherlock*. In both cases, we consider the fanboy auteurs' discussions of their own fandom, public statements about their series' fans, and representations of fans in the programs they produce. We assert that while digital culture may allow a softening of the line separating producers and fans, producers maintain their authority over their media productions by strategically differentiating themselves from fans with disparaging public comments and representations of fans in the texts they produce.

Russell T Davies and *Doctor Who*

Russell T Davies, a long-time fan of *Doctor Who* (1963–1989), helmed the new series (2005–present) as head writer and showrunner. Davies describes his own *Doctor Who* fandom as "geeky," saying, "I'm a fan myself but I'm very glad we've broadened the appeal… We've just restored it to its former glory" (Williams 2007, para. 6). Davies's interest in broadening *Doctor Who*'s appeal by courting new fans is positioned against his disdain for fans whom he feels take things too far. Davies says, "I think the great sadness about fandom is that it's a fantastic and constructive and passionate and loving thing, but there are 200 loud voices—I mean, *insane*, loud, voices—who dominate the entire conversation" (qtd. in Berry 2008). In his book *A Writer's Tale* (2010), Davies suggests that these insane voices thrive in online fan spaces, "It's those internet message boards. The forums. They destroy writers…. Creating something is not a democracy. The people have no say. The artist does. It doesn't matter what the people witter on about" (p. 104).

Davies's comments suggest that he struggles with the blurry boundaries between producers and audiences, and specifically with the deep investments of Classic *Who* fans, whose life-long relationships with the series have encouraged them to be vocal about their fears about the new series. Hills (2010) suggests that a common, but unfounded, concern of *Doctor Who* fans involves worries that the new series would descend into "fanwank" (a derogatory term describing content that appeals only to deeply invested fans). Davies's use of fanwank in the series and the few moments when he represents fans make it clear that he admires fandom but is also highly critical of those overly passionate fans.

For example, the very first episode of the new series features a die-hard *Doctor Who* fan: Clive (Mark Benton), whom Rose (Billie Piper) meets on the Internet. He fulfills the stereotype of the online, obsessed fan. Clive is obsessed with solving the riddle of the mysterious "Doctor" who pops up across history. There are multiple levels of fan representation associated with Clive. For starters, he is depicted as being "a lunatic" (Rose's word) and not someone worth Rose's time. He keeps a poorly lit shed behind his home filled with stacks of books and pictures of the Doctor. Clive is the first person killed when Autons attack later in the episode. There is no advantage to Clive being an apostle of the Doctor—he is ridiculed and then killed. This fan image is recurrent in Davies's character of Victor Kennedy (Peter Kay)—another fan who takes his fandom to an extreme, discussed below.

Beyond representing fans in the series, Davies also had to negotiate the long-standing fandom of which he was a part. Fending off fanwank fears, Davies's tenure on *Doctor Who* from 2005–2009 is marked by the careful maintenance of the balance between appeasing old and recruiting new fans. Davies, like the writers of *Supernatural* Felschow (2010) describes, demonstrated he had complete control of the series by using representations of fans in *Doctor Who* to acknowledge and celebrate them, but also to reject what he perceived to be extreme fan behavior, thereby instructing viewers on how to behave as fans (Booth 2015b). By doing so, he exhibited the reverence of the Classic *Doctor Who* fans, and also appealed to NuWhovians, audiences unfamiliar with *Doctor Who*. Consequently, there are multiple moments in the series when Davies clearly tips his hat to the fans.

The early episodes of the new series rarely addressed its long-term cult fans, underscoring that any fears that fanwank would alienate new fans were groundless; to the contrary, Hills (2010) suggests that "'non-fans' simply weren't reading [overt references to the previous series]" (61). While the first and second seasons paid homage to the early series and made occasional references that required previous knowledge of the series, other instances in the new series function both as an acknowledgement of Classic *Doctor Who* fans and as indoctrination for NuWhovians into what is clearly a world with a rich history, making potential "fanwank" into exposition. For instance, the premises of the early episodes, 1.6 "Dalek" and 2.3 "School Reunion," depend entirely upon previous *Doctor Who* knowledge—of the Doctor's arch nemeses the Daleks or of previous companions Sarah Jane Smith (Elisabeth Sladen) and K-9. Davies knows that not every viewer recognizes Sarah Jane or K-9, so neither does Rose. The Doctor explains the Classic *Who* characters' backgrounds gently to Rose and, thus, to new audience members. These explanations do not talk down to viewers, but encourage reverence for the old series. These episodes are full of subtle fanwank and the Doctor loves every minute of them, as evidenced by his beaming face and near squeals of glee when K-9 appears for the first time on *Doctor Who* since 1983. Classic Whovians likely would have done the same. But because Rose's confused reaction is, "Why does he look so disco?," the Doctor and Sarah Jane talk to her of K-9's long history. Rose acts as the new audiences' proxy in this unfamiliar world; meanwhile, Classic *Who* fans are encouraged to revel, right alongside the Doctor, in these asides filled with treasured history.

The most prominent depiction of fans is in the episode completely devoted to the *Doctor Who* fandom: "Love & Monsters" (2.10), which focuses on fans of the Doctor who seek to uncover the mysteries surrounding him. However, before "Love & Monsters" and the onscreen depictions of fans, the series still nods to these fans. While Davies may have included Whovian fan knowledge in the episodes between the pilot of new *Doctor Who* and episode 2.10, "Love & Monsters," he does so without representing fandom itself. "Love & Monsters" is an unusual episode because it does not overtly feature the Doctor or his companion, a move necessitated by *Doctor Who's* overlapping shooting schedule, which prohibits the main characters from appearing in one episode per season ("The New World of Who" 2006). The absence of the main characters in this episode allows Davies to explore new characters and situations, and encourages the audience to build relationships with these new characters. "Love & Monsters" centers on Elton Pope (Marc Warren), who had a childhood encounter with the Doctor and has since become obsessed with uncovering this mysterious figure. "Love & Monsters" is structured by Elton's video blog, which details his brushes with the aliens that have been invading London. Although the episode begins with Elton in relative isolation, his online searches for information about aliens lead him to Ursula Blake (Shirley Henderson), a blogger with a group of friends, all of whom are investigating the Doctor. Elton joins this group and they name themselves "London Investigation 'n' Detective Agency" (LINDA).

The members of LINDA each represent a different fan stereotype, as observed by various fan scholars (e.g., Jenkins 1992; Jensen 1992; Hills 2002a). Elton is the newcomer, eager for information, but also is lonely, searching for like-minded friends. Ursula is a blogger full of ideas, but primarily moderates the opinions of the others by uniting them. Mr. Skinner (Simon Greenall) is the fan-scholar who utilizes academically rooted ideas to create his own "scholarly fan identity" (Hills 2002a, 2); he is full of theories about how "the Doctor isn't a man, he's more a collection of archetypes." Bridget (Moya Brady) has researched the Doctor throughout history, cataloguing instances in which the TARDIS has been spotted. Finally, Bliss (Kathryn Drysdale) is an artist whose renderings of the Doctor have little resemblance to the man himself. In the audio commentary from the episode's release on DVD, director Dan Zeff suggests that the characterization of the LINDA members was intended to be affectionate, not critical, "They weren't people we were laughing at; they were people we were feeling for." Zeff's comments indicate that *Doctor Who's* creative team wished to position the LINDA members so as to avoid the common characterization of the series' fans as "pathologizations of fandom as 'sad,' infantile, and living in the past" (Hills 2010, 60).

Not simply a collection of fan archetypes, LINDA's members also represent the close-knit relationship that actual *Doctor Who* fans may form. The group eventually moves from sharing stories of the Doctor to simply enjoying each other's company. That is, until Victor Kennedy (Peter Kay) shows up. Kennedy is obsessed with the Doctor to the detriment of all else—the embodiment of the kinds of fandom Davies publicly disdains. Kennedy forces LINDA into a research mission much more intense and comprehensive than their previous half-hearted attempts, and ultimately changes the happy-go-lucky members of LINDA. Kennedy tasks Elton with becoming friends with Jackie Tyler to find Rose and, thus, the Doctor. Elton ends up using Jackie very poorly and comes to the realization that his actions are not healthy. He says, "I'd got so lost in conspiracies and aliens and targets, I'd been missing the obvious," that he's in love with Ursula. He turns on Victor Kennedy, and the remaining members of LINDA realize that Kennedy is an alien who wants to eat the Doctor. This dire outcome drives home Davies's warning about fandom: fandom is fine if you do it for fun, but obsession is unhealthy.

Unlike Davies's portrayal of Victor Kennedy, Elton Pope clearly exhibits the kind of "geeky" fandom that Davies both performs and condones—while Elton pursues knowledge about the Doctor, he says of his interests, "It's not all spaceships and stuff, because I'm into all sorts of things. I like football. I like a drink. I like Spain. And if there's one thing I really, really love, it's Jeff Lynne and the Electric Light Orchestra." He's a geek, surrounded by a diverse range of geeks in LINDA. While Davies celebrates Elton's form of dedicated fandom, he openly dislikes Victor's expression of fandom, positioning it as manipulative and dangerous. Davies thus constructs the members of LINDA as "fantastic and constructive and passionate and loving" fans, in contrast to Victor Kennedy, who is one of those "insane, loud voices" (Berry 2008).

Steven Moffat, Mark Gatiss, and *Sherlock*

The cocreators of the BBC's *Sherlock* (2010–present), Steven Moffat and Mark Gatiss, frequently describe themselves as fans of Sir Arthur Conan Doyle's stories and the numerous adaptations they have inspired. For instance, Moffat recalls that the pair's interest in remaking Doyle's stories evolved from a discussion of their enjoyment of them: "We'd always wanted to do Sherlock, and we're both huge Sherlock Holmes fans, so it began as a fan enthusiasm for Sherlock Holmes" (qtd. in Ittner 2014). In an interview, Moffat (who is also the current showrunner for *Doctor Who*) elaborated on his identification with fan stereotypes and his enduring love of Sherlock Holmes, "I'm a geek. I'm a writer. I spent all of my time in my childhood obsessing about Sherlock Holmes and Doctor Who. I was alone, I was an outsider..." (qtd. in Davies 2012). Likewise, Gatiss suggests it is their devoted affection for Doyle's stories that undergirds the series' popularity, "... I think why it's a success is because we live and breathe and love it" (qtd. in Arnstein 2014a).

In addition to readily claiming fannish identities, the creators describe their contributions to *Sherlock* as evolving from their enthusiasm for the stories, with Moffat recalling that the duo's work writing the series' third season came easily, "Like fan boys, we got excited about what we could do next with Sherlock Holmes" (qtd. in Heyman 2014). *Sherlock* star Benedict Cumberbatch has substantiated Moffat's claim of his and Gatiss's similarity to fanboys by suggesting that their writing contains "fanboy reverence" (qtd. in Ward 2014). And yet again underscoring their fannishness, Moffat has described their work on the adaptation of Doyle's original stories for the BBC series as "possibly the biggest sustained act of fan fiction" (qtd. in Arnstein 2014a).

Despite Moffat and Gatiss's connection to Sherlock Holmes fan culture and their identification as fans, they have adamantly distanced themselves from *Sherlock* fans, and online fannish activities, arguing that other fans do not influence the stories they craft. For example, Gatiss has emphasized that the two do not write with the fans' interests in mind because "shows go off the rails if you start trying to direct it towards what you think people will like or what you think they might fear" (qtd. in Arnstein 2014a). While Moffat has offered some praise for fans' writing about *Sherlock*, he has also stressed that his connection to fans is "a one-way thing" (qtd. in Jones 2014). Furthering this position, Moffat has insisted, "We know very little about the specifics of how the fans respond to Sherlock. So nothing they're seeing is in response to them" (qtd. in Ittner 2014).

While Moffat and Gatiss have feigned resistance to any possible influence or impact from the fan communities whose passion and transformative works surround the series, a push and pull between the series creators' fan identities and *Sherlock*'s enthusiastic fan communities plays out through the series' main characters. We argue that Sherlock Holmes serves as a proxy for the creators, his superior intellect unraveling unexpected stories through observation and inferences, while John Watson, Holmes's awestruck assistant and occasional critic, serves as a proxy for the fans. Confirming this, Martin Freeman, the actor who plays Dr. John Watson, argues that Watson sees Holmes as the audience does, viewing Holmes as alternately "brilliant" or "arrogant" (qtd. in Ward 2014). *Sherlock* positions Watson as fannish through his blogging activity, a modern adaptation of Doyle's depiction of Watson as commentator/publicist of Holmes's intriguing cases. Watson's blog is introduced in *Sherlock*'s first episode ("A Study in Pink"), when his therapist advises him to begin a blog to help with emotional recovery from his military service in Afghanistan. Uninspired by this task, it is only after Watson begins to work as a "consulting detective" to Holmes that his blogging begins in earnest. Watson's blog narrates the cases Holmes solves, building his public persona, making Holmes, as Moffat argues, "a celebrity" (Ittner 2014). Holmes's disdain for Watson's blogging activity, as well as his disparagement for anyone who lacks his superhuman deduction skills, places Holmes above the "normals" that surround him. In episode 1.3 ("The Blind Banker"), Holmes both acknowledges and belittles Watson's blogging activity and expresses indignation with Watson's characterization of him, yelling at him to "stop inflicting your opinions on the world."

As Watson's blogging endeavors gain a following, Holmes's disdain grows, along with his curiosity at the attention Watson's blog is getting. The resulting exchanges make clear that it is through the work of his most dedicated fans, embodied by Watson, that Holmes gains an eager and devoted audience. The playful opening montage in the second season's first episode ("A Scandal in Belgravia") demonstrates that "The Personal Blog of Dr. John H. Watson," has brought many new clients to 221b Baker Street, and with them, new fodder for Watson's blog. Frustrated and curious about Watson's blog commentaries on potential new cases, Sherlock asks, "Do people actually read your blog?" to which Watson retorts, "Where do you think our clients come from?" Sherlock defensively mentions his own website, "The Science of Deduction," and Watson scoffs, suggesting, with reference to Holmes's recent post about "240 types of tobacco ash," that "Nobody's reading your website."

Following this exchange, Watson underscores his site's popularity to Holmes, showing him that his blog received 1,895 hits in the eight hours previous, and emphasizes the visibility Watson's efforts have contributed to Holmes's career: "*This* is your living Sherlock." Holmes reveals his familiarity with Watson's blog by expressing his discomfort that Watson's posts about his unsolved cases may harm his reputation, but Watson emphasizes that such discussions give Holmes's growing fanbase a deeper, more personal knowledge of him. This conversation parallels frequent disagreements over transformative works like fan fiction that place producers' creations into scenarios and liaisons not imagined, and in some cases not sanctioned, by "the powers that be." In *Sherlock*'s case, the work of JohnLock shippers, fans whose writings imagine Holmes and Watson as lovers, has prompted abundant responses from the producers and cast—including reactions from Moffat, ranging "from snarky to baffled to annoyed" (Romano 2013b)—who feel this scenario, perhaps because of its assertion of homosexuality, strays too far from Doyle's original stories, potentially harming their reputation.

The fervent fanbase that Watson's blogging activity has quickly developed around Holmes is revealed in a later scene in which the duo investigates a case in a theater with Detective Inspector Lestrade (Rupert Graves), who remarks that members of the press have gathered outside to catch a photograph of Holmes. When Holmes expresses doubt that the press are there for him, Lestrade quips, "that was before you were an Internet phenomenon." Holmes's celebrity status is confirmed in episode 2.3 ("The Reichenbach Fall"), which opens with Holmes's characteristic lack of courtesy and gratitude as he receives public commendations and gifts for his detective work at a number of press conferences. Like a fan's fear that mainstream notoriety will diminish a beloved text's subcultural appeal, the press coverage prompts Watson to suggest they must become increasingly careful and work to stay out of the press, foreshadowing the misfortune to come in the episode. By the episode's end, Watson's fears are realized and he watches as his beloved friend (and object of his fannish devotion) jumps to his death, yet viewers learn in the episode's final scene, which also ends the second season, that Sherlock has, with his characteristic cunning, faked his death.

In the two-year gap between the second and third seasons, *Sherlock* fans debated Holmes's possible tactics in social media forums like Twitter and Facebook (Littlejohn 2012), prompting Gatiss to marvel at how fans' speculations about Holmes's methods for faking his own death became "a national talking point for months" (qtd. in Arnstein 2014b). The buzz around the series also led, as the *Radio Times* reported, to fears that the series would "become overly influenced by fan fiction and the numerous bizarre ideas that have emanated from obsessive viewers on the internet" (Jones 2014). Through his rejection of such assertions, Moffat revels in the recollection of how the creative team plotted to open the third season with an episode containing a number of conflicting accounts of Holmes's strategies for faking his death to purposefully confuse fans. Declaring the production team's ultimate authority over fans, Moffat becomes giddy when he offers his punch line, laughing, "And we wouldn't tell people how" (qtd. in Arnstein 2014b).

Sherlock's third season began with record-breaking ratings from the January 1, 2014 premiere on the BBC (Szalai 2014), which drew 9.2 million viewers; similarly, the series premiered on PBS's *Masterpiece* on January 19, 2014 to nearly 4 million viewers (de Moraes 2014). As promised, the much-anticipated third season premiere ("The Empty Hearse") returned Holmes to London to continue his work as a celebrity "consulting detective," and offered several opposing explanations for how he faked his death. The episode opens with Philip Anderson (Jonathan Aris), one of two members of the Metropolitan Police force whose long-standing doubts about Holmes contributed to Holmes's (faked) suicide, sharing his enthusiastic theory about how Holmes faked his death with Inspector Lestrade. When Lestrade suggests the theory is outlandish and accuses Anderson of building conspiracy theories out of his own guilt, Anderson reveals that he indeed realizes his mistake and that his theories may be compensation for a guilty conscience. Anderson protests Lestrade's insistence that Sherlock is dead with the simple line, "I believe in Sherlock Holmes." Anderson does what so many fans did in the series' two-year hiatus: imagine and discuss just how Holmes had tricked everyone.

Another theory unfolds later in the episode that references the fannish practice of shipping by casting Sherlock and Moriarty as lovers, their shared evil laughter turning unexpectedly to kisses. This theory is articulated by Laura (Sharon Rooney), a member of the fangroup The Empty Hearse, formed by Anderson. Anderson, who clearly wishes to focus only on Holmes, reacts with incredulity to Laura's theory in front of the group members in Anderson's flat. Interrupting his rant, the room's television announces that Holmes is indeed alive, and moments later the group members receive numerous phone alerts offering confirmation, as illustrated by an on-screen word cloud of hashtags like #sherlocklives.

The action of the case Holmes and Watson are investigating is broken later in the episode to offer yet another explanation for how Holmes faked his death; this time Holmes narrates the story to Anderson, who videotapes his "confession." Holmes signals the end of his story by asking, "Neat, don't you think?" Anderson shrugs and responds as a fan might to a revealed mystery in their favorite narrative, "Not the way I'd have done it…. Bit disappointed." Holmes playfully responds as a production team might, "Oh, everyone's a critic." Moments later, Anderson realizes the implausibility of Holmes's account and as he begins to question him, Holmes quickly sneaks out. Anderson realizes he has been tricked, his laughter indicating his enjoyment of being fooled by the superior Holmes. Anderson's amusement signals that, like many fans, he finds the unknown more productive and pleasurable than certainty.

With the theorizing over, the episode's story reassures that Holmes and Watson will begin working together again as a team. As they prepare to step out of 221 Baker Street to the press awaiting an explanation for how they solved their latest case, Watson says to Holmes, "Don't pretend you're not enjoying this. Being back. Being a hero again…. You love it… being Sherlock Holmes." For the first time since Holmes's return, Watson asks him to explain how he faked his death, but Holmes refuses. Ending the discomfort caused by the quick, but emotional conversation that ensues, Holmes says with a smile, "Anyway, time to go and be Sherlock Holmes." He begrudgingly puts on his deerstalker, and walks out to flashing bulbs and reporter questions. The scene symbolizes that *Sherlock* is back, and reminds that Moffat and Gatiss, as the keepers of Holmes's secret, are ultimately in charge of the story; yet Holmes's acknowledgment of fan expectations, through his willingness to don the iconic deerstalker, suggests that despite their decisive assertion of power, the series' creators wish to fulfill at least some of fans' wishes by grounding their novel interpretations in a respect for Doyle's legacy. And with this exchange, the familiar dance between producers and fans resumes.

Conclusion

Through exploration of producers' representations of fans in *Doctor Who* and *Sherlock*, contextualized in producers' discussions of their own fandom, we examined two cases of the long-standing antagonisms between industry and audience as manifested in contemporary digital culture. Our analysis demonstrates that the characterizations of fans that showrunners create are shaped by their perspectives on their series' fans and are undergirded by a desire to uphold their status as auteurs, which is easily accomplished through the maintenance of firm distinctions between producers and fans. In the examples we explored, Russell T Davies, Steven Moffatt, and Mark Gatiss used their public comments and series' storylines to draw sharp lines between the kinds of fans and fan activities they condone and those they do not; their actions reinforce, despite the possibilities offered by digital culture, the power differentials between industry and audience.

It may be that the long-lasting and invested fandoms created around the two cases we selected (*Doctor Who* beginning in 1963 and *Sherlock* stories originating in 1887) heavily influenced the nature of the producer/audience dialectics we found, and thus we suggest that future work explore representations in series with shorter histories. The duration of these cult narratives means that childhood fans have now become adult producers, incorporating their own fandom into their adaptations. Further, both series have broad audiences, containing a range of fans, from casual to passionate; the depth of passionate fans' attachments also creates intense emotions when the object of their fandom is recreated. Thus, our analysis suggests that while Davies's and Moffat and Gatiss's representations of fans offer both recognition and affection, they also make it clear that fans' values, desires, and behaviors do not influence them. In line with Scott (2013a), we believe that fanboy auteurs, upholding the practices they learned as fans, are less poised to explore the boundary-breaking possibilities of convergence culture than to uphold the familiar power imbalance between industry and audience.

Future work should continue to explore the intricacies of the power dynamics between producers and fans, specifically through interviews with fanboy auteurs and cult fans. One potentially fruitful direction may be to examine producers' attitudes and behaviors in social media. Although much has been written about the increased perception of closeness between celebrities and fans in social media, like Twitter (e.g., Marwick and boyd 2010b; Bennett 2014a), some fanboy auteurs, like Russell T Davies, refuse to use social media, while others, like Steven Moffat, abandon social media altogether after public clashes with fans. Tracing producers' and audiences' engagement in social media will certainly help to reveal if and how digital media have altered industry–audience relationships.

Finally, we suggest that future work explore the productivity of the power differences between producers and fans. If, as Jenkins (2006a) asserts, fandom is fueled—at least in part—by frustration, what would fandom entail if producers frequently bowed to audience demands, or regularly solicited fans' suggestions? As Hadas and Shifman (2013) suggest, some fans, in the process of venting their frustrations with producers, may actually work to enforce the boundaries between industry and audience. If some fans ultimately temper their critiques of producers to maintain the boundaries between producers and fans, perhaps it need not be entirely surprising that fanboy auteurs do the same. Convergence culture may offer possibilities for building more equitable and interconnected relationships, but if producers and audiences choose not to build them, we should endeavor to understand how both groups are served by the marked lines that separate them.

12

Hero-Fans and Fanboy Auteurs: Reflections and Realities of Superhero Fans

Ellen Kirkpatrick

The only difference between Virgil [Static's alter ego] and me is that he got lucky and woke up with superpowers one day.—Fanboy Bruce (Brown 2001)

I think fans want to see themselves represented on TV, and I think comic book fans want to see themselves represented in comic books... —Actor Candice Patton on playing Iris West in new *Flash* TV series —(Burlingame 2014)

Issues around representation and diversity affect all facets of the superhero genre, from creators and producers through to fans and scholars. These spheres do not sit in isolation, but rather intersect through many points. Within this chapter, I argue that the superhero genre, almost despite itself, speaks to the variety of ways of being a real-life superhero fan. Using tired and all too familiar negative stereotypes about fans as my departure point, I tackle issues of diversity and representation by approaching superhero fan representation from a new perspective, one scrutinizing the self-reflexive practice of diegetically representing superheroes as fans. Such an approach will shed new insights into how in-text fan portrayals speak to us about being and seeing superhero fans.

Superhero fans do not appear within superhero texts as often or in perhaps the ways one might imagine. Indeed, we are more likely to see superhero fans represented in other media and genres, in TV series such as *The Big Bang Theory* or *The Simpsons*, or in films such as *Kick-Ass* (2010) or *Super* (2010), than we are to see them represented in superhero texts.[1] But, they do appear in comics, and when they do they are, curiously, most likely to hold center stage, as protagonists and their sidekicks. Barry Allen and his fannishness for the Flash perhaps immediately comes to mind. Such characters, or "hero-fans" as I have termed them, are presented as having a passion for superheroes and/or the texts within which they appear.[2] As I advance in this chapter, hero-fan representation comes in two forms, *direct* and *indirect*. Characters are not, however, limited to occupying one position or another and may move between them, as narratives require. Barry Allen and Dino-Cop exemplify direct hero-fan representation. We see them enjoying, thinking, and talking about their beloved superhero characters and comics. Carrie Kelly and Tim Drake, on the other hand, epitomize indirect hero-fan representation.[3] Such characters tend to be fans of the heroes inhabiting their worlds, rather than of superhero texts. It is more "street" based than "text" based. Their fan status is consequently less conspicuous, and perhaps trickier to read. As I demonstrate later, this medley of representation speaks to the variety of ways in which people today become superhero fans.

Yet, despite such variety, one fan stereotype sits privileged among superhero fan representation, both within superhero texts and beyond, the fanboy: "a category that seems to have originated within the comics community to refer to some comics readers in a derogatory way" (Locke 2012, 849 citing Sabin 1993, 68). Adjectives used to describe fanboys include aggressive, territorial, loyal, and obsessed; used in combination, such descriptors style fanboys as fans with an overdeveloped passion and territorial attachment to their objects of fandom.

Creators and publishers play with ideas of fanboys variously, from subtly creating characters with fanboy traits (e.g., Bat-Mite, Ragnar) to blatantly referencing fanboy qualities within character names and series titles, such as Mysterious Fanboy from the *X-Statix* title (Marvel), or DCs miniseries entitled *Fanboy*, which narrates the fannish hopes and dreams of its main character, Finster. Fanboy characters, such as Bat-Mite and Ragnar, or even Buddy Pine (aka Syndrome), from the popular animated film, *The Incredibles* (2004), occupy the extreme end of the fan spectrum. Within their representation, adoration turns to all-consuming passion, and we see all types of risky behaviors and life-threatening doings (or in the case of Ragnar, murderous undoings).

I draw upon the fanboy in several ways: first in textual terms, by presenting an account of hero-fan representation, and second in industry-fan terms by exploring the impact of author as fan, or as Suzanne Scott (2012b) phrased it, the "fanboy auteur." Whereas Scott explores the author-fan dynamic in terms of transmedia production, I do so in representational terms, and, in so doing, foster new ways of seeing fans within superhero texts. Identifying connections and repetitions within stereotypes and representations of fictional and real-life superhero fans reveals how these accounts speak to each other and to our ideas of superhero fandom. For it cannot be just a case of interrogating representations as they appear on the page, it must also be about how these representations speak to the conditions of their creation and consumption.

Today, questions of diversity dominate discussions around media representation, production, and consumption, and so it is fitting to tackle representations of the hero-fan through diversity, and consequently its obverse, uniformity. In driving my discussion along race and gender lines, I query, for instance, why it is—beyond the fact that there are simply more of them—that male superheroes are historically more likely to be cast as superhero comics fans, and female characters less so, and further how this speaks to the androcentrism of real-life superhero comics fandom. It seems, until recently at least, that in the realm of the superhero genre, only male heroes read superhero comics, or were represented as superhero fans. This unrepresentative state of affairs is however being challenged. One need only look at the positioning of Kamala Khan—female protagonist of the 2013 *Ms. Marvel* title—as "out and proud" fangirl. Such characterization demonstrates not only the possibility of female superheroes but also the actuality of female superhero fans.[4]

Representation: Reflections and realities

Media representations are just one of many sources that we draw upon to shape ourselves and our realities. They are powerful conduits for conveying ideas, ideas affecting our perception of self and others.[5] They can also operate as systems encouraging particular ideological agendas, fomenting partisan cultural models, or "maps of meaning" (Gee 2001). As such, we need to study and interrogate the makeup of representations, for they are not without flaw, with lack of diversity and negative and affective stereotyping presenting as just two areas of deep concern.

Lack of diversity concerns categories of identity and their intersections, through dimensions of, for example, gender, sexuality, race and ethnicity, and disability. A repeating image overwhelms characterizations within our media texts—white, cis, straight, abled-bodied, and male—one unrepresentative of the social world. The supremacy of this image has had an eliding effect on media representation, no matter what the media platform. Varying efforts to unseat representational uniformity in favor of cultural diversity are however happening across all media, from mainstream films such as *Fast and Furious 7* (2015) to TV shows such as *Empire* (2015) or comics with Marvel's recasting of Thor as a woman (2014).[6] There is however much work still to do.

Fictional and real-life fan representations are further prone to negative and/or affective stereotypes. Within hero-fan representations, it is unusual to see a character read superhero comics just for the simple pleasure of it. If we do see someone enjoying comics, we can be sure there is a diegetic reason, purpose, or consequence to it. It is a pastime with ramifications. Mainstream representations of real-life superhero fans seem to echo this idea of superhero fans. Real-life superhero fans participating in extreme cosmetic surgeries in order to look like their heroes often receive disproportionate news media coverage, usually in the "shock" mode of journalism (e.g., Herbert Chavez as Superman and Henry Damon as Red Skull). And, one only has to reflect upon the international news coverage of real-life murderous incidents such as the Aurora Theatre Shootings, Shenandoah Park Killings, or the Rampaging Millers to see the mining of negative stereotypes of fans.[7] Even when it is not clear that the participants were superhero comics fans, the mere suggestion of them as fans is enough for mainstream media to attach and lead with the superhero fan label. Rarely do we see real-life fans engaging with the superhero genre moderately and without consequence—and they certainly exist. Instead, we see active fans, spectacular fans, where their fandom has had an effect, a consequence, upon the ways in which they live their lives. Not all superhero fans that attend conventions participate in cosplay, or have emotional reactions to seeing their fan objects or trailers for forthcoming releases, and yet these are the fans we see in convention media coverage. Warning, broadcasters and comics creators seem to be saying, being a superhero fan will affect your life and have an effect on your life.

Despite, arguably, more positive media fan representation, where more nuanced portrayals are replacing the freaks and geeks of yesteryear (Busse 2015), and academic work shading and reinterpreting negative fan stereotypes, matters of fan representation remain tricky (see, Hills 2012c; Busse 2013a; Booth 2015b). Not least because mainstream portrayals still tend to vacillate between the infantile and socially awkward, or pathological, but also because as Henry Jenkins notes, fans are considered to be "confused about the line between fantasy and reality" (Jenkins 1997, 506; see also Jensen 1992).

Superhero fandom is not alone in facing issues around uniform representation and stereotyping; it stands out perhaps in the labyrinthine nature of these issues. For, even within "negative" stereotypical representation, fans engage in life-affirming behaviors.[8] Considering the quality of superhero fan representation in terms of either/or (positive/negative), within this context, is itself perhaps limiting. What may be more valuable is to question how hero-fan representations speak to mainstream stereotypes of superhero fans.

Ways of seeing: Hero-fans and real-life fans

In the introduction to the twentieth edition of *Textual Poachers*, Henry Jenkins describes the word "fan" as "slippery and expansive enough to include a broad range of different kinds of relationships to media...." (Jenkins 2012d, xiv). Through its characterization of the hero-fan, the superhero genre, I contend, and counterintuitively perhaps, speaks to this range and variety. It demonstrates that there is more than one way of being a fan. For instance, indirect hero-fan representation—where the character is a fan of the hero inhabiting and protecting their world—evokes the ways in which contemporary real-life superhero fans are not necessarily fans of the comics in which their superhero fan object appears, but rather are fans of the characters as they appear in other media and settings (e.g., films, cartoons, TV series, and video games). Hero-fan Carrie Kelly is not a fan of fictional, text-based superheroes, but of Batman, the man, the hero, who protects her world. She is a superhero fan, yes, but in a different way to perhaps you and me. Whatever the source of their fandom however, hero-fan representation tends toward those compelled to action, those for whom their fan object acts as an impetus, as a driver toward some momentous life-change. This affective quality, where one's fandom impacts upon one's life, is dominant and aligns such representations with ideas of real-life fanboys and fangirls.

Yet, not all real-life fans are called to fandom; for some, the texts and the lore are reward enough. And, although rarer, we do see this type of fan representation within hero-fan characterizations, where their fan status has had no obvious effect on their superheroic disposition or its development: they are superheroes because they are superheroes, not because they are fans of the genre.[9] Red Racer (Earth 36) from *The Multiversity* series (Grant Morrison et al. 2014–2015) evokes this type of fan representation: he is not a superhero because he is a fan, but his fannishness definitely helps him be a hero.[10]

Opening up the discussion now to issues of diversity and quality of representation allows a review of the ways in which the makeup of creative teams speaks to on-page representations of fans and heroes, bringing in ideas of fanboys and indicating the sheer variety of fan representations presenting within superhero comics.

Red-letter days I: Direct hero-fans

An early example of the first category, the hero-fan as fan of superhero comics or characters, presents within the Silver Age's trailblazer Barry Allen and his transformation into the Flash (1956). Just like comic book readers reading *Showcase* #4 (1956), Barry Allen, the new Flash to be, was shown reading an issue of *The Flash* featuring the Golden Age Flash (Jay Garrick, 1940) and dreaming of becoming like his hero. A transformative accident subsequently endows Allen with "super-speed" and allows the fulfillment of his desire to become the, or a, Flash. This image and origin story knowingly and deliberately plugs into the desires of many superhero genre fans. Such knowing characterization not only confirms Barry Allen as a fan of the Flash and nods to the changing demographics of mid-1950s comics readers and popular opinions on their readership, but also represents an early idea of superhero fans as white and male.

The Flash title is just one of the many tackling contemporary concerns around lack of diversity, and showing perhaps more success in its on-page representations, than within its "off" page creative teams.[11] Similar observations have been made about the team behind Miles Morales/Ultimate Spider-Man (Ultimate Fallout #4, 2011) created by Brian Michael Bendis and Sara Pichelli.[12] Miles Morales as Spider-Man is valuable, and not just in terms of diverse character representation, but also because his portrayal as fan increases the visibility of minority fans within superhero texts. In creating Miles as a hero-fan, Bendis and Pichelli offer a much needed positive and potent representation of a non-white superhero comics fan.

Miles is not however the first representation of a black hero-fan, being preceded some eighteen years by Virgil Hawkins from the Milestone Comics stable.[13] Cast in a similar mold as Peter Parker/Spider-Man, Virgil is a teenager with a passion for reading superhero comics, and one who gains superhero powers through chemical exposure. Virgil's fan representation is significant given the white-centric climate in which he would have been reading superhero comics (late 1980s onward). Such superhero titles would have featured predominantly white characters created by white creative teams; for after all, wasn't that the very reason Milestone Comics was established?—to redress the dominance of the white superhero, the white creative team, and I would suggest by positioning Virgil as a comics fan, the white superhero fan. Virgil is a rare and potent representation of a fan, one set against the grain of the pervasive images of heroes and their fans as white. Virgil and Miles as hero-fans are important not only for showing superhero comics readers that there can be black superheroes, but also that there are black superhero comics fans.

Both Miles and Virgil read easily as wish-fulfilled fanboys, as does Superboy-Prime from the Superman mythos. Superboy-Prime's fanboy tendencies center on DC Comics; he not only dresses up as Superboy, but also shares his name with one of his heroes, Clark Kent. Over the course of his life, this Clark Kent is drawn into the superhero world, first through works of fiction, and later in reality; he becomes immersed in its histories, continuities, and customs, and finds that he cannot leave. Things can't get any better for this DC fanboy than when he gets to battle alongside his childhood heroes—

although he ultimately eschews the path of "good" to become a supervillain. This plot line reads like wish fulfillment for any superhero comics fanboy—to be inducted into the superhero world, and have their meticulous knowledge of superhero lore and continuity acknowledged and recognized as valuable—and exhibits strong Marty-Stu qualities.

Superman: Secret Identity (January–April 2004) explores similar ideas, again involving a character called Clark Kent who lives in a world without superheroes, but with superhero comics. This Clark also becomes a superhero, becomes a Superman, but he is resolutely not a fan of the fictional character or the comics in which he appears. While growing up, and before he discovers he possesses superpowers akin to the original Superman, this character's slight link to the superhero genre, his name, makes him vulnerable to bullying and physical attack. This abusive behavior causes him to despise the superhero genre and all it stands for. This character's frustration with the genre opens him up, I suggest, to a reading as a nonfan, or perhaps more accurately as an anti-fan. Jonathan Gray (2003) describes the anti-fan as someone who is bothered, insulted, or otherwise assaulted by the presence of certain media texts, or other fan objects (see also Sandvoss 2005; Hills 2012c; Harman and Jones 2013). This is a rare representation of an anti-fan, but counterintuitively, it is still coded and constructed along the lines of a fanboy's "dream come true," as true to form this Clark comes to embrace and (discreetly) enact his superhero status, paralleling his fictional counterpart.

Red-letter days II: Indirect hero-fans

Another way of seeing fans within superhero texts is to look at the somewhat rarer portrayals of hero-fans who are "fans" of their in-world heroes, such as Wally West and his fannishness about the Flash. Although sharing much with Barry Allen's origin story—surviving a speed inducing accident for example—Wally West is not a fan of a fictionalized Flash, but of Barry Allen, his soon-to-be uncle, as Flash. Wally even goes so far as to found the *Blue Valley Flash Fan Club*. Wally's fanboy dreams come true, first, when he learns that he is going to be related his hero (fan object), and second when he becomes inducted into the superhero world as Kid Flash.

This mode also presents some of the more exceptional occasions in which we see girls or women interpretable as hero-fans. It is uncommon to see female fans become hero-fans in the same way as male hero-fans (i.e., they discover they have superpowers, or gain them through some "accident") or to see them engage with the genre in the same way (i.e., their fannish knowledge saving the day). It seems that in order to become part of the narratives, female fans have to take more direct action, to insist that the narrative is re-written to include them, or to boldly insert themselves within the text—often against the wishes of the (male) protagonists and (male) fans (e.g., Stephanie Brown). Ragged Robin from Grant Morrison's *Invisibles* offers a compelling example of a female character authoring herself into a text.[14] Within superhero texts, as with female superheroes, female hero-fans are rare, and rarely represented in parity with their male counterparts.

Fan representations in this vein present characters driven to action through an "obsessive" fascination with their fan object. Their fan engagement is literally life changing. Characters such as Carrie Kelly and Tim Drake, both from the Batman mythos, engage in behaviors ascribed as "extreme" or "obsessive" fan practices. They routinely follow, or rather stalk, their heroes (fan objects). They investigate and gather information; they take photographs, snoop, and cross lines. In trying to impress, emulate, or catch the eye of their hero, they confront dangerous people or place themselves in risky situations—and often have to be rescued by their hero. In working to become known to their fan object, they may make costumes or adopt code-names, all to encourage their hero to adopt them, and enculturate them into their world. In such cases, fans eventually tend to gain acceptance into their hero's worlds; they become known, become beloved, and become an integral part of the story. Such practices are strongly reminiscent of "extreme" fan practices, and perhaps again of fanboy/girl dreams.

Comics authorship and fandom: The (super)man in the mirror

Originally aimed at children, the readership of superhero comics soon shifted to include and then become dominated by adolescent and adult male readers. Even though this genre is, and ever was, read, loved, and created by an array of fans, the male coding of the superhero genre and its fandom persists to this day. We are, in reality, still fielding the effects of the traditional, defining, and intersecting stereotypes of superhero creators and fans. And, although dealing in stereotypes, the resemblances between fan and creator are clear.[15] They are surely showing us, speaking to us of a deeper connection. Taking these shared stereotypes in conjunction with the way in which creators and fans also share creative spaces creates an image of a self-affirming community, or brotherhood. Jones and Jacobs (1997) in fact describe this community as a "self-perpetuating fraternity" (234) and it is hard to disagree with them. Suzanne Scott (2013b) too points to the male coding of comics culture in all spheres—industry, fan, and scholar—by presenting a sample of comics scholarship, noting,

> how this body of literature reinforces the cultural presumption that comic book fans are overwhelmingly, if not exclusively, male (see Jean-Paul Gabilliet's *Of Comics and Men: A Cultural History of American Comic Books;* Gerard Jones's *Men of Tomorrow: Geeks, Gangsters, and the Birth of the Comic Book;* Matthew J. Pustz's *Comic Book Culture: Fanboys and True Believers*).

The male codification of superhero fans (and culture), of fans as fanboys, is not only pervasive but also deleterious as it feeds into easy fan stereotypes and elides and subsumes all other fan identities. Not only fan identities however, but creator identities too—for they do not sit in isolation. Will Brooker (2013) describes comics fandom and comics authorship as "siblings locked into a relationship of debate and mutual dependence" (p. 61), and further that the idea of the comic book author is "slippery" and the boundaries encircling them as "thin." Although not as common as one might imagine, the author/fan border is passable from both sides. And, although scholars have written about the intricate connections between comics creators and their fandom (see Jenkins 2012c; Brooker 2013; Coker 2013), none have yet made, or explored the connections and implications of the hero-fan. Opening up this new site facilitates a discussion of the comics author as fanboy auteur (see Scott 2012b), suggesting ways in which this liminal position affects on-page (fan) representations.

Some superhero fans may dream of one day becoming fanboy auteurs, and indeed, it is not unheard of for those dreams to come true. One need only recall the fan-dream tales of creators such as Frank Miller or Grant Morrison. Frank Miller in his introduction to the groundbreaking *The Dark Knight Returns* (1986) describes how as a child he "opened a Batman comic and fell in, never entirely to emerge" (Miller 1986), and how Batman subsequently became his "favorite childhood hero" (Miller 1986). Miller moved from fan to creator and twenty-some years later went on to rework the Batman mythology, to re-create and rewrite his favorite hero, just the way he wanted him. Suzanne Scott (2012b) describes fanboy auteurs as creators who narrativize themselves as fans by publicly self-identifying as fans or "geeks," and this fan declaration—not uncommon within comics forewords—certainly suggests Miller as a fanboy auteur. Miller may not be cognizant that he is serving as "a textual double-agent, engendering fannish solidarity even as he monitors and manages fan responses to the text," but his positioning as fanboy auteur is certainly to the fore when considering his creative function.

Fanboy auteurs represent the superhero world (textual and fandom) as they know it and see it, and for some, due to the circles (and cycles) in which they move, it may still appear as largely white and male. They write themselves—or their fannishness selves—into their characters and narratives via categorical identity markers (e.g., race, gender, and sexuality), and in more metafictional or autobiographical senses, such as Grant Morrison's appearance in *Animal Man* #25, or as King Mob in *The Invisibles* (1994–2000). Besides making characters look like them (e.g., white, male), they might also make them talk like them, as is said of Stan Lee and his beloved Spider-Man, or even express their concerns as Peter Milligan is said to have done within the *Shade, the Changing Man* title (1990–1996). Taking the fanboy auteur as something of a wish fulfilled fanboy, it is perhaps not surprising that when given the opportunity to (re)write their heroes some draw upon the idea of "it could happen to you" mode of creating characters, because it (turning professional) quite literally did happen to them.

While all such examples speak to matters of uniformity and representation, in terms of fan representation perhaps the former—categorical identity—and the latter—wish fulfillment—do so most directly, where fanboy auteurs represent themselves within the categorical and allegorical landscapes of their characters. Such echoes, fluidities, and in-betweenness are, I suggest, at least coconspirators in engendering the overwhelmingly male-centric genre we have today. Given the decades of expectation and possible engagement that fanboy auteurs bring to the creative table, it is perhaps not surprising to see them locked into repeating the same patterns, the same representations of heroes as straight, white men. Mark Twain said, "write what you know," and in some ways perhaps these fanboy auteurs are doing just that: they write about the comics culture they know, and it is knowable as predominantly white and male.

Shifting representations, matching realities

When I first began considering the representation of hero-fans, I imagined I would write about the dominance of the white male within such representations, concluding that the supremacy of this image, while representing dominant *ideas* of superhero comics fans, ultimately fails to represent the actual diversity of this genre's fans. It would be another account of representations not matching realities. And, while this chapter does to some extent work with such ideas, it does so from a slightly different, less one-dimensional stance.

The current era of superhero comics is characterized by a—yet to be realized—desire and drive to increase diversity and improve representation, on-page and off-page. Recent flurries of recasting and rebooting characters along categorical lines (e.g., race, gender and sexuality) are indicative of an industry finally seeing its fans, seeing the diversity, and ultimately it seems seeing the economic advantage of representing that diversity.

Characters such as Miles Morales and Kamala Khan are indicative of this new drive, and while not perfect, their reception has been largely positive, particularly Kamala Khan as *Ms. Marvel*. Significant to my mind is their self-conscious positioning as superhero fans, a not insignificant move I would say. Kamala Khan's representation as a fan is telling; she is readable as representing a long-awaited industry acknowledgement of minority fans. She demonstrates, as do Miles Morales and Virgil Hawkins, that there are fans beyond the white male stereotype. The way in which Kamala Khan, fangirl, becomes *Ms. Marvel* is also noteworthy; for unlike historic female fan representation, her becoming occurs within the wish-fulfilled fanboy trope (i.e., she discovers her powers through an external event). The successful reimagining of *Ms. Marvel* is remarkable not only in terms of increasing on-page character diversity, but also for increasing the visibility of minority fans on-page and effecting popular ideas of superhero fans off-page.

The androcentrism of comics culture is multifaceted (industry, fan, scholar) and erases female, and other minority fan, contributions and presences within the superhero comics world. Challenges to this are also, however, multifaceted. From positive relaunches of extant female characters, from the afore mentioned Kamala Khan/Ms. Marvel, or Barbara Gordon/Batgirl under Gail Simone's adept custodianship (2011) to the independently produced reimagining of Batgirl found within the pages of *My So-Called Secret Identity* (Brooker, Zaidan, Shore 2013). Comics culture stereotypes are also being contested within its creative spheres, with the rising demand for more representative and diverse creative teams, and within its fields of commentary—from scholarly to fan-led.[16]

In all areas, there is still some way to go. It may be that we are entering an epoch where in-text representation of fans happens more often, and while this has definite advantages, we must be mindful that these will primarily be industry ideas of fans. In such an environment, it becomes as important to be attentive to the nature and quality of fan representations, as it is to the makeup of characters and the creative teams behind them.

Notes

1   Such representations tend toward the fanboy/girl stereotype; one need only think of fanboy Dave Lizewski who becomes Kick-Ass in the 2010 film of the same name, or female fangirl sidekick Libby who becomes Boltie in another 2010 superhero genre influenced film, *Super*.
2   Quite literally as "hero," for it seems that villains are less likely to pick up a superhero comic.
3   Such fans often gain admittance into the superhero realm, becoming partners, or sidekicks, becoming heroes just like their fan-objects. This usually occurs diegetically. There is however at least one instance where a real-life fan has crossed over into the fictional superhero realm. Samuel L. Jackson is a renowned superhero fan who not only routinely appears in superhero films (e.g., *Unbreakable* and the *Avengers* film series) but who has also sanctioned the use of his image as Nick Fury within the Marvel Ultimate comics series, set on Earth-1610. This is notable for several reasons, for not only do we see a fan crossing the fourth wall, but we also see a rare, and due to that rareness, an important representation of a superhero comics fan outside the dominant white-centric representation of superhero comics fandom.
4   It also, perhaps, suggests an industry awareness of the latent potency (in terms of economics and increasing readership) of representing the diversity of fans within texts.
5   This is not a passive process, but more a critical interrogation, a negotiation.
6   Mainstream publishers made attempts during the 1970s to appeal to minority fans by introducing more diversity and social "relevance" into their titles, and a number of self-conscious attempts were made to introduce prominent black characters and regularly racially themed storylines, but apart for a few rare examples (e.g., Green Arrow) these were poorly received, both critically and popularly. Significantly, those charged to create these titles were pooled from within the comics "fraternity" and so the idea of race espoused within these texts originated from a white-centric standpoint. This state of affairs still bedevils the mainstream comics world, with the same charges leveled at the decision to place Mile Morales (Ultimate Spider-Man) and Wally West (Flash) as African Americans in the hands of all-white creative teams. Matters of representation loom large for the superhero genre, both on-page and off-page, another reason why fan representation *within* these texts matters too.
7   See, "Man Dressed as Batman Character the Joker Shot Dead by Police." Accessed October 17, 2015. http://www.theguardian.com/world/2009/mar/13/police-shoot -man-dressed-as-joker, and "Married Las Vegas Street Performers Kill Tow Police in Bid to Start Revolution." Accessed October 17, 2015. http://www.telegraph.co.uk/ news/worldnews/northamerica/usa/10887842/Married-Las-Vegas-street-performers -kill-two-police-in-bid-to-start-revolution.html

8   Fannish activities, for instance, can lead participants to make new personal connections, work voluntarily for the benefit of their communities, or engage in creative practices, such as designing and making their own costumes—practices open to positive readings, and practices performed within real-life fandom, and by fictional hero-fans.

9   For such characters, being a fan has instead a more diegetic effect. We may see them refer to enjoying reading a superhero title, or delight in meeting a superhero they have read about in one of their comics, their knowledge may even help them solve some plotline.

10   Within *The Multiversity* series (2014–2015), creators play knowingly with the positioning of fans and heroes, with heroes shown reading superhero comics recounting their own lives.

11   The creative team behind the 2014 biracial reincarnation of Wally West (Flash #30) was entirely comprised of white males (Robert Venditti, Van Jensen, and Brett Booth).

12   Although receiving broadly positive receptions, such reimaginings remain dogged by questions of racial stereotyping and the lack of diversity within creative teams.

13   Founded in New York in 1993 by Dwayne McDuffie, Denys Cowan, Michael Davis, and Derek T. Dingle.

14   Ragged Robin is a fictional time-traveler who writes a fanfic version of the *Invisibles* comic and then travels back in time to occupy the role she has written for herself. Comics writer Grant Morrison is renowned for playing with ideas of authorship and textual control, see the authorial antics of King Mob from within the same title. King Mob himself is also routinely read as evidencing an author/fan textual insertion, or as a Marty-Stu.

15   Where fans are, "overwhelmingly male, overwhelmingly white… the quintessential geek: unwashed and scraggly bearded, thick glasses taped together, baggy slacks slipping low and a faded T-shirt stretched not all the way over a bloated belly" (Jones and Jacobs 1997, 233), and creators, "didn't look much better (read different) than their fans: ill-considered facial hair and over stretched superhero T-shirts" (Jones and Jacobs 1997). It is important to recognize the elision of gender and race from within the creator description, so ubiquitous is the white male in creative circles.

16   For example, websites such as *Autostraddle, The Mary Sue*, and *Geeked*.

13

We See You (Sort of): Representations of Fans on *Supernatural*

Katherine Larsen and Lynn Zubernis

Representing fans in canon is a risky business. While holding the tantalizing possibility of embracing, validating (and perhaps amusing) fans, representations can also fail to depict reality (thus alienating the very fans those representations were meant to appeal to). If what the viewers understand as "fan" and what the writers understand as "fan" do not align, the stage is set for confusion and hurt. Perhaps because of this inherent disconnect, few shows successfully write fans into canon. *Supernatural*, a genre show on the CW, has often tried to bridge the gap between representation and reality with mixed results. For the ten years that the show has been on the air, *Supernatural*'s writers have repeatedly featured their own fans in so-called "meta episodes," showcasing the writers' evolving (and at some points devolving) understanding of fans.

Supernatural is, on the surface, a show about Sam and Dean Winchester, two brothers traversing modern day America in a '67 Chevy Impala, hunting monsters and saving people (and each other) with help from an angel (Castiel) and occasionally from the King of Hell (Crowley). Beneath the surface, the show is about the relationship between the characters, and the theme of constructed family. A line from the show, "Family don't end with blood," is also the mantra for the fandom, which calls itself the "SPN Family," and operates as a (mostly) tight-knit community that has also formed close ties with the show's actors via a robust convention schedule. The writers however, are largely not a part of this community, rarely making appearances at these conventions or interacting directly with fans. And while SPN's interpretations of fans have shown a movement toward nuance, in the end these interpretations seem to be hobbled by a reliance on stereotypes.

In this chapter, we examine *Supernatural*'s representation of fans, in particular its female fans, and the frequent misalignment between signifier (the writers) and signified (the fans). We suggest that there exists an ongoing tug of war between the show's writers and their specifically female fans for control over the narrative and that this struggle informs the often negative and largely stereotypical representation of fans.

They know about us!

Five episodes of *Supernatural* have explicitly taken fandom's gaze and turned it back on itself, putting the fan in the spotlight, with predictably mixed reception from fans.[1] In a 2010 special issue of the *Journal of Transformative Works and Cultures* devoted to *Supernatural*, Jules Wilkinson (2010) describes the complexity of what the show has attempted:

> With *Supernatural*, [the] fannish fourth wall has been demolished.... What happens when the creators of the original work take the fans and their creative works and incorporate them into source material that the fans in turn will further transform?

In "The Monster At the End of This Book" (4.18), the show's tradition of meta episodes began by introducing both creator and fans into canon. This plot device allowed the writers to comment, in an only slightly displaced manner, on the series' own real-life fans. As the episode unfolds, Sam and Dean find out that someone has been writing the story of their lives in a series of books—the *Supernatural* series. And to make matters worse, "there are fans"—fan fiction-writing fans.

The writers not only dared to depict *Supernatural* fans in canon, but they also dared to talk about some fannish practices that were, at the time especially, both secret and shamed. Sam and Dean react as fans fear the real actors might react if they found out fans were writing "real person fan fiction" (RPF) about them. Dean expresses his horror—"I'm full frontal in this!" When Sam explains to Dean that some fans are writing stories about the two of them together "As in *together* together," Dean exclaims "Don't they know we're brothers?" This overt reference to one of the most hidden types of *Supernatural* fan fiction (known as Wincest) created a shock wave that ran through fandom, reaching far beyond the boundaries of the show itself.

Nevertheless, the reaction was mostly appreciative, since the episode poked fun not only at fans, but also at the show. As one fan observed:

> I was expecting something horribly angsty, and within the first five minutes I was pissing myself in laughter and disbelief. Taking the mickey out of the fans and themselves was pretty fun there for a while. Especially since an episode that was *fictionally* a crossover between fiction and reality was at the same time *in reality* a crossover between fiction and reality. Art and life imitated each other into a tangled ball of timey-wimey, wibbly-wobbly stuff (to quote The Doctor) ("Monster at the End of this Book," cited in Schmidt 2010).[2]

While fans may have been generally happy with the meta nature of the episode, it did highlight several issues surrounding representation. The writers used the occasion to speak back to actual fans of the real series. When Sam reads a critical post from one fan, Simpatico (an actual poster on the Television Without Pity forums), Dean's response is a defensive "Well screw you Simpatico, we lived it!" In this case Sam and Dean assert their authority over their own text (i.e., their lives), at the same time acknowledging that fans can and do critique the show and transform it to fit their own desires through fanworks. This acknowledgement, however, should not be confused with acceptance. When Sam and Dean are themselves mistaken for obsessed fans by the frightened author of the series, Chuck Shurley, they are quick to dismiss the suggestion that they are mere fans by revealing knowledge never written in the books. In other words, they demonstrate their mastery over the text of their own lives. One cannot help feeling that the writers and showrunner were also reclaiming ownership of the series, acknowledging, and admonishing fans for their noncanonical interpretations of their characters.

"Can you stop touching me?"

Another reason for the generally favorable reception of the episode may have been that fan practices were not overtly gendered, with one significant exception. In order to get to Chuck, the brothers have to convince his (female) literary agent that they are not just fans, but *superfans* before she will reveal the writer's true identity. She administers a trivia quiz during which her detailed knowledge of a culturally unsanctioned text is held up for ridicule. The scene makes clear that the Winchesters are too busy living their real lives to remember this kind of trivia (and that anyone who does must not have a real life) and makes clear that knowledge of the text is not equivalent to mastery or ownership of that text. While the implied criticism lurks behind the otherwise amusing scene, it is not a gendered criticism until the Winchesters are forced to reveal the protective tattoos on their chests, prompting the agent to reveal her own tattoo—on her backside. With this, the viewer is treated to a first glimpse of an obsessed female fan with questionable boundaries. This will not be the last.

In the Season 5 opener, "Sympathy For the Devil," Sam and Dean encounter another, and more broadly stereotypical female fan—Becky Rosen (see the interview with Emily Perkins, in Chapter 14). Becky is first shown in what looks like a young girl's bedroom, invoking one of the enduring stereotypes of fans—that they are infantile, not able to exist in the adult world, still "living in their parents' basements." That bedroom is a shrine to the series, littered with posters and memorabilia. She is sitting at her computer, in the act of writing Wincest fan fiction ("If this is wrong, then I don't want to be right!") when she is interrupted by Chuck, who knows her as webmistress of MoreThanBrothers.net. Becky is his Number One Fan and apparently sends him strange presents.

Chuck's interaction with Becky is dismissive ("I got your marzipan—yummy") and yet he is reaching out to ask for her help. He needs someone "crazy enough" to believe him and knows she is his only hope (a situation the writer and showrunner Eric Kripke certainly knew well in the early, struggling years of the series, when its devoted fanbase was instrumental in keeping the show on the air.) For a moment, Becky pulls back from the stereotype of the deluded fangirl, assuring Chuck that she knows the difference between fantasy and reality. However, when Chuck assures her "It's all real!" she needs no more convincing. "I knew it!" she triumphantly declares and we are back in the realm of stereotypes.

When Becky shows up to deliver Chuck's message to Sam and Dean, she is the model of the inappropriate fangirl—the one that other fans so diligently police. She criticizes the show—"the demon mythology was getting old"—and she can't stop touching Sam's chest.

> "Becky, do you think you could stop touching me?"
> "No."

Bethan Jones (2014) contends that portrayals of female fans have always "erred towards the sensational, drawing on women's sexuality (whether that's too much or too little) and our apparent inability to differentiate between reality and fiction." This is certainly the impression that Becky leaves, a woman unable or unwilling to draw those distinctions.

This episode drew a wide range of responses from fandom (c.f. Busse and Hellekson 2012). Some fans found the portrayal humorous, but others thought Becky was a creepy, unflattering portrayal of a fangirl. Fans were also disturbed by seeing previously cloistered parts of fandom, considered a safe haven for expression of sexuality, once again on their television screens. A provocative piece of fan art by Counteragent created in response to the "outing" of fan practices in this episode was polarizing for the fandom, with some taking issue with its internalized shame and others lauding it for expressing how they also felt (Figures 13.1 and 13.2).

The cartoon, depicting a husband's gradual realization of what his wife does online while he watches the episode with her, captured the fear of real-life repercussions when nonfans find out about fan practices.

> One of the things SPN's specific portrayal of *Supernatural* fandom did was contribute to the popular denigration of women's icky sexualized overinvestment in fiction. The episode foregrounded the extent to which female fans' investment is about sexual desire for the male leads *and portrayed that as laughable.* Unsurprisingly, this is messy! Because one thing that might happen when a man sees a portrayal of female fans' sexual desire, and connects that to his wife's fandom, is that he will conclude that *her* sexual desire is focused elsewhere: she doesn't want him, she wants *them.* (rivkat, 2010)

Other fans took issue with the shame expressed in the comic, pointing out that keeping such a big secret from one's partner may be more of a problem than the fact that a television show portrayed fangirls in a less than flattering light. Overall the conversation

Figure 13.1 Good Fourth Walls Make Good Neighbors, by Counteragent, panel 6.

was less about whether the writers had "gotten it right" with their depiction of a fangirl and more about the fact that they may have come uncomfortably close to an accurate depiction of a fan practice if not the actual fangirl engaged in it.

Figure 13.2 Good Fourth Walls Make Good Neighbors, by Counteragent, panel 7.

Transformative works

If in "Sympathy for the Devil" the writers, along with Sam, Dean, and Chuck, had to acknowledge the crucial role a fan can play in the life of the show (and the lives of the characters), in "The Real Ghostbusters" (Season 5, episode 9), we find out that Becky the fangirl is now literally in bed with the writer, having begun a romantic relationship with Chuck. Becky lures Sam and Dean to a *Supernatural* fan convention she has organized by sending a text for help from Chuck's phone.

In this episode, the fans attending the convention are overwhelmingly male, the reverse demographic for an actual *Supernatural* fan convention. Margaret O'Connell of "*Supernatural* Talk" offers one possibility for the gender reversal.

> Somebody who knew nothing about the *Supernatural* fandom beyond the fact that it exists might well come away from this episode with the impression that the show's writers and producers, at least, think that their audience is composed of a few women who want to sleep with the Winchesters (or otherwise sexually fantasize about them) and a lot of guys who'd like to be them. Unless they all have PhDs in denial, it's unlikely that anyone on the *Supernatural* staff seriously believes this. But, based on this episode, it certainly seems as if some of them would prefer it if that were the case. The striking dichotomy between the gender breakdown of real life *Supernatural* fandom and the way it's portrayed here seems more apt to be the product of the creators' uneasiness at their theoretically decidedly male-centric show being subject to, and significantly dependent for its success on, the female gaze. (O'Connell 2009)

O'Connell's point is well taken, and suggests that we might also see this as Eric Kripke's own entrance into the realm of writing fan fiction as well as his opportunity to turn the tables on his fans. In Kripke's version of fandom, Demien and Barnes, two fanboys who role-play Sam and Dean (and are also lovers—a safe shout out to Wincest), are the heroes, risking their own lives in order to save the real Sam and Dean and the rest of the convention goers. Their heroism also earns them the approbation of even the highly skeptical Dean.[3]

And while Becky offers a similarly important service to the boys, saving the day with her encyclopedic knowledge of the text (Chuck's books) and giving Sam and Dean a lead on finding the all-important, demon-killing Colt, this does not earn her the same validation as the male fans received. Instead, Becky is once again treated with a mixture of tolerance and derision. When Becky tells Sam that she and Chuck are now a couple, she worries, somewhat pathetically over how Sam will deal with the news.

Becky: Will you be all right?
Sam: Honestly I don't know. I'll just have to find a way to keep living, I guess.

Where Dean approved of Demian and Barnes, Sam humors (or quietly mocks, depending on the cynicism of the viewer) Becky, who is still too deep in her delusions to see Sam's response for the brush off it is. Even Becky's relationship with Chuck does not afford much to celebrate since there is no indication that it's based on anything other than need and opportunity and, as we find out later, it did not last.

Back to square one

Kripke departed as showrunner and writer after Season 5, but Becky returned for one more episode. This is not, however, the same Becky—nor the same episode writers. While Becky was gently mocked in her previous two episodes, in "Season Seven, Time for a Wedding" here she is a sad and pathetic figure, a woman with nothing but her fandom and her misplaced and inappropriate desires, and the treatment she receives is decidedly mean-spirited. She is alone, having failed in her relationship with Chuck, and desperately wants to appear happy and successful to others no matter how empty her life may be in reality. Inexplicably, this results in her making a deal for a love potion with a crossroads demon (apparently forgetting all her obsessive knowledge of the supernatural in her desperate need to bag the husband of her dreams). She drugs Sam, ties him to a bed, and hits him with a frying pan, essentially enacting the scary fan from *Misery*. When Becky finally confesses to Sam, the depth of her delusion is clear.

> Sam: "So you think I love you?"
> Becky: "Deep, deep down."

Sam is no longer concerned with humoring Becky or letting her down gently as he did at the end of "The Real Ghostbusters." Even the crossroads demon, who is supposed to butter up his marks, has trouble being nice to her for longer than absolutely necessary. When she realizes who he is, he snidely observes of her reaction: "That is so depressingly 'Becky.' It's so pathetic it actually loops back around to cute." This is certainly not cute for the viewer, who grows increasingly uncomfortable with this characterization of the sad, lonely fangirl who is entirely without boundaries. Compounding the mockery is Becky's wholesale acceptance of this treatment.

> I know what I am. I'm a loser. The only place where people understood me was the message boards. They were grumpy and overly literal but at least we shared a common passion. And I'll take it.

Not only is Becky portrayed as pathetic, but fandom itself is being positioned here as second best—something that is settled on rather than chosen.

There are islands of competence in Becky that continue to surface, perhaps indicating that the writers are as confused about how to feel about fans as the viewer is at this point in the episode. She again saves the day, and Sam's life, by tricking the demon into a devil's trap. This leads to a brief moment of self-esteem, as she declares, "I am awesome!" but she is immediately told to stand aside and she reverts compliantly back to ineffectuality, saying mournfully, "I'll be over here." She comes out of her corner in time to dispatch one of the crossroads demon's henchmen, but once again this moment of heroism is undercut when Crowley shows up. She is the only one there who initially knows who he is, remembering him from the books.

"You're Crowley!"

"And you're... well, I'm sure you have a wonderful personality, dear."

As the episode ends, Sam and Becky are signing annulment papers. "It wasn't all bad, right?" she asks, trying to salvage some vestige of self-worth. Sam barely allows it.

"Becky, you're not a loser. You're a good person. You've got a lot of... energy. So just do your own thing and you'll find the right person."

As this is being said, the hunter Garth, who himself has been the butt of jokes for much of the episode, repeatedly referred to as "that scrawny guy," casts a hopeful look in Becky's direction and is immediately warned off by Sam and Dean, for no real reason except perhaps that she's a "crazy fangirl" and fangirls, apparently, do not deserve happiness.

Not surprisingly, this left a terrible taste in the mouths of fans. Even the actress who played Becky, Emily Perkins, had mixed feelings. In an interview with us for this chapter, she allowed that, as a fan herself, she was excited to play a fangirl, but she expected a mixed reaction. Some fans, she thought, would be "constitutionally more able to laugh at themselves and pick up on the humor in the show, and others would not." She did understand how vulnerable fans—especially female fans—are to shaming, and how that impacted fan reaction to Becky. But she still tried to see the strengths of the character.

The shame is in there, and it's true to the experience, but it doesn't stop her. I think the writers were trying to be sympathetic to her, she was bullied in school, and it does sort of universalize the experience. And look what she got to do—she got to kill a demon, she got to save Sam. And she got Sam tied to a bed without any pants on, come on! So the last scene wasn't so positive, but if you take stock of the whole episode, she was actually triumphant, she did save the day. She's a pretty kickass girl. At least I like to see it that way. I think you have to be careful not to confuse the intention with the meaning that we take from it. (Interview with authors, 2013)

Nevertheless, many took their meaning from the fact that Sam and Dean have the power to deny Becky any potential happiness with Garth, and that her kick-ass qualities are ultimately diminished rather than affirmed. The fact that Sam and Dean retain this power over her (and by extension the writers over the fans) makes a positive reading of Becky across her three-episode arc difficult to support. While Judith Fatallah (2010) has argued that the figure of Becky serves to call into question "the masculinist epic" (3.1) and that her presence "could be read as refusing to take seriously the official, dominant story line, inviting those not privileged in mainstream society to appropriate the narrative for their pleasure" (1.2), it can also be argued that at no point does Becky question the narrative beyond a brief comment on the demon storyline "getting old." Indeed, her moments of heroism are predicated on the acceptance of the importance of Sam and Dean's quest to eradicate evil from the world.

And the fact remains that by Season 7, the show was at far less risk of being cancelled. Its fanbase was steadily growing and diversifying (more young fans and more male fans coming to the show as a result of the series' availability on Netflix) and there was no longer a need on the part of the writers to acknowledge Becky as anything other than pathetic and excluded. Little wonder that this episode has become the one that dare not speak its name.

"Getting it right?"

The struggle for authority over the text evident in the earlier depictions of fans is revisited in *Supernatural*'s 200th episode (10.05), "Fan Fiction," but with significant differences. Writer Robbie Thompson describes the episode as a "love letter to the fans" and for the most part, this show within a show seemed to succeed as such. While Sam and Dean investigate the usual unusual disappearances at an all-girls high school, they discover that the upcoming school production is based on Chuck's books, and once again, their lives. This time, while the girls take their production seriously, they do not take the book series seriously. There is no suggestion here that they have any difficulty with the boundary between fiction and reality. Indeed they burst into laughter when Sam and Dean claim that they're actually Sam and Dean, making it clear they're far from the stereotype of the "delusional fangirl"—i.e., not Becky, who is not present nor even mentioned.

This time, when the question of who has the right to interpret the text comes up, the fans are there to answer for themselves. When Dean bristles, "There's no singing in *Supernatural*," fangirl Maeve counters that "This is Marie's interpretation." She later answers Dean's complaint that some of what is in the play didn't happen in the books.

> "Well, not canonically no, but this is transformative fiction."
> "You mean fan fiction," Dean says.
> "It's inspired by canon," Maeve clarifies, "With a few embellishments."

These girls, unlike Becky, demonstrate an interest in sexuality and an expression of that interest that is not ultimately portrayed as inappropriate. There are references to fan shipping of Wincest and Destiel (the slash ship of Dean with the angel Castiel), though they are not the focus of the production. These fans are engaging in subversive play, calling canon into question in multiple ways. "Dean was with Lisa, Sam was back from hell, but not with Dean..." says the play's fangirl author Marie, as though it's obvious why some fix-it fic was needed. "And then.... Dean becomes a woman."

Thompson recognizes here how fandom subverts and plays with gender norms with Marie's matter-of-fact explanation. When Dean tries to assert the priority of canon (and authorship) by reciting what really happened to the Winchesters over the past four seasons, Marie laughs at him, calling his story "some of the worst fan fiction I've ever heard," reviving Kripke's tradition of incorporating digs at the show in the meta episodes. Clearly Marie's is the more plausible narrative.

Wincest is once again explicitly acknowledged, but more positively. As Sam and Dean watch the production, Dean comments on the actresses playing the Winchester brothers.

> "Why are they standing so close together?"
> "Reasons," Marie says, again using fannish parlance.
> "They do know we're brothers, right?" Dean persists, echoing his line to Sam from "The Monster At The End of This Book."

This time the fandom gets to answer, reiterating a clear understanding of canon versus fanon.

> "Well, duh," Marie answers, "But, subtext."

Dean also notices the young woman playing Dean and the girl playing the angel Castiel hugging and holding hands between scenes.

> "Is that in the show?" he asks.
> "No, they're a couple in real life. Though we do explore the nature of Destiel in Act 2."

Actor Jensen Ackles (Dean) breaks the fourth wall here (which apparently wasn't scripted) to look pointedly at the camera and to the fans, as if to say, *I see you. I know what you're doing.*

Quite a few fans tweeted Thompson to thank him for the recognition of queer fans in canon. In this episode, a (character) queer couple portray Dean and Cas, just as queer couple Demian and Barnes portrayed Sam and Dean in "The Real Ghostbusters," in recognition of both slash ships. Even the Winchesters have come far enough to joke about slash shipping in this episode, as Sam teases Dean with "Shouldn't it be Dee-stiel... or how about Sastiel?" Thompson uses the correct ship names, once again co-opting fannish norms and language but to generally more positive effect than the earlier invocations of Wincest produced.

Eventually, saving the day comes down to allowing—even encouraging—the fan production. In fact, shutting down the play (i.e., fannish creativity), the episode warns, will have dire consequences.

> Marie: I thought you didn't believe in this interpretation.
> Dean: I don't. Not at all. But you do. And I need you to believe in it with all you've got.

Then, Dean rallies the rest of the fangirl troops, assuring them that their interpretation of *Supernatural* is just as valid as his (i.e., canon), or anyone else's.

> I know I've expressed some differences of opinion, but this is Marie's *Supernatural*. I want you to stand as close as she wants you to [nod to Wincest]. You put as much sub into that text as you can [nod to Destiel]. You get out there and kick it in the ass!

This is an endorsement of fannish interpretation made even more powerful by the in-group reference to the signature phrase of the late, beloved *Supernatural* director Kim Manners, "Kick it in the ass!" After the curtain closes, Dean sums up the episode's message.

Dean: This has been educational, seeing the story from your perspective. Keep writing, Shakespeare.
Marie: Even if it doesn't match yours?
Dean: I have my version, you have yours.

Here the show explicitly acknowledges the existence of both canon and fanon, and the diversity of perspectives among fandom as well. The fan-created reflection of their lives gives the brothers a new appreciation of their story, and of each other. And the fangirls even get the seal of approval from author Chuck himself (i.e., Kripke), who turns up briefly at the end with a smile and a "Not bad." The creator of canon blesses the interpretation—the fan fiction, and the fans.

This validation was extended outside the boundaries of the episode as the cast and crew live-tweeted the episode along with fans when it aired first on November 14, 2014. Actor Misha Collins (Castiel) commented: "I feel like I'm in a Transformative Media graduate seminar. This canonical diatribe is a lot to chew on." And actor Osric Chau (Kevin) tweeted: "This episode is so mesmerizing. It's like Robbie Thompson dipped himself in a pool of fandom before writing it." Writer Robert Berens, well aware of the infighting that sometimes fractures *Supernatural* fandom, added: "This was a celebration of the show and its fans, and the brief respite from onscreen (human!) bloodshed is a metaphor for the episode itself as an occasion for peace and celebration across the fandom(s) itself."

The episode largely redeemed the image of fans, which had been arguably tarnished by the last Becky episode, though some questioned whether it was only redemptive for a certain segment of fans, that is, teenage girls who are behaving in age-appropriate ways. Most fans, however, felt that with this episode, the portrayal of fans on *Supernatural* moved in a positive direction. Writing in Fandomania Kimberly Workman applauded:

[Sam and] Dean finally learning to live and let live with the different interpretations of their life. Fan fiction of the Winchester Gospel is always going to be varied interpretations of the canon, but that's what we love. All our interpretations are just as valid, and the show set out to reinforce that fact. It was a love letter, through and through.

Fangirl 2.0

An entirely different, and far less controversial, version of the fangirl is represented by the recurring character of Charlie Bradbury. Charlie is a gamer with a sci-fi inflected name; she was "raised on Tolkien"; she LARPs; she has a Princess Leia tattoo acquired while drunk at Comic-Con. She knows the value of collectibles and isn't shy about showing her enthusiasm. Charlie is a self-proclaimed "nerd," a fully operational fangirl, and one who is not delusional or motivated solely by sexual desire.

Also created by Robbie Thompson, Charlie is Thompson's way of normalizing comments on fan practices such as fan fiction, collecting, and cosplay. While Sam and Dean are initially skeptical, they come to respect Charlie's intelligence, courage, and spirit of adventure to the point where they consider her a "little sister." This acceptance of the character of the fangirl is a far cry from the derision shown to Becky a season earlier. It certainly helps that Charlie is a lesbian, therefore removing all possibility of inappropriate sexual desire for either of "the boys," as well as being more reflective of the actual fanbase for *Supernatural*. The casting of Felicia Day, a real-life self-proclaimed geek fangirl, only served to solidify this positive message.

Charlie is also privy to the world of the Winchesters—and not from reading about it in Chuck Shurley's novels. She is a part of their lives rather than a dismissible character they encounter in passing. By Season 10, Charlie is the one who saves the day, by locating the Book of the Damned and then breaking the code through her superior research abilities. This stands in contrast to the ways in which Becky saved the day through her obsessive knowledge of the *Supernatural* books. While she was undoubtedly the hero, she was so via overinvestment rather than skill.

The character of Charlie was widely applauded by most fans. She was abruptly and horrifically killed off in Season 10's "Dark Dynasty" just as she was becoming a bona fide member of "the team." Fan reaction to Charlie's death was almost entirely negative. In fact, it accomplished something that sometimes seems like impossibility in *Supernatural* fandom: it brought the fandom together, unified in their rage at the show. Many fans felt that killing Charlie was like "killing us." It also reminded fans that in the end, the writers still control this particular text and that no matter how beloved this character was, she was still theirs to dispose of.

Conclusion

It seems clear that *Supernatural*'s understanding (and portrayal) of its female fans has evolved over the course of its ten seasons on the air. Charlie and the fangirls of "Fan Fiction" are set apart from Becky in several ways. They represent a form of fandom divorced from "belief," with clear boundaries between fiction and reality, unlike Becky's sometimes shaky negotiation of real and unreal. They have no delusions and are not engaging in a "parasocial relationship" with the objects of their fandom; rather, they are able to express their fannish passion and creativity in a way that enriches their lives and allows them to be themselves.

These are more positive depictions, but what message are we being sent about fans? There is no sexual component to Charlie's love for Sam and Dean. They are like brothers to her, in contrast to Becky's somewhat pathetic fixation on Sam in particular. So, is the only good fan a desexualized fan (in terms of the fannish objects) or, in the case of Marie, an adolescent fan who really can't control her hormonal responses anyway? And is the only good fan one who does not try to control the text as Becky did, inserting herself into the narrative of the boys' lives, but who understands that her interpretation is just that, an interpretation that has not had, and never will have, an impact on canon? Or perhaps writers never consider any of these questions?

Robert Singer, director, writer, and executive producer on *Supernatural* appeared recently at a fan convention in Chicago. When asked by fans about the handling of Charlie's character in particular, his response encapsulated the disconnect that will perhaps always exist between fans and creators. While acknowledging the fans' difficulty letting go of a much-loved character, he also took that response as an affirmation that the writers had done their job, creating a character with whom we all identified. He concluded with a shrug: "I'm sorry—it's just television."

Notes

1   The series has invoked images of fans and fandom many times over the run of the series, including derisive depictions of Dean as fanboy in several episodes. This chapter deals exclusively with representations of female fans of the series.
2   Television Without Pity deleted all of their forums on May 31, 2014, therefore this post is no longer accessible.
3   In a clever twist, Kripke writes real fans Demien and Barnes, frequent commenters on the Television Without Pity forums at the time into the episode, turning the tables on some fans who had written him into their own fan fiction.

14

Interview with Emily Perkins, Actor in *Supernatural*

Paul Booth and Lucy Bennett

Emily Perkins is a cult icon. The star of the horror film *Ginger Snaps* (2000), Perkins made a name for herself playing intense and quirky characters in both horror and comedy film and television. For readers of this volume, Perkins is perhaps best known for playing "superfan" Becky Rosen in *Supernatural*. Although some (Gray 2010) may criticize the character as being "an extreme in fandom" (17, also Tosenberger 2010a, 1.6), others (Zubernis and Larsen 2012) have called Becky "a love letter to fandom" (p. 170). Becky is unapologetically a fan: she writes fan fiction (Wincest in this case), daydreams about Dean and Sam Winchester (especially Sam), and is overtly sexual. Looked at through one lens, the character of Becky is thus an overly stereotypical fangirl, unable to control herself around "the boys" and an unabashed negative representation of overt feminine sexuality and power. Looked at through another lens, Becky is powerful, sexual, and in charge of her own desires. Love her, hate her, or laugh at (/with) her, there is no doubt that Becky Rosen's place in the *Supernatural* universe has cemented the representation of fandom in *Supernatural*. We spoke with Perkins over email about her experiences playing Becky Rosen, her past brushes with being a fan, and her impressions of fandom and the fan audience.

Q: *Supernatural* has become such a fan-centric show over the past few seasons. How has the production team understood the impact of fandom? Are there conversations about fan activities?
A: I heard a lot of conversation on set regarding fans, and because of the conventions the actors are enormously aware of fans and have a lot to say about them. The show's actors have very positive feelings toward their fans. When I came on set Jared [Padalecki] and Jensen [Ackles] rushed to tell me stories of fans—things they had sent (a quilt in the production office) or what they had written—and it was clear they have a lot of respect for their audiences. My sense was that the producers and writers keep well informed regarding fan activities and that the content of the show is very fan-responsive. The character of Becky with all the winks and nods to fan culture, and the incorporation of the fan lexicon into dialogue, was part of the show's desire to engage in conversation with audiences.

Q: Did you feel any sense of accountability in terms of representing the wider fan culture when you played the role of Becky?

A: I always feel a level of accountability with any part I play. I have turned down roles that I did not feel portrayed women fairly. Curiously, I often play roles that have something to do with sexuality—the *Ginger Snaps* series was a teen sexual coming of age story; on *Da Vinci's Inquest* I played a young sex-trade worker—and the sexual nerd-girl is a part I have played several times. You can't please everyone when playing with a more controversial aspect of human character, so I try to be true to my own experiences and my own sense of joy. Sexuality is often an aspect of fandom. The humor comes in when something that is normally repressed is instead expressed with abandon (surprise, nerd girls have a libido!). Do fans normally behave in such a hyperbolic way? Of course not. It was no one's intention to represent the typical fan's behavior. But are feelings of desire happening inside a fan? In many cases, yes. We are all sexual beings after all, and that's nothing to be ashamed of. Fandom is about excess in some ways, and it felt right to make Becky excessive; there is a certain truth in that, just not a literal translation of how it manifests. I really like characters that challenge assumptions or might provoke a strong psychological reaction: those are the ones that have the power to awaken new thoughts or ways of seeing. I don't feel accountable to any particular audience, but I do feel accountable to the role as I think performance should play as it reflects life.

Q: What was the response from the *Supernatural* fan communities afterwards? And the media in general?

A: I did not read many responses myself but what I have heard is that they were quite mixed. Some people felt that the production was laughing at them or mocking them through the character of Becky, which was definitely not the intention. Others were very positive about the character.[…] It is really cool to examine the gap between any reality and its representation. For me, it's about the fan-actor dynamic: not only does a fan make his or herself vulnerable in expressing their passion, the actor is equally vulnerable to the fan. Actors often try not to think about fans or read responses online because their job, their very identity, depends ultimately on fan approval. Negative comments are painful. Conversely, when fans tell actors that they have enriched their lives, it is wonderful, because we are engaging in an act of communication and we need to believe that we have something important to say, and that we are heard. In fact the approval of fans (i.e., "success" for an actor) is like a drug. We hear about so many actors using drugs, perhaps as a substitute for the approval of fans which they may not be getting enough of, or which may fail to be the unconditional sort of love we humans are always looking for. In a way, this part of the story exposes the artificiality of, or deconstructs, the fan/idol hierarchical binary.

Q: Representing fans of a text within the text itself is a challenging proposition. How would you respond to fans that may have had mixed feelings toward these representations?

A: I would like to really honor whatever response fans had to the character. All responses are legitimate and are informed by a much wider context, and are an important part of how meaning is made. No text has a single, fixed meaning. I can understand why Becky might be seen to be re-inscribing negative fan-stereotypes. But all meaning deals in stereotypes to some extent, and a more powerful stance than complaining about their employ is to reinterpret them: there are so many truths to be created or uncovered.

I think it's important to reflect on why Becky might offend. How does she fail to be an acceptable model of female desire? Is she not pretty and fashionable enough? Not demure enough? Not passive enough? Is she psychologically flawed—too needy? Perhaps some criticisms we might have of Becky are the unfair biases of male-dominated culture in which only women who behave in self-effacing and restricted ways are deemed acceptable. We are all deviant in some way—no one can be the ideal, and frankly, who'd want to? Becky was meant to be a loving poke, not a literal representation of fans as deviants. Fandom is an arena in which what makes us deviant, our particular loves, can be celebrated, and where we can take pride in them. What I love about Becky is that she is assertive enough to express her desire and have a fantastic adventure. In the end, Becky wins. Propriety Girl just had another boring weekend.

Q: Did you find representing a fan character any different to representing people in your other roles?
A: It was different in that I felt simultaneously like an insider and an outsider on set. […] When I walked on set I thought, however they treat me will reveal their true attitude toward fans. Fortunately, they were very sweet. But I had this consciousness that I did not really belong in the studio. I always have this nagging feeling as an actor that I don't belong, that I should not be there and was miscast. In my everyday life people seem surprised to learn I am an actress (you were expecting Megan Fox?) In this case, it came in handy, because on some level Becky knows she is violating the fan/idol barrier. That's me: the outsider… it made total sense. There is something really ineffable about being able to traverse the barrier between audience and performer; it felt truly unique and a tiny bit lonely.

Q: Would you consider yourself a fan?
A: In high school I was a *Next Generation* fan. Friends and I started a club and wrote scenes to perform for the school in costumes. Since that time, though, I've been a more casual fan. I'd say I'm a casual fan of the show *Sherlock*, for example. I am a book-lover and there are certain authors whom I see as god-like and with whom I would be completely tongue-tied if we ever met. George Saunders, wow! But I don't engage in distinctive "fan behaviors": excessive or binge (hate that term, so pathological sounding!) viewing, collecting paraphernalia or cosplay, committing extensive trivia to memory, writing fan fiction, etc. I think what changed in me was a growing suspicion that identification with a TV show, book, band, etc., has very little descriptive power. I stopped feeling that it bonded me with other fans in any meaningful way, and it felt like a bit of a trick, in the way we are tricked into thinking the nuances of fashion are meaningful in anything but the most superficial sense, at least on the individual level. I think for a long time I really questioned the value of placing emphasis on entertainment

and pleasure. I have this huge puritan streak! But it fascinated me that people are able to establish deep friendships and find creative expression within particular fandoms. I have since come to understand that fandom can be an incredibly deep and even spiritual experience, with even political and ecological implications. Entertainment is not a disconnected realm of human experience, and fandom really illustrates this. I guess what I'm trying to say is that fandom is really interesting to me as a cultural and psychological phenomenon—as a form of celebration and community—but for me fandom as an individual pursuit has lost a little of its charm. Or maybe (what I secretly hope) the right show just needs to come along to intoxicate me again!

Q: Were you aware of fan studies as an academic field and did you do any research before beginning the film?

A: I was aware of fan studies but not of the extent of the field. The idea of the aca-fan makes perfect sense, because academics and fans have something very particular in common: extraordinary consumption of a very narrow or specific subject of interest. So of course academics would create the field of fan studies! I didn't do as much research as I did reflect on my own experiences and those of friends who are fans, some of whom attend conventions and do cosplay etc. I think there are stages that fans go through—first, an unselfconscious adoration phase, like my own love of the *Star Trek* utopian fantasy. Second, there is an awareness of external criticism of fandom, of the attempt of others to shame fans for their excesses. I couldn't believe it when people said they didn't want to join our *Next Generation* club because people would think they were a nerd! For me, an ironic element of fan expression crept in during this stage. I started worshiping Elvis as a statement of my awareness of fandom as time/place specific. Third, a resolution of fan shame which brings a new understanding of what it means to be a fan, while reclaiming the pure and honest joy of fandom that was lost in the ironic phase. The doubt of others has this magical effect: it makes us take on their criticisms and question the meaning of what we are doing, allowing us to move forward in a more deliberate manner but with the same enthusiasm.

Q: While on set, did the actors/producers/creators discuss different ways of representing fans? What was that conversation like?

A: I asked Bob [Singer] if he wanted me to wear my fake braces from a previous role. He said, "No, we want you to look cute."

Spotlight On: Fan and Transmedia Works

15

Beyond Mary Sue: Fan Representation and the Complex Negotiation of Gendered Identity

Kristina Busse

Geek representation has changed in the past few decades: eighties high school nerd and outcast Anthony Michael Hall has given way to *The Big Bang Theory*'s (CBS 2007–) eccentric but loveable Sheldon Cooper, and fannish behavior is mainstreamed in network and cable shows from *NCIS* (CBS 2003–) and *Leverage* (TNT 2008–2012) to *Castle* (ABC 2009–) and *Psych* (USA 2006–2014). Yet most of these positive fan and geek characters are male; in fact, women are either cast as objects of nerd desire or, if they are depicted as fans, often derided as obsessive, silly, and loveless. Within such a televisual landscape, it is often difficult for women to see themselves in the media with which they engage, allowing them few potential female objects of identification and even fewer that may be like them: smart and geeky. One way female fans write themselves into contemporary media is by creating alter egos who can experience these worlds and characters. Alternately, fans take the protagonists out of their fictional universes and insert them into the audience's worlds: detectives, space explorers, and pop stars become fan fiction writers, beta readers, and bloggers.

Fan writers effectively feminize hypermasculine characters, give them primarily female geeky interests and writerly preoccupations, and, in so doing, revert the voyeuristic gaze while projecting their actions and emotions onto the characters. Internal community debates about issues of representation indicate how important it is for many fans to be able to relate to show characters—both male and female. At the same time, visual attraction remains important, so that the idea of Captain America as a Tumblr user or Dean Winchester as a cosplaying comic fan allows fan writers to merge attraction with identification. I suggest that fan fiction not only offers particular modes of interpreting the source texts but also ways to discuss and analyze theories of audience reception, especially as they relate to gender and the insufficient representation of women. Looking at Mary Sue as a particular instantiation of representing identificatory desires permits us to behold self-insertion fics not only as part of a larger spectrum of fan fiction, but also as an exemplary way in which fans explore and engage with their favorite media texts, their own identities and desires.

One of the central questions in literature is how to relate author and text. Beyond the most steadfast New Critical reading, it is apparent that excluding the author entirely will needlessly limit interpretations (Busse 2013b). At the same time an analysis that predominantly emphasizes the writer's conscious (or unconscious) thoughts and desires is equally fraught. Nowhere is this question more pertinent than when we look at the way fans represent themselves, other fans, and fandom in general. By design and necessity, this discussion is gendered. Mainstream media's more positive representation of male fans together with the larger number of female fan writers tends to create a scenario in which fans more easily notice and more quickly vilify female self-insertions.

I begin this chapter with a brief overview of community definition and responses to the Mary Sue trope. At once a character, trope, developmental stage, writing style, and all too easy dismissal of female characters, the Mary Sue has become all but useless as a descriptive or critical tool. In its stead, I look at the various ways in which fans represent themselves and their communities within fan fiction, both explicitly through self-insertion and implicitly by foregrounding crucial characteristics in protagonists. Whether fans cathect certain characters that share central aspects with them or project these aspects onto beloved protagonists, whether they create narratives in which fannish behaviors are played out or use the canon playing field to explore personal concerns, stories are always meaningful in ways that often also include its authors and their community.

Mary Sue: Definition, dismissal, defense

"Mary Sue" is a term coined by fan writer Paula Smith in her 1973 satirical *Star Trek* short story "A Trekkie's Tale." Initially only mocking a very specific type of female character insert, Smith responded to a type of fan fiction where the original female character would be exceptional in background, looks, and accomplishments, often sidelining the canonical characters or achieving a romantic relationship with the protagonist. As authorial self-insert, Mary Sue tends to be wish fulfillment, allowing the author (and, if successful, the reader) to enter the canon and participate in the action. Paula Smith describes the writer's faults as follows: "A story demands headspace, and the Mary Sue wants to come and occupy your whole head, so the writer gets the enjoyment and not the reader. It's a little too much like being used. I suspect that's why an awful lot of people agreed with our assessment" (in Walker 2011, 2.15).

What exactly constitutes a Mary Sue is widely debated, but its undesirability is generally acknowledged. Mary Sue is an easy insult that shorthands a variety of criticisms, but centers on the introduction of a non-canon infallible female character who takes over the action. As the term became more popular, fans tried to define it in various ways. Different groups use diverging definitions as they defend or dismiss the concept, but all of the definitions are equally limiting. If one defines Mary Sues as bad writing, then all Mary Sue stories are tautologically badly written. If one defines Mary Sues as a stage in most writer's learning process, then the immaturity is both cause and effect of the writer's developmental, if not biological, age. And if one defines Mary Sue as any female original character, then the critical specificity loses much of its power.

Given the overwhelmingly negative associations with the term, Mary Sue often simply describes characters and stories readers don't like, while those characters readers do enjoy are defended as transcending the Mary Sue trope.

In "150 Years of Mary Sue," Pat Pflieger (2001) establishes historical precedents for the Mary Sue character, whom she describes as "amazingly intelligent, outrageously beautiful, adored by all around her—and absolutely detested by most reading her adventures," and most often to be found in "fiction written by less-than-experienced writers." By expanding the term to include original stories, Pflieger foregrounds three characteristics: (1) the Mary Sue's extreme physical attributes, abilities, and, often, back story; (2) the reader's instant dislike; and (3) the writer's immaturity. If we add to this Paula Smith's characterization that Mary Sues take over headspace or, as fan writer p_zeitgeist describes, stories in which a "character den[ies] other characters the right to be central to their own stories" (LJ, May 21, 2005),[1] then we get (4) the story warps around the Mary Sue as the main character.

If, as Henry Jenkins (1992) suggests, at least part of the appeal of fan fiction is to "efface the gap that separates the realm of [the writer's] own experience and the fictional" (p. 173), and if we assume that a large number of writers identify to some degree with their characters (whether canon or originally created), then the question remains as to why the loathing and resistance is so particularly strong in regard to the Mary Sue. Fan fiction thrives on pulling beloved characters into new environments, turning them into werewolves and vampires, policemen and assassins, college professors and barista. It domesticates its intergalactic heroes and international spies by getting them married with children, buying curtains and homes with picket fences. Once the writer inserts a female avatar into the text, however, a line seems to be crossed. Jenkins describes this internal evaluation and policing: "So strong is the fan taboo against such crude personalization that original female characters are often scrutinized for any signs of autobiographical intent" (p. 173).

Given the vast number and diversity of fandoms, stories, and writers, there clearly cannot be a simple or singular explanation for any given fan fiction trends—not even the often seemingly unanimous derision of Mary Sue stories. And yet there may be some justifications and purpose for at least a number of Mary Sue stories that allow us to understand the vehement reactions many fans have against such obvious autobiographical inserts. Academic discussions of the Mary Sue trope are interested primarily in the psychological ramifications of the self-insert as a developmental stage and as romantic/sexual gratification. In one of the most positive descriptions of Mary Sue fiction, "Keeping Promises to Queer Children," Ika Willis (2006) looks at fan fiction's ability to respond to "a reader's desiring subjectivity" (p. 163) and its ability to allow (often younger) fans to create queer characters within their fiction where none may exist in the text.

Also looking at often younger writers, Camille Bacon-Smith (1992) reads Mary Sues as created by younger if not beginning writers, in that she "must be an adolescent, behaviorally if not absolutely chronologically, because she represents a transition in roles and identity specific to that period in a woman's life" (pp. 101–2). By contrast, Anne Kustritz (2003) understands Mary Sues as "idealized versions of the [authors] in order to fantasize about sex with the male protagonist" (p. 380). In so doing, Kustritz argues, she "represents and reproduces the worst aspects of female competition for desirable heterosexual relationship partners" (p. 380). Both of those are effectively oversharing the writer's personal issues without mediating and coding them properly. Generally, fannish negative sentiments toward the latter often expand to dismiss all Mary Sue stories, thus ignoring the fact that various forms of self-insertions are a central feature of fan fiction, if not fiction in general.

Canon Mary Sue: *Darcyland* and *Agents of S.H.I.E.L.D.*

Considering the fear of creating Mary Sues, fans are often torn between not wanting to self-insert while also not wanting to be completely left out. Fan writers thus put themselves into the text by altering and shaping the characters to resemble them or by placing the characters in situations that allow them to play out the fans' own needs, desires, and situations. Unsuccessfully done, the characters retain little recognizability to other fans: after all, it seems somewhat unlikely that forty-year-old astrophysicists will serenade their boyfriends with "My Immortal Beloved" or that bubblegum pop stars read *Finnegans Wake* in their off time. Fan fiction is always a tightrope walk between, on the one hand, adhering to canon facts and characterizations—however conflicted and subjective those may be—and, on the other hand, introducing different plots, themes, characters, and characterizations. If we accept that Mary Sue tends to describe an unpopular (or too individual and particular) tilt to the latter, there still are many ways in which fans can incorporate their own lives, backgrounds, and experiences; their beliefs, interests, and ideas; their cultural, sexual, and physical identities.

Attributing personal or community characteristics to characters ranges from the very specific to the very general. It includes characters reading or quoting beloved books, listening to one's favorite artist, or having hobbies such as knitting. It includes assigning specific identities with the characters, which are often referenced as head canon, a particular interpretation the writer believes to be true, one they want to see represented more widely, or one they may share with the characters, such as ace!Sherlock, trans!Carlos, or autistic!Will Graham. Often such works include subtle differences that merely shade the shared worlds and its characters as a little more liberal, more feminist, more queer than the canon worlds. Fan Betty P. explains in an essay how she purposefully alters her characters "in a certain way, a little more thoughtful than they probably are, a little more genuine, a little more confused. I write them trying harder to get through life than I think they really are… I write the way I write because it produces a story that I like and not because I think it mimics reality exactly" (LJ, January 23, 2004).

In the remainder of the chapter, I want to look at ways in which fan writers follow Betty P.'s model of making the characters "a little more"—thereby creating a story they like and readers, in turn, like as well. I begin with the most obvious and easiest form of self-insertion, namely choosing a character that invites fan identification. A popular example of a self-insert is the character of Darcy Lewis in the Marvel Cinematic Universe (MCU). Played by Kat Dennings, Darcy is first introduced in *Thor* (Marvel 2011) and reappears in its sequel *Thor: The Dark World* (Marvel 2013). She is a twenty-something political science graduate student who works as astrophysicist Jane Foster's lab assistant and mostly provides comic relief and commonsense commentary in this strange meeting of human science and magic. In fandom, Darcy quickly became an ideal point of view character that allowed writers to focus on a regular human getting to know both international spy organization S.H.I.E.L.D. and superhero group The Avengers. In a large number of stories, she joins S.H.I.E.L.D. and becomes an agent or gets employed by Stark Industries as a lab assistant or both, often serving as a form of babysitter for the Avengers and always bringing a commonsense mentality to the insanities of secret spy and superhero life.

As an ensemble text, MCU supports many pairings, but few characters get paired up as easily as Darcy does. There are dozens if not hundreds of stories each that have her romantically entangled with anyone from Jane and Loki to Hawkeye and Captain America. She is one of the few women to have become a "little black dress," a term originating with *The X-Files* (FOX 1993–2002)'s Alex Krycek and depicting a character who can be paired easily with multiple and various other characters. As an anonymous commenter describes: "she gets shipped with people she's never met because she's young and hip and likes cute things and has no powers, like the people who write her" (fail_fandomanon DW, October 01, 2014). And yet throughout most of these stories, the basic Darcy characterizations stay constant, some drawn and extrapolated from canon (social media savvy, quick-witted, and irreverent, but also smart, brave, and loyal), many becoming shared tropes within fandom (mostly related to her babysitting the Avengers, her general status as competent sidekick, and her extreme snarkiness). In fact, while the romantic aspects are certainly important in many Darcy stories, the focus is often on her coming of age and learning to fit into the Avengerverse in general.

Darcy thus fulfills two central roles for female fan writers and readers: she allows fans to imagine themselves, normal and ordinary, as they enter and become familiar with this world of exceptionally trained undercover agents and superheroes; and she allows fans to not only succeed in this world but also to find love with one of these heroes. Where it is difficult to imagine ourselves as a God, a multibillionaire, a serum-enhanced super soldier from World War II, a brainwashed assassin, a CEO of an international company, or a brilliant astrophysicist, Darcy is effectively fangirls everywhere: iPod listening, snarky, and big-busted, she looks, sounds, and feels like someone we might encounter on Tumblr or at ComicCon.

The only other MCU character who has a similarly mundane background and thus can function as an everyman character with whom we can identify is S.H.I.E.L.D. Agent Phil Coulson. Unlike Darcy, however, this middle-aged professional male has clearly been recognized by the showrunners in this function. In fact, Coulson's role has expanded throughout the Marvel Cinematic Universe, beginning with brief appearances as the obligatory man in black in *Iron Man* (Marvel 2008) and *Thor* to becoming a hero in his own right in *The Avengers* (Marvel 2012) to, finally, frontlining the TV series *Agents of S.H.I.E.L.D* (ABC 2013–). So whereas Darcy Lewis's inclusion in and interaction with the Avengers remains purely in fan speculation, Phil Coulson's has become canonical, in effect creating a fannish stand-in within the canonical universe itself. Moreover, whereas Darcy may become an easy figure of identification for female Millennials due to her specific interests and behaviors, Coulson is canonically a fanboy in *The Avengers*. Director Joss Whedon describes Coulson as "an everyman who people can relate to [with] a man crush on Captain America" (Wilding 2012). Coulson reveals his long-term obsession with Captain America when he confesses to an embarrassed Steve Rogers that he watched him sleep and then asks him to sign his mint condition Captain America cards. In fact, these bloodied collector's items are a central plot point when they become testimony not only to Phil Coulson's belief in the Avenger Initiative but also to his ultimate sacrifice.

Fans take Phil Coulson's canonical fannishness and use it to self-insert and project their own fannish experiences. Rageprufrock's "User Since" (AO3, October 21, 2013) uses and extrapolates Phil Coulson's canon characterization to ultimately tell a story about fans, fan communities, and fannish connections. The online epistolary story is a collection of posts, letters, emails, and texts by members of a fictional Captain America fan community, the Howling Commandoes, cofounded by Phil Coulson. It begins in the immediate aftermath of the Battle of New York, the culminating battle in *The Avengers* during which Coulson gets killed by Loki. The first post in the story is a general check-in post after the battle, but soon members are trying to figure out why their "fearless forum head mod" is missing. The story follows group's inquiries and subsequent memorial at Arlington, where they meet to read letters of Phil's online friends. One community member emailed Captain America, who ends up attending the service with all of the Avengers and many of Coulson's S.H.I.E.L.D. colleagues. The story concludes with Coulson's online profile, including his 100K+ posts and the final two lines: "**User since:** June 1998; **Last post:** May 3, 2012."

While the story may be about Phil Coulson's death and mourning by his online friends, it clearly taps into shared online fan experiences. The beginning check-in is a common enough occurrence whenever a disaster strikes. Given the ability of Internet communities to draw from widespread geographic locations, friends may be anywhere on the globe and a bombing in London, an earthquake in California, a tsunami in Japan may affect us equally because there are friends who live there. Louisa Stein (2002), for example, observed *Roswell* fan communities to discuss this phenomenon after 9/11, and describes how "*Roswell* fans drew on pre-existing online fan forums and on repertoires from *Roswell* fandom to mourn, to cope, to give support, to debate, to question and to organize community social action" (p. 478).

On a more personal level, the story resonates with fan experiences of losing loved online friends and often feeling helpless by not being there, challenging in particular the oft-repeated false dichotomy between online and real lives and friends. The immediate outpouring of grief and love after a fan passes is always staggering, and the last lines of the story recall the possibility of LiveJournals to be given Memorial status, which will preserve a journal and protect it from deletion. Often fans will get together to donate to a cause important to the deceased, rescue her fan works, or create fannish scholarships in her name. One reader addresses the actual get-together in the story as well as the commemorative letters in particular when friendships are created at a distance: "I think sometimes that distance helps those that have trouble connecting up close make real relationships for the first time. This is a very sweet piece about honoring someone's memory, both Phil's and Captain America's, and not just using words, but also actions to do it" (Basaltone AO3, October 22, 2013).[2]

Readers clearly responded to this parallel. Throughout, commenters referenced specific friends they had lost and their collective mourning. One reader describes how the story captures "how someone you've never met in person can be someone you care about so deeply and touch your life so thoroughly and the rest of the world can have difficulty understanding that" (daisydiversion AO3, October 25, 2013); while another explains "This fic is devastating for anyone who's ever been part of a close-knit fandom community or had friends they've never met online: the fear, the grief, the horrible separation of those experiencing Coulson's death from afar just hits so close to home" (emilianadarling AO3, November 4, 2013). Many comments praise the story for being gorgeous and beautiful if heartbreaking, and nearly every one mentions tears and crying.

Readers thank rageprufrock for relaying this experience and capturing these feelings via Coulson and these original fictional characters. Because while the story may be set in the Marvel Cinematic Universe, it ultimately is about the original characters: fans who work for big tech companies and universities, who change their babies' diapers, and who have gay partners tolerating their odd online hobbies and friends. Caltha accurately describes:

> I love that this isn't about the Avengers, not really.... It's about Coulson, and a bunch of people who cared about him, and about the community they'd built, and about a world where attacks like these are a little more common and the fannish infrastructure has adjusted a little in response. (Caltha AO3, October 22, 2013)

"User Since" may draw out most clearly the parallel between fanboy!Coulson and online fan communities, but "Fanboy Phil Coulson" is a tag on dozens of fan works at the Archive of Our Own, and many more employ the trope without necessarily tagging it.

Making them us: Fandom as storyverse

Even when the canon does not offer a ready-made stand-in for fans, writers will create stories in which they recast the main characters as media fans themselves. This "they are fans" trope effectively inverts the Mary Sue self-insertion: rather than projecting fans into the fictional world of the show, the stories take the source text's protagonists and directly immerses them in the fannish world. Some "they are fans" stories use random canon references to seamlessly extrapolate the show characters as also being fan fiction fans. Especially in Real People Fiction, the film, music, or sports star may find fan fiction about their friends and begins shipping them. More often, however, the story functions fully as an alternate universe, where the characters do not occupy their canon roles. The main pairing thus becomes an easy stand-in to explore and expose the intricacies of being an online fan, drawing much of its action from familiar interactions and drama.

In the popular anonymous *Merlin* (BBC 2008–2012) story, "Pairing Pendragon/ Merlin" (merlinkinkmeme LJ, January 19, 2011), Merlin Emrys and Arthur Pendragon are two British media fans of the show *Merlin*, who end up in a beta relationship and after slowly flirting online finally meet at a con and fall in love. While Arthur is a Big Name Fan, Merlin represents the more common anxieties and excitements that fan writers report again and again as they worry about popularity of their fan works and try to negotiate the complex social hierarchies of online fandoms. While each specific fandom may have its own idiosyncrasies and popularity and fame are usually relative and fleeting, the underlying emotions are often quite similar among different fan communities. "Pairing Pendragon/Merlin" expertly describes the anxieties, hopes, and desires of the social interactions with strangers online where a few random feedback comments and a beta request leads to long hours of instant messaging, a crush on an online friend's erotic writings, and an eventual meet-up that leads to a relationship.

The fact that the story was created as a Work in Progress on an anon meme increased the sense of parallelism between fans within and without the story. In feedback and recommendations alike fans repeatedly foregrounded the way the story mimics the interactive aspects of online communication and how it effectively fictionalized their own experiences. In particular, the form of multimedia rings true to many fans for whom social media networks are their central mode of fannish interactions: "I liked how a lot of the story is told through IM, lj posts and google docs, and it really gives the feel of being in fandom for me" (epic-recs LJ, October 11, 2011). Fan writer Pandarus captures the emotional resonance that the story quite clearly generated when she describes:

> It's terribly disarming, with its sense of fannish squee, and euphoria, and the whole hothouse atmosphere of fandom. Who hasn't been over the moon when a writer or artist they admire says something nice to them? This is a fic about that whole starstruck sensation, and about the ridiculousness of fannish prestige and hierarchy, and about the contrast between fandom and RL. (Pandarus LJ, January 18, 2011)

All of these are fannish interactions that occur regularly within slash spaces in particular, which bring together a shared passion for the source text, the intense intimacy of online social platforms, often strongly erotic writing, and a large number of queer women. The story thus enacts the realities of fan experiences and fan interactions from the erotic interaction between readers and writers (Lackner, Lucas, and Reid 2006), the performativity of online sexuality and sexual identity (Busse 2006), and the real sexual engagements that often follow (Lothian, Busse, and Reid 2007). BBC *Merlin* is, in fact, a particularly fertile canon source, because it features a narrative that already exist in dozens of literary versions, from Goffrey of Monmouth and Sir Thomas Mallory to

Mark Twain, T.H. White, and Marion Zimmer Bradley, adapted into many more TV and film versions. Likewise, Sir Arthur Conan Doyle's Victorian detective Sherlock Holmes is often considered to have spawned the first fandom, but most recently, it has generated an immense fandom in the Moffat/Gatiss BBC version *Sherlock* (BBC 2010–). The existence of multitudes of stories allows readers to not only pick their own versions to shape and alter, but also grants implicit permission to do so.

One popular story in *Sherlock* is "The Theory of Narrative Causality" (falling_voices LJ, July 31, 2011), which places Sherlock and Watson as media fans who are paired in a Big Bang, a collaborative exercise where artist and writer work together on a project. Like with Merlin, Sherlock lends itself to the conceit of both men being in their own fandom, so to speak, and the story they create, it turns out, happens to be the plot of the BBC series, a present-day AU to the Victorian detective series. In her book *Fic: Why Fanfiction Is Taking Over the World*, Anne Jamison (2013a) uses the story as a metonymy not only for fan fiction but for its show as well. After all, *Sherlock* itself is effectively a contemporary Alternate Universe of Sir Arthur Conan Doyle's stories, which creates a weird recursivity that Jamison foregrounds when she describes how "Theory" is "a fanfiction about fanboys writing fanfiction, and the fanfiction they write closely resembles the fanboy-penned (legal, professional) fanfiction of a television show that 'Theory' is fic for" (2013b, 11). What neither Jamison nor the story address is the way in which the BBC show and its creators engage in fan fictional pursuits yet also generate a level of authority not permitted the fan writers.

In contrast to Jamison's celebration of how the multifaceted narrative mirrors the actual show's online presence, some have criticized *Sherlock* for the way it distinguishes the fan fictional pursuits of its (male) authorial team from its (primarily female and heavily affective) fan fiction fandom. Matt Hills (2012b) argues that the "great game of fandom played via the production discourses of Gatiss and Moffat remains, finally, in the service of professional, authorial distinctions, while textually-disciplined codings of affectively flat fandom imply that fan passions should be kept under masculinized control" (p. 40). It might not be coincidental that both "Pairing Merlin/Pendragon" and "The Theory of Narrative Causality" feature male characters and pairings as stand-ins for female fandom. Slash theory, both within fandom and academia, cites many reasons as to why a primarily female viewership identifies with male characters, ranging from the more readily available complex male characters with often already existing male/male homosocial friendships and the ability to represent truly equal power relations to an identification with and desire for both protagonists by straight and bi women and the emotionally safe territory of unmarked bodies.

Mary Sue: Fan fiction par excellence

Given the variety of self-insertions, the continuous derision of Mary Sue stories may be surprising; however, popularity and general disdain are not mutually exclusive. Much fan fiction that could be labeled as Mary Sue fiction is repeatedly read, clearly beloved, and heavily commented upon. As long as the stories and its protagonists are not called

Mary Sues, various self-insert fiction remains ever popular. After all, the concept of personal and often quite specific head canons is more popular than ever and kink memes and Tumblr collaborative challenges often tailor to very specific and personal desires, clearly indicating the desire for finely tuned characterizations that often share important aspects with readers and/or writers.

Because for all the ways in which fiction can expose us to new ideas, beliefs, and worlds, there is comfort in familiarity, and self-inserts of the various sorts I've discussed allow readers easy entry and access to the narratives. Whether writers pick a canon character or create their own, whether they shape the characters or the worlds around them, the ultimate desire underlying all these self-insertions remains attempts to merge our own lives with that of the fictional universes, to address our own experiences and emotions within the worlds of our favorite texts. Moreover, by connecting the canon worlds with our own lives, fan writers often can address current and personal issues through their writings. And it is this resonance with current affairs and personal concerns that make fan writing an important but ultimately very intimate and specialized form of writing.

Mary Sue fiction at its extreme may only appeal to its author, but that it is also one of fan fiction's central virtues. While some stories appeal to many fans of a franchise or even cross-fannish boundaries in their readership, at heart fan fiction is a labor of love with an often understood small audience. In fact, one of the biggest fanfic exchanges, the yearly small fandom exchange Yuletide focuses specifically on smaller fandoms, unusual pairings, and the willingness of fans to gift its recipients the very story that they—and at times only they—always wanted to read. Likewise, when we look at kink fiction, it is obvious to its fans (and its nonfans alike) that a particular story may only appeal to a minuscule subset of the show's fandom, and yet it is all the more cherished for its fringe status.

Rather than focus on the failure of Mary Sue stories, we might more usefully behold its identifying feature of very particular and specific personalization as a characterizing feature of fan fiction. In other words, where critics of Mary Sue writing condemn its singular focus on the writer's specific identificatory desires that excludes other readers, we could simply understand that as a more extreme, less successful variant of what defines most fan fiction, if not fiction: the ability of the writer to translate their own fears and hopes, disgusts, and desires onto the fictional characters in order to share them with others.

Notes

1   I do not link fan works and commentary directly, but instead reference parenthetically with name, site, and date. Sites include Livejournal (LJ), Dreamwidth (DW), and Archive of Our Own (AO3).
2   This and the following quotes are comments to "User Since" and can be accessed on AO3, where the story is archived.

16

The Digital Literary Fangirl Network: Representing Fannishness in the Transmedia Web Series

Louisa Stein

The 2010s brought to YouTube a new genre of web series: the vlog-style literary adaptation. The Emmy award winning *The Lizzie Bennet Diaries* (2012–2013), *The New Adventures of Peter and Wendy*, *The Autobiography of Jane Eyre*, and *Frankenstein MD* (to name just a few) adapt classic works of literature to web series, and more specifically transform famed female literary figures into active participants in online fan culture.[1] From Lizzie Bennet to Wendy Darling to Jane Eyre to (the gender switched) Victoria Frankenstein, a host of female narrators tell the stories of their lives, and in so doing retell literary classics from a first-person perspective, adapted to present day. As they share their lives through the platforms of contemporary digital culture, Lizzie, Jane et al. participate in the online spaces of fandom, engaging with their own fans and declaring their fannish interests in other media texts. A far cry from the more ambivalent portrayal of fans in television series such as *Buffy the Vampire Slayer* and *Supernatural*, which often portray fans as obsessive and unbalanced, these web series transform iconic female characters into fangirls to lend relatability to the characters and verisimilitude to the series' narratives. The series also plant references to fandom and to a multitude of fan-favored texts throughout their episodes, signaling to viewers that not only do the fictional characters participate in fandom, but so do the creators who make the web series. Literary vlog-style web series offer a new spin on fan-representation: their lead characters are active participants in digital culture, with fannishness depicted as a necessary part of that participation.

Official representations of fans often strive to delimit and mold the proper industrial vision of fandom (Busse 2013a). To a certain extent, these limits are still in place in web series representations of fandom; most (although not all) of the fans represented in and narrating these series are middle class and white, and perform cisnormative gender roles. Yet these series do celebrate fangirls' affective participation in the queer collective communities of fandom and foster such communities for their own fandoms. Literary vlog-style web series like *The New Adventures of Peter and Wendy* and *The Autobiography of Jane Eyre* represent their characters as fans to signpost affiliation with desired audiences, and also to lend their characters a sense of authenticity. In addition, web series creators also represent themselves as fans to create relatable self-brands and to extend those brands to their production companies and multichannel networks. In turn, fans of these series welcome (or claim) their beloved characters and series' creators as fellow fans, and in so doing represent their own fannishness in series comments and Twitter conversations. Media fandom becomes a thread that links together web series producers, audiences, and viewers, in collective performance of fannishness and of collaborative community.

Courting and importing fans in participatory culture

The digital landscape has led to what both fans and broadcast media producers perceive as a heightened feedback loop, with the labor and perspectives of media producers seemingly available to fans and the labor and perspectives of fans seemingly available to producers. Moreover, both fans and producers are (often reluctantly) dependent on one another and aware of this dependence. They are also aware of their differing investments in the media texts in question. As others within this volume address, this has led to some ambivalent or downright negative depictions of fandom, for example in the TV series *Supernatural* and *Sherlock* (see Chapters 11 and 13). These ambivalent representations expose the fraught relationship between those producing broadcast or cable media within legacy models of media production and those producing for distribution within participatory digital culture. This latter category includes not only fans creating fan works, but also actors and independent producers experimenting with new forms of digital media entertainment for online communities, including web series. It also includes legacy media's attempts to harness the energies of digital culture for monetization and to gain control of digital audience culture (Russo 2009; Scott 2009).

Within the increasingly decentered landscape of participatory culture, the figure of the fan, rather than being reviled, comes to the fore as an ideal cultural participant, one who merges cultural engagement with community participation, readership with authorship, and emotional investment with critical literacy. Moreover, as digital media producers seek to find new and dependable modes of production and distribution, fandom's dedication offers the promise of a faithful audience, one that not only will view but also will serve as brand ambassador and will spend money to support productions that they are invested in.

The web series on YouTube is a rapidly evolving form that cultivates fandoms of the sort that form around TV series, but can cater to their niche interests and invite their productive response in more direct ways than can TV series. Independently produced web series, or web series produced by small production companies like *The Lizzie Bennet Diaries*' Pemberley Digital, seek smaller active audiences rather than the breadth of broadcast audiences needed to keep a TV series from being cancelled. Most web series' business models depend on crowd-sourced funding (using tools such as Kickstarter and Indiegogo) to gather individual contributions from fans, and also experiment with advertising sponsorships directed at niche markets (Chin et al. 2014; Scott 2015; Booth 2015a). In part because of this more direct relationship of financial support from fans, the mixed feelings that mark television's courting of fandom is for the most part absent in web series representations. Instead, web series court and celebrate fans in multiple ways. As we will see, they embed multifannish cues to hail fans of other media (especially TV) to become fans of a web series. They depict characters as participants in a range of fandoms and in millennial fan culture more broadly. Because these web series are often transmedia, story extensions amount to characters participating in existing fan cultures and digital interfaces—that is, Lydia Bennet, Jane Eyre, and many others not only vlog, but also tumbl, tweet, instagram, and pin. Their posts appear on social networking feeds alongside the posts of nonfictional participants who use the sites to represent their own lives and to share their fan works.

On top of this, web series creators and actors also represent themselves as participants in fandom, as they post on the same interfaces as the fans and characters, again in the form of vlogs, Tumblr posts, tweets, and pins. Their posts too appear on dashboards and feeds along with fan work, viewer's self-representation, and the posts of fictional characters. The actors and creators of these web series author their own engagement with culture, their own fannishness, and their own processes of productive labor, and in so doing fostering a sense of intimacy with and among the fans of their series (Marwick and boyd 2010b; Bennett 2013b). Thus web series characters, creators, and viewers all to different degrees represent themselves as participants in online communities, colored as they are by media fandom.

Lizzie Bennet and the fan(girl) network

The Lizzie Bennet Diaries (2012–2013) adapts Jane Austen's *Pride and Prejudice* to contemporary media culture. In so doing, the series transforms Lizzie Bennet and her sisters into participants in online culture and fandom: Lizzie's outspoken personality finds new outlet in her video blog (vlog) on YouTube, and sisters Lydia and Jane post on YouTube, Tumblr, and Pinterest.[2] *The Lizzie Bennet Diaries* is striking for its depiction of female transmedia authorship online. Elsewhere I have written about Lydia's significance as celebratory embodiment of the "culture of feels"; Lydia performs unabashed emotion in her own supplementary YouTube vlogs, and where in *Pride and Prejudice* Lydia is not usually understood as a sympathetic character, fans of *The Lizzie Bennet Diaries* celebrate Lydia's braveness in being herself and not hiding her emotion.

By celebrating Lydia's affect, *The Lizzie Bennet Diaries* addresses and undermines the long-standing gendered stereotype of the overly emotional, incoherent fangirl. Negative depictions of fans often feature either the excessive emotion of fangirls or the taboo feminized masculinity of fanboys. Depictions of fans and fannishness in web series tend to move away from these negatively gendered stereotypes, in part because their authors include self-professed fangirls and fanboys (Busse 2013a; Scott 2013b). While film and television production are still dominated by male producers, the digital landscape of web series means that more young women can be audiovisual authors, depicting their own creative visions in close to the same medium as TV and film, and creating representations that undermine and reject gendered stereotypes. Many of these web series are indeed created and produced by young women.[3] More broadly, because fan (and fangirl) audiences are seen as the lifeblood of web series, web series' representations of fans, fannishness, and fandom move beyond (and sometimes tackle and dismantle outright) gender taboos. As a result, what has emerged is a network of representations of articulate, impassioned self-authoring fictional fangirls who retell their own embodiment of classic literature to viewers who respond in kind. Moreover, by depicting these characters as fans, these web series take female figures that were limited to the private sphere and recast them as public figures speaking in and for a culture that insistently undermines long-standing divides between intimate and public, individual and collective.

Writing in 2006 (i.e., right around the advent of YouTube), Mary Celeste Kearney (2006) argued that the contemporaneous generation of young women, rather than being "restricted to writing and the domestic arts," were using a wide range of media "to express themselves, explore their identities, and connect with others" (p. 3). Part of the significance of this shift, as Kearney put it, was that "girl-made cultural texts" now circulate beyond the domestic spaces of girls' bedroom cultures and private circles (p. 3). These works are also significant in the way their content fights back against gendered tropes; according to Kearney, many girls make media that specifically demonstrate "their resistance to, if not refusal of, the traditional ideologies of gender and generation" (p. 3). Before the coming of YouTube and online fan cultures, fan video production (as well as fan authorship more broadly) already functioned as a collective process practiced by specific communities of young and adult women who together reworked popular media to better articulate their visions and desires (Lothian et al. 2007; Coppa 2011). Digital technologies and cultures made such collective fan processes more widespread and moved them into (online) public spaces where more viewers could access them, contribute, and participate in the fan community, celebrating its sense of collective growth. The digital literary fangirl network—including fictional characters and their fans and creators—represents a coming together of these two evolving traditions of female authorship, significant for the media they produce and for the networks they create.

From this light, *The Lizzie Bennet Diaries* is significant because it depicts Lizzie Bennet as a vocal author, producing and sharing her narrative with an audience of friends and fans. But it is also significant because it offers a multiplicity of vlogging voices, of digitally armed young women connected together in a network. Not only Lizzie, but also her best friend Charlotte Lu, her sister Lydia Bennet, and latecomer to the narrative Gigi Darcy—each of these represents a different variation of a the "girl vlogger" trope. Lizzie is sardonic and smart, a graduate student in Communications with a critical mind and a ready wit who shares her professional and personal story on YouTube. Charlotte edits Lizzie's videos and (sometimes reluctantly) shares the screen with her; Charlotte is depicted as technologically savvy and professionally driven. Lydia is unabashedly emotional, a performer of millennial feels who ruptures cultural assumptions about proper femininity in her buoyant vlogs. Gigi deploys and experiments with vlogging technology; she is the face, voice, and test user of a (fictional) vlogging app, Domino, which she uses for her vlog posts (Klose 2013, 50).[4] Each of these characters is significant as an individual representation of a young woman wielding technology to write her own self-representation and to connect with others. But they're also significant as a networked collective. Thus, *The Lizzie Bennet Diaries* not only reframes Jane Austen's *Pride and Prejudice* as a story of contemporary female digital experience and authorship, but it depicts both as multiple, varied, and interdependent. Many viewers laud this multiplicity and collectivity as central to their appreciation of *The Lizzie Bennet Diaries*.

Beyond Lizzie Bennett: Fandom as cultural connector

The Lizzie Bennet Diaries' authoring collective expanded from its core focus on Lizzie and her sisters to include more minor characters and also the series' (imagined) audience.[5] The authoring collective included the audience that interacted in comments to the characters, sometimes posing themselves in-world, sometimes out-of-world, offering advice and support to characters or praise, critique, and questions to series producers. Actors and producers also participated in this networked collective, commenting, vlogging, tumbling, and tweeting, highlighting their own labor as media producers, and their own status as fans, within the larger networks of millennial fan cultures.[6]

Although there were limits to the impact fans could have on *The Lizzie Bennet Diaries* narrative, nonetheless, *The Lizzie Bennet Diaries* cultivated a sense of culture shared between character, creator, and viewer (Seymour et al. 2015). In turn, the series inspired many emulators, on a spectrum from independent and fan-created to more professional with commercial intent. *The Lizzie Bennet Diaries'* production company, Pemberley Digital, went on to adapt *Welcome to Sanditon*, *Emma Approved*, and *Frankenstein MD* (coproduced with PBS Studios). In addition, fans, independent producers, and college students have created literary adaptation series including *Autobiography of Jane Eyre*, *Carmilla*, *Classic Alice*, *Green Gable Fables*, *In Earnest*, *Jules and Monty*, *March Family Letters*, *From Mansfield with Love*, *The Misselthwaite Archives*, *The New Adventures of Peter and Wendy*, *Nothing Much to Do*, and *A Tell Tale Vlog*. All of these feature female lead characters who use digital media to (fictionally) author themselves and to interact with each other and their viewers in shared transmedia landscapes. Starting with *The Lizzie Bennet Diaries* and spiraling outward, a plurality of fictional vlogging girls model digital skill, fannish investment, and self-authorship online. As the characters use the same platforms that their viewers and producers use for self-expression and cultural engagement—YouTube, Tumblr, Twitter, Instagram, Pinterest—these platforms create a sort of cross-platform cross-reality intertextuality. On this shared interface, fandom serves as the cultural thread that weaves participants together.

Not all of the representations of participatory networked culture in web series feature media fandom in the strictest sense; these series depict and create a millennial cultural engagement shared by creators, characters, and viewers in which fandom is one dimension. Rather than silo or marginalize fandom, this multiplicity serves to weave fandom into a larger multifannish cultural mode of experience and larger cultural network. Thus the fangirls featured in these web series are not necessarily singular fans of particular media texts—indeed, sometimes we only see hints of their fannishness— in their clothes, in their dishware, in the posters on the wall. In other cases, they quote fan-favored media or use their Tumblrs to locate themselves within digital multifannish culture. Web series reference to fannishness occurs in varying degrees, but in each case it amounts to a fostering of affiliation between web series viewer and fictional vlogger. For example, the web series *Green Gables Fables* transforms Anne Shirley's (of L.M. Montgomery's *Anne of Green Gables*) famed effervescence into fannish engagement with Tumblr culture; it's not so much that Anne is depicted as a fan of a particular media text as that she models fannishness as a life stance.

Paul Booth (2010) writes that fannishness is something "we can all relate to" (p. 17). In the literary web series examined here, fandom becomes shorthand for the characters' seeming claim on the authentic and the real, embedding them in the lived experienced and mediated culture of their viewers. These series pose their lead characters—and their actors and creators—as participants in the same cultures by posing them as fans. Moreover, these fictional vloggers do not just share the position of fan, but more specifically, of fans as authors, if not of fan fiction and art then of their own narratives of self. Lizzie, Lydia, Jane, Anne, and Wendy are all (represented as) digital authors who work with and remix media culture to represent themselves.

On top of this, the creators and actors in these many web series also represent themselves as authoring participants in fandom, as they post on the same interfaces as the fans and characters. They have their own Tumblrs and Twitters not unlike Jane and Anne's, and not unlike their viewers. Their posts also appear on dashboards and feeds along with fan work, viewer's self-representation, and the posts of fictional characters. The actors and creators of these web series author their own engagement with culture, their own fannishness, and their own processes of labor in the production of the series. They interact with one another across series, and with their fans, forming a larger sense of an intertextual producing community.[7]

Fan address as niche audience building

Web series use fan representations to reach out to niche fan audiences in a range of ways: transmedia extensions are often situated within fan spaces in the form of characters' social networking accounts; creators embed fannish references in web series episodes via set dressing, dialogue, and by depicting characters as fans; series cast actors familiar from other fan-favored web and even TV series; producers announce and perform their fandom in comments or in their own online presences; sponsorship and affiliated advertising or funding campaigns affiliate a series with fan/geek media culture; and a particular fan/geek ethos can characterize the brand of a web channel or multichannel network on YouTube, including its sponsorship and affiliated advertising (Hills 2012b; Scott 2012b).[8]

Early episodes are especially key for signposting fannishness to viewers in order to spread buzz and bring in audiences for past and future installments. Within the often quite short prologues, teasers, and opening episodes, web series embed multiple references to similar web series and also reference television series popular among fans. For example, the opening episode of vampire/mystery web series *Carmilla* features main character Laura clutching her *Doctor Who* Tardis mug as she narrates the strange occurrences at Silas University to her viewers. She name-drops Veronica Mars within the first five minutes of the series and also quotes *Buffy the Vampire Slayer*, thus shouting out to various televisual fan communities and vampire fandoms who could be imported into *Carmilla* fandom. The series continues to build in references to main character Laura as Veronica Mars (and as a *Veronica Mars* fan), and also continually invokes fan favorite series *Buffy*, *Xena*, *Game of Thrones*, among others, suggesting that the *Carmilla* characters are fans of these series as well.

Likewise, *The New Adventures of Peter and Wendy*'s first episode features vlogger Wendy Darling pretending to be her mother in a hat, scarf, and glasses in an homage to Lizzie Bennet's similar performance of her mother in her first vlog;[9] it also features Wendy wearing a *Doctor Who* t-shirt with a Dalek positioned in the background. *The New Adventures of Peter and Wendy* has continued with its cross-fan address through casting, with the season two featuring fan-favored TV actors Jim Beaver (of *Supernatural*, *Deadwood*, among others) as Mr. Darling and Percy Daggs Jr. (Wallace of *Veronica Mars*) as Captain Hook, as well as YouTube lifestyle vlogger Strawburry17 as pirate Billy Jukes.

In the opening episode of *The Autobiography of Jane Eyre*, Jane positions herself as a *Lizzie Bennet Diaries* fan and as a participant in literary fandom and in Tumblr and YouTube culture. In her opening video, entitled "This Is Me, an Introduction," Jane introduces her viewers to herself through images of the various things that she surrounds herself with, including the books, tea, and *The Lizzie Bennet Diaries*. We see *The Lizzie Bennet Diaries* playing on her computer, as Jane says:

> I watch the Lizzie Bennet Diaries, and laugh, and cry, and then I spend a lot of time sitting around wishing I was her. I mean, not just because she's surrounded by extremely attractive men, and because her hair, and let's be honest, the hair of everyone around her is flawless, but because she's brave, and I don't think she even knows it.

This moment positions Jane as a fan of *The Lizzie Bennet Diaries* and spells out the motivations and pleasures behind her fandom. The episode integrates her fandom within its larger depiction of Jane as millennial cultural participant. "I spend a lot of time on Tumblr," she says, as we see her scrolling through Tumblr, although the images aren't fannish but rather of natural landscapes. As she says "Mostly I own books," the camera pans, hand held, across her book collection scattered on her floor, which includes more than one volume of *Harry Potter*, as well as *The Fault Is in Our Stars*, *Lemony Snicket*, Margaret Atwood, Shakespeare, among others. In addition to these overt references, creator/actor Alysson Hall has said (in YouTube comments on the video) that the opening video was based on a "Self Image 2013" video trend, in which vloggers spoke about themselves, layering on a soundtrack, while showing images of their living space and the things they love.[10] Thus this opening episode signposts Jane's fannishness and also situates her within the larger cultural conversations taking place on Tumblr and YouTube.

Viewers pick up on all of these references and share their appreciation for them in the comments. In so doing, they also perform their own fan allegiance and thus represent themselves as fans to the series' creators and to each other. For example, the first episode of *The New Adventures of Peter and Wendy* (which included allusions to *Doctor Who* and *The Lizzie Bennet Diaries*) received comments such as:

- DR WHO SHIRT!
- Dalek!!!! You put a Dalek!!!! That's so whovian wooooow
- I recently binge watched The Lizzie Bennet Diaries, got caught up with Emma Approved, and started The New Adventures of Peter and Wendy. Any of you ladies fans of these shows? I'm completely obsessed.
- I've finished The Lizzie Bennet Diaries and Emma Approved and just started this. Because of the Doctor Who reference though… I already love it!!!!

These comments celebrate the inclusion of multifannish references, affirming the connection between *The New Adventures of Peter and Wendy* and *The Lizzie Bennet Diaries* and to *Doctor Who*/cult television.

Viewers of *The Autobiography of Jane Eyre* similarly highlight in their comments the series' various cultural and fannish references. For example, one commenter shares her love of tea and her appreciation of the books on Jane's shelf, while another claims Jane as a "Potterhead" and "Nerdfighter." Another fan comments, "I hope Hank Green (coproducer of Lizzie Bennet) sees this. He has started something," positioning *Autobiography of Jane Eyre* as inheritor of *The Lizzie Bennet Diaries*' legacy.

In such comments, fannishness emerges as a thread that connects viewers and producers. Fan declarations offer opportunities for producers to dialogue with their viewers in the shared role of fans. For example, in the episode of *The New Adventures of Peter and Wendy* introducing *Supernatural*'s Jim Beaver as Mr. Darling, fans pointed out what they saw as many *Supernatural* references. In return series' creator Shawn DeLoache commented confirming each reference, declaring his own status as a *Supernatural* fan. This back and forth demonstrates the way in which the performance of fannishness serves as connective thread binding producer and fan, creating a sense of shared community and cultural outlook.

Fannishness as commodification and critique

One key way in which web series signpost character and series fannish associations is through fashion and set dressing. This commodified fan reference can be folded into efforts toward funding and sponsorship. For example, *The New Adventures of Peter and Wendy* appeals to commodified geek and fan culture through brand affiliation with online youth fashion marketplace ModCloth and "monthly geek and gamer subscription box" LootCrate. Episode posts on YouTube include links to "Our hip clothing sponsor: ModCloth" and "The geeky set dressing sponsor: LootCrate." While neither ModCloth nor LootCrate are specific to particular fandoms, both foster a sense of multifannish pop cultural identity that bolsters the web series' fan/geek ethos. In addition, *The New Adventures of Peter and Wendy* produced LootCrate unboxing videos both with the series actors and with the series' characters, infusing all dimensions of the series and brand with its LootCrate sponsorship while also emulating the YouTube DIY video "unboxing" genre.[11]

Fans are often wary of commodified fannishness, deeming fandom for profit inauthentic (Stanfill and Condis 2014; Busse 2015, 11). But this taboo against monetization has begun to shift in small degrees within the seemingly decentered creative spaces of digital culture (De Kosnik 2009; Noppe 2011). *The New Adventures of Peter and Wendy* addresses fans positively as a perceived market capable of funding new modes of production, and in turn many of the series' fans celebrate their participation in a fan commodity market as a way to support their favorite series (Scott 2012b; Kohnen 2014). *Peter and Wendy*'s multifannish and geek commodity culture approach did not prevent and indeed perhaps contributed to the series' successful fundraising endeavors, which increased multifold (raising 900 percent more funding) from the first season Kickstarter campaign to the second season Indiegogo campaign.[12] Likewise, lesbian-vampire-mystery romance web series *Carmilla* incorporated overt sponsorship from Kotex, which included making "public service announcements" in which characters shared the history of menstruation (including vampire menstruation), thus weaving in the series' commercial sponsorship with its feminist politics and its supernatural genre play. In the comments, fans thanked Kotex for sponsoring *Carmilla* and spontaneously included the hashtag #ubykotex in their comments, for example:

- I love this PSA!… Thank you to U by Kotex! Please give us Carmilla Season 2 and more period PSAs! #SaveCarmilla
- I would sell half my soul to #ubykotex to get more of these videos. I already use their products so it just makes me that much happier to know that they sponsor one of the greatest shows in my life!! #carmillapocalypse

While the Kotex affiliation in these *Carmilla* extras wasn't in itself a fannish one, fan responses allowed fans to perform their fannishness as a form of targeted consumer power (Jenkins 2012a; Savage 2014). Some fans did critique Kotex as a company or the pseudo-PSA spots as awkward commercials compromising the series' integrity, but the overarching reception of the Kotex PSAs was positive and spun into the now familiar "save our show" framework, with the #savecarmilla hashtag deployed to support the series and its Kotex sponsorship.

Fan self-representation through critique

Fans may not critique the commodification of fan and geek preferences within the more intimate sphere of a well-orchestrated YouTube series, but they are likely to critique the web series' adaptation of beloved texts. While some fans come to a literary adaptation web series without prior knowledge of its source text, many are already familiar with and invested in the literary original. Indeed, in their comments, many fans position themselves as experts on the literary source text being adapted. Fans assert their knowledge of the source text, of production processes, of narrative structure, of genre tropes, of product placement, and a whole host of other elements that characterize the digital space over which fans feel they share authority with producers.

These articulations of invested fan expertise at times result in performative struggles for authority within the sphere of the web series. However, they can also serve as thread binding fans and producers into a perceived shared community. The synthesis of producers and fans into a community bound by shared fannishness is not always a frictionless union, but rather an unstable but dynamic one, bound by performances of authority, expertise, and media literacy. This came to the fore in *The Autobiography of Jane Eyre*, when the actor who played Jane's main love interest, Rochester, left the show near the end of its production. Fans channeled their disappointment into expertise-fueled critique. The second to last video—the long awaited reunion between Jane and Rochester—was shot with a newly cast actor playing Rochester in such a way that viewers would not see his face or hear his voice. This choice denied viewers the intimacy otherwise cultivated by the series, and by the vlogging-style web series genre in general. Fans watched Jane and Rochester unite at a distance, in the background of a long shot, their two-minute conversation an inaudible mumble.

Fans criticized this episode quite harshly, even after series creator Nessa Aref explained on Tumblr the unfortunate production issues that led to the recasting.[13] Some fans called the refusal to depict the reunion a betrayal of character and narrative, and of the literary original.[14] Others offered critique based on their sense of what web series should offer, and the contract between a web series and its audience. However, others expressed their sympathy for the producers, emphasizing their knowledge of the issues facing web series producers rather than their knowledge of *Jane Eyre*. Still others celebrated the ending for what they saw as its canonically appropriate and/ or feminist focus on Jane and her character's growth and journey, rather than on the romance between Jane and Rochester. All of these critical responses (in the broader sense of the term) emerge from the web series' shared transmedia landscape and the sense of shared fan expertise and authority it fosters. Fans perform their cultural and media literacy and speak with intimate knowledge of the narratives being adapted and of the modes of media production deployed in those adaptations.

Indeed, web series viewers' self-representation as fans complicate any perceived simple unity between producer and fan of web series. The celebration of media literacy inherent in these series empowers fans to critique and assert their own authority. Likewise, producers' performance of fannishness as well as professionalism often means they respond in kind. These moments of open critique and dialogue, fueled by shared expertise, underpin successful new transmedia communities of authorship. While web series fans may be critical of the producers and vice versa, in the larger scheme of things they align themselves as participants in a shared digital network that fosters creativity, reflection, analysis, and critique, and thus media literacy.

Conclusion

In the literary adaptation web series examined here, representations of fannishness hold weight; they serve as invitation for audiences to migrate from television to YouTube viewing, and as route to integrate product sponsorship and crowd-sourced funding in ways that feel organic and authentic rather than intrusive. Fan representations help create imagined communities of viewer, text/character, and producer bound by fannishness and fan identity into evolving independent and commercial media structures.

The literary web series as a genre, form, and commercial structure is in its infancy. While some literary web series are created by fans for fans, others exist in an in-between state of independent production aspiring to be commercial production or commercial production aspiring to have an independent, "authentic" feel. It remains to be seen whether these series will flourish as commercial endeavors, perhaps dominated by legacy media, or as the domain of fan and small independent productions, or some combination of both. At the moment, the literary adaptation web series offers experimental ground where fan, independent, and commercial productions meet and experiment with evolving interdependent relationships.

Notes

1 This essay is part of a larger project on literary web series in which I examine these seventeen series. At the time of data gathering (May 2015) breakout success, *Carmilla* had received over 6 million views, and combined views for the series examined in this study equaled approximately 15.7 million.

2 Lydia also has her own YouTube channel with supplementary episodes that many hail as the heart of the series (Stein 2015).

3 *Green Gables Fables* is created by Marie Trotter, Alicia Whitson, and Mandy Harmon, *Carmilla* by Jordan Hall and Ellen Simpson, and *The Autobiography of Jane Eyre* by Allyson Hall and Nessa Aref, to name only a few of the many women working on these literary web series in all levels of production.

4 The fictional "Domino" becomes the medium of narration and communication in the *Lizzie Bennet Diaries* spinoff, *Welcome to Sanditon*. http://www.pemberleydigital.com/welcome-to-sanditon/ (accessed July 6, 2015) (Klose 2013).

5 For example, fans were invited to pretend to apply to work with the in-story fictional "Better Living with Collins and Collins" by creating parody instructional videos. https://www.youtube.com/playlist?list=PL-kgvWgodA8ZQKIDd62w04VJ27IhT9bkC (accessed July 6, 2015).

6   Coproducer Bernie Su shared his perspectives on the production process on his Tumblr account. Coproducer Hank Green was well known as one half of the thevlogbrothers and as co-creator of the expansive fan culture community, Nerdighteria. Stars Mary Kate Wiles (Lydia) and Ashley Clements (Lizzie) participate actively in Tumblr culture, and Mary Kate Wiles also began vlogging toward the close of *The Lizzie Bennet Diaries.*

7   For an example of cross-series interactions, see https://www.youtube.com/ watch?v=s4JQivBfGn8 (accessed July 6, 2015).

8   While producers of film and television also increasingly position themselves as fans, this fan affiliation is more accentuated in communities of all digital/online production, distribution, and reception.

9   It is left open to interpretation whether this is a subtle nod on the part of the Peter and Wendy producers to fans, or if Wendy Darling is herself performing a (fictional) self-conscious homage to *The Lizzie Bennet Diaries.*

10   *The Autobiography of Jane Eyre*'s opening video closely resembles Rosianna Halse Rojas's Self Image 2013 video (https://www.youtube.com/watch?v=xSomh5dXTCgO) (accessed July 6, 2015). Following episodes of *Jane Eyre* for the most part use a more traditional vlogging aesthetic.

11   For an example of a Lootcrate unboxing featuring the actors as themselves, see https://www.youtube.com/watch?v=G_0YdY6IzQQ (accessed July 6, 2015); for a Lootcrate unboxing by a series' character, see https://www.youtube.com/ watch?v=MeXax8b_bYM (accessed July 6, 2015).

12   *The New Adventures of Peter and Wendy*'s first season Kickstarter campaign raised $9,230 from 162 backers, while its second season Indiegogo campaign raised $57,027 from 1,637 backers.

13   "Some Notes on Today's Episode," Inking Ideas, http://inkingideas.tumblr.com/ post/88102118642/some-notes-on-todays-episode-steps (accessed July 6, 2015).

14   The comment conversation, which includes all of these perspectives in multiple variations, is available on *The Autobiography of Jane Eyre*'s penultimate episode, "Steps," YouTube.com, https://www.youtube.com/watch?v=hQV8Ja9DDSk (accessed July 6, 2015).

17

Interview with Luminosity, Fan and Vidder

Paul Booth and Lucy Bennett

Luminosity is a well-known fan vidder and an outspoken participant in a number of fandoms. Prominent fan scholar Henry Jenkins (2007b) has called her "among the best of this current generation of fan video-makers" (p. 2). In fan circles, she has made a name for herself by creating some of the most watched (and taught) fan videos: "Women's Work," a critique of the representation of women in *Supernatural*, "Vogue/300," a take on masculinity, violence, and aesthetics, and "The Red Shoes," a video about the obsessive nature of fandom and fan audiences. Luminosity has been interviewed about her vidding work before, most notably by Logan Hills (2007) in *New York Magazine*. We've had the pleasure of meeting Luminosity in person at a vidding convention in Chicago, and she is a warm and candid proponent of fan cultures. The following interview was conducted by email, and we spoke about the act of vidding, changing activities of fans, and the role (and responsibility) of fan vid creators in representing fandom.

Q: Can you tell us how you first got into fandom and fan communities? What made you start vidding?
A: I've always been a fan, even before I knew it had a name. My awareness of popular culture/media is probably rooted in the pleasant times I spent watching old movies with my mother and reading Rudyard Kipling with my grandmother. We would talk about the way the movies looked and the way the books were written, the stories they told beneath the story they told, which I now know was "meta" discussions. Thanks, Mom! I drew my favorite characters, actors, etc., and made up stories about them. By the time I was in high school, I had taught myself guitar and wrote filks with my aunt. My father-in-law gave me my first computer back in the late 80's, and it had a modem! I connected with BBS's in northern California, and I stumbled upon FidoNet and EchoNet, both of which carried newsgroups, including fannish ones. Online fandom was in its infancy at that time, and I frequented alt.star-trek.creative, alt.mindless-chatter, alt.callahans, etc., where I read the first fan fiction that I hadn't written myself. I don't know that I could call alt.mindless-chatter a fannish community, but it had elements of fandom in that it flourished creatively in its observations and reactions to popular culture.

In 1994–1995, a friend of mine asked me to "beta" her *Highlander* slash story. I had no idea what that even was, but I said yes. Through her, I discovered the *Highlander* fannish listservs and egroups lists. I was active on several *Highlander* lists [and] via those lists, I joined a *Highlander* tape tree, which was how many of us shared the "Euro-minutes" versions of the *Highlander* TV show. One day, I received a VHS tape full of *Highlander* vids. I had never seen such a thing! The first vid I ever saw was the Central Consortium's "Sympathy for the Devil," featuring Methos. I felt like I had been hit by a creative lightning bolt. I knew without a doubt that I could do that.

Five years passed before I hit critical mass and bought a computer powerful enough to make videos. I was about to explode creatively and needed that outlet!

Q: What are some of your fandoms?
A: My first "official" online fandom was *Highlander*, and then I discovered *X-Files* and *Buffy*. I was active in *Angel* fandom, *Farscape*, and most recently, *Supernatural*. Now, I am more of a fannish butterfly, dipping into various TV shows and movies. At this point, my true fandom is vidding, and the media is just part of that.

Q: You have consistently made very popular fan videos—When you make these videos, do you have an imagined community you're creating them for?
A: No. Unless I'm making a vid specifically for another person, e.g., auctions and fundraisers, I make them for myself and seldom even consider someone else. Creatively—artistically speaking—if I allowed myself to feel "accountable" to a larger community, it would be just one more constraint. It's not that I don't privately feel that way sometimes, but if it's between being fannishly politically correct and the art itself, the art wins. Also, no one ever got anything done by being beholden to an ill-defined, constantly-reinventing-itself, sometimes petulant zeitgeist.

Q: Some of your most popular videos, like "Women's Work," critique some systemic issues in the media. What do you see as some of the major issues in the media today?
A: I'm just a fan, but I do have opinions! On the one hand, I love the (seemingly) open dialogue fandom has with the creators of the source because I'm curious about their "process," but I think that the openness is just a facade, really. The real dialogue is between the creators and the money, and they listen to fans only when it's convenient and their plans match fandom's desires. They like having fans, but they're not beholden to us, especially when fannish desires dictate a different vision of the work from what they're doing. I feel the same way about my own creative work. I'm not a fan of the destruction of the fourth wall, though. It's fun as an entertaining aberration, but too much of it feels both forced and self-conscious, and I think that it detracts from the material—unless the entire point of it is breaking the wall.

Although I don't have a horse in this race, I feel that one of the bigger issues in media today, fannishly speaking, is queerbaiting. For good or bad, TPTB [The Powers That Be] have been made aware of slash in fandom. It's unavoidable. They've utilized a carrot-and-stick approach to those fans/viewers in order to keep them. Will they or won't they? They won't. Trust me. They won't. We fans are knowledgeable viewers; we read subtext dialogue and visual clues rather easily, and it's offensive and disrespectful to us for a show to give nearly contextual hints about a popular slash pairing's sexuality and where it's going, only to deny it later. I've seen this heavy-handed bait-and-switch in a few shows already, and I'm sure it's not going to go away any time soon, sad to say. Not when there's money to be made!

[For example, in 2012, *Teen Wolf* released a promo video], urging fans to vote for them for the Teen Choice Awards, and blatantly used "Sterek" to get votes, and then dissing and dismissing the fans who voted for them. I hope this is just a phase because it's dishonest and bad storytelling.

Q: One of your newest videos, "The Red Shoes," focuses on a type of obsessive fandom—how do you think fans tend to represent fandom in their own work? Should fans have a responsibility to particular types of fan portrayals?
A: Thank you for watching "The Red Shoes." It's one of my favorite vids of my own, a story about the Gift demanding its toll. I can only speak for myself, but I look at fandom as a gift that keeps on giving. None of us works from within a vacuum, and the constant back-and-forth among us keeps my creativity piqued.

These words. Accountability. Responsibility. (I'm tempted to go into my Inigo Montoya rant.) I don't know that we fans represent ourselves in our work as much as our work is us. Like any art, what we do reveals a part of who we are. As far as being responsible to particular types of fannish portrayals, I'm not sure I even understand that question. I'd like to see a truthful portrait of what keeps a show on the air or makes a movie number one from the creators of those things, but I think that, as fans, our only responsibility to each other is the attempt to entertain each other, understand each other, and do no harm.

Q: What are your views on the ways fans have been represented in the media and popular culture?
A: Media is presented to us to consume, and we consume it. The biggest change is that now the creators of the media are able to get real-time reactions to their work. They are accountable to *us*. They have a responsibility to *us*. They don't like that we know that now. That they take the well-worn path of least resistance in their portrayals of (mostly female) fans is laughable and points out how ill-informed they are. The older I get and the longer I'm involved in fandom, the more infuriating this becomes. Media fans, as I'm sure you know, are cross spectrum. In my own fannish circles, I can count lawyers, librarians, homemakers, soldiers, teachers, doctors, novelists, physicists, software engineers, journalists, students, visual artists, chefs, historians, and general polymaths! And that's just off the top of my head. There really *is no* cliche of a fan anymore except the one that the media tries to foist upon us. For every slack-jawed Becky, there's a rock-solid rocket scientist. For every tech-savvy Charlie who designs computer systems, there's an overworked mom who just presses "play."

It's also quite interesting to me that the shirtless, beer-bellied, tempera-painted, howling MALE football fan has garnered so much respect, and we mostly female media fans are dissed regularly. I saw a commercial for a fantasy football league just yesterday, and what is that but fannishness writ large on the (mostly) male psyche? I feel that it's just one more dictate that women can't have passions—or can't show them, anyway. It's sort of short-sighted, though, since women have more disposable income and are more likely to spend it on fannish pursuits.

Q: Were you aware of fan studies as an academic field and have you done any research before making your videos or participating in fandom?
A: I was not aware of fannish academics when I was first involved in online fandom, but as time has passed, you can't swing a dead cat without hitting a media/fandom academic. I find the work quite interesting because I'm a "meta" fan as well as a media fan, but I don't do the writing. I'm the person the academics write about.

I do not research what academics are going to think of my work before I do the work. I try to remain unaware of anyone observing my work, hopefully avoiding some sort of fannish Hawthorne effect.

Q: How do you think the reception of fan audiences has changed over time?
A: I think we are in-your-face visible now, and we're not always seen in a positive light. I had this same conversation with a fan-friend just recently. We're seen as childish and demanding and we're mocked for what we love on the one hand and teased, promises made, fleeced for our money on the other hand. The disdain is public, too. One Direction is a billion-dollar supergroup, their success riding on the backs of teenaged girls, and those girls are mocked for their passion. *Twilight* became a movie franchise, making over three billion dollars so far, and its fans, with money in their pockets, have been mercilessly made fun of. *50 Shades of Grey*? Fan fiction. Terrible, *money-making* fan fiction. And the author and readers are lampooned. That being said, we've always been ridiculed, only now it's more public. "We'll take your money, but we won't respect you in the morning."

We've always been here, though. Cavemen painted those pictures on the cave walls for an audience. Ovid wrote fan fiction. Every painting of the Madonna is fan art—just one more take on a story that has existed for thousands of years. We've always been here. Mock us already. We're not going anywhere.

Part Three

Cultural Perspectives on Fan Representations

18

Straighten Up and Fly White: Whiteness, Heteronormativity, and the Representation of Happy Endings for Fans

Mel Stanfill

Characters with deep affective attachments to media objects—who we might term "fans"—have proliferated in recent years. If, historically, fans were rarely present in media and frequently somewhere between lonely losers and pathologically violent when they appeared (Jenkins 1992; Jensen 1992; Lewis 1992a), fans are now increasingly often main characters in television and film. That fans are now both present and not solely the villain or punchline seems like improvement. As Joshua Gamson (1998) notes, when a previously excluded or marginalized group suddenly seems to be everywhere, "It looks, for a moment, like you own this place" (p. 5) However, as those studying representation of many marginalized groups have argued, mere presence in media is not the entire story. Instead, we must ask *how* the category appears in order to understand what that presence means.

Here, through analyzing representation of both sports and speculative media fans in fictional films, documentaries, and news coverage, as well as examining statements about fans by industry workers in interviews and supplementary DVD features, I consider how—despite fans becoming central to media processes in the Internet era and increasingly seen as mainstream (Jones 2000; Sandvoss 2005; Coppa 2006a)—the equation of fandom to *failed* masculinity, heterosexuality, and whiteness persists. Through deliberate mash-up of disparate sources I argue that, while fandom is constructed as failed whiteness through failed masculinity and heterosexuality, contemporary representations include a redemption narrative for white men (and only such fans). The features of the social category "white" condition both the specific forms fan nonnormativity takes and why and how redemption is possible for such fans. Consequently, the redemption narrative works both to reinforce cultural common sense that privilege is a "natural" property of white, heterosexual masculinity and to produce "fan" as a white category.

Doing fandom, (Mis)doing whiteness

Even the most cursory look shows that fans as visually represented are overwhelmingly white. Against that baseline, I interrogate how whiteness *functions* in popular understandings of fandom. Fans are not simply white but often more specifically what Richard Dyer (1997) calls "skin" white but not what he terms "symbolically" white—though fans are most frequently represented as *phenotypically* white, and though fans of color are marginalized, images of fandom generally do not demonstrate the positive valuation of whiteness in dominant American culture. I argue that this is because these white fan bodies fail at other components of normativity: masculinity and heterosexuality.

Though whiteness is generally understood as a position of dominance in contemporary US culture, not all representations of white people demonstrate this privilege. Some scholars argue that such constructions demonstrate, as backlash against the perceived destabilization of white men's privilege, a belief that white men are now victims of discrimination (Frankenberg 1993; Savran 1998; Wiegman 1999; Rodino-Colocino 2012). Others contend that representations of white men's nonprivilege disrupt the equation of whiteness with superiority and provide an opportunity to rework and undo white privilege (Hill 1997; Newitz and Wray 1997a; Newitz and Wray 1997b). Though the former point of view argues that nonnormative whitenesses obscure continuing white privilege and the latter contends that such representations actually undo privilege, both assume that whiteness is the only structure shaping these representations, and that it is monolithic. However, intersectionality tells us privilege and domination are produced by multiple factors (Crenshaw 1991; Cohen 1997; Collins 2000). As Ross Chambers (1997) argues, "In the end, identity becomes a bit like a poker hand, in which the value of the ace (whiteness) can be enhanced, if one holds a couple of face cards or another ace (masculinity, heterosexuality, middle classness) or, alternatively depreciated by association with cards of lower value (ethnicity, lack of education, working classness)" (p. 191). Fandom, I contend, is understood to entail deviance from normative gender and sexuality, and behaving in such a way "diminishes the value" of fans' whiteness.

Fandom, as was originally described in the early 1990s, has historically been stigmatized (Brower 1992; Jenkins 1992; Lewis 1992a). Fans are associated in the popular imaginary with danger, violence, and pathology or just loneliness, alienation, and loserdom. Fans have traditionally been depicted as "brainless consumers who will buy anything associated with the program or its cast" (Jenkins 1992, 10). Fans "devote their lives to the cultivation of worthless knowledge." They "place inappropriate importance on devalued cultural material." They are "social misfits" and "feminized or desexualized." They are "infantile, emotionally and intellectually immature." Perhaps most dramatically, fans "are unable to separate fantasy from reality" (see Jenkins 1992, 10; Jensen 1992; Lewis 1992a; Johnson 2007). As has been demonstrated by more recent research, these tropes are still with us (Sandvoss 2005; Driscoll 2006; Johnson 2007; Punathambekar 2007; Scott 2008).

This cultural construction of fandom seems opposite to that of whiteness. In particular, fandom and normative whiteness come into conflict—and fandom becomes constructed as insufficient whiteness—with respect to self-control. Whiteness has traditionally been predicated on self-control (Roediger 1991; Dyer 1997; Savran 1998; Floyd 2009). Normativity rests on a "notion of whiteness having to do with rightness, with tightness, with self-control, self consciousness, mind over body" (Dyer 1997, 6). Whiteness was invented as part of larger trends to "eliminate holidays, divorce the worker from contact with nature, bridle working class sexuality, separate work from the rest of life and encourage the postponing of gratification" (Roediger 1991, 96).

As Dyer's and Roediger's formulations suggest, whiteness requires *sexual* self-control in particular. "Sexual stereotypes commonly depict 'us' as sexually vigorous (usually our men) and pure (usually our women) and depict 'them' as sexually depraved (usually their men) and promiscuous (usually their women)" (Nagel 2003, 10). Under this construction, white men's sexuality is "vigor" without "depravity," is modulated and controlled. This framework relies on the affiliation of whiteness with civilization and rationality as opposed to sexuality (Sandell 1997; Ferguson 2003; Nagel 2003; Floyd 2009). The counterexamples reinforce this association: failure at normative expectations of sexual self-control undergirds the "failure" of whiteness in "white trash"—a group typically constructed as prone to bestiality, incest, and rape (Sandell 1997; Newitz and Wray 1997a; Newitz and Wray 1997b). Thus, while people deviate from norms of whiteness for different reasons—class in the "white trash" case or hobbies for fans—the form the supposition of deviance takes is often sexual.

Because fandom and whiteness are somewhat discursively antithetical, the prevalence of phenotypically white people as fans emphasizes that whiteness is not just pigmentation but behavior. Extending the insight that gender is constituted through enactment (West and Zimmerman 1987; Butler 1990), the need to repeatedly perform whiteness in order to construct and reaffirm it makes it possible that a white-skinned person can "fail" at that enactment and therefore at whiteness (Dyer 1997; Ahmed 2006). In particular, because normativity yokes together race, gender, and sexuality, they must all be "right" to achieve it. Nonnormative gender or sexuality undermines an enactment of whiteness, as nondominant racial or sexual status would undermine the normativity of an enactment of masculinity. Fandom, as a practice associated with nonnormative gender and sexuality, is one way of *doing* whiteness "incorrectly." Much like white trash is "a naming practice that helps define stereotypes of what is or is not acceptable or normal for whites in the U.S." (Newitz and Wray 1997a, 4)—in which it is not simply that they *are* poor, but *how* they are poor—so too is the particular nonnormativity of the fan the way they fail at white self-control. The discursive construction of fans as white produces a notion of "appropriate" fandom through whiteness and "appropriate" whiteness through fandom, tying both to self-control. In what follows, I will address the role of gender and sexuality in constructing fandom as insufficient whiteness in turn.

"I was trying to be a man, a plan with a fundamental conceptual flaw": Fandom and failed masculinity

The first failure at normative whiteness is that in fiction and nonfiction, representation and industry commentary, fans are overwhelmingly not quite gender-normative men. Here, much like their phenotypic whiteness, fans *seem* to get gender and sexuality "right" in that they are heterosexually oriented men, but there's a "fundamental flaw" in their execution of constructed-as-white normative, heterosexual masculinity, as in the quote from character Seth Cohen of *The O.C.* (2003–2007) that titles this section.[1] Fans fail at doing manly things—even at knowing what manliness *is*. Sometimes fans are directly termed insufficiently masculine, as when characters in *Fanboys* (2009) question whether each other have "the nut sack to go through with" their plan to steal a copy of *Star Wars Episode I: The Phantom Menace* (1999) prior to its theatrical release. A similar logic animates a scene in *The O.C.* in which fannish character Seth suggests, "Let's do what guys do," only to then ask his more conventionally masculine adopted brother: "Ryan, what do guys do?" Fan failure at gender is a key component of the dissociation of fandom from normativity that constitutes their failure of whiteness.

Fan characters are also routinely called women or compared to them. The men of *Fanboys* get insulted as "ladies," "Spice Girls," or the perennial favorite "pussies." While non-masculinity is a staple insult among men, it is unevenly distributed, and being open to such accusations marks one's manliness as vulnerable to challenge. This is reinforced when a woman is the one to call fans "a little bitch" (*The O.C.*) or "ladies" (*Fanboys*). Fan characters in *Chuck* (2007–2012), *Forgetting Sarah Marshall* (2008), and *My Name Is Bruce* (2007) are all described as sounding like women or girls when they scream (in fear) or cry (in sadness). Often, women outdo fans at masculinely gendered activities. Penny in *The Big Bang Theory* (2007–present) chides her fannish neighbors, "Look, guys, for the future, I don't *mind* killing the big spiders, but you have to at least *try* with the little ones."

Similarly, fans tend to lack the physical prowess of "proper" masculinity. In *The Big Bang Theory*, Leonard insists to Sheldon that they can retrieve Penny's TV from her ex-boyfriend because "There's not going to be a scene. There's two of us and one of him." Sheldon replies, "Leonard, the two of us can't even *carry* a TV." Visibly overweight fans are impressively consistent for both sports and speculative media, in both fiction and documentaries, a seemingly indispensable part of any flock of fans. Much of the humor of Comic Book Guy from *The Simpsons* (1989–present) comes from how he waddles and wobbles, his constant eating, or jokes like sweating through his jumpsuit with half a jumping jack at fat camp ("The Way We Weren't" 2004) or when pointed wizard caps get stuck on his flabby chest to produce a look reminiscent of Madonna circa 1990 ("Radioactive Man" 1995). Much the same idea appears with Paul in *Big Fan* (2009), played by portly comic/actor Patton Oswalt—who joked that he had to "get fat for the part," reinforcing the idea that such a physical state is necessary for a sports fan character.

This is similar to understanding fans as indoorsy and/or unathletic. In *Fanboys*, the fans' friend comments, "This is, like, the most exercise you guys have had all year" as they run through *Star Wars* (1977–present) creator George Lucas's production facility Skywalker Ranch. Importantly, Patton Oswalt was not only "willing to bulk up for the role" as the lead in *Big Fan*, but also, as writer Robert Siegel joked, "stay out of the sun. He had a pretty healthy, glowing tan at the time and he promised he would go method and stay in his basement for a few months to kind of get rid of that" ("Patton Oswalt and Robert Siegel: Serious Funny Men" 2010). Oswalt was already both large and pale, but the joke demonstrates expectations about fans by assuming this look is indispensable to the role, such that he would generate it if necessary. Indeed, writer/director Siegel said Oswalt was cast because "I just thought he looked like he could be an obsessive, you know, nerdy sports fan." Paleness and tan-ness are distinctly white phenomena. Though historically being pale was associated with upper-class freedom from outdoor work, by the late twentieth century, being tan had been articulated to health and fitness and became the privileged condition, but the reversal in valuation did not sever the attachment to whiteness (Dyer 1997). Thus, being both a man and white does not guarantee normativity. The fan, in the popular imaginary, "does" normative masculinity incorrectly through deviations from a white norm of bodily control.

God hates fans: Heterosexual failure and fandom as nonnormative sexuality

Fan behavior also fails at the control expected of whiteness through failed heterosexuality. Harry Knowles of entertainment website Ain't It Cool News, consulted as a "web guru" in documentary *Fanalysis* (2002), ties together fan unsuccessful heterosexuality and liminal adulthood, identifying a fan as "Someone who has a nine to five job in the real world, and they want to have the wife, but they're still hanging on to being a child," suggesting fans, as children, can't achieve their desire for heterosexual marriage. This attitude was already established when William Shatner appeared on *Saturday Night Live* (1975–present) in 1986, playing himself at a *Star Trek* (1966–1969) convention, admonishing "Trekkies" to move out of their parents' basements, kiss a girl, and get a life, foregrounding this belief that fans have never had (hetero)romantic success. If whiteness is grounded in vigorous-but-controlled sexuality, fans are failures.

Thirty years later, this notion of fan sexual inexperience persists. The lead character in *The 40 Year Old Virgin* (2005) is a fan, though *The Simpsons* Comic Book Guy outdoes him, numbering himself among "45 year old virgins who still live with their parents" ("Mayored to the Mob" 1998). Even if not strictly virgins, fans are generally understood as sexually inexperienced. The characters in *Fanboys* decidedly lack sexual knowledge. When they are caught at Skywalker Ranch, the security guard informs them that the breaking and entering charges will be dropped if they can prove their status as "fanboys" with "a simple quiz." The scene equates fans with failed heterosexuality when said quiz includes not only *Star Wars* trivia they are supposed to know, such as "What is the name of the gunner in Luke's snow speeder?" (which they can indeed answer without hesitation), but sexual trivia they are supposed to *not* know, such as "Where is a woman's g-spot located?" (which provokes head-scratching). To emphasize this cluelessness, fans are frequently shown as less sexually knowledgeable than younger people. In particular, adult fans know less about sex than teens or tweens in *The Benchwarmers* and *The Guild* (2007–present). Ben in *Fever Pitch* (2005) asks for relationship advice from a high school student, constructing him as less mature and knowledgeable than a teenager. High school senior Seth in *The O.C.* asks younger boys who haven't even completed puberty.

Fans are framed as wanting heterosexual sex, but unable to succeed with women. A comedic version is *The Big Bang Theory*'s Howard Wolowitz, who creator Chuck Lorre describes on the first season DVD as like Pepe Le Pew; in the same special feature, actor Simon Helberg describes Wolowitz as "a genius, but he's an idiot with girls, because he thinks he's as brilliant with them as he is with, you know, science." Alternately, this notion can be more sinister, as in *Buffy the Vampire Slayer* (1997–2003) when three fannish villains use a "cerebral dampener" to make a woman do what they want; when the effect wears off she tells them: "You bunch of little boys, playing at being men. Well, this is not some fantasy. It's not a game, you freaks. It's rape. You're all sick." Desperation for heterosexual contact conditions the behavior of these fan men, clearly distinguishing them from the sexual control expected in whiteness.

Furthermore, the homosociality of fandom forever threatens to collapse into homosexuality. In *Big Fan*, when Paul is jailed after shooting a rival fan with paintballs in his team colors, all the other prisoners are visited by women (presumably intending to suggest wives and girlfriends), but Paul's visitor is his football friend Sal, paralleling their relationship and the heterosexual ones surrounding them. More explicitly, Chuck and best friend Morgan are repeatedly called "boyfriends" or "life partners" in *Chuck*, including by Morgan himself. Certainly, the show played with this dynamic, staging a reunion between the two after a fight in slow motion, their eyes meeting across the room in a clear invocation of romance tropes, which creator Josh Schwartz described as "our romantic finale, because at the end of the day, you know, the relationship between Chuck and Morgan really is a huge part of the show." The romantic framing in fan homosocial pairs thus exceeds the "buddy relationship" template, linking fandom to homosexuality.

Contemporary discourses of fandom similarly demonstrate Joli Jensen's (1992) argument that representations construct "fandom as a surrogate relationship, one that inadequately imitates normal relationships" (p. 16). Many argue fandom is believed to substitute for real romantic and sexual relationships fans lack (Jenkins 1992; Lewis 1992a; Hills 2002a; Driscoll 2006). Fandom is offered as consolation when relationships go awry in *The Big Bang Theory* and *The O.C.* There is also a consistent notion that fans tend to choose the object of fandom over romantic entanglements. Paul in *Big Fan* desires his object of fandom more than women, declining a lap dance and even peering around the dancer to look at his favorite player; actor Oswalt joked that Paul's attitude was "Please get your gorgeous, naked body out of my way, so I can look at the giant guy who's about to pummel me into a coma" ("Patton Oswalt and Robert Siegel: Serious Funny Men" 2010). Prioritizing fandom over relationships or having fandom be the primary relationship in one's life easily slides into the concept that fans eroticize their object of fandom. This appears when a fan in *Fanalysis* exclaims "I love you!" to actor Bruce Campbell and tries to kiss him. Similarly, the Trekkie antagonist in *Fanboys* tenderly cradles the severed head of his prized statue of the character Khan, screams "Khan!" like Captain Kirk did in *Star Trek II: The Wrath of Khan* (1982), then, after using his inhaler, kisses the statue full on the lips.

Such images suggest that at least part of the pleasure fans derive from fandom is sexual, and the decision of Fred Phelps's Westboro Baptist Church to picket San Diego

Comic-Con 2010 implies that the far right, at least, has made the same judgment. Certainly, fandom's discursive construction appears to demand such analysis. The logic of eroticizing fandom produces the scene in 1998 *The Simpsons* episode "Das Bus," in which Comic Book Guy's attempt to download a racy picture of *Star Trek: Voyager* (1995–2001) commanding officer Captain Janeway is thwarted by slow Internet. The scene thus uses the idea that fans seek out erotic iterations of the object of fandom to advance a plot about Homer becoming an Internet service provider. More subtly, Paul in *Big Fan* has a dream in which his gaze lingers on various body parts of player Quantrell Bishop in a way that would set anybody's Mulvey sense to tingling, which is supplemented in another scene when Bishop's poster is the last image before Paul begins to masturbate, implying that it aids his process. This scene, like the way three fans in *Fanboys*, in a catalogue of their fan practices, acknowledge that they had "named their right hand Leia" after the *Star Wars* princess, is reinforced as nonnormative by the cultural common sense, described by Rubin (1993), of masturbation as inferior to partnered sex.

More intensively, Summer in *The O.C.* tries to catch a fanboy's attention by dressing up as a comic book character, and exasperated Trish in *The 40 Year Old Virgin* asks, "What do I have to do for you to have sex with me? Do you want me to dress up like Thor? I'll dress up like Thor. I'll dress up like Iron Man." This equates fandom to a fetish, as when in *The West Wing* (1999–2006) episode "Arctic Radar" (2002). White House Deputy Chief of Staff Josh Lyman asks a staff member wearing a *Star Trek* pin:

> Tell me if any of this sounds familiar: "Let's list our ten favorite episodes. Let's list our least favorite episodes. Let's list our favorite galaxies. Let's make a chart to see how often our favorite galaxies appear in our favorite episodes. What Romulan would you most like to see coupled with a Cardassian and why? Let's spend a weekend talking about Romulans falling in love with Cardassians and then let's do it again." That's not being a fan. That's having a fetish. And I don't have a problem with that, except you can't bring your hobbies in to work, okay?

This scene, too, constructs fandom as deeply, inevitably, tied to nonnormative sexuality, both through directly calling certain fan practices as a "fetish" and the way Lyman's "And I don't have a problem with that" echoes the *Seinfeld* (1989–1998) "Not that there's anything wrong with that" quip about homosexuality. Thus, fans are tightly linked to incapacity for "proper," normative heterosexual sex.

Redeem yourself now! (restrictions may apply)

The "happy" ending (for representations that have one, generally the fictional films that are comedies) comes when fans are recuperated into self-control. If whiteness depends on self-control, and fans are constructed as out-of-control white people, then fans who are white men are simultaneously represented as fully able to "achieve" normative white, heterosexual, masculine self-control, as their deviance comes from correctable bad decisions. Though heterosexual romance coming to fruition commonly drives happily-ever-after in film, fandom is often positioned as the specific impediment in these sources, doing particular cultural work that rewards closer examination.

Fans are often presented as needing to get perspective and diminish fandom's role in their lives. Jeff in *My Name is Bruce* learns to be brave and solve his own problems rather than relying on actor Bruce Campbell to be a hero like the characters he plays. Fan characters in *Kickass* (2009) and *Knocked Up* (2007) refocus on their relationships in place of "immature" fan-dreams. Andy in *The 40 Year Old Virgin* sells his extensive toy collection, makes half a million dollars, and uses it to finance the wedding his move away from fannish virginity permits. The trajectory of modulating all-consuming fandom into contained appreciation compatible with heterosexuality even occurs in documentaries. In *Trekkies* (1997), we meet Gabriel Koerner, who is excessively nerdy and focused on fandom, but by *Trekkies 2* (2004) he has become a man, calmed his appreciation of *Star Trek*, begun a career, and found a girlfriend, achieving gender, class, sexual, and racial normativities.[2]

The most explicit articulations of a positive outcome to diminished fandom are distinctly tied to heterosexual success. In *The Big Bang Theory*, Leonard's acquisition of an oversized movie prop blocks the stairway in his building and ruins Penny's day, causing her to scream at him and his fan friends: "My God, you are grown men. How could you waste your lives with these stupid toys and costumes and comic books and-and now that- that-" before trailing off in disgust. Later, though Penny has apologized, saying, "You are a great guy, and it is things you love that make you who you are," Leonard decides to sell his fannish possessions, declaring, "Still, I think it's time for me to get rid of this stuff and, you know, move on with my life." Penny replies, "Oh. Wow. Good for you" and kisses his cheek, positively reinforcing his decision with affection from his unrequited love interest. In *Fever Pitch*, Ben loses his girlfriend Lindsey and decides that he must grow up and give up fandom by selling his lifetime season tickets to the Red Sox. Ultimately, Lindsey does not let him make the sacrifice, saying, "If you love me enough to sell your tickets, I love you enough not to let you," but—much like Penny's approval of Leonard—his *willingness* to abandon his "childish" pursuits proves to her that he is worth it.

In all of the cases, though fandom doesn't have to be abandoned, it does have to be brought under control; this alignment with the white norm, made possible by being white men, makes these fans eligible for "redemption" into heterosexuality. People of color and women who are fans never "reform" and get their fandom "under control." Japanese fan Hiro of *Heroes* (2006–2010) never does become less childlike, and fannish women like Liz Lemon of *30 Rock* (2006–2013), Cyd of *The Guild*, and Becky of *Supernatural* (2005–present) make no appreciable "progress" either. The exclusion of fans other than white men from the recuperation narrative can be understood either as constructing other fans as incapable of being normalized or as assuming everyone will identify with and want to emulate the white man's narrative trajectory. In either case, it reinforces the construction of self-control as a characteristic of white men.

Conclusion

"Deviant" whitenesses like fandom seem to disrupt the normativity and dominance of whiteness. However, constructing fans as lacking privilege relies on an assumption of heterosexual white men precisely *as* privileged. As Dyer (1997) points out, "Going against type and not conforming depend upon an implicit norm of whiteness against which to go" (p. 12). The norm makes fan deviance intelligible *as* deviance, and it is reinforced by the possibility of recuperation. Privilege is regainable for fans in the happy ending of normativity because their skin whiteness makes them eligible for symbolic whiteness, such that these narratives reinforce rather than undermine the connection of whiteness and privilege. Kyle Kusz (2001) argues, "Constructions of Whiteness as unprivileged, victimized, or otherwise disadvantaged—images that seem to contradict the ideology of Whiteness as privileged—can work in particular contexts as a mechanism to resecure the privileged normativity of whiteness in American culture," and images of fandom constitute one of those contexts (p. 394). Ultimately, the articulation of white bodies, fandom, and nonheteronormativity in contemporary representation constructs the supposed inadequacy of fans as resulting from substandard—but standardizable—self-control.

In some sense, then, this discourse of fandom is a story about that most neoliberal of buzzphrases, "personal responsibility." The construction of fans as normative failures due to bad decisions they *personally* made figures their deviation from the white norm of self-control as ultimately correctable. Because their phenotypic whiteness carries a cultural expectation of an innate capacity for self-control, fan redemption in these narratives seems to actualize that capacity, getting the enactment of whiteness "right." As Sara Ahmed (2006) points out, some bodies are more interpellated than others. Simply by having white skin, then, normativity and redemption become possible for fans, for "Bodies that pass as white, even if they are queer or have other points of deviation, still have access to what follows from certain lines" (Ahmed 2006, 136–7). By being heterosexual white men, these fans have access to normativity, if only they can straighten up and fly white.

Notes

1   This failed masculinity is particularly interesting when sports fandom is commonly understood as integral to normative American masculinity. Thus it is clear that masculinity must be enacted—though attached to a normatively masculine object, sports fans as discursively constructed don't act very manly about it.

2   In an interesting parallel, fan Darryl Frazetti has also "become a man" between the two *Trekkies* films through transitioning from female to male. The documentary does not address Frazetti's changed presentation, and it is difficult to know how the distinctive scratchy transman voice reads to someone unfamiliar with the changes a transitioning FTM body undergoes; it may be that the average viewer interprets Frazetti as reaching puberty late—which would, of course, be consistent with notions that fandom is arrested development and masculine failure.

19

Outdoor Queuing, Knicker-Throwing, and 100th Birthday Greetings: Newspaper Narratives of Mature Female Fans

Ruth A. Deller

In this chapter, I explore the way mature (50+) female fans are depicted in a range of local and national English-speaking newspapers from around the world.[1] I focus specifically on female fans of male solo singers, particularly to explore how gendered fandom is presented when the women are older than the teenage female fans most often associated with male artists (Ehrenreich et al. 1992; see also the One Direction fans discussed by Jones and Proctor in Chapters 5 and 6). Hodkinson (2011) notes that participation in music subcultures has often been "regarded as a temporary accompaniment to the broader experience of being adolescent" (p. 262) and Cavicchi (1998) argues that:

> The obsessive activities of fandom—collecting artifacts and photographs, imitating a star's dress and manners, camping overnight for concert tickets, creating fanzines, joining fan clubs—are accepted only as the temporary behavior of hormone-driven (usually female) teenagers, who, when reaching adulthood, are expected to settle into the more mature behavior of work or motherhood. (p. 6)

Yet, it is clear that music fandom is no longer the sole preserve of the young. Indeed, there is a growing body of research into older/long-standing fandoms, including work on long-standing fan communities and subcultures (Anderson 2012; Baker 2014; Deller 2014), fan identities, practices, and age (Bennett 2006; Hodkinson 2011; Connell 2012), nostalgia, memory, and the role of music in people's lifecourse (Harrington and Bielby 2010; Pope and Williams 2011; Forman 2012). However, what is less common is an exploration of the way older fans are presented in wider media.

Many authors have observed the way fans have been stigmatized in media and popular culture. In her oft-cited chapter "Fandom as Pathology," Jensen (1992) argues these representations fall into two key categories:

> the obsessed individual and the hysterical crowd ... these two images of fans are based in an implicit critique of modern life. Fandom is seen as a psychological symptom of a presumed social dysfunction ... Once fans are characterized as deviant, they can be treated as disreputable, even dangerous "others." (p. 9)

Cavicchi (1998) echoes similar concerns, arguing:

> At worst, fans are characterized as pathological and deviant... At best, they are
> amusing and quaint, suitable for a three-minute slot on *Entertainment Tonight.* (p. 6)

In this chapter, I explore how similar representations to those described by Jensen can be
found in newspaper narratives of older fans, but the emphasis is less on fans' "deviance" or
"other" ness as a source of *threat*, but as a source of *humor*. I argue that fans are presented
more as the "amusing and quaint" type Cavicchi identifies, particularly in regional and
local press where they provide a source of feel-good amusement, allowing readers to
position these women as eccentric curiosities who've never grown out of teenage crushes,
while also offering a sympathetic nod to their roles as wives, parents, and grandparents—
these fans may be "other" but they are an "other" familiar to the reader.

Methodology

I performed a Nexis search on all English-language newspapers using the key term
"[Artist name] fan."[2] The artists selected were Tom Jones, Rod Stewart, Michael Ball,
Cliff Richard (UK); Donny Osmond, Neil Diamond, Barry Manilow (USA), and
Daniel O'Donnell (Ireland).[3] They were chosen for the longevity of their careers, the
genre of their music (middle-of-the-road pop/rock), and their appeal to a largely
female audience. Articles dated from 1982 until February 2015 although the bulk of
results were from 1995 onwards, due to institutional subscription. Articles came from
179 publications.

I read the headline and first paragraph of every article for each star. For the three
stars with the median number of results, I conducted a textual analysis of every article
to identify key themes, categories, and mentions. For the remaining stars, a stratified
sample of 20 percent of articles were analyzed to provide qualitative material.

The fandoms chosen for the content analysis were Tom Jones (235 results), Barry
Manilow (297), and Daniel O'Donnell (308). Richard, Stewart, and Diamond returned
more results; Osmond and Ball significantly fewer. Repeat articles (e.g., where multiple
regional papers ran the same story) were removed from figures as were mentions in the
letters pages and classifieds.[4]

Table 19.1 Summary of article content.

	All articles	Cursory mentions only (%)	National press (%)	Regional or local press (%)	Articles not referring to mature female fans (%)	Derogatory reference to fandom (%)	Fan "excess" (%)
Jones	235	37	41	59	14	4	21
Manilow	297	39	48	52	12	14	18
O'Donnell	308	19	36	64	5	5	36

Table 19.1 gives an overview of key article content. "Cursory mentions only" refers to articles where only a passing mention was made, such as a profile of another celebrity or a local resident (in the case of local press) making a brief reference to their fandom, or (as I return to later) a reference to these fans as a joke in an article that isn't about fandom or the artist concerned. A small minority of articles did not mention mature female fans, such as those referring exclusively to younger fans or male fans. "Derogatory comments" refers to any explicit criticism of fans. "Excess" refers to examples where fan excess was highlighted—such as references to someone being a "superfan," the star's "biggest fan," owning large amounts of memorabilia, etc.

Other types of articles about fans included gig and album reviews; announcements of tours; obituaries of fans; "feel-good" stories such as fans celebrating milestone birthdays; interviews with tribute artists;[5] fans meeting the artist; fans hosting charity events; interviews with the artist where fans are mentioned. Certain types of fan practice are notably absent from these stories, including fanfic/slash, fan video, and fan art. Fans are presented as somewhat chaste in their behavior, preferring to queue politely rather than scream at their idols (except for Tom Jones fans, repeatedly presented as knicker-throwing—to which I will return). The omission of these activities could possibly be because of the newspapers' interests, but may also be due to the age of the fans concerned. In the following sections, I look at these key themes in more detail.

"Camping out in wind and rain"—Narratives of excess

Perhaps unsurprisingly, narratives of excess were common in stories about all fandoms. Fans are positioned as being willing to travel anywhere in order to see their idols:

> ROD Stewart fan Barbara Clarke-Tune is used to trotting the globe to catch a glimpse of her idol. She has travelled to America, Canada and across Europe during her 30-year obsession with the gravelled-voiced rocker. (Cronin 2004)
>
> IF MICHAEL Ball—the tenor with the god-given voice—ever feels the need for the company of an older woman, he will be spoiled for choice. He is followed across the globe by an army of mostly middle-aged women who are willing to go to great lengths to hear his voice, admire his boyish good looks, and—with the case of one groupie yesterday—run both her hands through his golden curls. (Verity 2004, 3)[6]

In addition to travelling, they are associated with block-booking tickets for stars and camping out overnight for tickets. While Cavicchi's (1998) account of Springsteen fans associates queuing overnight with young fans, such stories are common in newspaper accounts of older fans. Queue stories were connected with all fandoms studied, although were most common in stories about Cliff Richard and Daniel O'Donnell fans, possibly because these fandoms are associated strongly with long-standing fan clubs, and because both artists tour Britain regularly. In O'Donnell's case, a third of articles mentioned queuing—mainly in local or regional press, although they occasionally made British and Irish national papers:

DANIEL O'Donnell fans—many of them pensioners—have been camping out in wind and rain for three nights to get front row seats to see their hero. The women, wearing up to four layers of clothing, sleep on deckchairs.... (*Mirror* reporter 2007, 30)

THREE die-hard Daniel O'Donnell fans who have pitched camp outside Plymouth Pavilions have said "nothing" will stop them queuing to secure front-row tickets—even a bomb ... So far they said they'd been soaked by rain and kept awake by high winds, but they passed the time, chatting and reading. (Radford 2010, 3)

In such narratives, "die-hard" elderly fans display not youthful excess, but preparedness—bringing deck chairs, flasks, and layers of clothing—and "blitz spirit"—not letting weather or even bombs deter them. These stories are usually presented as "feel-good" accounts of devotion and camaraderie, possibly because of the age of the fans, who are not seen as "vulnerable" or "threatening" in the way a group of teenagers might be. However, sometimes this devotion was deemed to be unnecessary:

DIE-HARD Daniel O'Donnell fans spent three nights camped in the cold for tickets—but they needn't have bothered, as only half were snapped up. (Ridley 2013, 23)

Narratives of queuing situate it as a practice for the elderly by comparing older fans to younger ones who prefer to use the Internet, thus implying queuing is not only unnecessary, but out-dated:[7]

[Venue] spokesman, said: "The days of people camping out in large numbers and queuing for tickets are becoming more of a thing of the past with the popularity of internet and telephone booking. There are still a handful of customers who enjoy the camaraderie and atmosphere of queuing up outside the theatre to be the first to get tickets in their hands. They see it as part of the experience when it comes to a popular performer like Daniel O'Donnell." (Nolan 2013)

Attending concerts is not the only activity of excess participated in by older fans. Memorabilia collections are frequently mentioned, often described as "shrines," extending the fandom as religion metaphor noted by many authors (O'Guinn 1991; Cavicchi 1998; Löbert 2012):

To her, singer Rod Stewart—or her Roddy—is sustenance, like air or food; her fandom is practically a career. Her address labels and stationery allude to as much. "Jo Wilhelm, Rod Stewart Fan," they state. (Gregorian 2007, E1)

CROONER crazy Kathleen Collins reckons she's Ireland's biggest Daniel O'Donnell fan—after converting her pub into a SHRINE to the singer. (Milton 2010, 26)

In these articles, the excess of fandom is discussed in terms of devotion and need—Stewart as sustenance; O'Donnell and Diamond as idols. While memorabilia stories tend to highlight these fans as different or eccentric, these eccentricities can be used for good, as in the case of this Tom Jones fan whose home became a tourist attraction to raise funds for charity:

> WALES' biggest Tom Jones fan is inviting people to visit her "shrine" to the pop legend in aid of Children in Need ... There is no charge but people will be asked to make a £2 donation and to buy a raffle ticket. (Powell 2009, 7)

The excessive nature of fans is replicated in their depiction as devotees. Several articles about older fans refer to fandom as if it should normally be the preserve of teenagers—but for these "obsessed" women, it is something they have never grown out of:

> YOUR LIFE: OBSESSED! TREASURING LOCKS OF HAIR, TREKKING TO SEE THEIR IDOL AND CREATING A SHRINE IS JUST NORMAL LIFE FOR THESE FANS, WHO NEVER GOT OVER A TEENAGE CRUSH. (Monti 2007, 28)
>
> IT was a love affair which began decades ago and for hundreds of Donny Osmond Fans at Glasgow's Clyde Auditorium last night their puppy love had not died. (Anderson 2003, 3)
>
> [A]lthough the Irish crooner inspires the type of near-frenzied adoration usually experienced by teen idols such as Justin Timberlake and Gareth Gates, his fans tend to be—how should I phrase this?—more on the mature side. O'Donnell's sell-out gigs attract vast numbers of women who in the 1960s probably considered themselves rather too grown-up to get overexcited about The Beatles. (*Stoke Sentinel* [author unattributed] 2003, 11)

Although some fans are presented as being part of couples, there is a recurring narrative in which husbands are seen as being in "competition" with stars, albeit in a lighthearted way:

> [A]ccording to husband Dan, [she] has the pop singer's pictures plastered all over the laundry room of their Saanich home. "Do I think you're sexy, not as sexy as Rod Stewart," she sang. (Young 2005, A3)
>
> There was Ann Edwards, 49, of Aspley, who was the envy of most in the crowd when she puckered up and planted one on 62-year-old Sir Cliff's cheek. Still reeling like a love-struck teenager 30 minutes later, she said: "If there's one thing we have a lot of in the Cliff Richard fan club, it's long-suffering husbands." (Williams 2003, 20)

These accounts replicate Löbert's (2012) analysis of Cliff Richard fans and O'Guinn's (1991) account of Barry Manilow fans in which the lack of husbands at gigs is seen as important for many female fans, who see gigs as a space to scream, to bond with other women, or let themselves have fun away from the normal duties of life:

> [F]irst of all, the transformation of the women into a self-mode they perceive as pleasant, one that involves unreserved, "crazy" and unrestrained behavior. Secondly, the event is exclusively for the girls; the husbands are deemed unwelcome. Thirdly and finally, the women describe the event's three-hour duration as a period when they are released from their everyday cares and leave their worries behind. (Löbert 2012, 128; see also Zubernis and Larsen 2012)

These wives whose (mostly chaste) love for male singers is "indulged" by their husbands are a contrast to the younger Barry Manilow fans whose more explicitly lust-filled letters appear in the Vermorels' (1985) *Starlust*. However, this is not to say there were no references to the sexuality of older female fans in newspaper accounts. Tom Jones fans were repeatedly represented as being "knicker-throwing," something mentioned in 14 percent of articles featuring them:

> [T]he Tom Jones Fan Club is tense, poised to fling their laundered pink, white and beige silk underpants at their idol. (Dennis 1993, 1)
> Those who have been with Tom from the start must be hoisting up big pants these days rather than lobbing their knickers towards the stage. (Hitt 2009, 26)

However, these accounts serve to desexualize the act of knicker-throwing through mentions of underpants being laundered, and coming in unflattering shapes and colors. Neither the fan object nor the fans are deemed attractive or sexual in any way that could be considered *serious*—a combination of age and lack of relevance. Indeed, fans are told to accept that they, and the object of their affections, are growing old:

> TOM JONES fans have been complaining that the Ponty Pelvis's latest publicity shot makes him look, well, his age. "It's not the sexy-looking Tom that we know and love," whined one devotee. They have to learn that it's not unusual for a 68-year-old bloke to look slightly haggard. This pussycat hasn't been new since 1967 so why, why, why can't they let him grow old gracefully? Even with access to the finest nip'n'tuckers money can buy, our idols do grow old as we grow old. (Hitt 2009, 26)

In some accounts, speculation about stars' love lives is seen less as the preserve of women who fancy the star, more that of the concerned grandmother hoping he will settle down:

> GRANNY Sarah Carville is looking for a straight answer from her heart-throb singing hero about his love life. The 89-year-old Daniel O'Donnell fan wants the Donegal bachelor to come clean about his romance ... (Roberts 1998, 9)

As we have seen, accounts of fan excess persist when discussing older fans. While this excess is not seen as "harmful," the accounts often serve to humor these fans and present them as different from "ordinary" people, or as immature women who've not yet grown out of a teenage crush. In the next section, I explore how similar ideas are developed in articles that are more explicitly critical of fans.

"Don't dream of suggesting such heresy to his fans"—Critical narratives

In her account of the way fans are presented in media narratives, Jensen (1992) notes the way (mainly female) fans are presented as organized mobs. This image can be found in several newspaper narratives, from campaigns to get Tom Jones knighted (*Daily Post* 2006, 7) to Donny Osmond fans who promote his new releases "tirelessly" (Simmons 2005, E1) and Cliff Richard fans responding to allegations of sexual abuse by trying to get an old song charting:[8]

> Fans of the pop star have been showing their support by buying copies of his 1992 Number 7 hit I Still Believe in You … (Webb 2014)

However, many critical newspaper narratives of fans as a mass focus on issues of "taste." Drawing on Bourdieu's (1984) discussion of taste, the likes of Hills (2002a) and Van den Bulck and Van Gorp (2011) have noticed how fans can often be characterized by how "credible" or not their fan interests are seen to be—something these particular stars are not:

> ABOUT 23,000 Rod Stewart fans descended on the RDS last night for an occasion of questionable taste. (O'Kelly 1995, 5)
>
> If you're a Michael Ball fan, which you shouldn't be … (Holden 2003, 13)
>
> Fans like these don't care that—to the unenlightened—Barry Manilow is sometimes seen as a kitsch icon, a human punch line. With his poofy hair, substantial nose and unblinkingly earnest songs, some see him as a living example of all that is, well … uncool. (Sotonoff and Rees 2004, 1)

Such sentiments are not just found in articles about fans or stars, they can be used as derogatory examples in otherwise unconnected articles:

> More than half the people on unemployment benefits have been on the mooch for over a year. Like being a drug addict or a Barry Manilow fan, it becomes an acceptable way of life for them. (Ruehl 2003, 64)
>
> Frankly, it was a bit of a cliché that Bill, a fanatical devotee to the chugging doomy sounds of Black Sabbath, would be a Satanist. It's like the Rod Stewart fan who also happens to be semi-catatonic—too predictable. (Hunter 2007, D1)

The most detailed articles about older fans as an undiscerning mass come from Tanya Gold, who wrote two similar accounts of watching concerts with older fans:

of Barry Manilow and Cliff Richard. In each, Gold positions herself as an outsider and lists the various reasons why she doesn't like the singer. She attempts to provide humorous commentary on the alien subcultures of mature female fans:[9]

> They wear long cocktail gowns under sensible coats and have neatly curled hair, like the Queen. Most are elderly, or nearly elderly. Quite a few are in wheelchairs, or on crutches, and one is blind. It is an odd sight and the young people sauntering past stare politely, as if the women have been beamed down en masse from BHS... Eventually I give up asking them why they love Barry Manilow. In truth, I don't think they actually know... Fanilows are a global network, like a weird Barrythemed version of SMERSH, the evil organisation in James Bond. (Gold 2008)[10]
>
> Some are wearing Cliff Richard's face. Not his real face obviously, but a mask, although if he had several I'm sure he'd auction them, because he is famously courteous to his fans. There are Cliff scarves, T-shirts, earrings, watches, jackets, and his own branded perfume, which I sincerely hope isn't actually made of essence of Cliff. The whole impression is rather like being inside Cliff Richard's face... Soon, a little old woman comes up to the edge of the stage with an envelope. Cliff saunters over and does a little dance for her. I decide Cliff loved his mother very much. Either that or he is in 24-hour therapy. (Gold 2010)

Gold's positioning of these women is clear—they are slightly delusional (or blind), their fan objects' appeal inexplicable, and the stars need therapy for indulging fan behavior.

Although many articles discussed thus far position fans as a humorous curiosity upon whom the reader (and writer) can look down, these are not the only accounts of older fans. In the next section, I explore how fandom forms part of stories about the lifecourse of fans.

"The perfect surprise for a fan's 100th birthday"— Narratives of lifecourse

Local and regional newspapers are more likely than national newspapers to feature stories of fans, as fan stories offer a human-interest angle more beloved of the regional press than the national (Ross 2006). Fan stories give a local face to reports of a famous singer touring in the region (as in stories of fans camping outside venues). Feel-good stories look at fans' charitable endeavors, discuss memorabilia collections, or mention experiences of meeting stars, such as this article, surely written with the intention to give the reader a warm glow inside (while also slightly patronizing its subject):

> AN 85-year-old woman has fulfilled her dream of meeting her idol, singer Michael Ball... and was even given a hug and a peck on the cheek... Edna said: "I couldn't believe it when I was told I was going to be able to meet him face to face... He is a

good looking chap, even though he is many years younger than me. I had my hair done before the concert to look my best for meeting him ..." (Turner 2009)

Feel-good narratives in local papers are often connected to key life events. Harrington and Bielby (2010) note the importance of fandom in helping people navigate through life's milestones: "Becoming a fan thus re-directs the life course, gives new meaning, structure and purpose to specific life stages, and marks periods of one's personal past ... fandom is shaped over time by modifications in the self" (p. 438). This sense of fandom as accompaniment to major life events is a recurring feature of newspaper stories, with local and regional press in particular mentioning fandom in obituaries and stories about retirement:

> A HALESOWEN teacher has called it a day ... The avid Cliff Richard fan was bought a piece of pottery by staff and pupils ... (Hales News Roundup 2009)
>
> MORE than 200 people are expected to attend the funeral of a popular Clevedon dog trainer ... Janet was also an avid Daniel O'Donnell fan and Bristol City supporter. (PR Script Managers 2014)

Another common "life course" narrative was of fans celebrating milestone birthdays with their favorite music, or receiving (or hoping to) cards or greetings from stars—much as, in the United Kingdom, local newspapers regularly cover centenarians receiving birthday messages from The Queen:

> A great-grandmother celebrated her 100th birthday with a dance. Annie Bailey got up to dance to one of her favorite Cliff Richard tunes at a party held at a care home in her honor. (Statham 2014)
>
> An international singing star sent a personalised video message as the perfect surprise for a fan's 100th birthday. Country and Irish folk singer Daniel O'Donnell recorded the message for huge fan Doris Stanczyk after a request from friends. (O'Donoghue 2014)

Situating lifecourse events within the context of fandom gives readers a lens through which to understand the person mentioned as well as presenting fandom as the preserve of ordinary—or at least identifiable—women: mothers and grandmothers in particular. Indeed, grandmothers are repeatedly referenced throughout these articles, both in feel-good stories where they are people we can enjoy reading about and as figures of amusement serving to emphasize the outdated-ness of their fan object:

> CLIFF Richard fan Jill Stolworthy drives around with a life-sized doll of the singer in her motor to scare off carjackers and other criminals. The star-struck gran loves the wrinkly hitmaker, 73. (Young 2014, 27)
>
> In Neil Diamond's case, the upbeat songs, the Seventies bouffant and the squeaky-clean image combine to produce an entertainer a grandmother could love. That's a big enough turnoff for any self-respecting rock fan. (Honey 2001, R3)

Tom Jones's staying power is quite incredible. He is as huge an idol to modern teenagers as he is to salivating grannies. (Coren 1998, 24)

While these comments are clearly humorous, they reinforce the idea of "granny fandom" (sometimes with no evidence the fans mentioned *are* grannies) as laughable—even if, as in the lifecourse stories mentioned earlier, it can offer us an opportunity to have our hearts warmed.

Conclusion

In this chapter, I have discussed key newspaper narratives about older female fans. While some present heart-warming human-interest stories, many depict these fandoms as sources of fun, mocking the fan object's lack of credibility and therefore the fans' perceived lack of taste. Fans are still characterized by excesses and eccentricities. Their queuing for tickets, spending money on travelling, or constructing shrines of merchandise are positioned as activities at best quaint, and at worst ridiculous. Mature fans are frequently humored and patronized, treated as teenagers who've never really grown up while simultaneously described as drooling grandmothers throwing their deeply unsexy lingerie at old-aged stars. Despite the caution expressed by some fan scholars (Cavicchi 1998; Hills 2012c; Duffett 2013) about the problems of conflating fandom with religion, such narratives persist in mainstream media discourse. References to idols, shrines, pilgrimages, relics, worship, and devotion permeate these articles as do well-worn terms such as "die-hard."

These narratives work together in making these women an eccentric curiosity whose devotion to a star is almost childlike. Newspaper accounts position fans as "other" to the author and reader, yet unthreateningly so—they may be a neighbor, a parent, or more often, a grandmother—a seemingly "ordinary" person whose "unusual" devotion to a star allows for a humorous human-interest narrative to be constructed around their curious fandom.

Notes

1   50+ was chosen as the core age group, as products and services aimed at "mature" markets (e.g., magazine subscriptions or holidays) are directed at this group. Therefore, it was deemed to be an age at which people might be considered "mature" by the press. However, as the article spans over twenty years, in some earlier articles, the fans and the artists are younger than this cut-off point.

2   For some publications, such as the *Guardian* and *Daily Mail*, Nexis also returned results from their associated websites.

3   Other similar artists, including Michael Bolton and Chris de Burgh, returned few relevant results.

4   The letters pages provided interesting material, as has been noted in other fan studies (Vermorel and Vermorel 1985; Sabal 1992) but did not fit the scope of this chapter.

Common themes of letters from fans included praising stars and their latest releases/tours; criticizing the newspaper's coverage or reviews of a star; complaining about poor service at gig venues or criticizing the newspaper's coverage of fans.

5   Mainly relating to Tom Jones, whose tribute artists had fourteen separate articles dedicated to them.

6   The use of "groupie" here seems humorous when positioned in contrast to the traditional image of the rockstar groupie as a young, sexual being. That this "groupie" runs her fingers through Ball's hair only serves to reinforce the humorous and desexualized nature of older fandom.

7   On the subject of technology versus fans, several newspapers covered the story of a naïve (43-year-old) Neil Diamond fan whose technological illiteracy led to a £2,000 phone bill for downloading his album on holiday. Such accounts often run contrary to the fans' own accounts of employing technologies in fandom (Bury et al. 2013; Deller 2014).

8   At the time of this writing, no conviction has been made.

9   Both columns attracted a number of complaints to the letters pages of the newspapers concerned, claiming Gold misrepresented both fans and artist.

10 Gold echoes Bourdieu (1984) in this piece when she offers this passing thought: "I find myself wondering if Manilow Mania is a class thing and whether, when we mock the Fanilows, we are mocking the working class." However, she quickly justifies her criticisms of the Fanilow phenomenon by claiming there are constant calls throughout the show for fans to part with money.

20

Squee from the Margins: Racial/Cultural/Ethnic Identity in Global Media Fandom

Rukmini Pande

Any scan of the international pop culture scene today reveals that there is no better time than the current moment to be a fan. Entertainment companies are increasingly eager to embrace once reviled productions of fannishness, from cosplay and fanart contests to fan fiction on Kindle Worlds. As interest in the topic grows, ideas about fannish identity, spaces, and productions are becoming increasingly complex both within and outside of fan studies. It is important to note that the referents of those terms have shifted quite a bit from when the first wave of fan scholars (Bacon-Smith 1992; Jenkins 1992) conceptualized them. Initially examined as subcultural practices, fan interactions with pop cultural media texts through fanworks (including fan fiction, fan art, fan vids, etc.) have a high level of visibility in mainstream popular culture today. Stereotypical representations of fans in pop cultural texts (and the surrounding mediasphere) as irrational and deluded still persist, particularly in the case of female media fans producing erotic fanwork. However, these fan communities and their labor are also increasingly seen as "valuable" to producers as entertainment companies often seek to build (often exploitative) relationships with them (De Kosnik 2012; Booth 2015b).

Fandom scholarship has contributed to the mainstreaming of fans and fanworks, undermining unflattering stereotypes by stressing their subversive potential and self-reflexivity. However, this interruption has remained partial, allowing certain assumptions to stand unquestioned. Fan studies scholarship has failed to adequately interrogate the racial demographic makeup of these communities, which has led to significant erasures and biases in their representation. Further, newer models of distribution driven by globalization and the rise in the use of the Internet have affected both the spread of media texts and the functioning and makeup of media fan communities around the world. While these communities have always been multi-racial/ethnic/cultural, and today are also transnational and transcultural, fan studies has not engaged critically with those dynamics, nor with the effects of neo/colonialism and neoliberal capitalism.

To clarify further: the foundational studies of media fandom communities saw them as comprised of mainly heterosexual, cisgender, white,[1] middle class American women (Russ 1985; Lamb and Veith 1986; Penley 1986). In some cases, this assumption led to skewed conclusions about fan motivations for participating in certain types of transformative fanworks. Salmon and Symons (2001), in a much-critiqued analysis, speculated that writers of slash fan fiction (stories that pair male characters together in romantic and/or sexual relationships) viewed these characters in highly reductionist and gender essentialist ways, based primarily on the assumption that the women writing this fan fiction were heterosexual. This view has since been challenged (Lothian et al. 2007), and recent fandom surveys (Melannen 2010; Centrumlumina 2013) also support the idea of media fandom as a queer space. However, these challenges have remained limited to fans' sexual and gender identities, leaving the assumed—white and USA-centric—racial/cultural and ethnic makeup of these communities in place.

In this chapter, I argue that dominant theoretical formulations that frame media fandom spaces as progressive and fan repurposing of popular cultural texts as inherently subversive have limited critical engagement with the fact that not all fans are on an equal playing field. While conflict within fan spaces has received some attention, this has concentrated mainly on the gendered ways in which fan practices are policed (Gray 2005; Busse 2013a). What is notably absent in media fan studies is an engagement with, or even an acknowledgment of, the varied demographics of English-language fan communities formed around the media texts that are most commonly encountered in fan studies readers or conferences.[2] In most cases, fans of *Supernatural* or *Star Trek* are examined as just that—fans—undifferentiated by any other aspect of their identity except for gender and perhaps a reference to their sexuality. This rhetorical practice allows readers to "default" to the norm, which remains white, middle class, cisgender, and American. What remains unexamined is that media fandom spaces, theorized as inclusive and liberating, are not immune to hierarchies structured by privilege accruing to income, class, racial, ethnic, and cultural identity, disability, etc. Ironically this lags behind actual fan practice where these debates have never been more energetically pursued. The critiques of these intra-fandom dynamics range from commenting on the problematics of cosplayers using blackface/yellowface and other appropriative behavior to pointing out when fan fiction authors use racist stereotypes.[3]

This chapter addresses that gap and is, in effect, an interrogation of the representations of fans in fandom scholarship. I will be using interview data and examples of fan critiques to illustrate how transnational fan communities negotiate extremely messy real-world structures of power that do not just go away within "safe spaces." I present a brief overview of contemporary fandom scholarship, arguing that this discussion must question the use of nationalistic boundaries to limit studies of identity performance within fandom spaces, as this division does not hold up in the face of media fandom practices. I am not proposing that the categories I discuss here are absolute; identity (as performative) is based on shifting markers and none of these can be construed as singular, absolute measures of coherent definition. As such, it is important that researchers maximize the flexibility of our own theoretical structures so as not to construct artificial boundaries. I then analyze the ways in which the specific platforms that fandom has utilized has influenced discussions around racial dynamics and use this to demonstrate how a postcolonial theoretical lens enables a dynamic and productive engagement with these shifting identity markers while also keeping in mind the effects of neo/colonialism and neoliberal capitalism.

Different strokes: Conceptualizing fan diversity

Media fandom has been theorized as a resistant force, beginning with Jenkins's (1992) view of participants as "textual poachers." This framework has most often appeared in work on slash fan fiction (Russ 1985; Penley 1986) but also on fan vids (Coppa 2008) and other transformative fanwork. Increasingly, however, "fans as activists" have also been theorized as an engaged audience that can be "recruited" to band together behind different social causes, from raising awareness about HIV to the Darfur conflict in Sudan (Hinck 2012; Jenkins 2012a). As Chin and Morimoto (2013) argue, this tends to set up a "good vs. bad fan practice" hierarchy. This has a twofold effect: on the one hand "bad" fan practices that are seen to be rooted in "fantasy and escapism" are excluded entirely from analysis, while the problematic features of "good" fan practices are unexamined.

Consequently, what remains undertheorized is the manner in which identity articulation within these fannish communities affects notions of subversiveness and resistance. What happens when fan repurposing is subversive in one context (interrupting heteronormative canons) but coercive in another (reinforcing racial power structures)? In the context of a networked world where new communicative possibilities are linked inextricably with capitalist globalization, issues of racial, cultural, ethnic, and religious identity matter more rather than less, and this extends to how fan communities receive, consume, and repurpose media.

Within the larger field of fan studies, sports (Sanderson 2010; Redhead 2014) and gaming (Leonard 2003; Everett 2005) fandoms have produced work considering racial, cultural, and ethnic identity. In the specific case of media fan scholarship, there have been some attempts to engage with the diversity of media fan communities, but these have largely chosen nationalistic frames of identity. Most studies have chosen to frame their analyses as discrete nationalities interacting with a "source" culture. Korean pop or K-pop scholarship is one example of this.[4] While useful, these studies tend to compartmentalize what is a transnational and transcultural phenomenon mediated by Internet technologies and so eminently porous and "spreadable" (Jenkins et al. 2013).

Anne Kustritz (2015b) also underlines concerns about scholarly practices perpetuating certain erasures in the context of European transcultural fandoms:

> The term *fan* ... mediates between local and international media and audiences; it encapsulates a broad range of diverse activities, histories, and practices, which become invisible by attending only to English-language fan spaces, or by assuming that because conversations there take place in English, the participants all come from Anglophone countries. Likewise, European fandoms illuminate many of the pitfalls, and much of the unevenness and uneasiness, that accompany globalization of media and globalization of fan identity and community. (3.1)

Kustritz identifies two key themes that I would like to explore further. First, fandom scholars must keep in mind the question of language and the assumptions made about the participants in English-language fandom spaces. A failure to do so in effect *makes* invisible the diversity of fan demographics. Second, fandom scholars must remember that the global fannish media landscape is an uneven and uneasy one, and globalization is one of its key driving forces. Terming it a "global" mediascape without interrogating this obfuscates the fact that it is dominated by USA-produced texts.

I would like to further interrogate this unease and link it to the growing influence of USA neo-imperialism on the global mediascape. Indeed, it would be almost impossible not to do so when examining the effects of global media flows controlled by largely USA-based conglomerates, especially in light of Hardt and Negri's (2000) analysis of imperial nodes of power no longer being restricted to the actions of specific nation-states, but also how these are intertwined with the operations of multinational companies. Hollywood films portray world events in ways sympathetic to USA state interests (Lee 2008), and it is important to stress that link in this context. For instance, when the email communications of the entertainment behemoth Sony Pictures Entertainment (SPE) were recently hacked and released to the public by WikiLeaks, one of the most discussed revelations concerned the level of collusion between the company and the USA government.[5] Given this scenario, it is interesting to see what kind of pushback, if any, these texts receive in fan communities often lauded for their self-reflexivity.

It is not my intention here to propose an overly deterministic model of fan consumption in the face of such massive geopolitical forces. Fan scholars have contended repeatedly with the question of how fan activities can be subversive within a neoliberal capitalist consumer culture. In their consideration of fan activism, Brough and Shershtova (2012), quoting Mukerjee (2011), posit that "Commodity activism … complicates our understanding of resistance, forcing us to consider 'civic politics in the neoliberal era' as possibly 'enabled by, and nurtured within, modes of consumer citizenship'" (4.7) Likewise, by incorporating an awareness of how neo-imperialism also influences both the texts that media fandom engages with and how those engagements proceed, fan studies can further complicate ideas of subversion and resistance. This calls for a broadening of scope in two important ways: firstly, in our conception and knowledge of who media fans are, and secondly, in the theoretical lenses we consider for analyses.

Methodology

I draw from primary data in the form of personally gathered fan interviews and theorize my findings using postcolonial cyberculture theory (Fernández 1999; Sardar 2000; Nayar 2008). This data was collected as part of a broader research project that focuses on the demographic diversity of media fandom. I also examine the effects and experiences of marginality stemming from identification with minority racial/cultural/ethnic and religious identities in fan communities that have so far been shown to skew white, cisgender, middle-class American.[6]

I used narrative analysis (Riessman 2008) to examine this data because fan discourse revolves around the act of storytelling. I used purposive sampling (Palys 2008) to select my interview group and conducted semistructured interviews of thirty-nine respondents, located in nine countries. The respondents ranged in age from eighteen to forty-three, with most identifying as using she/her pronouns, two clarifying that they were genderqueer, while one identified as intersex, and another as male. Twenty-three respondents identified as queer in some form, ranging from asexual to demisexual. In terms of racial/cultural and ethnic identity, the data reflected twenty-five different self-classifications. The primary markers of self-classification varied from single nationality (Indian/Singaporean) to hyphenated nationality (Chinese-American) to racial/ethnic categories (Latina/Black) to skin color (brown).

My findings indicate that non-white fans do have an "uneasy and uneven" relationship, to echo Kustritz, to the media texts that they engaged with in a transformative framework. This encompasses both the interactions that individual fans had with larger fan discussions on issues like representations (or lack thereof) of minority cultures in source texts and fanworks as well as the various media within which these interactions took place. It is the latter that I will take up first, as the question of medium is a vital aspect of online fan culture that has not been addressed adequately.

Medium matters: Use of fannish platforms

To riff off a favorite Austen quote, it is a truth universally acknowledged that the move of media fandom communities to the Internet changed *everything*. This has been examined in terms of the Internet connecting media fandom participants, allowing unprecedented community building and sharing of fanworks (Hellekson and Busse 2006) as well as platform-specific examinations (Booth 2010). However, scholarship has treated it as neutral medium and therefore has not interrogated its variable effect on different demographics. My interviews reveal that changes in platform have had significant effects on how fandom debates its own norms and practices.[7]

Online fandom communities have moved (broadly) from platforms like mailing lists (ONElist eGroups, Yahoo Groups) to journaling sites (Livejournal, Insanejournal, Dreamwidth) and standalone archival websites of individual fandoms or groups of fandoms, to the current preferred platforms of Twitter and Tumblr, along with broad-based archive sites for hosting fanwork (Archive of Our Own, Wattpad). Fandom interactions on all these platforms have differed according to current norms and practices, however the platforms themselves also mediated these interactions, allowing for greater or lesser autonomy, connectivity, and exposure to different ideas. In the case of mailing lists, Busker (2008) comments that they were hard to find and that:

> Perhaps just as problematic was an implied and even overt hostility to critical discussion. Any non positive reaction to an individual story tended to be greeted with recriminations, and even a discussion of the problems of a particular theme or genre was likely to be shouted down. (1.3)

It is not difficult to see how this hostility to critical discussion and insularity of focus would have manifested when participants wished to discuss potentially "non-positive" aspects of a source text such as racism. Indeed, such policing, both in terms of content (responses like "this is not an appropriate topic for discussion here") and in terms of tone (rules like "please keep this list friendly and supportive") have been recalled by respondents who participated in such spaces. That is not to say that these arguments have not continued to come up in other online forums, but the capacity for enforcement was greater in moderated mailing lists.

The increasing popularity of journaling sites over mailing lists allowed fans to curate their experiences by choosing other journals to connect to, and by creating their "own" space in which to host fanworks, meta discussions, or more personal posts. Busker notes that these sites made fandom more "porous," allowing for individual fans to be more aware of events in other fandoms. This mix of the personal and the political leads to more strongly felt opinions being expressed and circulated, perhaps contributing to one of the watershed moments in fannish history in terms of discussing racial dynamics: RaceFail '09.

To summarize, RaceFail '09[8] refers to a series of blog posts written by SF/F fans in response to SF/F author Elizabeth Bear's (2008) advice about "writing the other" in fiction. These posts pointed out both Bear's apparent hypocrisy, critiquing her record of portraying people of color, and encompassed the failings of the SF/F genre as a whole on the issue of race. While it is not within the scope of this chapter to discuss the specific series of events that made up RaceFail, the discussions that took place, which involved fans, writers, and editors, have impacted the ways non-white fans engage with such issues across media fandom (Reid 2010).

The fact that this discussion took place mainly on Livejournal, where individual posts are heavily interlinked, is overlooked when discussing the ways in which these arguments were disseminated. Busker argues that the journal format was influential because, "in many ways it has served to take the focus off the source and put it on the fan, and in turn, on fandom" (2.2). While I would argue that the source text remained very much in focus in the context of RaceFail '09, the foregrounding of fan identity as it intersected with issues of racial, cultural, and ethnic representation was facilitated by the journal platform in unique ways.

Keeping this in mind when formulating the initial questionnaire for my research, I attempted to track the effects of RaceFail '09 in my survey. Several respondents did mention its impact on their interaction with fandom, but were more inclined to discuss contemporary debates. When asked about the perceived rise in levels of fannish discourse around issues of privilege, respondents consistently identified fandom's move to even more dialogic platforms like Twitter and Tumblr as a turning point. These platforms offer greater visibility, both in terms of a willingness of individual fans to "claim" a non-white identity within a fannish space and, in doing so, find others who share or understand their experiences:

> I don't know if this is related at all, but I didn't come across many FOC [Fans of Color] until I started engaging in tumblr and twitter! I've found that in many of my fandoms, most of the people who were active were white, especially on LJ and dreamwidth. It wasn't until I got a twitter account that I came across so many FOC, and maybe it's bad to say this, but I was very surprised to see how many were in fandom. I knew that I was one, and logically there would be more just based on the sheer size of fandom, but it's different when you actually come across them in another space! (lquacker, Interview with author 2015)

It is clear that the discovery of "others like me" was an important one in terms of articulating a differential fannish identity. It is also clear that the presumed default representation of fans is a powerful influence on media fandom participants themselves, even if "logically" it does not hold up to interrogation. Another respondent, stepquietly, also remarked on the effect of "knowing" a community/audience existed for fanwork dealing with non-USA material. She started writing fan fiction about Bollywood movies noting that "the production of fanworks can be deeply personal but it also requires the possibility of an audience, and knowing the audience I was writing towards were people with shared markers of linguistic and cultural experience helped" (Interview with author 2015).

The second aspect concerning the broad dissemination of, and therefore access to, discussions problematizing source texts is also linked to the ease with which Tumblr posts can be reblogged. Respondents reflected on the ways such fan critiques often functioned as consciousness-raising, leading them to consider more nuanced understandings of the texts under consideration. This is not to say that Tumblr as a platform is viewed as unproblematic; respondents have identified issues around usage stemming from both its limitations as a platform (such as a lack of control privacy and inability to circulate longer, more nuanced arguments) and problems in broader individual usage (like the amplification of misleading information due to a lack of fact-checking).

One fan, identified as snackiepotato, commented on what she perceived as a lack of contact between fandoms and individual fans on Livejournal, citing the creation of "individual echo chambers" (Interview with author 2015) that then validated their own preconceived opinions. This term has also been used to describe Tumblr fan communities, where certain types of ghettoization can occur around ideas of essentialism, language use, cultural hierarchies, and fanwars. An example of the simultaneous nature of Tumblr as an "echo chamber" *and* "interruptible" is that of a fan-made gifset that imagined an Indian "Wizarding School" riffing off on the *Harry Potter* universe.[9] The gifset repurposed material from Bollywood films and the accompanying description leaned heavily on eroticizing stereotypes like "enchanted saris that shift colors sporadically" and the presence of a magical mango tree. This gifset was popular and received more than 30,000 notes exemplifying the "echo chamber" effect where un-nuanced ideas of "diversity" are amplified. However, the wide circulation of the gifset also resulted in criticism by some Indian fans who used it as a springboard to discuss issues like the effects of British imperialism on the development of Indian magic.[10]

Clearly, the degree of "interruptability" of a circulating idea is seen to be greater on more dialogic platforms like Tumblr and Twitter. Respondents identified Twitter as a more personal space than Tumblr, as access can be controlled through privacy settings and sensitive discussions can be carried out without the attendant anxiety of being "on display." In most cases, fans reported using both Tumblr and Twitter, simultaneously leveraging each platform's strengths. In the above example, for instance, the initial discussion about the problematic aspects of the gifset took place on Twitter before moving on to Tumblr (Swatkat interview with author 2015). The use of locked platforms to discuss problematic aspects of fan culture also underlines the fact that fandom spaces continue to be hostile to these debates.

This analysis makes explicit the multiple issues that need to be taken into account when approaching contemporary fandoms, in terms of both the fanworks themselves and the platforms utilized in their circulation. Most crucially, it points to the need to expand the scope of fandom theorization to fully encapsulate the variability of its participants.

Zooming in, zooming out: Theorizing 'global' fandom

One way of theorizing this increasing multivocality is in terms of postcolonial cyberculture theory, a theoretical paradigm that has had to grapple with the dualistic nature of the Internet. While historically used in cultural and literary studies, postcolonial perspectives in theorizing aspects of cyberculture are vital in order to center its embedded inequalities. Postcolonial digital theory has had to balance the liberating potential of the Internet with the reality of it being inextricably linked to neo/colonialism, capitalism, language use, and technology that functions within global networks to retain the status quo in favor of the global North (Fernández 1999; Nayar 2008). As Marianne Franklin (2004) notes, technological networks that are hailed as entirely new and revolutionary communicative innovations do in fact "overlay older ones put in place by the British Empire a hundred years ago and then developed by post-World War II military-based satellite communications. The ensuing skewing in 'global' coverage continues today" (p. 23). However, a cornerstone of postcolonial theory has always been the negotiation of shifting centers and flows of power within such uneven, even hostile terrains. To summarize Nayar's argument, he contends that it is possible for digital spaces that are interactive and multimodal to be seen as postcolonial if they are used for resistant political purposes. Nayar further identifies the qualities of heterogeneity, contestability, and contingency as key to shape these spaces as polyphonic and open-ended.

It is quite easy to see how the qualities of heterogeneity, contestability, and contingency inform the dynamics of online fan communities. Postcolonial critiques have often taken the form of "talking back" to discourses of power, interrupting canonical framings of knowledge and history. The fan critiques cited enable non-white fans to "interrupt" both hegemonic popular cultural texts *and* fanworks that reify privileged racial and cultural representations. Taking these dynamics into account, I posit that online media fan communities can be theorized as postcolonial spaces. To clarify, postcolonial spaces are not unproblematic, reciprocal, or equal fields of debate but do acknowledge the complex ways in which individuals negotiate "global" flows of media and information. For instance, to return to the example of the "Indian wizarding school" referenced earlier, while the original gifset was interrupted and critiqued, that critique did not get equal circulation. The burden of education inevitably rests on the postcolonial or minority subject, and interrupting this dominant discourse can still lead to being penalized or tone-policed. Therefore, to frame fandom spaces in this way is not to (re)signify them as inherently subversive, but rather demand more nuance from our analyses.

This has multiple effects. For one, it forces fan scholars to take seriously our usage of descriptors like *global, globalized,* and *international* when speaking about both the circulation of media texts and fan communities. It is not enough to acknowledge that national boundaries are being superseded in both contexts, but also important to engage with what aspects of fan identity remain unmentioned and therefore invisible in our work. Postcolonial theory stresses the value of glocal (Robertson 1992) perspectives when discussing the effects of informational "flows," pointing out that there is often a reciprocal process whereby the meaning of media texts is influenced by both local and global contexts. When analyzed from this perspective, the ways in which fans work both to deconstruct and to reify aspects of "global" media texts produced by multinational corporations, informed by their "local" circumstances—racial/cultural and ethnic identities, religion, class, disability, etc.—would broaden the scope of fan studies.

In my own research, a broadening of the scope of identity markers demonstrated the diversity within even a somewhat limited dataset. Part of my analysis interrogated respondents' levels of public engagement in discussions about representations of marginalized subjects in fandom texts. The sample was split evenly in terms of fans with medium and high levels of engagement and those with low levels. Figure 20.1 shows the distribution of respondents in terms of geographical location, while Figure 20.2 shows

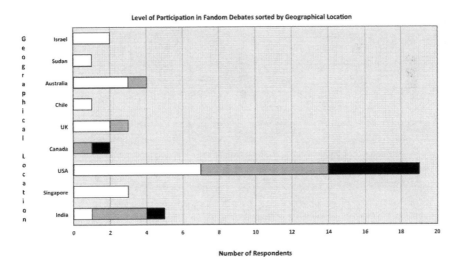

	India	Singapore	USA	Canada	UK	Chile	Australia	Sudan	Israel
Low	1	3	7	0	2	1	3	1	2
Medium	3	0	7	1	1	0	1	0	0
High	1	0	5	1	0	0	0	0	0

Figure 20.1 Distribution of respondent participation in fandom debates according to geographical location (created by the author).

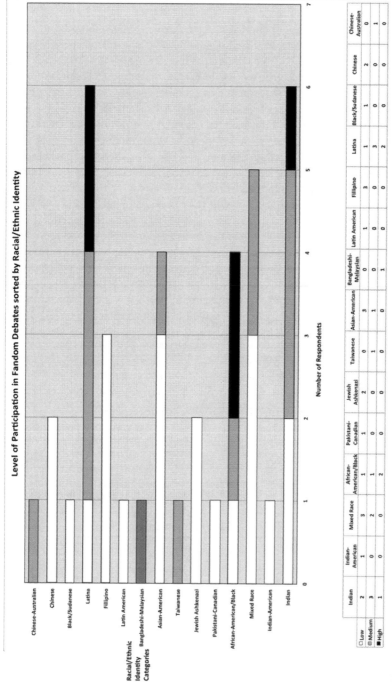

Figure 20.2 Distribution of respondent participation in fandom debates according to racial/cultural/ethnic identity (created by the author).

the distribution of respondents according to racial/cultural/ethnic identity. Both figures are sorted by levels of public engagement in fandom.

As can be seen in these charts, there initially seemed to be a predominance of people with high and medium levels of engagement located in the USA. While this might be seem to indicate the merits of concentrating on only the geographical area of the USA in such studies, when the distribution is examined in terms of racial/cultural/ethnic identity as shown in Figure 20.2, it is possible to come to a much more nuanced idea of who is engaged in these conversations.[11] Indeed, I would argue that even when the level of engagement is low, it is equally important to analyze why fans hesitate or choose not to participate in the discussion. A transcultural framework therefore would enable us to interrogate these hesitations rather than accept them as unavoidable silences.

Therefore while studies that concern themselves with nationalistic markers of influence have important stories to tell, we also need to expand our frames of reference to show the constructedness of current analytical boundaries. Using a postcolonial frame of analysis would also allow for more flexible and nuanced ideas of what individual racial/cultural and ethnic affinities look like and how they might operate, foregrounding their slippery and shifting nature as markers. The examination of these terms in only one national context leaves us open to the danger of reifying them. For instance, one fan attempted to undercut the highly positive critical reception of *Mad Max: Fury Road* (2015) as a feminist movie by critiquing it on the basis of non-white representation. This, however, was based on USA-centric ideas of race and sparked angry reactions by non-American fans who pointed out that there were actually three non-white women—Zoe Kravitz, Courtney Eaton, and Megan Gale—in the movie. Further, the fact that Eaton and Gale are biracial Maori women had critical resonances in a film set in a post-apocalyptic Australia.[12] An Australian respondent also echoed this sense of frustration in a broader context noting, "The USA-dominated discussions of racial identity and representation are particularly frustrating because it does not always speak to my context and it can be really simplistic" (Interviewed by author 2015).

Conclusion

As previously stated, it is not my intention to set up a "hierarchy of authenticity" regarding either the representations of marginalized racial/ethnic/cultural/religious identities in media texts or the ways they are discussed in fandom spaces. It is, in fact, vital to my argument that these interactions be seen as messy, overlapping, and problematic. Media fandom communities have been repeatedly analyzed as safe spaces, built on principles of gift-giving and shared passions for media texts and as close-knit and progressive in their politics (Hellekson and Busse 2006; Jenkins 2012a). Part of this depiction has developed out of the need to "reclaim" the image of fans as uncritical consumers, and has been facilitated by scholars with roots in these communities who have been careful not to feed into stereotypes. This is not to say that those characterizations of fan spaces are inaccurate, but perhaps the time has come to talk about how media fandom spaces are *also* spaces of contention and of conflict. I feel it is precisely by discomfiting ourselves and expanding our frameworks conceptually, geographically, and theoretically that fan studies will be able engage with fan cultures that are already "global" in all the utopian and dystopian potentials of that word.

Notes

1   "Whiteness" as a monolithic category has been complicated by numerous theorists (Roediger 1991; Ignatiev 1996) and this also applies to fandom participants. However, as Spivak (1990) has theorized, identity positions are often articulated "strategically" by minority groups in order to gain visibility.

2   A notable exception is Lori Kido Lopez's (2012) examination of the fan protests around the whitewashing of characters in the live-action adaptation of the animated series *Avatar: The Last Airbender* (2005–2008). However, this analysis concentrated on one site of activism for a limited amount of time and was not followed by similar studies. Rebecca Wanzo's (2015) recent article on expanding the accepted critical genealogies of fandom criticism is also a vital intervention.

3   Critiques are often authored by individual fans and circulated via informal networks. Curated Tumblr blogs—Racebending.tumblr.com, Cosplayingwhileblack.tumblr— also signal to boost such critiques.

4   These include Indonesian (Jung 2014) and Israeli (Lyan and Levkowitz 2015) fans.

5   A summary can be found here: http://motherboard.vice.com/read/the-us -government-asked-sony-to-help-counter-isis-propaganda (accessed May 13, 2015).

6   I interviewed fans who engage with fanwork in some way (not limited to producing it). Their experiences of marginalization concern English-language based media (mostly produced in the United States and United Kingdom) and their transnational fan communities.

7   I am well aware that fandom participants frequently use multiple platforms simultaneously. However, we can plot an increase and decrease of use of certain platforms over time.

8   The date is used to differentiate this from other discussions around race that had happened before 2009 but had not gained as much traction.

9   http://zorana.tumblr.com/post/97054380985/asheathes-wizarding-schools -around-the-world (accessed May 13, 2015).

10 http://thepostmodernpottercompendium.tumblr.com/post/94196004347/they -trip-over-the-words-the-syllables-and-sounds (accessed May 13, 2015).

11 The data record even further variation within the graphically represented categories, which have had to be aggregated due to the restraints of printing.

12 http://fangirljeanne.tumblr.com/post/119506756812/ranting-about-feminism -its-racist-for-you-to-ask (accessed May 13, 2015).

21

Interview with Laurent Malaquais, Director of *Bronies* (2012)

Lucy Bennett and Paul Booth

Laurent Malaquais is the director of the crowdfunded documentary *Bronies: The Extremely Unexpected Adult Fans of My Little Pony* (2012), which focuses on male adult fans of the aforementioned children's animated series, a community that has received growing attention and expansion in recent years (Gilbert 2015; Jones 2015). In addition to documenting their well-attended yearly conventions, the film focuses on a range of individual international Bronies, with Malaquais visiting them in their homes and hearing their personal stories, in an attempt to unravel the meanings and values behind their fandom. In order to learn more about the processes and challenges surrounding representing fans in documentaries, we spoke to Malaquais about his experiences of making the film and how it was subsequently received by the wider Brony community.

Q: Could you tell us how you got the idea for the documentary, and how it came to fruition?

A: The documentary began with John De Lancie—Q from *Star Trek*. He was pretty famous for his character Q, and Lauren Faust, who created *My Little Pony: Friendship Is Magic*, was a big fan of the character. She sent the script to John De Lancie, he liked the writing, and he went in and essentially did 6 hours of voiceover work. And then, completely forgot about it. And I think three or four months later, he started getting tons and tons of fan mail. And so he goes to his wife and he's like. *What, what is this little girls' show?* And she's like *you did that three months ago*, and he's like *I completely forgot. Because these aren't little girls that are messaging me, these are twenty-year-old men.* So it blew his mind that he had these fans that were in their twenties for a little girl's cartoon that he had voiced. He just couldn't wrap his mind about it. And he's been in the *Star Trek* fandom for years and has gone to tons of conventions, and dealt with stereotypical nerd, geek culture, and people that are introverts, people that have a hard time relating to the world and need that fictional world to live in and relate to, to understand their place in the world. So he was very familiar with all that, but he couldn't wrap his mind around Bronies, because they're so different.

He went to this producer I work with, Mike Brockhoff, and they were talking about it over dinner, and Mike said, *wow, that's crazy*. And then [De Lancie] goes, *what's even crazier is that I've just been invited to a convention where there will be six thousand Bronies in New York*. And Mike thought, *this could be a documentary*. He called me and said *what do you think, is this something you'd be interested in?* And I didn't really know what Bronies were, kind of vaguely, but not really. So I got online and the first thing I encountered were these *Fox News* affiliates that were bashing Bronies and just asserting this jock/bully mentality of their pundits, and they were just nasty and blaming the state of the economy, the economic global decline, on Bronies and this type of mentality. I just thought that this was so unfair. When you get to find out more about the Bronies, you realize that they are going to love and tolerate the hell out of you. That's their motto. So you have the bullies beating up on a fandom that's loving and tolerating. It just seemed so unfair. And the damage that they were creating was that a lot of these Bronies, their families watch *Fox News* or hear about it. I felt like they needed a voice and so that's why I said, *alright, I'll jump aboard*. I knew there was much more to this fandom. My parents are hippies, they're French hippies that came to America, and I sort of grew up in that love, tolerance, and friendship kind of culture, that part of it I could relate to. It was like, *I want to give them a voice*.

The documentary began as John De Lancie going to meet the Bronies and that for me was the vehicle for how the audience could see it, because here's this man who knows nothing about Bronies, and he's going to basically open the door to the audience and show them who they are and who's coming in with prejudice—like suspicion of the fandom, it was just like what the outside would think. So I think this would be a great way to introduce who they are and get to know them and, as he made this arc into understanding and appreciating them and their fandom and why they appreciate him, the audience also could be on that journey and then they could come to the same sort of understanding.

Q: In other documentaries about fans, there's a problematic element that creators tend to focus on very extreme cases. But in your Bronies documentary you show more different shades of fandom—extroverts, introverts, and so on. How much of that was a conscious decision and how much of that was just happenstance?
A: I would say by nature I tend to go for the grittier, darker stories, but I think that it was fair to have a spectrum of who the Bronies are, from a dramatic level—the Pinky Pie, the Fluttershutter—seems fair, because I was sort of modeling my characters after the actual ponies because everybody relates to a different pony, and I think that each pony represents an archetype and a challenge in someone's life. It's a life lesson for them. So most people identify with a certain pony. You can see in their lives why that pony takes on so much meaning for them. It's either something that they already are or something they aspire to be. If somebody wants to be a Rainbow Dash, and in their life they're not a Rainbow Dash, then you can immediately go—it's almost astrological— well, this person is perhaps really shy and might be like Fluttershy but wants to be Rainbow Dash, so you start realizing when you spend time with them, this person

really is a Rainbow Dash, and is a very outgoing person that wants to be out in the limelight and fly around and make a lot of noise and be seen. But they are stuck in this other archetype that's clearly not who they are and it seems to create a lot of internal conflict.

Then it's like, what's their obstacle in becoming their true selves? To me that's really important. I mean, we see Daniel—he was really "walk away" and isolated from the world, and not connecting. But once he got to the convention at the end, he was running around bro-hoofing everybody, you saw him come out of his shell and it was almost shocking to him to recognize the potential of who he could be, and sort of who he knew he always was. And seeing that, his higher self and his lower self connect in one moment; to me that's what's so beautiful about-what I loved most about that scene.

Q: How did you select what fans to include? What kind of process did you use to select them?
A: We put posts on Equestria Daily, the news site for all the Bronies, and it just spread like that because the Bronies are so viral that you put one thing up and it just bounces all over the place. Daniel, funnily enough, he didn't even submit—we were asking people, do you have an interesting story and do you feel like you should be included, please tell us why, and a little bit about yourself, and that's pretty much the gist of how we solicited people. And Daniel's mother, she's all over the Brony fandom, and she found our post and she submitted her son. So he was too shy to submit himself. But she knew that reading it that he would be a great … he was perfect.

Q: Did you face any struggles when representing the fans, either internal struggles about how you're going to represent them, or were there things that your film subjects didn't want on camera?
A: Lyle's father was very resistant. They didn't want to be part of the documentary—let's be real. I mean, at one point, when I was filming him, I filmed Lyle's [interview] before, and they actually asked me to leave. The dad was really uncomfortable; the mom was like, as soon as the husband got home, she was even more uncomfortable. I had to be really tenacious, and I had to keep going and not give them a moment to realize what was going on. Because I could feel the energy was slipping away, and the fact that, I wasn't even certain they were going to show up to BronyCon afterwards. It was a hard situation and he was so resistant—that's when I came up with the idea of that other Brony father who was very supportive of his son. He probably grew up driving muscle cars, and doing whatever manly things he did in the 70s, and to realize that his son, who he wanted to be the spitting image of himself, a gun enthusiast, a history buff of wars, is now into colorful ponies? And playing with Legos and everything else that comes with that culture. I don't know … I wonder if it's opened his eyes, it's hard to think that this experience changed him. But it must have in a small way, I don't know. It would be interesting to film Lyle's father now, and see what his whole take on it is.

Q: What was the response from the Brony community afterwards?
A: It's just like anything. There were people that loved it and people that hated it. It was the entire spectrum. But for the most part, very positive. Then there's people outside of the fandom that have no interest in Bronies and were upset that the film didn't cast them in a more negative light—it was more of a fair and balanced documentary— which for me was never my goal. I wasn't going to get people to comment on why it's negative. Sure, there's negative things in everything, I felt like telling the audience going into it, *I'm making a documentary about men in their twenties and they're into a little girl's cartoon, that's meant for 8-year-old girls.* I felt like my obstacle already was the audience. There's nobody I could tell that to that wouldn't ask me, *are these pedophiles?, This is weird, there's some weird sexual deviancy going on, and there's just some sort of furry sexuality. It just sounds like a den for pedophiles.* Just on and on and on. I found myself trying to convince people and it would take me like an hour, and they'd still walk away from it going, *yeah, I'm still not convinced.* And so that was my approach to why I felt like I didn't need to weigh heavily on the negative stereotypes that people think of when they think of Bronies.

Q: Do you hear anything from the actual subjects? Did they contact you afterwards?
A: Yes, I'm still in contact. Facebook friends with Lyle and Daniel, and Daniel's mother talks to me all the time on Facebook. It's like I'm part of the Brony family. They do charities and stuff, they invite me to be on a radio show, I'm invited to all the Brony conventions. It's part of my community. Funny enough, I still talk to the manliest Brony—I still talk to all of them, anyone I talked to. I'm considered part of the family, I guess.

Q: As a filmmaker, how do you negotiate making an interesting narrative with representing fans accurately?
A: I mean, I have my intent. I have my Joseph Campbell hero's journey, and intend my little plots, my little twelve story beats and I'm trying to do that to show a change and then that's how I go about a documentary. Or any story—narrative or scripted or whatever, I want to see somebody in this, then they're going to a certain point or event, with the intention of something larger than themselves happening. Then afterwards there's going to be some sort of aftermath and with that aftermath there's going to be change of some sort, and it can be negative or positive, it doesn't really matter. I just don't want to see them in the same place at the end. And they may end up in the same place. If I'm making a documentary I have to be willing to accept that and take that risk, that there might not be a change, and I may not be able to see that happen. That's part of it.

A lot of it is just, you talk to your subjects, you try to figure out what they're going to try to do, you get a good sense of who they are, you find out what their challenges are. Like Daniel, for instance, told me that he had a hard time in open spaces with lots of strange people he didn't know. He'd start to get paranoid and it would freak him out. And that's when I was like, *okay, so, I'm going to follow you to B.U.C.K.* [Brony convention] *and you're going to figure this out.* And I just laid back, and I could see him sort of panic, and then I would pull back. I would just step back, so when he looked around, he was all by himself, having to negotiate his path in a sea of strangers. I wanted to see him confront these fears. I wanted him to experience that in a visual way so the audience could really feel. It's kind of sadistic, but at the same time, when it's really good, it's showing not telling. And then you're showing, it's also making the audience feel what the character's experience is. So that's one example.

And the other thing is, when I was in North Carolina filming with Alex, I took him back to the spot where these rednecks had bullied him and threatened his life, and I brought him right back to that spot. So some rednecks were there in the background getting gas, and I think it was like bringing his anxiety up, so I was trying to get him to re-experience that moment so it would take on more weight, we could feel this fear. So I'll do stuff like that. And then a lot of it was his moment when he was dancing around all the Bronies and BronyCon, it was just sort of following him around, listening to what he was saying, just trying to capture those moments, so I'm really at the disposal of the character.

Once the journey starts, you just set it up and let it go, whatever they do—all they do, you just hope that you're there capturing and it unravels, and what they're feeling, and whether it leads to an arc or not. It's all about finding those defining moments. I really like those moments where they're being themselves, even if the camera wasn't there. So I walk in and spend a lot of film—I'll film somebody for hours, like five hour interviews, just burn them out to the point where they don't care about the camera anymore. They just want it to stop. And then after awhile, they just stop talking, they forget the camera, and we're just having a conversation. That's really important in getting those moments that you can relate to.

Q: The aspects of fandom that you put in the Bronies documentary, was there anything you wish you'd put in? Any other elements of Brony fandom that didn't make the film?
A: I would've liked, but we didn't have time, a whole bunch of story lines that didn't make it in there. I mean, I overfilm my stories, there are too many stories, but I would've liked to have made it more experiential, where we just really get into their heads more. Or there are those silent moments where you can almost read their thoughts, and they make you uncomfortable, and you can really feel their pain and you can really feel their reason for turning to this. I would've done that. And there are some beautiful moments with Daniel I would've put in. He took me on a walk to the top of that mountain where he was—we got up to the top—and I felt like it was a very dark moment for him, where he basically turned to *My Little Pony* for wisdom because it was the only bit of hope in his life. And it seemed very clear to me, the alternative, at that moment. That making that decision was very dark. And just to put it like that, it seemed morbid. And it seemed like a spot where people came to end all their problems, with finality. So, I would've put more of that in there.

I would've liked to have gone with Alex and tried to explore the rednecks more, and gotten their side of it, and seen him interact with them, which was really tricky because they didn't want to be on camera. I'm not even sure how I would've done that. But I would've liked to have had time.

Q: Did you become a Brony after making the documentary?
A: In the process of it, I got more steeped in the culture and I started to feel like a Brony. And when I'm around them, I could relate to them. I could say that when I'm in their presence I feel like a Brony, and I definitely have a fondness for them. But it's not like I'm running around doing Brony things on a regular basis. I don't know, as a filmmaker, I'm more of a Gypsy. I have to relate to the things I'm doing and feel a part of them as I'm making them, and there's always that fondness for [them]. I'll always take a piece of it with me.

Part Four

Global Perspectives on Fan Representations

22

Slashy Rotten Pervs: Transnational Media Representation of *Sherlock* Slash Fans and the Politics of Pathologization

Darlene Hampton

Due in large part to global convergence—which Henry Jenkins defines as "the multicultural flow of cultural goods around the world" (Jenkins 2006a, 116)—"fans"—a word that once signaled fanaticism and pathology (Jensen 1992)—have become a cultural and economic force that flows across national borders and cultures. Both scholars and the mainstream entertainment press discuss fans in terms of their economic value—especially fans' influence on the content, shape, and direction of media texts. In short, media production and promotion has become all about the fans.

Yet, within this context, not *all* fans are catered to, lauded, and empowered; not *all* fan influence is valuable and welcome. More often than not, the determining factor in a fandom's value and the legitimacy of its practices is gender. Fans and fan practices have historically been and continue to be bound up with discourses that construct gendered identities and values under patriarchy. Female fans, for example, are still subject to associations with pathology (with terms such as *hysteria*, *rabid*, and *obsessive* used to characterize behavior) while a majority of male-associated fan practices are not. These representations not only police and contain the textual and legal threats female fans represent to media industry (Scott 2010), but cultural and ideological ones as well.

Extending this discussion of gender, fandom, and value to include the relationship between gender and nation, I read the continued pathological representation of female fans as inextricably enmeshed in discourses of both gender and nation. Within transnational media representation, the body of the fangirl acts as a global site for the performance of overlapping cultural, economic, and geopolitical anxieties—anxieties rooted in the economic power of the female consumer, the increased visibility of women's sexual desires and pleasures in the public sphere, and a sense that the balance of power in the world is becoming more fluid and unstable (particularly between the "east" and "west"). As a product of converging discourses, I argue that the figure of the fangirl is deployed to disavow the economic significance of female consumers, police the desires and pleasures of women, *and* promote specific national interests. In order to tease out these connections, I compare British and US media representations of Chinese female fans of the BBC's *Sherlock* (2010–) against the backdrop of the US and Great Britain's response to China's mass industrialization and rise as a global superpower. Analysis of the China-focused media blitz surrounding the release of the show's long-awaited third series illustrates how the figure of the fangirl is woven into both patriarchal and national discourse.

Sherlock and slash

Sherlock is a modern adaption of Arthur Conan Doyle's classic British detective stories. Created and produced by self-proclaimed Sherlock Holmes "fanboys" Steven Moffat and Mark Gatiss (see Click and Brock, this volume), the show has achieved immense worldwide popularity and transformed actor Benedict Cumberbatch into a superstar. *Sherlock* has active and vocal female-dominated fanbase that crisscrosses national boundaries and cultures, making it a prime example of a *transcultural* fandom (Chin and Morimoto 2013). Within this group, there is an ardent and vocal contingent of fans engaged in the culture of slash—the practice of producing and engaging with homoerotic storytelling inspired by popular media. *Sherlock* fandom's most visible and prolific slash pairing is Johnlock—or Sherlock Holmes/John Watson which produces fanworks in a variety of genres, media, and languages.

Although the origin story of slash fandom traces the practice to science fiction fandom in the late 1960s and early 1970s, homoerotic fan practice is a global phenomenon. Erotic male/male fiction has a rich history in manga fan culture. Distinct from slash culture, *yaoi* (boys' love) culture has flourished in Japan, where *doujinshi* (fanzines) have been printed and sold by fan creators since at least the 1980s. The emergence of yaoi culture in Japan, unlike slash, was strongly linked to professionalism. The practice began as a way for female manga artists, who were largely marginalized from the industry due to their gender, to use the "amateurish" market of *dōjin* manga publication to jumpstart professional careers by selling their zines and marketing their work (Zheng 2013).[1]

Contemporary Chinese slash culture, known as *danmei*, is strongly linked to yaoi culture in Japan—imported in the late 1990s and early 2000s via expanding access to Internet technologies. Fans of boys' love culture in Japan refer to themselves as *Fujoshi* (rotten girls), a moniker that has been taken on by fangirls in China, where it is translated to *Fu Nu* or "rotten women." Today, homoerotic fan art in various incarnations is produced and circulated all over the world; it is also subject to containment—largely by pathologizing the fans who express their desires and pleasures publicly.

There is no lack of fan scholarship examining slash fandom as cultural practice, subcultural community, subversion, activism, and queer performance (Bacon-Smith 1992; Jenkins 1992; Busse 2006; Lackner et al. 2006; Lothian et al. 2007). In fact, slash is one of the most-studied and written about practices associated with fandom. Yet, there has been very little work done on how slash is represented by those outside of fandom. Although the focus of this study is on the significance of how representations of slash fandom align and differ transnationally and *not* on its subversive potential, it is important to acknowledge that the characterization of slash as a resistive subculture *is* significant because it determines how slash fandom becomes enmeshed in national discourse.

Gender, value, and fangirls

Within the framework of patriarchy, everything is seen as less valuable when it is associated with the feminine. Scholarship examining the reception of media across genres and texts demonstrates that media with female-driven commercial success suffers a significant hit to its cultural legitimacy and value. This holds true for "casual" video games (Vanderhoef 2013), films like *Titanic* (Nash and Lahti 1999) and *Twilight* (Click 2009; Pinkowitz 2011; Busse 2013a), or pop stars and celebrities like Justin Bieber (Jones 2014). This gender-based devaluing speaks to cultural anxiety over the power of female pleasure and desire over the entertainment market.

Mainstream press outlets such as *The Guardian* and *National Public Radio* (NPR) have recently expressed anxiety over the power of female desire to affect the production of television texts by publishing reviews bemoaning instances of overwhelming "fan service"[2]—especially concerns over the transformation of action-oriented characters (such as the Doctor in *Doctor Who* and Sherlock Holmes in *Sherlock*) into "whimsical and romantic heroes." Anecdotally, this indicates a generalized anxiety over an imagined impending feminization of media—an anxiety that consistently appears whenever gender roles begin to shift (Hansen 1986). Yet, this devaluing of the feminized includes not only taste and fan practices, but a range of other gendered associations and identities, including that of the nation. Sherlock Holmes and the Doctor are, after all, explicitly British characters; their feminization threatens a feminization of the nation they represent.

In the context of global convergence, the female consumer is now a transnational one whose economic power, visibility, and public desire have global implications reflecting back on the nation itself. Thus, it is not surprising that the discourse surrounding the global popularity of an explicitly national property—like *Sherlock* (2010)—leverages this desire in a way that both incites nationalism and contains the cultural threat of feminization in ways unique to the nation in which the discourse is produced.

The containment of female slash fans is consistent across genres and texts; it is carried out largely through media representation that shames, dismisses, and pathologizes. In the case of *Sherlock*, this includes confronting celebrities with erotic fan art, repeatedly asking producers how they feel about slash interpretations of their text, and writing dismissive portrayals of slash fans into the narrative of the show itself (Jones 2014). Slash fans' homoerotic interpretations are cast as misreading (Strudwick 2013), dismissed by show's stars and producers as absurd, and ridiculed for the purposes of comedy. The discourse produced by these representations is not unique to *Sherlock*. As slash has become more visible, we see similar discourse produced about slash fans of a variety of texts—from cult shows like *Supernatural* to works of literary fiction such as Annie Proulx's *Brokeback Mountain*. The commonality of these representations demonstrates an underlying cultural anxiety about the public desires and economic power of women and girls—especially when they breach the boundaries of interpretation as set by media text's producers.

What is unique about the representation of Chinese slash fans is how it differs from this model and how the discourses produced are incorporated into national discourse. The representation of Chinese slash fans dedicated to *Sherlock* quickly became absorbed into international discourse in ways that performed (however unintentionally) the work of soft power for both Great Britain and the United States. In Great Britain, it is enmeshed in the nation's deployment of *soft power*—the ability to attract and persuade by cultivating positive feelings toward national culture, values, and policies (Nye 1990); in the United States, it is co-opted as self-congratulatory reinforcement of the country's imagined social/political superiority. One of the most common ways in which soft power is exerted is through cultural exports—especially, in the age of digitization and global networks—entertainment media.

Between November 2013 and April 2014, media coverage of the release of the *Sherlock* series three premiere appeared in entertainment, current affairs, and general news across multiple outlets in both the United States and the United Kingdom. As both a fan and a fan scholar, I watched and read this coverage as it appeared. I was interested in observing both the behavior of different segments of the fandom, and the representation of *Sherlock* fangirls in general. In my observations, I noted that a large amount of the coverage focused specifically on the show's reception in China—especially its reception among young, female slash fans. As I followed these articles, content patterns began to emerge: viewing statistics, romance-inflected language, repeated fannish characterizations (young, sweet, innocent), and excerpts of the same slash fictions. To create a representative sample, I initiated Google searches using combinations of the terms: *Sherlock, China, Fangirls, Fans, Slash*. I pulled press articles from each nation that appeared in the first two pages of searches with each combination. Analysis of these articles revealed key differences between those published for US audiences and those published for audiences in Great Britain. What follows is close analysis of the distinct national discourses produced through these articles.

A nation in love: Representing the Chinese fangirl in Great Britain

The pervasive coverage of China's love for *Sherlock* fits seamlessly into the discourse produced through David Cameron's interviews with both British and Chinese press preceding and during his much-touted December 2013 trade visit to Beijing. Speaking on Beijing Television's (BTV) "Yang Lan One on One" in London on November 28, Cameron characterized his vision of an expanded relationship between the two countries as a "win-win"—emphasizing cultural exchange, reciprocal investment, and extending offers of British guidance and support for sustainable development. This same message was delivered to the Chinese public in a more casual way by Cameron when he answered questions put to him by users of the microblogging network Sin Weibo. In each response, Cameron takes the opportunity to characterize Great Britain as China's wiser mentor or guide and promote British cultural products. These same themes are mirrored in the press coverage of Chinese *Sherlock* fans.

The British discourse on *Sherlock*'s Chinese reception unfolded across multiple magazines, newspapers, and blogs but stems from one originating source: a November 15, 2013, piece entitled "Benedict Cumberbatch is a Gay Erotic God in China" (Carter 2013) which appeared in *Foreign Policy Magazine* (FPM). The article leads with Chinese viewing statistics, noting that the series had (at the time of writing) been viewed 24 million times since its 2011 release on Sohu TV. The popularity of *Sherlock* star Benedict Cumberbatch, specifically, is credited with inspiring a "new wave" of both Chinese viewers of British television and "gay romance stories" (Carter 2013).

The bulk of the piece is largely focused on slash—pulling badly translated quotes directly out of Chinese fan fiction, describing explicit examples of slash artwork and fan vids on Youku (a Chinese video-sharing site). The article frames slash as strange, new, and explicitly subversive—characterizing fans' taking on of the label *Fu Nu* as a kind of resistance to traditional feminine roles. Yet, Carter still takes a dismissive tone when she quips that the homoerotic stories must be important as the women are willing to risk jail in order write them—reminding readers that in China, LGBT individuals still face discrimination (Carter 2013). There is no mention of the roots of the term *Fu Nu*, its relationship to Japan, or the fact that Chinese danmei has been fairly popular since the late 1990s.

Following Carter's piece, there was a rash of short pieces in the British press cherry-picking its content while adding embellishments—many of which directly addressed the Sin Weibo response to Cameron's trade delegation to Beijing. Using hyperbolic language and a condescending tone, each piece represents Chinese fans as obsessive and sex-crazed. However, these descriptions also cast them as silly, sweet, and adorable. A December 2013 piece in the *Radio Times*, "Introducing Curly Fu and Peanut—better known as Sherlock's Benedict Cumberbatch and Martin Freeman," begins with the tagline: "As Chinese fans go potty for the BBC's *Sherlock*, it emerges that they have some rather endearing nicknames for its two stars" (Dowell 2013). It briefly explains the reasoning behind the Chinese nicknames for Benedict Cumberbatch and Martin Freeman,[3] but quickly moves on to cite viewing statistics and discuss the interactions between Cameron and Chinese citizens on Weibo—characterizing citizens as oblivious to the seriousness of his diplomatic visit and only interested in the Prime Minister's power to speed up the production of *Sherlock*.

Chinese appeals to the Prime Minister for more *Sherlock* are mentioned again in a January 2, 2014, blog post on the BBC News *China Blog* titled "Gay love theory as fans relish Sherlock in China" (BBC 2014). Alongside references to the stars' "cute" nicknames, the piece includes Chinese reactions to the long-awaited episode such as "Curly Fu is my only male god. He represents beauty and wisdom, but better with his clothes off" and "the human race cannot stop the invasion of Curly Fu" (BBC 2014). Another piece published the same day by *Public Radio International*, "Why is China obsessed with *Sherlock*," is taken nearly verbatim from the FPM article (Porzucki 2014). On January 3, 2014, the top story in the arts and entertainment section of *The Independent* is "Chinese fans give Sherlock and Watson bizarre nicknames and hail

Benedict Cumberbatch as erotic icon" (Dunham 2014). A January 19, 2014, article published on metro.co.uk entitled "The Chinese have fallen in Love with *Sherlock* and Benedict Cumberbatch who they call 'Curly Fu'" (Staff 2014) repeats a majority of the same content, leading the story with: "Chinese audiences are *lapping up Sherlock*, with the third series of the Benedict Cumberbatch-led show becoming a phenomenon in the country" (emphasis mine).

Looking closely at the repetitious content of these articles we see two intertwining discourses emerge. The first—which we see in words like "erotic," "relish," "obsessed," "potty" (child-like), and "fixated"—reinforces the representation of female fans as immature, sex-focused, shallow, and irrational consumers. There is also a fair bit of orientalist exotification with the multiple repetitions of the stars' Chinese nicknames, the use of the word "exotic" in titles, and the allusions to *Fu Nu*. The second, underlying, discourse represents Chinese fans as adorable and sweet—if not a bit clueless—and the sexual pleasure they derive from slash is represented as less perverse and more *quaint*. Whereas the first discourse continues to do the work of pathologizing and dismissing female fans, the second echoes the British government's ongoing efforts to increase trade relations with China.

In each of these media representations, the pathological identity usually mapped onto fangirls is applied to China itself—which becomes personified as a "fan" of Britain. Fannish identity is collapsed into national identity and China is figured as a *fangirl* of Britain, feminized through its characterization as a romantic consumer (rather than producer) of cultural goods. China as a fangirl is "obsessed," "in love," and "fixated" on British culture. Of course, like any fangirl, China's interest is cast as sexual, silly, and shallow. However, it is also framed as explicitly unthreatening and economically valuable—an open and desiring market for British goods.

What is also very important to note about the British coverage is what is glaringly missing. Whereas the traditional discourse on fangirls frames female fans as economically and ideologically threatening, this aspect is curiously absent; the fangirl's desires or pleasures are exoticized and discussed as an oddity, but are not framed as negative. Even more importantly, the British discourse minimizes (or ignores altogether) any discussion of the ongoing Chinese crackdowns on homoerotic fan art, the nation's much-publicized discrimination against LGBT citizens, or the intermittent arrest of online danmei artists and archive administrators—topics which, as we shall see, are the *central* focus of the American discourse.

Obsession versus repression: Representing Chinese fangirls in the United States

On January 19, the Associated Press (AP) published, "China Falls in Love with Sherlock Holmes" (Fu 2014), an article that echoes the piece from *Foreign Policy Magazine* by including condescending references to nicknames and emphasizing viewing statistics. However, it refocuses the discourse to highlight particularly *American* concerns— noting that *Sherlock* has stimulated commercial ventures in China and positing the superiority of Western media (and its distribution) over Chinese properties; it explicitly praises capitalist business models and critiques Chinese censorship policies:

> Even the Communist Party newspaper People's Daily has heaped praise on [Sherlock], saying the first episode of season three exhibited: "Tense plot, bizarre story, exquisite production, excellent performances." (Fu 2014)

and:

> Yu Fei, a veteran writer of TV crime dramas for Chinese television, said […] "Our writers and producers face many restrictions and censorship. We cannot write about national security and high-level government departments." (Fu 2014)

These quotes extol the quality of the drama and lament the fact that censorship prevents the production of its like in China, complimenting the BBC while issuing a not-so-subtle jab at China's domestic policy. The piece barely touches on the slash, only briefly mentioning that Chinese fans write their own fiction that sometimes "play on the complicated relationship of Holmes and Watson by making them a gay couple" (Fu 2014).

The tone of this piece is reminiscent of Cold War rhetoric—praising the virtues of capitalism while characterizing communism as a stumbling block to national success. This rhetoric is repeated across the sample, especially prevalent in articles published between January and April 2014; if slash is mentioned, it is consistently in the context of censorship and LGBT discrimination. For example, on January 15, *The Wire*—a subsidiary of the Cable News Network (CNN)—published "Chinese Women Can't Stop Reading and Writing Gay 'Sherlock' Fan Fiction" (Abad-Santos 2014). The piece appears in the sample more than once, as it was re-run in *The Atlantic* and picked up by Yahoo News and other blog and information sites. As the title indicates, the piece's draw is, again, Chinese fascination with *Sherlock* slash fiction. It begins by quoting a Chinese fan (as quoted in a BBC piece) as saying "The *gaycitement* has finally returned. PS: Thank you Prime Minister Cameron, for visiting China" (Abad-Santos 2014).

Abad-Santos acknowledges that slashing is widely practiced by fans across the globe but notes that slash is different in China due to discrimination and censorship, linking directly to a 2012 article on a Chinese news site describing the arrest of slash website administrators for distributing pornography.[4] The article ends by framing "raunchy Curly Fu-Peanut fan fiction" as representing "an improvement in the country's attitudes toward the LGBT community" (Abad-Santos 2014). In this way, slash is not only subversive; it is characterized as a signifier of grassroots social change.

Throughout US media discourse, a theme begins to emerge: Chinese slash fans have been inspired by Western media to explore and express their (arguably) queer sexual desires and the communist regime is trying to shut it down. This unfolds across multiple press articles beginning with the *Sherlock* series premiere in January 2014 and peaking in mid-April when twenty more slash authors were arrested and more fiction archives were shut down as part of a "cleaning of the internet" initiative enacted by the Chinese government to eliminate pornography. Representative examples include *LGTB Weekly's* "Gay Sherlock Holmes Fan Fiction Irks China's Media Regulator" (Editor 2014), *The Comic Book Legal Defense Fund's* "Chinese Same-Sex Slash Fic Targeted in Porn Crackdown" (Williams 2014), and *Buzzfeed's* "Inside China's Insane Witch Hunt for Slash Fiction Writers" (Tang 2014). Many of the articles include the same quote attributed to a slash fan on Sin Weibo: "This is not cleaning the cyberspace. This is pure discrimination. I may never see a rainbow flag fly above China in my life time."[5]

A day after *The Wire* piece, self-described feminist news site *Jezebel*—part of the blog conglomerate Gawker Media Inc.—published "Women in China are really into Gay *Sherlock* Fan Fiction" (Davies 2014), leading with:

> Extra, extra! Breaking news from the East! Women in China really love their Sherlock slash fic. As do plenty of women in the U.S., England, France, Mexico, Brazil, South Africa or pretty much anywhere else on the planet where people are able to watch the show. SHOCKING! It looks like women's sexuality is more complex than most cultures would care to admit, at least when it comes to Benedict Cumberbatch porking Martin Freeman. Rrrrrrread all about it! (Davies 2014)

This opening paragraph undermines the rhetoric of Chinese exceptionalism and takes a tongue-in-cheek swipe at the manufactured sense of shock surrounding slash. However, once the snark is over the article reinforces the nationalist discourse by calling attention to China's arrest of fan fiction writers and claiming the country's anti-homosexuality laws have forced gay and lesbian citizens into fake heterosexual marriages.

Explicitly fan-friendly sites covered the arrests as well. *The Daily Dot* published "Chinese Authorities Are Arresting Writers of Slash Fanfiction" (Romano 2014) and *The Mary Sue* posted "Several Women Arrested for Writing Fanfic in China" (Pantozzi 2014). These articles begin with lines such as "Recent reports of crackdowns by Chinese officials on young female fans who write slash have sent waves of alarm throughout international fandom waters" (Romano) and "Quick! Hide your fic!" (Pantozzi). These pieces engage in the same rhetoric, as *The Wire* article. The *Mary Sue* piece even ends with a quasi-inspirational call to arms, asking fans to "double our slash efforts to support their freedom to fic. Who's with me?" (Pantozzi 2014). To *The Daily Dot's* credit, they do acknowledge similar legal issues affecting slash erotica in Canada and Australia by noting the arrest and imprisonment of a yaoi fan for bringing comics across the Canadian border. However, this acknowledgment that censorship is not unique to China gets lost in the overwhelming flood of indignation over the arrests.

Even more revealing than the content of these pieces are comments such these,[6] which appear at the end of the *Mary Sue* piece: "Welcome to China and we complain about the lack of freedom in the West," and, "Aw, China thinks they can fix the internet by arresting a few people? That's cute, China. You're adorable," and ending with: "It's so easy to forget the freedoms we often take for granted around these US parts. Long live slash and all it's [sic] wacky fic incarnations."

So, how does this coverage perform the work of soft power for the United States? Just like the British narrative, we see a double discourse. First, the pathological fangirl is invoked with extreme examples of fan works, the dismissal of slash interpretations, and allusions to fangirls' lack of attention to serious matters of state; the second discourse, however, explicitly incorporates the Chinese fangirl into anticommunist rhetoric. Here, the figure of the slash fangirl fighting for her freedom to porn is used to highlight human rights issues in China in ways that clearly separate "us" from "them." China is characterized as the great oppressor and, the result—as we can see in the comments above—is a sense of: it could be worse, look at those poor women in China, arrested for writing porn.

Conclusion

At the ideological level, both sets of discourses frame fangirls (freedom fighter or not) as silly, shallow, and sex-obsessed consumers who "lap up" Western media; they are unable to control their appetites for both media and sexual gratification (they just "can't stop" reading gay fan fiction), and are so "obsessed" with *Sherlock* that a significant international figure's visit is simply an opportunity to ask for *more*. Simply put, these representations indicate that the representation of fangirls—regardless of country of origin—disciplines in the Foucauldian sense; it shames women and girls, reinforces the characterization of female fans as hysterical and hormone-fueled, and seeks to reestablish their cultural powerlessness, raising the specter of the pathological fangirl only to dismiss the threat as laughable, disavowing the economic power of female consumers ideologically, while exploiting their consumption economically and politically.

Great Britain's characterization of China as its biggest *fangirl* celebrates the global success of British media and culture *and* disavows China's global economic power. This mirrors how pathologizing female fans disavows the economic power of female consumers. Metaphorically transforming China into a silly, obsessive teen girl devalues and defangs the nation and positions Great Britain as the wiser, colonial (father) guide. The United States' representation of Chinese fangirls as freedom fighters in a homophobic and repressive society reinforces the nation's construction of China as *Other*. Casting Chinese fangirls as innocent victims of unjust persecution incites feelings of both nationalism and patriarchal protectionism. This conceals the nation's own domestic failings at both combating discrimination and maintaining freedom of expression.

Although this analysis is based on a small sample of articles published and circulated during a specific time period, it clearly demonstrates how representations of fangirls function both ideologically and politically when incorporated into national discourse. Discourse produced through representations in both nations construct Chinese fangirls as other by employing the language of exoticism, condescension, and hyperbole; both explicitly gender China as feminine, rendering the nation both out of control and in need of Western (male) guidance or a damsel in need of rescue—

demonstrating the ongoing deployment of gender as a means of devaluation—not only at the ideological level, but also in the realm of global politics.

Notes

1   http://henryjenkins.org/2013/02/the-cultural-context-of-chinese-fan-culture
    -an-interview-with-xiqing-zheng-part-one.html (accessed March 23, 2015).
2   http://www.npr.org/blogs/monkeysee/2014/01/23/265221943/thanks-for-the-fan
    -service-but-what-about-the-story and http://www.theguardian.com/tv-and-radio/
    tvandradioblog/2014/jan/03/sherlock-doctor-who-fans-influencing-tv (accessed
    March 23, 2015), being the most blatant examples, but these discussions are also
    rampant in Yahoo chat boards, YouTube comments, Twitter, and various other sites of
    Internet chatter.
3   "Curly Fu" a combination of the Chinese translation of "Holmes" and a reference
    to Cumberbatch's curly hair and "Peanut" deriving from the Mandarin word *hua
    sheng*—which translates to "nut" and sounds like the word for "Martin."
4   http://www.northnews.cn/2012/0408/744375.shtml (accessed March 13, 2015).
5   Quoted in Romano (2014).
6   Article and comment thread found here: http://www.themarysue.com/fanfic
    -writers-arrested-in-china/ (accessed March 15, 2015).

23

The Good Fandom: Depicting Japanese Female Fans in *Moonlight Express, Moumantai,* and *Hong Kong Star Fans*

Lori Hitchcock Morimoto

In the early to mid-1990s, Japanese journalists began reporting on the growing popularity of Hong Kong films and, in particular, male stars among urban female fans. Even at its peak, the so-called "Hong Kong star boom" was little more than a niche fandom.[1] Yet, it coincided with Japanese critical appreciation of the cosmopolitan cinema of such filmmakers as, in particular, Wong Kar-wai in such a way that the fandom became emblematic of what was characterized as a wholly positive sea change in the Japanese reception of Asian films and stars. Ultimately, this fandom was the impetus for a handful of film and television coproductions in the late 1990s and early 2000s, among them *Mōichido aitakute* (*Moonlight Express*, Daniel Lee, 1999), *Moumantai* (*No Problem*, Alfred Cheung, 1999), and the two-part, made-for-television drama, *Honkon myōjō-mei* (*Hong Kong Star Fans*, Shingo Matsubara, 2002).

As in the case of English-language female fandom,[2] Japanese female fans of popular culture have been "diagnosed" as suffering from maladies and disorders for at least a century, in press descriptions ranging from the sexual deviancy of early twentieth-century fans of the all-female Takarazuka theater troupe (Robertson 1998, 146–7) to the early twenty-first century "Yonfluenza" afflicting fans of South Korean star Bae Yong-joon at the height of the Korean Wave (Miller 2008, 17). Against this, media discourse that praised women's love of Hong Kong films for challenging its kitschy stereotypes linked female fans' love of male stars to a socially sanctioned, if nascent, awareness of these fans' own (East) Asian identities. As a 1997 article in the widely circulated newsweekly *Aera* explained,

'95 and '96 are years to remember, as this is when Japanese awareness of Hong Kong popular culture completely changed. Chief [among the reasons for this] was the success of Wong Kar-wai's *Chungking Express* and *Fallen Angels*. ... These two films, which stylishly depict young, single urbanites, erased stereotypes of *kyonshī* [Chinese vampires], kung fu, and hardcore action from Hong Kong cinema.[3]

Articulated with newspaper and magazine discussions of Japanese women's film-induced defection to Hong Kong, the female fandom of Hong Kong stars was positioned as the vanguard of a new East Asian cultural regionalism in Japan. Yet, the films inspired by this discourse tell a more complex story. This chapter examines how sympathetic mass media characterization of Japanese female fandom of Hong Kong stars was mobilized in *Moonlight Express*, *Moumantai*, and *Hong Kong Star Fans* to purposes specific to their (almost exclusively male) writers and directors. In so doing, it reveals the contradictory nature of this media discourse, foregrounding its malleability to idiosyncratic ends.

The coproduced fan

From as early as the late 1980s, Japan–Hong Kong coproductions were made with the intent of capitalizing on the growing fandom of Hong Kong cinema and stars in Japan (as well as Hong Kongers' somewhat less passionate love of Japanese popular culture). The Yuen Biao vehicle, *The Peacock King* (Lam Ngai-kai, 1988), used his martial arts prowess and boyish good looks to tap in to a kung fu "boom" in Japan that was only just beginning to wane at the time of its production. Subsequently, films such as *The Christ of Nanjing* (Tony Au, 1995), starring Tony Leung Ka-fai and Japanese actress Yasuko Tomita, showcased actors who enjoyed no small popularity within a then-thriving Japanese female fandom of Hong Kong stars.

In the late 1990s, these coproductions introduced fans themselves to the diegetic world of the Hong Kong stars they loved, their passions portrayed through a lens of overseas-oriented self-actualization that had heretofore been the sole purview of West-directed women. The mid-1990s had witnessed an exodus of Japanese women to Hong Kong that was captured in articles dubbing them "The Japanese Runaways"[4] and associating their migration to Hong Kong with a broader phenomenon of female "internationalism," described by Karen Kelsky as a mode of "'defection' from expected life courses" enacted through Japanese women's professional and personal encounters with the West (Kelsky 2001, 2). Kelsky argues that the emergence of East Asia–oriented internationalist discourse in the mid-1990s was linked to "the 'Westernized' aspects of these sites" (p. 6). Yet, while Hong Kong exerted a particularly potent semiotic lure in Japan based on its alternative experience of East–West relations (Iwabuchi 2002, 194–8), East Asia–directed female internationalism coincided with the rise of discourses of Japanese economic and political "Asianization" that were closely aligned with the growing popularity of East (and, to a lesser extent, Southeast) Asian popular culture in Japan. It was this articulation of mass media discourses of women's self-actualization and Hong Kong film (stars) that constituted the narrative focus of *Moonlight Express*, *Moumantai*, and *Hong Kong Star Fans*.

It is perhaps no surprise that *Moonlight Express*, the earliest (by several months) of these three works, was also the least explicit about its protagonist's personal growth as an offshoot of her film (star) fandom. Largely a product of the Hong Kong film industry, *Moonlight Express* was financed in conjunction with Japan's Hakuhodo and Media Factory, but otherwise produced with minimal input from Japanese contributors. As such, it did not depict Japanese female fans so much as it invited them to identify with the film's (nonfan) protagonist, Hitomi (Takako Tokiwa). This invitation was extended both through Hitomi's own Japaneseness and through the affective appeal of its Chinese star, the immensely popular Leslie Cheung. By invoking the assumed fan-audience's star-centered fantasies within the narrative trajectory of Hitomi's personal growth, *Moonlight Express* firmly fixed Hong Kong (star fandom) as the locus of her/fans' happily-ever-after.

At the beginning of *Moonlight Express*, Hitomi has just become engaged to her Japanese-Chinese fiancé, Tatsuya (Leslie Cheung). While in the midst of preparations to relocate to Hong Kong with Tatsuya, he is suddenly killed in an automobile accident; subsequently, a mourning Hitomi makes the decision to go through with her plans and travels to Hong Kong. There she meets an uncouth undercover detective, Kar-bo (Leslie Cheung), who kisses Hitomi as means of avoiding discovery by gangsters who are pursuing him. The pair eventually strike up a somewhat tortured relationship that eventually ends in Hitomi's decision to remain in Hong Kong with the now much-softened Kar-bo.

Only a handful of scenes in *Moonlight Express* explicitly reference Hong Kong star fandom, but each foregrounds Hitomi's Hong Kong-oriented process of change and self-discovery. The first comes at the end of a Cantonese language class in Tokyo, where the instructor is finishing up a lesson with a clip from a Chow Yun-fat film. This filmic articulation of Hong Kong star fandom with language learning recreates a scenario eminently recognizable to Japanese fans of Hong Kong stars (down to the scene's instructor, Anny Tang, who was a relatively well-known language teacher within Tokyo fandom) (Cantonese Center online). In so doing, it at once validates fans' own experiences of film-motivated language learning, and it situates Hitomi on an Asian road-less-taken characterized by her growing appreciation for Hong Kong once she has relocated there. At every turn, her outdated expectations of the city are supplanted by the very cosmopolitanism that characterized reporting on Hong Kong popular culture and its female fandom in Japan throughout the 1990s (Iwabuchi 2002). Here, too, cinema is the impetus for Hitomi's observation that Hong Kong movie theaters are "unusually clean—I thought they'd be more … dirty," marking her recognition of a "capitalist coevalness" between Japan and Hong Kong—one that, as Koichi Iwabuchi argues, in fact elided very real asymmetries (pp. 194–5).

Japanese female fandom of Hong Kong stars is perhaps most tacit in scenes of Kar-bo/Cheung in various stages of undress as the object of Hitomi's—and the camera's—female gaze. Here, star and character are all but indistinguishable, echoing an expensive, fan-targeted Japanese photo book entitled *All About Leslie Cheung* (Resurī Chan no subete) that was published shortly after the film's release, featuring similarly revealing photographs of Cheung smiling lazily at the camera from his bed. Similarly, when the soon-to-be married Hitomi consoles a friend over her continued singlehood, proclaiming that the music box she holds can make dreams come true, she turns the crank on the small box and blissfully whispers "Tatsuya," before her friend grabs it, shouting, "DiCaprio!" Hitomi's rejection of the more mainstream Leonardo DiCaprio/Hollywood star situates her/fans' taste in Tatsuya/Cheung at the top of a hierarchy of Japanese/fan authenticity-as-East Asian regional belonging (Hitchcock 2002). In the end, prior to their final reunion, Kar-bo flips through a photo album left him by Hitomi, coming across a page with a picture of him, topless and sleeping, captioned, "You in my Bed!" Opposite is a picture of Hitomi herself, captioned, "Me in cinema!" the two photographs capturing the film's elision of sociopolitical commentary in its emphasis on the fantasy of women's star fandom.

In contrast with *Moonlight Express*, *Moumantai* is all about fan migration to Hong Kong; yet, where Hitomi embodies a kind of internationalist female fan, living out fans' film-induced, Hong Kong-centered dreams through both the film's narrative and Chinese star, *Moumantai* effectively contains the threat to Japanese social stability inherent in women's foreign-focused ambitions through its own protagonist, the hapless Daijirō (Takashi Okamura). Daijirō is a shop clerk and avowed Hong Kong film fan who wakes up one morning to a letter from his girlfriend, Reiko (Yasue Satō), telling him she has left to become a receptionist at Jackie Chan's production office in Hong Kong. Daijirō eventually follows her to Hong Kong and there becomes a stuntman for the legendary Sammo Hung (in a rare cameo role). Determined to become the best stuntman in Hong Kong and thus win back Reiko, he overcomes his natural limitations to succeed in the first goal; in the meantime, he meets a down-on-her-luck Mainland Chinese illegal immigrant, Ching (Jessica Sung), looking for her boyfriend, which ultimately results in romance for the cross-cultural couple.

Moumantai was the brainchild of popular comedian Okamura—a self-proclaimed fan of Hong Kong cinema—and producer Isao Takenaka. It was targeted at an audience of male martial arts and action aficionados in Japan who, while no fewer in number than the female star fandom, had been all but overlooked in the Japanese press. Indeed, that sense of invisibility is palpable in the film's opening scenes: panicked after receiving Reiko's note, Daijirō phones several of her friends, exclaiming to one in his broad Osaka accent, "She's left to meet Jackie Chan!" to which the woman replies, "I'd like to meet him, too!" Another ignores his plight entirely, instead asking Daijirō to have Reiko send her a Leslie Cheung poster. His indignity culminates in finding himself surrounded by posters of his nemesis at the film paraphernalia shop where he works. When a fashionable young woman approaches him asking for a *Rumble in the Bronx* poster, Daijirō informs her that they don't sell Jackie Chan posters. She sheepishly points to the Chan poster behind him, to which he responds, "That's Jackie *Cheung.*" He tells the woman that the only Jackie Chan paraphernalia they have in stock is one doll that she is free to take, repeatedly beating it on the counter until she and her boyfriend scurry out of the store, the heartbroken clerk calling after them, "You shouldn't watch too many Jackie Chan movies!"

This sense of Japanese men having been supplanted by Hong Kong film stars in the minds of Japanese women in fact echoes contemporary articles in women's magazines such as *Cosmopolitan*, which compared the raw masculinity of Hong Kong stars to the "fake Westernness" of "handsome, but shallow" Japanese stars,[5] and *Elle-Japon*, in which journalist Mitsue Hashimoto wrote:

> Interest in Hong Kong and Asian entertainers isn't limited to a handful of crazy
> fans, but is spreading among ordinary young women—particularly women who

are attuned to changing times, who wince at the weakness of metrosexualized Japanese man-boys and sense a sexuality in Asian men—who have become cool and beautiful along with their growing economies—that is lacking in Japanese men.[6]

Yet, where such articles lambast apparently weak and even effeminate Japanese men, Daijirō himself is anything but typical. Okamura's short stature and famously funny face combine with the character's arguably excessive knowledge of Hong Kong martial arts/action movies and stars to establish the object of critique not as Japanese men per se, but a specifically *otaku* iteration of Japanese masculinity (Condry 2011, 263–5).

This, in turn, is what makes *Moumantai* a singularly contradictory text about Hong Kong-centered self-discovery. On the one hand, the film is ultimately a celebration of the films and stars that put Hong Kong cinema on the global map, one that revels in its affective appeal. This is exemplified in a short scene at the now-defunct Bruce Lee Café, in which Daijirō responds to the subtle call of a fan imitating Lee with his own impression of Lee's famous "cat-call," abandoned mid-"*wa-chow*" by Reiko's arrival. It is a delightful moment of recognition for any fan of Hong Kong cinema, interactive in a way that the emphasis on style in a film such as *Kill Bill Volume 2* (Quentin Tarantino, 2004) cannot invoke. Here, Daijirō is a differently gendered, exuberant, and largely unrepentant fan of Hong Kong films *and* stars, not unlike female fans themselves.

At the same time, the narrative effectively nullifies Reiko's, and by extension Japanese female fans', attempts at achieving Hong Kong-centered self-actualization when Reiko, jealous of the far more dependent Ching, turns all her attention to winning Daijirō back. Early scenes of Reiko speaking fluent Mandarin on the phone in her Hong Kong workplace and insisting to Daijirō that she wants "to begin a new life, see new things," give way to suspicion and subversion of this new threat to Reiko's emotional hold on Daijirō. Particularly when, acting as go-between for Daijirō and Ching, Reiko deliberately mistranslates Ching's question, "Are you in love with me?" as "I never loved you," the narrative makes clear that it is Reiko's selfishness that continually forces Daijirō into unhappy situations not of his own making. That the resolution to his predicament is to reject what the now-independent Reiko is offering, however speciously, in favor of Ching's more undemanding charms hews a bit too close for comfort to a then-rising, and not untroubled, trend of importing Southeast Asian brides for unwed men in Japan (Yamashita 2008, 107–9). Thus, while the film recuperates passionate film and star fandom for Daijirō, it does so at Reiko's expense, and then further suggests, if not explicitly reinforces, a paternalistic, Japan-centered regional dominance through Daijirō and Ching's politically and economically unequal partnership.

Neither *Moonlight Express* nor *Moumantai* is concerned explicitly with Japanese female fans of Hong Kong stars. Yet this fandom haunts the narratives of these films in a shared trope of female (fan) self-actualization in Hong Kong. In this sense, they reflect not the zeitgeist of the period per se, but diverging responses to mass media discourses of women's internationalist fandom. These responses, in turn, speak to broader gender conflicts and concerns within Japan of the late 1990s. Women's dissatisfaction with the status quo is exemplified in Hitomi's drive to go to Hong Kong upon the death of the singularly gentle, loving Tatsuya—a subtle indictment of Japanese gender relations. At the same time, the displacement of the dissatisfied fan from women to men in *Moumantai* at once reinforces lazy stereotypes of "selfish" young professional women in Japan and neutralizes the social disruptiveness of women's defection overseas.

Yet, while Japanese gender relations are obliquely revealed and resolved within the narratives of *Moonlight Express* and *Moumantai*, their East Asian regional locus remains uninterrogated in each. The Hong Kong of these films is little more than a backdrop against which both Hitomi and Daijirō discover themselves, their engagement with it never exceeding the level of interpersonal relationships. By contrast, *Hong Kong Star Fans* is explicit both in its central concern with Japanese female fans of Hong Kong stars and in how their fandom engenders an Asian regional identification that effectively justifies women's otherwise excessive fannish activities.

Hong Kong Star Fans

While a Japan–Hong Kong coproduction mainly in terms of the local assistance it received during Hong Kong location shooting, the TV Tokyo-produced *Hong Kong Star Fans* (Shingo Matsubara, 2002) exemplifies more than any other work the discursive link between female internationalism and Hong Kong popular culture advanced in Japanese mass media of the mid-to-late 1990s. The story, written by Taichi Yamada, invokes his penchant for narratives foregrounding the tension between women's professional and personal lives through its protagonist, career woman Satomi Kudō (Hiroko Yakushimaru). The executive manager of Asian regional marketing for a French shoe manufacturer, Satomi longs to regionalize design operations, arguing that East Asian women appreciate a different aesthetic than European women. Yet her company's European management repeatedly rejects her ideas, leaving Satomi frustrated and her talents untapped.

Chief among Satomi's consolations is her fandom of Hong Kong star Ekin Cheng. Following the latest rejection of her ideas at work, she embarks on a quick trip to Hong Kong in order to attend an invitation-only birthday party for Cheng at which he is scheduled to appear. There, she finds herself in the company of two women: Akane Onuma (Shigeru Muroi), a middle-aged housewife excited to be on her first fannish trip to Hong Kong, and Keiko Shibasaki (Mirai Yamamoto), a former professional rival and closet Ekin Cheng fan. Despite Satomi's initial animosity toward her fellow fans, the three are briefly united in concern for the star when they learn of his hospitalization in Shanghai upon arriving at the event site. Disappointed, they leave a gift of flowers for Cheng and retreat to a nearby restaurant. There, the women are approached by one of Cheng's entourage, who says in Japanese that the star has arrived and wants to thank them personally for their gift. Cheng, in a cameo appearance, appears in pajamas and overcoat, and Satomi and Keiko excitedly address him in Cantonese, translating for the monolingual Akane. After several minutes, Cheng excuses himself, and the group subsequently returns to Japan and their disparate lives.

Back in Tokyo, the women's enjoyment of their time in Hong Kong is underscored by glimpses into their quotidian lives: Keiko is shown working listlessly at a desk in an anonymous securities firm, while Satomi encounters Akane sitting alone on a bench in a park, smoking a cigarette to postpone the inevitable moment when she must continue caring for her ailing mother-in-law. For Keiko and Akane, fandom is an escape from the dissatisfactions and drudgery of everyday life, liberating them from the roles they are obliged to perform. By contrast, albeit to similar effect, Satomi's fandom is a cover for her clandestine attempts to woo a Chinese shoe designer whom she hopes will strengthen her case for East Asian–designed footwear. When her gamble fails, Satomi is dismissed from the French company for her insubordination, then later offered work in a new company along with her Hong Kong designer. This happy ending arrives almost simultaneously with the announcement of Cheng's recovery and his rescheduled birthday party, and the drama concludes with the three fans reunited in Hong Kong, delightedly cheering for Cheng.

Throughout, Satomi, Keiko, and—to a lesser extent—Akane each engage in self-recriminations for their fandom, repeatedly voicing their embarrassment at being such passionate fans at their age. Satomi and Keiko go to great pains to hide their fannishness: Keiko slinks around during her travels in oversized sunglasses, while Satomi hides her stash of Ekin Cheng-related paraphernalia even within the privacy of her own home. Rather than contesting the need for such obfuscations, *Hong Kong Star Fans* instead characterizes the unseemly excess they overlay as symptomatic of deeply felt dissatisfactions with the gender constraints of women's personal and professional lives. A means to an end, rather than an end in itself, these women's fandom affords them a temporary respite from the unceasing demands of women's workaday lives and, at best, marks a jumping-off point from which they may remake themselves.

In fact, such characterization of Hong Kong star fandom closely mirrors contemporary mass media discourse in its representation of fans as single, urban professional women in their twenties and thirties, whose independence from the constraints of mainstream corporate and family life afforded them both the time and money to pursue their extracurricular interests. As reported in a 1997 *Shūkan bunshun* essay, women were well positioned to indulge in fannish activity and, in the case of transcultural fandoms, travel "precisely because of the monetary reserves of single OLs [office ladies]."[7] This perception was reinforced in a 2002 essay in *Aera*, where it was observed that "older female fans are efficient workers who have built up a surplus of time and money. This period in their lives when they can relax and seek out pleasures (*asobi*) without destroying their lifestyle coincides with a relaxing of demands to succeed.... That may be why career-minded thirtysomethings have awakened to the pleasures of unexpected fandom".[8]

What is noteworthy here is the subtle shift from a discourse of parasitic "OL" autonomy and consumerism, in which young, single women living with family utilize their salaries in the single-minded pursuit of their own selfish interests, to one of well-deserved emancipation from social expectations—so long as they meet exacting standards of uncomplaining service and thrift.

This discursive shift is particularly interesting when contrasted with the derision historically directed at female fans in Japan. Female fandom of popular culture in Japan is overwhelmingly personality-based, centering on kabuki stars, luminaries of the all-female Takarazuka theatrical troupe, the "Johnny's" boy band idols of producer Johnny Kitagawa, television actors, and *enka* (folk song) stars, in addition to Western film and music celebrities. As Jennifer Robertson has noted, the passion brought to star-centered interests and activities has been subjected to pathologization by both journalists and cultural critics alike (Robertson 1998, 152), and fans of Hong Kong stars were as susceptible to such discourses as any other. Indeed, it was partly the perception of Jackie Chan's 1980s Japanese female fandom as immature and excessive that precipitated his excision from subsequent fan and press discourses of Hong Kong star fandom in Japan. Thus, it was the intersection of otherwise typical star fandom with women's well-publicized drive for professional success and frustrations with the gender status quo that afforded both fans and their media interlocutors a means of articulating fandom with internationalist discourses of defection.

In one sense, internationalist fandom gave women a way of talking about their fandom that was immune to outside criticism and, when effectively deployed, cast fans in a vaguely progressive, feminist light. In books such as the *Kinema jumpō* (Movie Times) 1994 publication, *Work in Hong Kong: A Guidebook for Women Working in Hong Kong*, as well as the 1995 *Let's be OLs in Hong Kong!*, personal anecdotes describe women's interest in Hong Kong cinema and stars as one impetus for the discovery of a "new self" in Hong Kong that was the embodiment of "a woman's natural abilities and desires 'freed' from or discovered under layers of oppressive tradition" (Kelsky 2001, 121–2).

In the Hong Kong film fan context, this "new self" finds its most complete iteration in *Racing Cinema Girl*, the memoir of film distribution company Prénom H's CEO, Hiroko Shinohara. In a subchapter tellingly titled, "Divorce, resignation from work, and looking for a new start at age 29," Shinohara succinctly captures the main tropes of discontentment and self-actualization that characterized women's internationalist discourse, writing,

> At that point in my life, I was looking for work that I could devote myself to heart and soul—work that would span a lifetime.…So I quit my job of seven years at Seibu Department Store. At the same time, I also put an end to my four-year marriage, freeing myself from the gender role of wife. (Shinohara 1998, 18–19)

In September 1987, together with a small coterie of influential Hong Kong film fans, she embarks on a trip to Hong Kong with the intent of becoming further acquainted with Hong Kong cinema. The tour marks Shinohara's first trip to the city, and the revelation of her own "new self" arrives on the heels of the group's marathon screening of Hong Kong films:

> Everything was fresh and new, and we discovered that there were dozens of actors just as charismatic as Tony Leung, Leslie Cheung, Chow Yun-fat, and Yip Tong.

And as I watched these films, I realized—like a shock of electricity running through my body—that even though we're all Asians, these people live by a different logic, a different mentality. (p. 22)

Shinohara thus makes it her "life work" (p. 18) to bridge these differences through a film distribution venture that was successful through the early 2000s, her personal transformation inextricably linked with Hong Kong cinema and stars.

The specifically East Asian bent of women's internationalist discourse of this period is most clearly voiced in writing that posited cross-cultural identification as the main appeal of Hong Kong stars to Japanese women. Journalist Chieko Kobayashi observes that Hong Kong stars "have the same black hair and the same black eyes [as us]," making them "feel closer to us than Hollywood [stars]" (Kobayashi 1996, 14). Tomoko Hara takes this one step further in her own observation that

One key reason [that women became fans of Asian idols] is perhaps that, for the last several years, cultural exchange between Asian nations has progressed apace.... Because of this, in Asian countries where a Western orientation has dominated, people become aware of other Asian cultures. And there is no doubt that it has been women who have responded to this trend with the greatest sensitivity. (Hara 1996, 17)

Articulating a pan-Asian female fandom of East Asian stars with women's internationalist discourse, Hara implicitly aligns Japanese female fans with their (cosmopolitan) East and Southeast Asian counterparts in an argument for women's innate Asian orientation. Here, Japanese "Asianization," with all its ambivalent history, becomes the purview of female consumers, the social legitimacy of which acts as a mode of "auto-legitimation" (Hills 2002a, 38) on the part of fans that deftly elides mass media pathologization of fandom through its appeal to cosmopolitan regionalism.

Ultimately, however, it is the effectiveness of such a discourse of fannish auto-legitimation as a means of deflecting negative attention in the mass media that begs the question of its underlying semiotic function in Japan. *Hong Kong Star Fans* effectively illustrates the contradictions of female fans' internationalist Asianism in Satomi's desire to regionalize the design of shoes marketed to East Asian women. While a clear means for her to achieve self-actualization via her own star fandom, it nonetheless overlays more troubled popular and political discourse of Japan's role within the East Asian (cultural) sphere. Satomi envisions herself as an intermediary between her European employers and the unconnected, resolutely "Asian" designer she discovers in Hong Kong, her unique ability to communicate effectively with both belying the assumption that neither can communicate effectively without her. In this way, Satomi unwittingly reflects "Japan's mission as a mediating leader" (Iwabuchi 2002, 14) within the East Asian regional context, a characteristic of Japanese regional imagination from at least as far back as its wartime project of pan-East Asian cooperation and expansion.

Conclusion

Hewing closely to the discourse of women's internationalist emancipation from Japanese social, gender, and professional constraints, the experiences of Satomi, Keiko, and even Akane paint a picture of personal and professional fulfillment as the end result of a journey beginning in Hong Kong film fandom. In this sense, their experiences of transcultural media fandom recall Ella Shohat and Robert Stam's argument that "transnational spectatorship can ... mold a space of future-oriented desire, nourishing the imaginary of 'internal émigrés,' actively crystallizing a sense of a viable 'elsewhere,' giving it a local habitation and a name, evoking a possible 'happy end' in another nation" (Shohat and Stam 1996, 164–5).

At the same time, Kelsky observes that in spite of the ways in which women's internationalist discourse "construct[s] an alternative reality under which all that had been maligned is now revered, and all that had been revered now rejected ... ironically, invocation of female international 'adaptability' has ... become talismanic in the mainstream, male-dominated Japanese media." She attributes the mainstream embrace of this otherwise counter-hegemonic discourse to the ways it "deflect[s] onto women the distasteful imperative of internationalization" (Kelsky 2001, 119). Similarly, the discourse of women's internationalist Asianism that runs through *Hong Kong Star Fans* was a means by which broad claims of deepening (popular) cultural ties with "Asia" could be made by those bearing none of the onus of such work. In this sense, this drama reflects the kind of "soft" Asianization that characterized mass media accounts of the Japanese female fandom of Hong Kong stars, satisfying an ultimately fleeting engagement with Japan's regional neighbors.

Eventually, this Asianist discourse was resurrected in the Korean Wave that supplanted a dying Hong Kong star fandom in the early 2000s. Here, at least initially, the Japanese mass media made even more of South Korean star fans' embrace of Korean language, food, and (popular) culture as the vanguard of a new appreciation of Japan's historically maligned former colony. However, particularly because of historically fraught relations between Japan and South Korea, it was an ill fit that opened up room for not only Japanese backlash against what some perceived as nationalistically manipulative soft power (Hayashi and Lee 2007, 208), but also renewed pathologization of the "gullible housewives"[9] who flocked to a new generation of East Asian stars.

Notes

1 Given the grassroots nature of this phenomenon, the precise size of the fandom is difficult to ascertain. However, based on membership data from the Yumcha [Dimsum] Club, a female fan-centric organization sponsored by then-Wong Kar-wai film distributor and financier Shinohara Hiroko under the auspices of her company, Prénom H, there were at least 12,244 card-carrying fans of Hong Kong cinema in Japan as of December 1997.

2 See, for example, Hansen 1986; Nash and Lahti 1999; Busse 2013a.

3   Hiromichi Ugaya, "*Chūka poppu daisuki Nihonjin ga kyūzō*" (An explosion of Japanese who like Chinese pop)," *Aera*, January 20, 1997.

4   Dick Chan, "The Japanese Runaways," *South China Morning Post*, October 8, 1994.

5   Chieko Kobayashi, "*Honkon mūbī netsuai sengen*" (A declaration of love for Hong Kong movies), *Cosmopolitan* (Japan), July 1996, 14–31.

6   Mitsue Hashimoto and Junko Murata, "*Rinrinshiku otoko no iroke afureru Honkon sutā ni muchū*" (Obsessed with Hong Kong stars overflowing in masculinity), *Elle-Japon*, November 1997, 94–9.

7   Takako Hanaoka, "*Otona no josei ga hamaru 'Honkon myōjō' no miryoku*" (The appeal of "Hong Kong stars" to adult women), *Shūkan bunshun*, July 3, 1997, 63–5.

8   Nao Irokawa, "*Barikyari to totsuzen okkake*" (Career women who suddenly become star-chasers), *Aera*, January 28, 2002, 46–8.

9   Motosaru Nashi, "*Itsu made tsuzuku Hanryū sutā no zeni geba shōhō*" (How long will Korean stars' money-grubbing business persist), *Shūkan jitsuwa* December 9, 2004, 54–5.

24

Otaku: Representations of Fandom in Japanese Popular Culture

Nicolle Lamerichs

Fans of Japanese popular culture or "otaku" are often stereotyped as obsessive adult fans who are unable to connect with reality. First used in 1983 in a journalistic article by Nakamori Akio in a soft-porno magazine *Manga Burriko* (Neojaponism 2008), the term "otaku" was not widely popularized until the late 1980s. Its widespread use and negative connotation stems from the media's reporting on Tsutomu Miyazaki's "The Otaku Murder" in 1989. Between August 1988 and June 1989, Miyazaki had abducted, sexually molested, and killed four young girls in Tokyo.

This national incident alarmed the media. The killer had been a fan of anime and horror films. Mass media played into this image, desperately trying to explain what went wrong. Gailbraith and Christodoulou (2012) contextualize this negative media response:

> Commentators and experts explained that Miyazaki was alienated from human contact and common sense. He was dependent on media and technology. He was a sociopath and sexual deviant. Miyzaki Tsutomu was an "otaku." (p. 16)

The discourse on otaku in the 1990s continued along these lines and often reflected concerns in Japanese culture. Individualism had been pressed too far and young people were failing to assume adult responsibilities (Kinsella 1998).

In the new millennium, the discourse on otaku became less negative. Japan was in state of economic stagnation and otaku were spending money, thereby spurring innovation of technology and media. In his book *Otaku: Japan's Database Animals*, Hiroki Azuma (2009) describes several key moments that influenced the millennial discourse, such as Miyazaki Hayao winning the Academy Award for *Spirited Away*, Murakami Takashi achieving recognition for otaku-like designs and the Japanese pavilion in the International Architecture exhibition of the Venice Biennale which was themed "otaku" (p. xi). While otaku culture is often portrayed as a youth culture, Azuma explains that its core consumers are mature and knowledgeable fans who have social freedom and are economically able (p. 3).

The terminology of otaku also helps shed light on this changing discourse. Otaku is an honorific second-person pronoun that literally means "your home" (Gailbraith and Christodoulou 2012, 20). This word is often used metaphorically, its literal translation being "you." In subcultures of science fiction, the word has been used sporadically in the 1970s and 1980s (ibid.). Examining the use of the word in different historical essays and accounts, Gailbraith and Christodoulou write: "We gather from a review of the discourse that the term 'otaku' is consistently associated with the private space of the home and difficulties communicating with others in public" (p. 21). Many language traditions adopted the word "otaku," but foreign fans tend to use it as a more positive term to emphasize their engagement with Japanese popular culture.

While foreign fans connote otaku with fans of anime and manga, the verb has broader connotations in Japan. Otaku is not solely reserved for media fans, but can mean any type of fandom or even hobby. Izumi Tsuji (2012), for instance, wrote in detail about the history of train otaku who enjoy train spotting and model-building. "Otaku," then, is a general term which describes being a fan of something. There are many types of otaku, but one that I will often refer to is *Fujoshi*, which is often equated with female fans of manga and anime. This term literally means "rotten girl" and is a self-mocking pejorative. Specifically, Fujoshi refers to fans of "boys' love": a genre of Japanese popular culture that includes homosexual themes (see also Hampton, in this volume).

While this study focuses on Japanese fiction, it positions itself as a fan study. This means that I actively engage with the theories and concepts that Anglo-American and European fan studies have developed. There are many lessons to be learned from Japanese culture that run parallel to phenomena in Western countries. Like other fan cultures, otaku are subjected to stereotyping both in journalism and politics, and in popular culture itself. Similar to Western fans, the otaku are characterized as overly invested or emotional. Such fans are considered escapists, who seek to flee from everyday life by indulging in fiction. From the study of otaku, we can gain more insights in how fandom is seen, represented, and subverted in mass media.

Drawing from studies on fans of Japanese popular culture (Galbraith 2012; Ito et al. 2012; Tamagawa 2012), I explore the cultural context and representations of otaku in Japanese fiction. I argue that while the political and journalistic discourse on otaku became more positive in Japan in the new millennium, popular culture itself still affirms some of the negative and gendered connotations that are associated with otaku culture.

Otaku in popular culture

Representations of fandom in popular and journalistic discourses are often far from positive or realistic. Fandom itself has a long and stigmatic history. The word "fan," after all, is an abbreviation of *fanaticus* or "fanatic," which has connotations of religious zeal and overactive engagement (Bailey 2005, 48–9). Fans have often been understood as overly invested, and representations of fan culture often emphasize this stigmatic history. Examples include the murderous fangirl from Stephen King's *Misery* (1987), who kidnaps the writer whose work she admires; the nerdy antagonists in *Buffy: The Vampire Slayer* (Larbalestier 2002); or the obsessive Mel in *Flight of the Conchords* (2007–2008). The different chapters in this book make visible that fan representations are still highly diverse and often contested.

In his article on *Inspector Spacetime* fandom, Paul Booth (2013a) argues that the "representation of fans as active components of the media economy has increased, popularized, and valorized fandom across the media landscape" (p. 147). For example, a show such as *The Big Bang Theory* (2007–) may carry negative and gendered portrayals of geek culture, but the show also communicates this culture to outsiders. While largely shot at the character's apartments, the show also includes spaces such as comic shops, conventions, and universities, thereby demonstrating that fans are smart and able consumers. The sitcom is self-aware and exaggerates its fan characters in such a way that a geek audience can still identify with them.

The representation of Japanese fans has a different cultural context, but similar patterns emerge when compared to Western fandom. Historically, media fandom emerged almost simultaneously in the 1970s in rich, industrial countries such as North America and Japan (Ito et al. 2012). Japanese fans resemble Western fans in that they can be understood as an organized fandom and engage in creative practices together. On several levels, the representation of Japanese fans displays similar themes as its Western counterparts, such as social isolation, aggression, and sexual deviance. While there was a positive revaluation of otaku in the 2000s, the image of an otaku in Japan is still partly constructed as that of an inept fanboy (Galbraith 2012, 24–5).

Studying otaku, however, also means turning away from Japan. The popular culture of Japan is an exemplary nexus to study the construction of fan culture through the East Asian capital. Manga is a transmedial phenomenon that originates in comics but has spread to animation, games, and consumer articles (Steinberg 2012). This visual language has hailed consumers all over the world. Japan's global influence has also been described as a soft, transnational power. This influence of Japanese pop culture has been amply theorized as "cultural globalism" (Burn 2006), "transculturalism" (Hills 2002b; Jenkins 2006b, 156; Chin and Morimoto 2013; Noppe 2014), or even a "global space" (McLelland 2001). Though anime fandom is a global phenomenon, it is innately tied to local identity. All over the world, non-Japanese fans celebrate manga culture and contribute with their own fan practices, such as creating fan comics and costumes (Lamerichs 2013). In many countries outside Japan, "otaku" therefore carries more positive connotations, and signposts a creative cult-fan.

To understand how this increasingly global fan identity is captured within Japanese media, I will close-read various manga and anime.

Methodology

This research relies on ten titles published in the period 2001–2014. The sampling was based on a wide variety of manga and anime. I chose titles by reading synopses, watching snippets, and familiarizing myself with the content. Furthermore, the sampling was based on availability. For the purpose of this study, titles needed to be translated in English officially. In one case (*Princess Jellyfish*), an English fan translation by Hachimitsu Scans was used, alongside the official French translation of the manga.

Many of the selected titles do not consist of one source text or primary text. The different texts belong to larger franchises and may consist of an anime, television series, or game. For the purpose of this chapter, I have analyzed the original text when it was available. In some cases, however, the source text was not translated or available. *Light novels* (popular young adult literature) especially are seldom published abroad, but inspire many manga and anime adaptations.

While I draw my primary material from one version of the text, I have also acquainted myself with the other versions by selectively analyzing other installments. In this process, I was guided by secondary texts, such as synopses by fans. This helped me to contextualize the fiction better and be aware of obvious differences in the plot and characterization among different media installments (Table 24.1).

Table 24.1 Selection of anime and manga titles.

Manga	Anime
Genshiken (Kyo, 2002–2006)	Melancholy of Haruhi Suzumiya (Kyoto Animation, 2006)
Comic Party (Inui, 2001–2005)	Welcome to N.H.K. (Gonzo, 2006)
Princess Jellyfish (Higashimura, 2008–)	Lucky Star (Kyoto Animation, 2007)
Spotted Flower (Kyo, 2009–)	Ouran High School Host Club (TBS, 2011)
Durarara!! (Nariga & Satorigi, 2009–)	Monthly Girls' Nozaki-kun (Dogakobo, 2014)

My selection consists of the manga *Genshiken* (Kyo, 2002–2006), *Princess Jellyfish* (Higashimura, 2008–), *Comic Party* (Inui, 2001–2005), *Spotted Flower* (Kyo, 2009–), *Durarara!!* (Nariga and Satorigi, 2009–), and the anime *Monthly Girls' Nozaki-kun* (Dogakobo, 2014), *Welcome to N.H.K.* (Gonzo, 2006), *The Melancholy of Haruhi Suzumiya* (Kyoto Animation, 2006), *Lucky Star* (Kyoto Animation, 2007), and *Ouran High School Host Club* (TBS, 2011).

In my analysis of these series, I have paid attention to how otaku culture itself is represented: its spaces of consumption, common fan practices, and fan values. Moreover, I have examined how otaku characters are portrayed in terms of gender and sexuality, and in terms of social and creative activity. For the purpose of this chapter, I have divided the analysis into four sections that broadly cover the stereotypes and themes, namely the representation of otaku culture, gender and sexuality, social isolation, and violence.

Otaku culture

The sampled stories emphasize the social aspects of otaku culture and its spaces of consumption. Such sites may include maid cafes, manga libraries, and doujinshi shops where fans come together to enjoy and buy fiction. Particular districts that function as cultural centers for otaku are also well represented, such as Akihabara, a shopping district in Tokyo for games, anime, manga, and computer technology.

Genshiken, for instance, follows the everyday lives of a college club for otaku, the "Gendai Shikaku Bunka Kenkyūkai" ("Society for the Study of Modern Visual Culture"), abbreviated to "Genshiken." The series starts when main character Kanji enrolls in college and becomes interested in otaku culture. His friends at the genshiken club bring him into this lifestyle slowly. Being a closeted otaku, his fellow-students give him tours of doujinshi shops, recommend erotic games, and eventually take him to Comiket, the largest fan event in Japan. Hardcore otaku Madarame warns Kanji: "Stay in line even if it kills you" (chapter 5, 6). They hunt for fanzines and regularly meet up.

Genshiken features new fans, such as Kanji, and also nonfans. The girlfriend of one of characters, Saki, has no interest in otaku culture but hangs out at the club frequently so she can see her boyfriend. She befriends the otaku, and while she adamantly insists on not being an otaku herself, becomes more interested in their culture. Saki often ends up at Comiket, and even engages in cosplay to amuse the others. She is a member of the community, even if she does not identify as otaku.

Being an otaku, then, means participating in this culture and self-identifying as a member of it. It means shopping at the right places, going to the right festivals, and expressing knowledge about Japanese pop culture. Comiket is framed as a core event in the sampled fiction. *Comic Party* was originally a "dating sim" (a video game genre that simulates romance) and is set in Tokyo Big Sight where Comiket is held. The characters attend a large comic festival, "Comic Party," which is clearly inspired by Comiket. The anime stars many female doujinshi artists, but focuses on a male main character that interacts with them. While female fans are actively represented and voiced in *Comic Party*, the otaku that we are supposed to identify with is male. Similar to *Genshiken*, then, *Comic Party* also genders its fans, but even goes a step further. Female fans are sexualized as the ideal romance candidates for heterosexual fanboys.

Intertextual connections between these shows also support a shared otaku culture and canon. *The Melancholy of Haruhi Suzumiya* focuses on the members of the school club "SOS Brigade," who are interested in discovering supernatural entities and phenomena. The eccentric titular character Haruhi especially strikes as an otaku at points, obsessed with the supernatural. Early on in the show, it becomes clear that something is not quite right with Haruhi and finally she is revealed to be a Goddess. She has the power to alter reality, but her fantasies are kept in check by her friends. The character and the anime have become very popular in actual otaku culture. Fans started a mock religion in honor of the show, "Haruhiism," with its own rites and festivals. Popular in Japan and abroad, this phenomenon is similar to other mock religions that originated in popular shows, such as *Seinfeld*'s Festivus and dudism from *The Big Lebowski*.

Several anime follow up on the massive fandom of "Haruhi," most particularly *Lucky Star*, whose anime has been produced by the same studio as *The Melancholy of Haruhi Suzumiya*. The character Konata Izumi especially appears to be a Haruhi fan, who has many figurines of the show, and attends live concerts of it.

That is to say, otaku have a large participatory culture that is represented in these stories. What is striking is that the stories are self-aware about this culture and parody fan practices and events frequently to draw attention to fandom itself. Through humor, exaggeration, and positive accounts of fandom, these stories validate their fan audience.

Social isolation

The different series play with themes such as reclusion from society, social awkwardness, and unemployment. The otaku characters are portrayed as people who have a lot of time to spend on fiction. Since they are often students (e.g., *Genshiken*) or unemployed adolescents (e.g., *Princess Jellyfish*, *Welcome to N.H.K.*), they are not well-off and have to save money to buy figurines, comics, and anime.

In the fiction that I examined, otaku are still stereotyped as loners who may be involved in otaku subculture to some degree, but generally stick to themselves. These representations may be carried out further to the degree that otaku are depicted as having phobias or mental illness. Fear to go outside, for instance, is a theme in many of the stories. In the first shots of *Princess Jellyfish*, main character Tsukimi walks through the crowded district Shibuya, in Tokyo. She is on her way to an exhibition of jellyfish, which she loves, but the busy streets of Shibuya are too much for her. Defeated, she goes home before she has seen it.

The rise of mental illness in Japan among young people and the phenomenon of "hikikomori" have led otaku to become even more stereotyped. Hikikomori (literally "being pulled inwards") refers to acute social withdrawal of adolescents or adults from social life, seeking extreme degrees of isolation. *Welcome to N.H.K.* particularly addresses these issues, because its main character Tatsuhiro Sato is a hikikimori. He has withdrawn from social life since he could not cope with the pressure of college. Now he lives in his student room and hardly ever goes outside. The first episode depicts him slowly going paranoid in his small room. One day, as he watched the network N.H.K., he comes to believe that this was all a conspiracy. N.H.K., he reasons, does not stand for Japanese Broadcasting Society (*Nippon Hoso Kyokai*) but for the Japanese Society for Hikikomori (*Nihon Hikikomori Kyokai*).

Tatsuhiro, however, gets support from his neighbor and high school friend Kaoru as well. Kaoru is a hardcore otaku, who gradually introduces Tatsuhiro into Japanese pop culture. Together, they aspire to produce a game that is easy to make, but profitable: a dating sim. For inspiration, they play a large amount of games, go to Akihabara, buy erotic figurines, and visit maid cafes.

Tatsuhiro slowly starts to become an otaku himself, immersed into the pornographic culture of manga and anime. Still, he cannot shake his fear of a conspiracy. This mass culture of excessive consumerism both fascinates and haunts him. These sentiments bring to mind Azuma's (2009) theory on otaku as postmodern animals. Inspired by Hegel's philosophy, he argues that modern Japanese subjects, characterized best by otaku, are constantly looking for meaning in Japanese society. Otaku find this meaning in the flat worlds of anime and manga. For Azuma, otaku represent a "virtual, emptied-out" humanity, in which subjects navigate as if through a database (p. 95). The grand narratives of modernity are lost, and it becomes harder to connect to others.

Welcome to N.H.K. portrays these cultural fears. When Japanese youth cannot live up to the country's strict cultural expectations, they isolate themselves. Throughout the series, fandom becomes a way to escape the hardships of life. Ironically, the anime is also wary of the consumer practices and emotional attachment that define the otaku by phrasing it as a conspiracy. While the strongly visual and erotic culture of mass media seems enjoyable at first, it is not a remedy for social isolation. In fact, fiction encourages isolation throughout the show. The otaku become so emerged in entertainment and fiction that they only leave their apartments to go on a shopping spree in Akihabara.

The large participatory culture of otaku is well known and represented in fiction. Although otaku can enjoy many events together, pop culture still tends to portray them as introverted, and even isolated.

Gender

The stories represent female fans as different from male in terms of interest in practices. The depiction of female otaku often relies on fan practices that are associated with women. Cosplay and doujinshi in particular are hobbies that female otaku engage in. For instance, *Ouran High School Host Club* stars Renge who is depicted as a Fujoshi. Renge enjoys cosplay and often fantasizes about the other characters. She is also the editor of a fanzine of the host club (*Moe Moe Ouran Nikki*). These are fan practices commonly associated with women in Japan. Similarly, *Genshiken* has female characters that cosplay or draw doujinshi, while the men are more interested in collecting statues, building model kits, and playing video games. A male cosplayer is also part of the club, but his representation is clearly gendered. He creates costumes to make women look pretty and enjoys taking pictures of them in his outfits.

In line with these gendered fan practices, the series also depict female otaku as having other interests than male otaku. Fujoshi, for instance, are considered to be more obsessed with romance. They favor pairings and couples, and are frequently fans of boy's love. By contrast, the male fans adore different versions of one cute character. They may buy statues of their favorite character or *dakimakura* ("hug pillows"). Examples of these practices are found in *Welcome to N.H.K.* and *Genshiken*, among others.

A deconstruction of these gendered fan practices can be found in *Monthly Girls' Nozaki-kun*. This anime focuses on a student who is secretly the author of a popular romance manga under a female pen name. When a girl falls in love with him, he believes her to be his fan, and recruits her to help him produce the manga. *Monthly Girls' Nozaki-kun* portrays a male author of romance manga, who believes that all women admire his work, while in actuality they hardly care about it.

Princess Jellyfish most clearly discusses femininity and sexuality of otaku. The story depicts how a cross-dresser, Kurasoke, befriends a Fujoshi woman, Tsukimi, and her roommates. Tsukimi writes: "Happily, all of the residents are, like me…fujoshi!!" (chapter 1, 15). The women have different objects of devotions: trains, dolls, historical drama series, and Korean pop culture. Since no men are allowed in the building, Tsukimi insists that Kurasoke always shows up in drag and pretends to be an actual woman for her roommates.

Being a comedy, *Princess Jellyfish* often uses fandom as the butt of its jokes. The women are portrayed as socially awkward, afraid of public places, single and unfeminine. Believing herself to be an unattractive otaku girl, Tsukimi often contemplates the femininity of herself and others. She is passionate about jellyfish, we found out, because her mother loved them and took her to see them at the aquarium. After her mother's passing, Tsukimi learned to cope with her grief by visiting the jellyfish at the pet store or aquarium. While jellyfish symbolize the mother–daughter relationship in this manga, they also tie into womanhood on another level. Ever since she was young, Tsukimi saw a resemblance between jellyfish and princesses. Jellyfish are like "lace from a princess dress," she reminisces.

When she first meets Kurasoke, Tsukimi fondly compares him to a princess, and a jellyfish. The cross-dressing Kurasoke is arguably the most feminine character in the manga, even though he does not identify as female: "I just have a taste in women's clothing. I'm normal" (chapter 2, 13). Kurasoke's femininity is important, but not linked to a specific subcultural or sexual identity. He often emphasizes that he is not a drag queen or queer, but a man who enjoys wearing female clothing. In drag, he uses a male vocabulary in Japanese by referring to himself as "ore," much to the confusion of Tsukimi's roommates who code him as female. *Princess Jellyfish*, then, is clearly not just a story about female fans, but about what it means to perform femininity.

While female fans are adequately visible in Japanese fan culture, the stories show a gendered account of fandom. Female fans are often cast in the roles of side-characters, and when they are main characters, they are partly coded as unfeminine and unsocial.

Sexuality

In mass media, being an otaku has been aligned with sexual deviance and inexperience. Being a sexual deviant is often seen as inherent to being an otaku. This has a gendered component. While female otaku may be coded as asexual, and swooning over homosexual content, male otaku are often seen as masturbating to erotic games. Sexual inexperience is often the starting point of the stories. *Princess Jellyfish*, for instance, is a romantic comedy, rife with assumptions about otaku sexuality. They all live in one apartment building, "amamitzukan." They call themselves "amar" as an abbreviation, but "ama" is written in the kanji for "nun." Being a Fujoshi, then, is explicitly aligned to discourses of asexuality and celibacy in this story.

The Fujoshi in this manga are virgins, which is quickly joked to be the most sensitive topic that you can ever discuss with a female otaku. In chapter 2, Tsukimi lists the "best 5 ranking questions you must not ask a Fujoshi," which is ranked by: "Are you a virgin?" It also includes: "Have you ever gone out with a guy? What kind of make-up do you use? Want to go to a sale at 109? Why don't you try contact lenses?" (p. 15). This list is filled with gendered stereotypes about female fans, who are framed as improper women and sexually inexperienced.

The idea that otaku find fictional characters more attractive than actual people—either on a visual, physical, or emotional level—is common in the stories that I investigated. In Japanese, this is called *nijikon*, which is often translated as a 2D complex. For example, in *Genshiken*'s fourth chapter, the guys get excited over a manga character. This confuses nonfan Saki: "I don't get it. How could you get excited over a picture like this?" (p. 98). Hardcore otaku Madarame explains to her that they are "guys with a 2D complex," who are interested in fictional female characters. The 2D complex emerges in other series as well. In the sixth episode of *Welcome to N.H.K.*, Tatsuhiro refers to this complex when he hears that his otaku best friend is dating. Envisioning Kaoru with his many figurines, hugging pillows and manga, Tatsuhiro believes that he could not possibly be dating a real girl: "After he dragged me into the world of 2D, he himself gets a flesh-and-blood chick? Unforgivable!"

While most of the cases stigmatize otaku sexuality, the manga *Spotted Flower*, by Shimoko Kio of *Genshiken*, focuses on the everyday life of a newly wed otaku and his pregnant, ordinary wife. Like any couple, they face the challenge of parenthood and see their life change. This also affects their fan behavior. They quarrel about how to redecorate their spare room—stocked with collections of doujinshi and figurines—into a baby room.

Becoming a parent, then, creates insecurities for the otaku character. In the fifth chapter, he admits his fears of having a son: "I'm just fully aware of how hopeless I am as a role model, that's all." His wife reassures him: "You say you don't think you can raise your son right, but you're not going to be raising him alone. I'm here too. You used to be a hopeless otaku, but now you're married, you've had sex, and you've even gotten your wife pregnant with your kid. How you explain this incredible turn of events?" Being an otaku, and a father, is still presented as an anomaly in this scene, as if a "hopeless otaku" is not entitled to be a spouse.

For otaku, sexual deviance appears to be the norm. *Spotted Flower* stands out as a manga that features a mature otaku that has settled down, but at points returns to similar problematic imagery as the other titles. Fans are believed to be either desperate, single fanboys, or virgin fangirls. While they are interested in erotic fiction, otaku are believed to shy away from intimacy and sex.

Violence

In a popular discourse, otaku are also perceived to be violent. Several incidents, particularly the before-mentioned Otaku Murder, heavily influenced how otaku are seen and understood. The selected cases differ from the discourses in journalism and mainstream media. In manga and anime themselves, otaku are seldomly represented as violent. There are some exceptions that play with this theme, though, such as *Durarara!!*

Originally a light novel, the anime and manga of *Durarara!!* tells the story of an underworld courier in Tokyo's Ikebukuro neighborhood. The main characters are involved in an Internet-based gang called The Dollars and involved with some of the most dangerous people in Ikebukuro. *Durarara!!* features some fantasy elements, but primarily focuses on the underworld in Tokyo. The show has a large cast, but most relevant for this research are the otaku Erika and Walker, who are both members of The Dollars gang.

Erika and Walker are first introduced when they are walking across the street with a life-size carton plait cut-up of a manga character. They are trying to force the cut-up into their van and take it home. The two of them are clearly geeks, who make references to their favorite stories continuously, and regardless of who they are with.

While Erika and Walker both come across as bright and enthusiastic people, they have a darker side, though, which has been toned down for the anime. In the manga, they like to perform torture by letting their victims choose a light novel or manga to inspire their methods. For example, in the seventh chapter of the *Durarara!!* manga, Erika and Walker torture a business man in their van. They let him choose from a selection of manga: "My recommendation is *Darker than Black!*" Erika smiles (p. 20). The victim chooses the seemingly innocent *Black Butler* manga, which amuses the otaku. In the story, main character Ciel has a demonic eye, and they choose to re-enact this. During the graphic torture scene, the otaku threaten to carve a pentagram into the man's eye. While they approach the eyeball, they explain their sadism. They emphasize that "ames, manga, and anime are not to blame" (p. 23). They could have taken inspiration elsewhere, be it period drama or educational text books. "It's us that are twisted" (p. 24).

While *Durarara!!* portrays its otaku in violent scenes, their acts serve a purpose. Even during the torture scenes, it is made explicit that popular culture itself is not to blame. Erika and Walker are sadists and gang members. They are not violent otaku, but professionals. While their methods are inspired by manga and anime, they emphasize that fiction did not trigger their aggression. Through these scenes, the author also provides an image that counters the moral panic around otaku in Japanese culture. Violence is not triggered by media content, but has more complex social and psychological causes.

Conclusion

Otaku have long been stigmatized. Mass media have represented members of this community as sexual deviants, loners, and aggressors. What these manga and anime show is that being otaku means adopting a very social and unique lifestyle too. Otaku perform their fan identity by demonstrating specific knowledge, but also by sharing spaces such as the stores in Akihabara or Comiket's Tokyo Big Sight. By foregrounding the participatory culture of manga fandom, the cases do show that being a fan means more than being isolated or lonely. Through inside jokes and references, the stories validate otaku culture and show its diversity.

Considering that the audience of this fiction partly consists of otaku, and that its creators have often been fans or fan artists themselves, it is striking that the stories do not correct certain stereotypes more. The representation of otaku in terms of gender and sexuality especially has hardly enabled new readings and understandings about these fans. Sex-positive imagery of otaku, for instance, is difficult to find. Still, there are also counterexamples, such as *Spotted Flower*, that show otaku as aging fans with a family life. While Japanese popular culture partly reproduces negative imagery of otaku, many of the stories that I examined also show corrective traits. By framing the subculture and spaces of otaku, these representations serve as a helpful introduction for new fans and outsiders.

25

Interview with Jeanie Finlay, Director of *Sound It Out* (2011)

Lucy Bennett and Paul Booth

British filmmaker **Jeanie Finlay** has directed a range of documentaries that focus on music, people, and their stories, such as *Goth Cruise* (2008), *The Great Hip-Hop Hoax* (2013), and *Orion: The Man Who Would Be King* (2015). In 2011, Jeanie released *Sound It Out*, a crowdfunded documentary exploring the last surviving independent record store in Teeside, in the North East of England. The film focused on a number of male music fans that frequented the store and interviewed them about their musical passions. During October 2014, we interviewed Jeanie via email about her experiences of making *Sound It Out*, and the processes that can occur when representing local music fans in documentaries.

Q: How did you get the idea for *Sound It Out*, and how did it come to fruition?
A: I grew up with Tom (the store owner) and Sound It Out Records is in my hometown. I was spending a lot of time up north—my Mum was going through chemo at the time and the shop offered me a real haven. I looked around and realized that it was a haven for everyone else in there. After a few years of joking that I was going to make a film I did just that, staying in my old bedroom at my Mum and Dads and spending lots of time in the shop.

It was the first time I'd filmed anything without a crew and was interested about giving it a go—the camera work may be a bit shonky at times but so is the shop. After about a year of filming on and off I thought I had something interesting—it just offered so much, an opportunity to make a film about my home, men, music, and Mákina. I pitched it a couple of times to broadcasters and was told that there was no story that could sustain an audience. I disagreed and realized that continuing to pitch the film would kill the love I had for the project so I decided to crowdfund a micro budget to get the film finished. I honestly thought we'd have a local screening and sell the film in the shop. When we got into *South by Southwest* everything changed and the film has now been seen all over the world.

I hope that the film demonstrates what Tom says—"it's emotions, emotions and memories… records hold memories." Tom and Sound It Out (and other shops like it) are very important to many, many people. I still get emails about it and it nearly always makes me cry, it means so much.

Q: Could you tell us about the place that music fandom has in your life? And how does this infuse with your documentary filmmaking?
A: I would say that I'm much more a fan of people than music really. My films usually start as a very personal response to something or a notion that catches me out of the corner of my eye and once I've seen it I can't shake it.

Teenland, *Goth Cruise*, and *Sound It Out* are all hugely personal and connected to my life in one way or another. *The Great Hip Hop Hoax* was something I read about but I kept thinking about my (Scottish) father and the improbability of him ever sacrificing his "Scottishness." *Orion* was triggered by my husband buying a mysterious record at a car boot sale with a masked man on the cover. Sometimes, when I've spotted something with potential I start looking around to see if everyone else is seeing the same thing too!

I'm interested in telling small and shy stories. I sometimes feel like a shy person in the role of an extrovert, as a filmmaker. I've found a way of connecting with an audience—a film can make a very small and intimate story accessible by thousands, but without the need for shouting. I really enjoy interviewing people who have never been on camera before and might see themselves as unlikely contributors. Who really wants to hear from someone who wants to be in a film? All the films I've made, even if they have a lot of music in them have to have a driving narrative or a compelling reason to form a narrative.

In terms of my own taste I'm a huge Dolly Parton fan as well as of The Shangri Las. I've entertained perhaps making films about either or both—but I would have to find a way in to the story that is narratively driven. Fandom or interest is not enough on its own—what is the third act?

Q: What are your views on the ways fans have been represented in documentaries? Had you watched any prior to making this film?
A: I think that broad brushstroke portraits of whole subcultures or fan bases can be very damaging. Where are the individual stories?

Q: How did you select what fans to include in *Sound It Out*?
A: I thought of them much more as customers than fans and it was very instinctive. I wanted a spread of the different types of people I had met—either distinctive characters—Chris the accountant who came in every day, Shane the Status Quo fan. Or fans of particular music—the metal lads, the Mákina boys, the shed DJs. Almost everybody said "no" first of all, that's how I knew they were the right people!

Q: Did you face any struggles when representing these fans? For example, was there anything that your film subjects did not want on camera?
A: It's all been good and I've never really faced difficulty, once the contributors are on board for them to talk about anything. The only exception was *Goth Cruise*. Most of

the cruisers were polyamorous and only one person was willing to talk about this on camera. I did worry that it may be misinterpreted that ALL Goths are polyamorous, which is of course not true. I once had an awful screening of the film in the UK. It was made for the US and concentrated on The "Goth Cruise," an American initiative attended by 150 self-identifying Goths. The UK audience didn't like the American Goths at all and felt that I had misrepresented their subculture and I had a responsibility to make a film that told their story. I actually have next to no interest in telling the story of a whole subculture or creating an essay. The cruise was an excuse to make a personal film about five very different individual's experiences of being Goth and going on the cruise. The scenario was an excuse for a portrait.

Q: As you filmed these individuals, did you feel any sense of accountability, in terms of representing individuals, and the wider fan culture?
A: I do to the individuals—I guard and defend their stories like a tiger. I want them to recognize themselves, for good or bad, in the final cut. I only feel responsibility to the individuals I've met, not fan culture at large.

Q: One criticism that has surrounded the general representation of fans in documentaries is that sometimes creators focus on extreme cases—as a filmmaker, how did you negotiate making an interesting narrative with representing fans accurately?
A: You have to be able to sleep at night with choices you have made as a filmmaker. My responsibility lies with the individual I am filming or depicting at that moment.

I look for people who are able and willing to be themselves on camera and I endeavor to honor that openness and integrity in the finished film. I don't particularly look for extreme cases but I am more interested in whether people are "playing up" to the camera. I am drawn to shy and quieter people who may have never told their story onscreen before.

I rarely think about the wider "fans" community, e.g., Shane in *Sound It Out* is a Quo fan but his experience is personal and that is what he reflects in the film. I think about him and the band and their relationship—not whether he is one of many other Quo fans out there.

Q: *Sound It Out* **focuses quite a bit on the male music fan experience. What are your thoughts on the way gender influences (or doesn't?) fandom?**
A: The men in *Sound It Out* and *Orion* were usually completists, looking for rare artifacts and "completing" their collections. *Sound It Out* is about men as I was the only woman in the shop at the time of filming. The clientele at the time of making *Sound It Out* in 2011 was 99 percent male so the film reflects the reality I found. It's now shifted. I can make observations on the experiences I had but don't want to make sweeping generalizations about gender.

The women I interviewed for *Orion* had more personalized collections—locks of hair, handmade t-shirts, signed and personalized memorabilia. It seemed to be more about finding a community through a shared connection.

Q: How much did the people you spoke with consider themselves "fans"? Did they have other terms to describe themselves?

A: A few, but they were more likely to identify with a subculture—"Goths," "Metallers," "Mákina," etc.

Q: What was the response from record communities afterwards? And the media in general?

A: The community was very positive. There was a bit of "you should do this shop next" and "why didn't you cover all shops?" but those people were kind of missing the point. I'm really not interested in making the film equivalent of a shopping list. The overwhelming feeling I had was that the film reflected the way that people feel about Sound It Out Records.

The press was completely and utterly overwhelming. We were film of the week in *The New York Times* and had four or five star reviews, pretty much across the board. When the film broadcast it trended higher than *Children in Need*. Amazing for a film I was just going to sell in the shop on DVD.

Q: Can you update us on how the record store Sound It Out is doing? Is it still around? Do you still hear from the customers in the documentary?

A: It is doing well: it has expanded and has welcomed vinyl tourists from all over the world. I could never have estimated the impact the film, the theatrical release, and international broadcasts would have on the shop.

Afterword: Participating in
Hybrid Media Logics?

Matt Hills

This volume of essays has eloquently demonstrated the range of fan representations circulating through contemporary culture, showing how fandom is articulated with many other themes and topics, whether these involve images of disability and locality (Chapters 1 and 2) or threatening/appealing transnational images of China and Hong Kong (Chapters 22 and 23). Pathologizing stereotypes of fandom may not have entirely been supplanted—remaining more powerfully fixed in place, perhaps, in relation to certain types of fan object such as those belonging to young girls—but such problematic, negative, and patriarchal devaluations seemingly coexist with more positive, celebratory iterations of fandom (see Chapter 9, for example, and Geraghty 2014).

Writing in the early noughties, I suggested that images of fictional fans had become oxymorons (Hills 2003, 65), uniting contradictory positive and negative imagery, and Paul Booth's recent discussion of the "hyperfan" (Booth 2015b, 80) argues that different fan characters within a relational or coupled system of meaning can carry older stereotypes of excess versus "mainstreamed," normalized versions of "the fan" (*The Big Bang Theory* is one of his persuasive examples). Of course, neither such approach—each committed to complicating prior accounts of pathologizing/celebratory fan representations—fully captures the array of diverse ways in which fans are now seen. Arguments around "good" and "bad" fandom—or discussions of the emotionally "excessive" or socially "atomized" fan—seem a touch outmoded in such a context, where "the subcultural fan and the cultural mainstream fan" can be variously portrayed, and where such "dual portrayals reflect the changing media environment" (Booth 2015b, 83).

I suspect that what we need here is a stronger sense of how fandom is represented not simply in relation to what's been dubbed "convergence culture" (Jenkins 2006a), but rather within an increasingly "hybrid media system" where multiple media logics are at work. That is, we need "to try to be as specific as possible about the combination of media logics in flow in any given event, process or context" (Chadwick 2013, 210). Media studies has certainly been alert to the need to rethink established logics of mass mediation (Merrin 2014), with Graeme Turner (2016) echoing Andrew Chadwick's approach when he notes:

> The hybridity of… actual patterns of contemporary media use has been under-examined, perhaps as a consequence of media studies' preferred focus on

convergence, but... hybridity does seem to me to be a key attribute of the re-invented media and it needs to be used more actively to organize analysis. (p. 126)

Contradiction and duality at the level of fan representations, as well as restrictive commercialism and pluralist Web 2.0 diversity, all call for a contextual understanding of hybrid media logics and exactly how they are intersecting in particular cases. In a number of interviews with media practitioners in this volume (e.g., Chapter 4), people talk about creating images of fans as "entertainment," where this is shorthand for a professional, commercial practice leading to sensationalist, individualizing images of fans that are disconnected from any explicit ethic or responsibility of representation. Equally, in other cases (Chapter 7), practitioners are reflexively aware of a mass media system that requires fan images to be "sexed up" in terms of deviance or "craziness"—the implication being that to get one's work broadcast, and to function effectively as a media professional, one has to assent to a commercial media logic of (fan) stereotyping. This media logic requires particular *performances* of professionalism, which are either naturalized and internalized or felt as a kind of institutional imposition (Jenkins 2012b, 54). Elsewhere in this volume, though, we encounter very different performances (see Chapters 3 and 5), and hence very different media logics. Fans' tweets and assorted online responses, for instance, can instead display what Joseph Reagle (2015) terms "*drama genres* of comment.... In the age of comment, people are always performing front of stage, and much of it is sensational" (pp. 178–9).

Such fan performances of intense emotionality, or "authenticity-as-excess" (Fishzon 2013, 186), have a longer cultural history and certainly are not restricted to today's social media or even to particular platforms such as Tumblr and Twitter. Noting this, Louisa Ellen Stein (2015) accurately points out how

What I refer to... as feels culture thrives on the public celebration of emotion previously considered the realm of the private. In feels culture, emotions remain intimate but are no longer necessarily private; rather, they build a sense of an intimate collective, one that is bound together precisely by... processes of shared emotional authorship. In this equation, emotion fuels fan transformative creativity, and performances of shared emotion define fan... communities. (p. 156)

"Feels culture" can enable fans to transform out-of-copyright characters into modernized refractions of media fandom within fan-produced web series (Chapter 16), inverting usual anxieties around the "Mary Sue" character by depicting key characters in these dramas as fanlike, and engaging in new debates around established intra-fandom pathologizations of fans who allegedly don't "do" fandom properly (see also Chapter 15).

Although we might assume that "feels culture" and its performances of identity are antithetical to the performances of professionalism required by commercial media institutions, this is not entirely the case. Stein (2015) observes that:

Just as professionalism as an aesthetic may move through commercial and fan work, so too may the ethics of professionalism extend into fan communities and to the creative works of fans. These ethics can come directly in[to] conflict with even such a seemingly core fannish value as the… right to transform [canonical and commercial popular culture]. Rather than being uniformly held millennial fan values, affective collectivity and fan transformation exist in tension with discourses of individual professionalism and idea ownership, all of which fans hold as valuable in an expansively diverse millennial culture. (p. 160)

In short, no fan is an island within contemporary neoliberal culture. Values of individualism, self-branding, and career progression premised on an internalized entrepreneurial self can coexist (sometimes uneasily) with more "traditional" lineages of fandom as resistant to capitalist norms. Not all fans would represent commercializing fan-careerists as "selling out," and hybrid media logics are evidently in play here. Fans able to "make it pay" as bloggers, artists, or writers may be recognized as "one of us," made good as Big Name Fans.

There is a related kind of hybridity on show across this volume: interviews with media producers and actors (e.g., Chapters 8 and 14) sit side-by-side with interviews with fan creators (Chapter 17), while critical analyses are variously carried out by scholar-fans and practitioner-fans (Chapters 6 and 7). Although there are still very different performances of identity that can, and will, tend to occur within media-institutional cultures or a "culture of feels," say, there remains a sense here in which identity categories and performances can be porous and permeable. Rather than clear-cut distinctions between "mainstream" and "subcultural" fandom, fan representations take on a fluidity and mobility—One Directioners may be mocked by *GQ*, but aspects of their performative culture nevertheless circulate outside its cultural filter bubble in this case—the same goes for *Trekkies*, *Bronies*, and the fans of *Sound It Out* (see Chapters 21 and 25). And by the time of series 3, *Sherlock*'s creators, Steven Moffat and Mark Gatiss (Chapter 11), are willing to describe the show as fan fiction: "We did this as possibly the biggest sustained act of fan fiction, and as a result there's fan fiction about our fan fiction. And I do think that's where storytelling comes from" (Moffat 2014).

It seems increasingly difficult to maintain a notion of "one true context" (fanfic in its own safe or "underground" spaces) at such a moment. Fan vids and fanfic are discoverable outside their communities and archives, and fan-cultural terms have arguably shifted into broader consciousness via the "fanboy auteur" (Chapter 12) or the "showrunner" or the "spoiler." Fandom has been reflexively incorporated, connotatively and denotatively, into shows such as *Stargate SG-1* (Chapter 10) and *Supernatural* (Chapter 13), bringing the details and controversies of media fandom to wider audiences. Indeed, writing in *The Guardian*'s "Comment is Free" section online, Catherine Shoard (2015) goes so far as to argue that over "the past decade the public sphere has undergone a compulsory conversion into a sort of Comic-Con-style convention centre" where fannish discussions of blockbuster movies, quality TV, and glossy pop music (Seabrook 2015) are no longer contained within fan cultural spaces, but instead circulate widely across social media, trending, being shared, and attaining an eminently "spreadable" status (Jenkins et al. 2013). This fluidity generates a situation where "the very definition of 'fan' is shifting, with many shades of gray emerging whereby multiple and sometimes contradictory understandings of fandom exist" (Ross 2008, 260). To argue that a monolithic public sphere is now "Comic-Con-esque" may be rather hyperbolic, and some might want to question how good a model the industrial domains of Comic-Con would make for such a transfer, but Michael Saler's (2012) concept of multiple "public spheres of the imagination" (pp. 97–8) surrounding different franchises and diegetic universes remains highly evocative.

Perhaps we are often invited to see *as* (specific kinds of) fans in today's news and commentary media, especially given that there are so many specialized niche websites where debates can be staged, while mass media news outlets have responded to social media logics by emulating populist, entertainment-driven approaches—it is now reasonably common for "event" *Doctor Who*, *James Bond*, or *Star Wars* (such as an anniversary, a premiere, or even a trailer) to offer up a BBC TV news headline in the United Kingdom: franchises and brands are seemingly newsworthy culture in action (Turner 2016, 38–9). And although there may well be problematic limits to the versions of fan creativity and fan practice that can become "spreadable," or endorsable by commercial media systems (Scott 2012b), many controversies in fan activity and representation are nonetheless debated across a range of blogging sites today—the "fake geek girl" has been subjected to widespread blogging takedowns, for example, and the "Sad Puppies" phenomenon in the science fiction fan community was also widely debated across blog-dom, as was GamerGate.

Likewise moving across contexts, this book also performs a hybridization of media professionals, fans, and professional academics, from Orlando Jones's "fanboy" and "fangirl" binary (which we might not want to reinforce too strongly: see Jones's Foreword) through to Daisy Asquith's self-analysis, and beyond. And a similar "context collapse" (Marwick and boyd 2010a, 124) marks out Andreas Halskov's (2015) study *TV Peaks: Twin Peaks and Modern Television Drama*, in which TV professionals, fans, and scholar(-fan)s are treated similarly—in each case, people are interviewed and quoted. It also marks out Joanne Garde-Hansen and Hannah Grist's (2014) *Remembering Dennis Potter Through Fans, Extras and Archives*, where TV extras who had appeared in Dennis Potter's dramas are discussed alongside the "hyperlocal" and international fandom of "Potterites." Such a "context collapse" between fandom, academia, and media production/commentary seems, to me, highly indicative of a hybrid media system where differing media logics now incessantly intersect and interact, and where fan representations can be caught up in these hybridizations. More than merely a "double visibility" of producers and fans "within shared and overlapping digital networks" (Stein 2015, 138), this is *a triple or extended visibility* where digital scholars, as well as digital fans and media producers, all contribute to public spheres of the imagination (Booth 2010; Weller 2011).

In this hybrid space, fans themselves might draw on fan studies scholarship, or deliberately ignore it in order not to color their creative processes; at the same time, fans may stereotype rival fandoms (Hills 2012c) or police "correct" ways of being a fan (Bennett 2014b). But fandom becomes so multiple and hybridized itself—permeated by commercial culture, differently gendered, classed, aged, and raced (see Chapters

18–20)—that no singular and "authentic" image of the fandom can be produced or sustained, even if "fake fandom" can still be constructed as an "Other" (Dixon 2013, 58). Moving from "structured polysemy" (dominant images; see Morley 1992, 123), to "neutrosemy" (where ambiguous meanings of fandom can be read so as to reflect viewers' self-identities; see Sandvoss 2005, 127), to "connective polysemy" (where shared, negotiated group meanings circulate via social media; see Papacharissi 2015, 87), fandom's representations work today to bring together (or appall) different communities engaged in immediate discussions, deconstructions, or dismissals.

But hybridity does not mean the loss of all distinctions and boundaries. Quite to the contrary, *in a hybrid media system boundaries are actively redrawn in a series of ways.* One DVD/Blu-ray "value added material" producer dismissed fans who were trying to exert influence over his professional activities, remarking that they displayed a "bizarre entitlement" (Halskov 2015, 174). This reinstates a pathologizing image of "excessive" fandom, but also attempts to draw a line around the otherwise chaotic or contested exercising of media power (Freedman 2014): fans were seemingly "entitled" if they didn't know their "proper" place as an appreciative audience. Allegations of fan "entitlement" seem to be one way in which, within a hybrid media system, the stereotyping suggestion that fans should "get a life!" is updated and retooled (Jenkins 1992). And the sense that fandom can be performed and articulated with many other identities—alongside scholar-fans we may encounter journalist-fans, publicist-fans, transmedia producer-fans, and so on—also seems to have led to the newly ascendant figure of the "superfan": when fandom permeates pro-am mediatized culture then a kind of "grade inflation" or "fan inflation" appears called for, in order to reinstate fan-cultural distinction and difference in the face of so many shades of fandom. The "superfan" can be stereotyped without fear of impugning "rank-and-file fandom," perhaps, or extensively monetized (and narrated) by commercial schemes such as crowdfunding (Lovell 2014; Kustritz 2015a). Indeed, the "superfan" seems to reproduce older images of the fan-as-excessive-consumer, albeit within neoliberal ideology where the power to massively consume can be (insecurely) celebrated as well as pathologized.

Rather than seeking to conceptualize the cultural agents who shape, circulate, and resist fan representations as, variously, fans, academics, aca-fans, producers, or media practitioners, we might alternatively take a different and less classificatory tack. In *Media and Morality*, Roger Silverstone (2007) ponders what terminology to use for those caught up in media cultures, concluding:

> I will… talk of *audiences and users as participants*… We cannot but be participants in this world of mediated appearance… There is, however, something of a catch to participation, for it implies and requires something else… [S]uch activity, such agency, implies some kind of responsibility. Participants in media culture… must be understood to be taking responsibility for their own participation…. For the refusal of responsibility is itself an act for which one has to take responsibility. (pp. 107–8)

Perhaps, then, in a world of "context collapse" and hybrid media logics, we are all participants who are called upon to display responsibility for our actions and representations of fandom, where disavowing responsibility means merely that other participants will potentially attribute it to us. But this also means being responsible for how we circulate and recontextualize representations (rather than only producing them)—how are critical academics speaking about the work of flesh-and-blood media practitioners?; how are journalists appropriating fans' tweets?; how are documentary-makers, or cult/quality TV franchises, imaging and imagining fans?; how are fans responding to media producers and to other fans? It may frequently seem that we remain miles away from "public spheres of the imagination," as sensationalist practices of trolling and provocation roll across pro-am cultures of media creation/commentary (W. Phillips 2015), and as fractious dissent is performed across contexts and across media logics.

In such a massively multiple and probably ultimately unmappable terrain, terms such as *superfans*, *hyperfans*, *uberfans*, or even *otaku* (see Chapter 24) offer a reassuring inflation of fandom within hybrid media systems. Such terms seek to replay and restore a bounded, contained sense of what it means to be represented as a fan who has conspicuously worked on their identity—rather than fandom being naturalized here, it is visibly worked at entrepreneurially, economically, and across the life course (Benzecry 2011). The neoliberal affective work of being a "superfan" overwrites different shades, politics, and experiences of fandom, often representing a singular image of dedicated and delimited consumption. Such images of fandom still need to be challenged and contested, which is one of the strongest lessons I have taken from this excellent collection—fandom may not be as strenuously or obviously pathologized today as it has been in the past, but its many mainstreamed embraces and "positive images" still mask a host of representational and cultural-political exclusions, absences, and ideologies. Fans have long since got themselves interesting and rewarding lives, but the terms on which such things are represented by participants in a hybrid media system (including fans themselves) call for further analysis, critique, and the taking of responsibility with (and without) power.

Editor and Contributor Bios

Editors

Lucy Bennett completed her PhD in online fandom at JOMEC, Cardiff University, where she is working as a researcher. Her work on fan cultures appears in journals such as *New Media & Society, Journal of Fandom Studies, Transformative Works and Cultures, Social Semiotics, Continuum, Cinema Journal, Celebrity Studies*, and *Participations*. She is the co-founder/chair of the Fan Studies Network and coeditor of *Crowdfunding the Future: Media Industries, Ethics and Digital Society* (Peter Lang, 2015).

Paul Booth is Associate Professor at DePaul University. He is the author of *Playing Fans* (University of Iowa Press, 2015), *Game Play* (Bloomsbury, 2015), *Digital Fandom* (Peter Lang, 2010), and *Time on TV* (Peter Lang, 2012). He has edited *Fan Phenomena: Doctor Who* (Intellect, 2013), and has published numerous articles on fans, social media, and technology. His research interests include fandom, new technologies and media, popular culture, and cult media. He is currently enjoying a cup of coffee.

Contributors

Daisy Asquith has made more than twenty documentaries for British television on a wild array of subjects that include concentration-camp survivors, gay dads, immigrant children, and most recently her own long-lost family in County Clare. She has won the Royal Television Society award for Best Documentary series twice, and has a BAFTA nomination and a Grierson Award. She began her university education at the age of thirty-five and is undertaking AHRC-funded doctoral research at the University of Sussex into the response of the One Direction fandom to her documentary about them.

Nettie Brock is a PhD student in the University of Missouri's Communication Department. She studies popular culture, with an emphasis on television shows and genre/narrative techniques. Her master's degree is in Cinema Studies from San Francisco State University. She studies *Doctor Who, Community*, and *Sherlock*.

Robert Meyer Burnett has worked in Hollywood for twenty-five years. Beginning as a production assistant on such films as *Leatherface: Texas Chainsaw Massacre III* and *Army of Darkness*, he worked his way up through the ranks, eventually becoming an award-winning editor, writer, producer, and director. His first feature, the cult favorite

Free Enterprise, came out in 1999. Since then, he was a producer on both of MGM's *Agent Cody Banks* features, produced *The Hills Run Red* for Warner Premiere, and most recently edited director Gary Entin's dark thriller *My Eleventh*, executive produced by Bryan Singer. He spent fifteen years producing content for special-edition DVDs and Blu-rays, including work on *The Usual Suspects*, *The Fellowship of the Ring*, and *The Two Towers, Tron, Superman Returns*, and all seven seasons of the award-winning High Definition restoration of *Star Trek: The Next Generation*. Most recently, he edited the time travel thriller *Paradox* and is directing the crowdfunded independent Star Trek feature film *Axanar*.

Kristina Busse is an active media fan and has published a variety of essays on fan fiction and fan culture. She is the coeditor of *Fan Fiction and Fan Communities in the Age of the Internet* (2006), *Sherlock and Transmedia Fandom* (2012), and *The Fan Fiction Studies Reader* (2014), as well as founding coeditor *of Transformative Works and Cultures*, an Open Access international peer-reviewed journal about fan cultures and fan works.

Melissa A. Click is Assistant Professor of Communication at the University of Missouri. Her work on popular culture, audiences, and fans has been published in the *International Journal of Cultural Studies, Men and Masculinities, Television & New Media, Popular Communication, Popular Music & Society, Transformative Works & Cultures*, and in NYU Press's *Fandom*. She is the coeditor of *Bitten by Twilight*.

Ruth A. Deller is Principal Lecturer and Program Leader for Journalism, Media and Public Relations at Sheffield Hallam University, UK. She has published on a range of media and journalism-related topics including religion and the media, reality and lifestyle television, and social media cultures. Her fan and audience studies research has looked at a range of fandoms, including Cliff Richard, *Neighbours, Fifty Shades...*, and *The Sims*. Her own fandoms include Kylie Minogue, *Doctor Who*, and Roxette.

Mark Duffett is Reader in the Department of Media at the University of Chester. He is the author of *Understanding Fandom* (Bloomsbury, 2013) and two edited volumes for Routledge: *Popular Music Fandom: Identities, Roles and Practices* (2014) and *Fan Identities and Practices in Context: Dedicated to Music* (2015). He was the keynote speaker at the MARS 2012 conference in Finland. Dr. Duffett is working on a book about Elvis Presley for the Equinox series, Icons of Popular Music.

Jeanie Finlay is a British artist and filmmaker who creates intimate, funny, and personal documentary films and artworks. Her work includes *The Great Hip Hop Hoax* for BBC Scotland and BBC Storyville (BIFA-nominated best documentary), *Sound It Out*, a documentary portrait of the very last vinyl record shop in Teesside (official film of Record Store Day), and the recently released *Orion: The Man Who Would Be King*.

Sam Ford is VP of Innovation and Engagement for Fusion. He is also a research affiliate with the MIT Program in Comparative Media Studies/Writing and an instructor for Western Kentucky University's Popular Culture Studies Program. Sam is the coauthor of *Spreadable Media* (2013, NYU Press) and coeditor of *The Survival of Soap Opera* (2011, University Press of Mississippi). He has frequently written about and taught classes on the genre of pro wrestling and has, himself, performed in pro wrestling shows, as a fan and as an on-stage character.

Lincoln Geraghty is Reader in Popular Media Cultures in the School of Media and Performing Arts at the University of Portsmouth. He serves as editorial advisor for *The Journal of Popular Culture, Reconstruction, Journal of Fandom Studies*, and *Journal of Popular Television* with interests in science fiction film and television, fandom, and collecting in popular culture. He was recently appointed as a senior editor for the new online open access journal from Taylor & Francis, *Cogent Arts and Humanities*. He is author of *Living with Star Trek: American Culture and the Star Trek Universe* (IB Tauris, 2007), *American Science Fiction Film and Television* (Berg, 2009), and *Cult Collectors: Nostalgia, Fandom and Collecting Popular Culture* (Routledge, 2014). He has edited *The Influence of Star Trek on Television, Film and Culture* (McFarland, 2008), *Channeling the Future: Essays on Science Fiction and Fantasy Television* (Scarecrow, 2009), *The Smallville Chronicles: Critical Essays on the Television Series* (Scarecrow, 2011), and, with Mark Jancovich, *The Shifting Definitions of Genre: Essays on Labeling Film, Television Shows and Media* (McFarland, 2008). He is currently serving as editor for multivolume *Directory of World Cinema: American Hollywood* from Intellect Books (2011 and 2015), and his most recent collection, entitled *Popular Media Cultures: Fans, Audiences and Paratexts*, was published by Palgrave in 2015.

Darlene Hampton completed her PhD in English with a concentration in Film and Media Studies at the University of Oregon in 2010. Her scholarly work examines media fan practices as sites of cultural work and identity performance and is particularly interested in the relationship between patriarchal and post-feminist ideologies of gender and the valuing and policing of fan practices in the digital public sphere. She holds concurrent faculty appointments in American Studies and Film, Television, and Theatre at the University of Notre Dame, where she enjoys teaching courses on gender, film, new media, and fan cultures. Her current research focuses the role of social networking technologies such as Tumblr on the evolution of fan practices and cultures.

Karen Hellekson is founding coeditor of the fan studies journal *Transformative Works and Cultures*. She has published in the fields of science fiction, media studies, and fan studies. Her latest book, a reprint anthology coedited with Kristina Busse, is *The Fan Fiction Studies Reader* (Iowa, 2014).

Matt Hills is Professor of Film and TV Studies at Aberystwyth University. He is the author of six books, from *Fan Cultures* (2002) to *Doctor Who: The Unfolding Event* (2015), and the editor of *New Dimensions of Doctor Who*, published in the show's fiftieth anniversary year. Matt has published more than a 100 journal articles/book chapters in the areas of cult media and fandom, and is working on the book *Sherlock: Detecting Quality TV* (forthcoming 2017).

Bethan Jones is a PhD candidate at Aberystwyth University working on her PhD by publication. Her work focuses on hatred, tension, and fractures within and across fandoms, and between fans and producers, and she has written extensively on anti-fandom, gender, and new media. Bethan's work has been published in *Transformative Works and Cultures, Sexualities,* and *New Media and Society,* and her coedited collection on crowdfunding was published by Peter Lang earlier this year.

Orlando Jones began his Hollywood career at nineteen writing on NBC's *A Different World,* Fox's Martin starring Martin Lawrence and writing/producing Fox's *Roc Live* starring Charles Dutton. Orlando later combined his writing and acting talents when he was handpicked by Quincy Jones to join Fox's fourteen-year-long sketch comedy franchise MADtv. Orlando also wrote, produced, and stars in the graphic novel action comedy *Tainted Love,* which was released by Machinima in 2013 and played Det. Frank Irving on the hit Fox series, *Sleepy Hollow.*

Ellen Kirkpatrick (MPhil, Bristol University) is a PhD candidate in comics, culture, and "identity" at Kingston University, London, and Assistant Editor at *Cinema Journal.* Her research interrogates the concept of identity, centering on notions of borders and matters of their blurring and crossings. Ideas circulating the dressed body loom large in her work, and within her thesis, she examines dressing and costuming practices to explore the implications of the dressed body within the performance of "identity." She has had work published in *Transformative Works and Cultures* and *Cinema Journal,* where she coedited and contributed to an In Focus section on gender identity and representation in the superhero genre. She also coedited and contributed to an *InMediaRes* themed week on gender identity and the superhero genre.

Nicolle Lamerichs holds PhD in media studies at Maastricht University. Her doctoral thesis *Productive Fandom* (2014) explores intermediality and reception in fan cultures. She currently works at International Communication and Media at HU University of Applied Sciences, Utrecht. Her research focuses on participatory culture and new media, specifically the nexus between popular culture, storytelling, and play.

Katherine Larsen teaches writing and media studies at The George Washington University. She is the editor of *The Journal of Fandom Studies* and the coauthor of *Fandom at the Crossroads: Celebration, Shame and Fan/Producer Relationships* and *Fangasm,* and the editor of *Fan Culture: Theory/Practice* and *World Film Locations: Washington D.C.*

Luminosity is a fan vidder. In 2007, her vid Vogue went viral. She was nominated to be profiled in a double-page spread in *New York Magazine* and Vogue was rated by the magazine as one of the funniest videos, and the best fan video, of the year. Luminosity returned to *New York Magazine* in 2008 to pick the best fan vids of that year. In 2008, she judged the Video Remix Challenge alongside Larry Lessig, Henry Jenkins, Pat Aufderheide, JD Lasica, Kembrew McLeod, Mark Hosler, and Matt Mason.

Laurent Malaquais is Director of *Bronies: The Extremely Unexpected Adult Fans of My Little Pony*. Laurent studied theater at the University of Southern California, and also with Sanford Meisner, before working in low-budget cable television as a segment/field producer, segment director, and cinematographer. He has made scripted short films and short form documentaries that have screened at the US and various international film festivals including: The Tiburon International Film Festival; Vision Fest Los Angeles; Group 101 Film Festival, Los Angeles; Off-Courts Trouville, France; Cannes Film Festival Short Film Corner; and The Festival International du Film D'Afrique.

Lori Hitchcock Morimoto is an independent scholar of transcultural fandom. She has published on Japanese multicultural film, female fandom, and transcultural fandom in *Scope, Transformative Works and Cultures*, and *Participations: Journal of Audience and Reception Studies*, and her current research centers on the Japanese female fandom of foreign stars from the 1980s to the present.

Roger Nygard has made several award-winning independent films, including a comedy called *High Strung*, an action picture called *Back to Back: American Yakuza 2*, a movie about car salesman called *Suckers*, a documentary about UFO fanatics called *Six Days in Roswell*, and a documentary about *The Nature of Existence*, in which he asks why are we here, and what are we supposed to do about it. But he's probably most notorious for his *Trekkies* documentaries about the most obsessive sci-fi fans in the Universe. In television Nygard has directed shows like the HBO series *The Mind of the Married Man*, the FOX series *The Bernie Mac Show*, the NBC series *The Office*, the DisneyXD series *Zeke & Luther*, as well as having edited the FX series *The League* and Emmy- and ACE-nominated episodes of HBO's *Curb Your Enthusiasm*.

Rukmini Pande is pursuing a PhD on Intersections of Identity in Media Fandom Communities at UWA. Her recent publications include coauthoring an article titled "From a Land Where Other People Live: Perspectives from an Indian Fannish Experience" in *Fic: Why Fanfiction Is Taking Over the World* (ed. Anne Jamison) on racial dynamics in media fandom and "In Your Face: Empire Is Proving that Diversity Isn't a Dirty Word" about the TV show *Empire* and its provocative use of Black-American race and sexualities at *The Conversation*. She also has forthcoming publication with the *Electronic Book Review* titled "I will tell your story: New Media Activism and the Indian 'rape crisis'" about erasures inherent in transnational feminisms co-opting Indian feminist issues.

Emily Perkins is a Vancouver-based actress working in feature film and television. She is best known for her work in horror (Stephen King's *It*, *X-Files*, the *Ginger Snaps* trilogy, *Supernatural*) and comedy (*She's the Man, Another Cinderella Story, Hiccups*). She has received a Leo award for her recurring role in Da Vinci's Inquest and has been inducted into the Fangoria Hall of Fame. She has a BA in Psychology and Women's Studies from the University of British Columbia.

William Proctor is Lecturer in Media, Culture and Communication at Bournemouth University, UK. He teaches on a variety of topics including transmedia, new media, adaptation, fan cultures, and popular culture. William has published various articles and book chapters on reboots, *Batman, Star Wars, The Walking Dead*, and *James Bond*. He is currently working on a monograph based upon his PhD thesis titled *Beginning Again: The Reboot Phenomenon in Comic Books, Film and Beyond*. William is also director of "The Force Re-Awakens: World Star Wars Audiences," and editor of Disney's *Star Wars: Forces of Production, Promotion and Reception*.

Mel Stanfill is Post-Doctoral Research Associate in American Studies at Purdue University. Stanfill engages in critical media industry studies, investigating the articulation of speculative media and sports fandoms to industry in the Internet era through heteronormativity, whiteness, consumption, intellectual property law, and labor. Stanfill's work has appeared in venues such as *Cinema Journal, Transformative Works and Cultures*, and *New Media and Society*.

Louisa Stein is Assistant Professor of Film and Media Culture at Middlebury College. Her work explores audience engagement in transmedia culture, with emphasis on questions of gender and generation. Louisa is author of *Millennial Fandom: Television Audiences in the Transmedia Age* (University of Iowa Press, 2015). She is also coeditor of *Sherlock and Transmedia Fandom* (McFarland, 2012) and *Teen Television: Programming and Fandom* (McFarland, 2008). She has also published in a range of journals and edited collections including *Cinema Journal* and *How to Watch Television*. Louisa serves as book review editor for *Transformative Works and Cultures* and *Cinema Journal*.

Rebecca Williams is Lecturer in Communication, Cultural and Media Studies at the University of South Wales. She is the author of *Post-Object Fandom: Television, Identity and Self-Narrative* (2015, Bloomsbury) and editor of *Torchwood Declassified* (2013, IB Tauris) and *Transitions, Endings, and Resurrections in Fandom* (forthcoming, University of Iowa Press). She has published in journals including *Popular Communication, Celebrity Studies, Television & New Media, Continuum, Critical Studies in Television*, and *Journal of British Cinema and Television*.

Lynn Zubernis is an Associate Professor at West Chester University. She is the co-author of *Fandom At The Crossroads: Celebration, Shame and Fan/Producer Relationships* and *Fangasm: Supernatural Fangirls* and the co-editor of *Fan Phenomena: Supernatural* and *Fan Culture: TheoryPractice* and has also published a counseling textbook, *Case Conceptualization and Effective Interventions*. She has a new book on the television series Supernatural coming out soon, *Family Don't End With Blood: How A Television Show Changed Lives*.

Bibliography

"200." 2006. *Stargate SG-1*, 10.06. Directed by Brad Wright, Robert C. Cooper, and Joseph Mallozzi. Beverly Hills, CA: MGM Worldwide, August 18.

Abad-Santos, Alexander. 2014. "Chinese Women Can't Stop Reading and Writing Gay 'Sherlock' Fan Fiction." *The Wire*, January 15. Accessed March 17, 2015. http://www .thewire.com/culture/2014/01/chinese-women-cant-stop-reading-and-writing -sherlock-gay-fan-fic/357046/.

Adorno, Theodor. (1938) 2001. "On the Fetish-Character of Music and the Regression of Listening." In *The Culture Industry: Selected Essays on Mass Culture*, edited by J. M. Bernstein, 29–60. New York: Routledge.

Ahmed, Sara. 2006. *Queer Phenomenology: Orientations, Objects, Others*. Durham, NC: Duke University Press.

Amesley, Cassandra. 1989. "How to Watch *Star Trek*." *Cultural Studies* 3 (3): 323–39.

Anderson, Ole, with Scott Teal. 2003. *Inside Out: How Corporate America Destroyed Professional Wrestling*. Hendersonville, TN: Crowbar Press.

Anderson, Tonya. 2012. "Still Kissing Their Posters Goodnight: Female Fandom and the Politics of Popular Music." *Participations: Journal of Audience and Reception Studies* 9 (2): 239–64.

Andrews, Maggie, and Rosie Whorlow. 2000. "Girl Power and the Post-Modern Fan: The 1996 Boyzone Concert Tour." In *All the World and Her Husband: Women in Twentieth-Century Consumer Culture*, edited by Maggie Andrews and Mary M. Talbot, 253–66. London: Cassell.

Appadurai, Arjun. 1986. "Introduction: Commodities and the Politics of Value." In *The Social Life of Things: Commodities in Cultural Perspective*, edited by Arjun Appadurai, 3–63. Cambridge: Cambridge University Press.

Arnstein, S. 2014a. "Fans, Villains, & Speculation." DVD commentary. BBC, UK: *Sherlock* Season Three.

Arnstein, S. 2014b. "The Fall." DVD commentary. BBC, UK: *Sherlock* Season Three.

Asquith, Daisy. 2013. *Crazy About One Direction*. London: Channel 4.

Asquith, Daisy. 2016. *This Is Not Us*. Forthcoming film.

Austin, Thomas. 2007. *Watching the World: Screen Documentary and Audiences*. Manchester: Manchester University Press.

Azuma, Hiroki. 2008. *Otaku: Japan's Database Animals*. Minneapolis: University of Minnesota Press.

Bacon-Smith, Camille. 1992. *Enterprising Women: Television Fandom and the Creation of Popular Myth*. Philadelphia: University of Pennsylvania Press.

Bailey, Steven. 2005. *Media Audiences and Identity: Self-Construction in the Fan Experience*. Basingstoke: Palgrave Macmillan.

Baird-Stribling, Eleanor. 2015. "Valuing Fans." *Spreadablemedia.org*. Accessed March 17, 2015. http://spreadablemedia.org/essays/stribling/.

Baker, Andrea J. 2014. *You Get What You Need: Stories of Fans of the Rolling Stones*. Virginia: Minniver Press.

Baker, Sarah. 2013. "Teenybop and the Extraordinary Particularities of Mainstream Practice." In *Redefining Mainstream Popular Music*, edited by Sarah Baker, Andy Bennett, and Jodie Taylor, 14–24. New York: Routledge.

Barker, Martin, and Julian Petley. 1998. *Ill Effects: The Media/Violence Debate*. London: Routledge.

Barker, Martin, Jane Arthurs, and Ramaswami Harindranath. 2001. *The Crash Controversy: Censorship Campaigns and Film Reception*. New York: Wallflower.

Barnes, Colin. 1992. *Disabling Imagery and the Media: An Exploration of the Principles for Media Representations*. Halifax: Ryburn Publishing.

Barthes, Roland. 1957 (translated 1972). "The World of Wrestling." In *Mythologies*, translated by Annette Levers, 15–25. New York: Hill and Wang.

Baudrillard, Jean. 2005. *The System of Objects*. Translated by James Benedict. London: Verso.

Bear, Elizabeth. 2008. "Whatever You're Doing, You're Probably Wrong." *Livejournal*. http://matociquala.livejournal.com/1544111.html.

Beeler, Stan. 2008. "*Stargate SG-1 and the Quest for the Perfect Science Fiction Premise*." In *The Essential Science Fiction Television Reader*, edited by J.P. Telotte, 267–82. Lexington: University Press of Kentucky.

Benjamin, Walter. (1936) 2007. "The Work of Art in an Age of Mechanical Reproduction." In *Illuminations: Essays and Reflections*, edited by Hannah Arendt, 217–52. New York: Harcourt, Brace, Jovanovich.

Bennett, Andy. 2006. "Punk's Not Dead: The Continuing Significance of Punk Rock for an Older Generation of Fans." *Sociology* 40 (2): 219–35.

Bennett, Lucy. 2013a. "Discourses of Order and Rationality: Drooling R.E.M. Fans as 'Matter out of Place.'" *Continuum: Journal of Media & Cultural Studies* 27 (2): 214–27.

Bennett, Lucy. 2013b. "'If We Stick Together We Can Do Anything': Lady Gaga Fandom, Philanthropy and Activism through Social Media." *Celebrity Studies* 5 (1–2): 1–15.

Bennett, Lucy. 2014a. "Fan-Celebrity Interactions and Social Media: Connectivity and Engagement in Lady Gaga Fandom." In *The Ashgate Research Companion to Fan Cultures*, edited by Linda Duits, Koos Zwaan, and Stijn Rejinders, 109–20. Burlington, VT: Ashgate.

Bennett, Lucy. 2014b. "Tracing *Textual Poachers*: Reflections on the Development of Fan Studies and Digital Fandom." *Journal of Fandom Studies* 2 (1): 5–20.

Bennett, Lucy, and Paul Booth, eds. 2015. *Transformative Works and Cultures* 18: "Performance and Performativity in Fandom." http://journal.transformativeworks.org/index.php/twc/issue/view/19.

Benzecry, Claudio E. 2011. *The Opera Fanatic: Ethnography of an Obsession*. Chicago, IL: University of Chicago Press.

Berg, Louis. 1942. *Radio and Civilian Morale*. Self-published pamphlet.

Berry, Dan. 2008. "Unreality SF – Russell T Davies & Benjamin Cook Interview." *Unreality SF*, October 15. Accessed October 20, 2015. http://unreality-sf.net/2008/10/15/russell-t-davies-benjamin-cook-interview/.

Blassie, Freddie, and Keith Elliott Greenberg. 2003. *Legends of Wrestling—"Classy" Freddie Blassie: Listen, You Pencil Neck Geeks*. New York: Pocket Books.

Booth, Paul. 2010. *Digital Fandom: New Media Studies*. New York: Peter Lang.

Booth, Paul. 2013a. "Reifying the Fan: Inspector Spacetime as Fan Practice." *Popular Communication* 11 (2): 146–59.

Booth, Paul. 2013b. "*Star Trek* Fans as Parody: Fans Mocking Other Fans." In *Fan Phenomena: Star Trek*, edited by Bruce Drushel, 72–81. Bristol: Intellect Press.

Booth, Paul. 2015a. "Crowdfunding: A Spimatic Application of Digital Fandom." *New Media and Society* 17 (2): 1–18.

Booth, Paul. 2015b. *Playing Fans: Negotiating Fandom and Media in the Digital Age*. Iowa City: University of Iowa Press.

Booth, Paul, and Peter Kelly. 2013. "The Changing Faces of *Doctor Who* Fandom: New Fans, New Technologies, Old Practices?" *Participations: Journal of Audience and Reception Studies* 10 (2): 56–72.

Bourdieu, Pierre. 1984: *Distinction: A Social Critique of the Judgment of Taste*. Cambridge, MA: Harvard University Press.

Bourdieu, Pierre. 1986. "The Forms of Capital." In *Handbook of Theory and Research for the Sociology of Education*, edited by John G. Richardson, 241–58. New York: Greenwood.

boyd, danah. 2008. *Taken Out of Context: American Teen Sociality in Networked Publics*. PhD dissertation., University of California.

boyd, danah. 2010. *Social Steganography: Learning to Hide in Plain Sight*. Accessed April 23, 2015. http://dmlcentral.net/blog/danah-boyd/social-steganography-learning-hide -plain-sight.

British Broadcasting Company (BBC). 2014. "UK Sent BBC's Sherlock to North Korea." *BBC News—Entertainment and Arts*, July 3. Accessed October 12, 2015. http://www .bbc.co.uk/news/entertainment-arts-28147177/.

Brooker, Will. 2000. *Batman Unmasked: Analyzing a Cultural Icon*. London: Bloomsbury.

Brooker, Will. 2002. *Using the Force: Creativity, Community and Star Wars Fandom*. London: Continuum.

Brooker, Will. 2007. "A Sort of Homecoming: Fan Viewing and Symbolic Pilgrimage." In *Fandom: Identities and Communities in a Mediated World*, edited by Jonathan Gray, Cornel Sandvoss, and C. Lee Harrington, 149–65. New York: New York University Press.

Brooker, Will. 2013. "Fandom and Authorship." *In The Superhero Reader*, edited by Charles Hatfield, Jeet Heer, and Kent Worcester, 61-72. University Press of Mississippi.

Brooker, Will, Zaidan, Sarah, and Suze, Shore. 2013- present. *My So-Called Secret Identity*. http://www.mysocalledsecretidentity.com/.

Brough, Melissa M., and Sangita Shresthova. 2012. "Fandom Meets Activism: Rethinking Civic and Political Participation." *Transformative Works and Cultures* 10. doi:10.3983/ twc.2012.0303.

Brower, Sue. 1992. "Fans as Tastemakers: Viewers for Quality Television." In *The Adoring Audience: Fan Culture and Popular Media*, edited by Lisa A. Lewis, 163–84. London: Routledge.

Brown, J. A. 2001. *Black Superheroes, Milestone Comics and Their Fans*. Jackson: University Press of Mississippi.

Bruzzi, Stella. 2006. *New Documentary*. London: Routledge.

Burlingame, Russ. 2014. "The Flash's Candice Patton: 'It's about the Story and Race Is Irrelevant.'" *Comicbook.com*, July 28. Accessed October 17, 2015. http://comicbook .com/blog/2014/07/28/the-flashs-candice-patton-its-about-the-story-and-race-is -irrele/.

Burn, Andrew. 2006. "Reworking the Text: Online Fandom." In *Computer Games: Text, Narrative and Play*, edited by Diane Carr, 72–87. Cambridge: Polity.

Bury, Rhiannon. 2005. *Cyberspaces of Their Own: Female Fandoms Online*. New York: Peter Lang.

Bury, Rhiannon, Ruth A. Deller, Adam Greenwood, and Bethan Jones. 2013. "From Usenet to Tumblr: The Changing Role of Social Media." *Participations* 10 (1): 299–318.

Busker, Rebecca Lucy. 2008. "On Symposia: LiveJournal and the Shape of Fannish Discourse." *Transformative Works and Cultures* 1. http://journal.transformativeworks .org/index.php/twc/article/view/49.

Busse, Kristina. 2006. "My Life Is a WIP on My LJ: Slashing the Slasher and the Reality of Celebrity and Internet Performances." In *Fan Fiction and Fan Communities in the Age of the Internet: New Essays*, edited by Karen Hellekson and Kristina Busse, 207–24. Jefferson, NC: McFarland.

Busse, Kristina. 2013a. "Geek Hierarchies, Boundary Policing, and the Gendering of the Good Fan." *Participations* 10 (1): 73–91.

Busse, Kristina. 2013b. "The Return of the Author: Ethos and Identity Politics." In *Companion to Media Authorship*, edited by Jonathan Gray and Derek Johnson, 48–68. Oxford: Blackwell.

Busse, Kristina. 2015. "Fan Labor and Feminism: Capitalizing on the Fannish Labor of Love." *Cinema Journal* 54 (3): 110–15.

Busse, Kristina and Karen Hellekson. 2012. "Identity, Ethics and Fan Privacy." *In Fan Culture:Theory/Practice*, edited by Katherine Larsen and Lynn Zubernis, 38-56. Newcastle upon Tyne: Cambridge Scholars Publishing.

Butler, Judith. 1990. *Gender Trouble: Feminism and the Subversion of Identity*. New York: Routledge.

Butler, Judith. 2004. *Precarious Life: The Powers of Mourning and Violence*. London: Verso.

Cann, Victoria. 2015. "Girls and Cultural Consumption: 'Typical Girls,' 'Fangirls' and the Value of Femininity." In *The Politics of Being a Woman: Feminism, Media and 21st Century Popular Culture*, edited by Heather Savigny and Helen Warner, 154–74. London: Palgrave.

Carey, Diane. 1997. *Ship of the Line*. New York: Pocket Books.

Carter, Liz. 2013. "Benedict Cumberbatch Is a Gay Erotic God in China." *Foreign Policy Magazine*, November 15. Accessed October 12, 2015. http://foreignpolicy .com/2013/11/15/benedict-cumberbatch-is-a-gay-erotic-god-in-china/.

Cavicchi, Daniel. 1998. *Tramps Like Us: Music and Meaning among Springsteen Fans*. Oxford: Oxford University Press.

Centrumlumina. 2013. "AO3 Census: Masterpost." October 5, 2013. http:// centrumlumina.tumblr.com/post/63208278796/ao3-census-masterpost.

Chadwick, Andrew. 2013. *The Hybrid Media System: Politics and Power*. Oxford: Oxford University Press.

Chambers, Ross. 1997. "The Unexamined." In *Whiteness: A Critical Reader*, edited by Mike Hill, 187–203. New York: New York University Press.

Cherry, Brigid. 2005. "The Other End of the Wormhole: The Case of *Stargate SG-1* on British Television." *Spectator* 25 (1): 61–70. http://cinema.usc.edu/assets/097/15732 .pdf.

Chin, Bertha. 2010. *From Textual Poachers to Textual Gifters: Exploring Fan Community and Celebrity in the Field of Fan Cultural Production*. PhD diss., Cardiff University.

Chin, Bertha, and Lori Morimoto. 2013. "Towards a Theory of Transcultural Fandom." *Participations* 10 (1): 92–108.

Chin, Bertha, Bethan Jones, Myles McNutt, and Luke Pebler. 2014. "*Veronica Mars* Kickstarter and Crowd Funding." *Transformative Works and Cultures* 15. http://dx.doi .org/10.3983/twc.2014.0519.

"Citizen Joe." 2005. *Stargate SG-1*, 8.15. Directed by Andy Mikita. Beverly Hills, CA: MGM Worldwide, February 18.

Click, Melissa. 2009. "'Rabid,' 'Obsessed,' and 'Frenzied': Understanding Twilight Fangirls and the Gendered Politics of Fandom." *Flow*, December. Accessed October 12, 2015. http://flowtv.org/2009/12/rabid-obsessed-and-frenzied-understanding-twilight -fangirls-and-the-gendered-politics-of-fandom-melissa-click-university-of-missouri/.

Cohen, Cathy J. 1997. "Punks, Bulldaggers, and Welfare Queens: The Radical Potential of Queer Politics?" *GLQ: A Journal of Lesbian and Gay Studies* 3 (4): 437–65.

Coker, Catherine. 2013. "Earth 616, Earth 1610, Earth 3490—Wait, What Universe Is This Again? The Creation and Evolution of the Avengers and Captain America/Iron Man Fandom." *Transformative Works and Cultures* 13. http://journal.transformativeworks .org/index.php/twc/article/view/439/363

Coleridge, Samuel Taylor. 1817. "Chapter XIV." In *Biographia Literaria, or Biographical Sketches of My Literary Life and Opinions*. Charleston, SC: BiblioBazar.

Collins, Patricia Hill. 2000. *Black Feminist Thought: Knowledge, Consciousness, and the Politics of Empowerment*, 2nd ed. New York: Routledge.

Condry, Ian. 2011. "Love Revolution: Anime, Masculinity, and the Future." In *Recreating Japanese Men*, edited by Sabine Frühstück and Anne Walthall, 262–83. Berkeley: University of California Press.

Connell, Matt. 2012. "Talking about Old Records: Generational Musical Identity among Older People." *Popular Music* 31 (2): 261–78.

Coppa, Francesca. 2006a. "A Brief History of Media Fandom." In *Fan Fiction and Fan Communities in the Age of the Internet: New Essays*, edited by Karen Hellekson and Kristina Busse, 41–59. Jefferson, NC: McFarland.

Coppa, Francesca. 2006b. "Writing Bodies in Space: Media Fanfiction as Theatrical Performance." In *Fan Fiction and Fan Communities in the Age of the Internet*, edited by Karen Hellekson and Kristina Busse, 225–44. Jefferson, NC: McFarland.

Coppa, Francesca. 2008. "Women, *Star Trek*, and the Early Development of Fannish Vidding." *Transformative Works and Cultures* 1. doi:10.3983/twc.2008.0044.

Coppa, Francesca. 2011. "An Editing Room of One's Own: Vidding as Women's Work." *Camera Obscura* 26 (2/77): 123–30.

Coren, Victoria. 1998. "The Sultan of Sex." *The Evening Standard*, July 17.

Couldry, Nick. 2001. "The Umbrella Man: Crossing a Landscape of Speech and Silence." *European Journal of Cultural Studies* 4 (2): 131–52.

Couldry, Nick. 2004. "Teaching Us to Fake It: The Ritualized Norms of Television's 'Reality' Games." In *Reality TV: Remaking Television Culture*, edited by Susan Murray and Laurie Oullette, 57–74. New York: New York University Press.

Couldry, Nick. 2005. "Media Meta-Capital: Extending the Range of Bourdieu's Field Theory." In *After Bourdieu: Influence, Critique, Elaboration*, edited by David L. Swartz and Vera L. Zolberg, 165–89. New York: Kluwer Academic Publishers.

Couldry, Nick. 2007. "Media Power: Some Hidden Dimensions." In *Stardom and Celebrity: A Reader*, edited by Sean Redmond and Su Holmes, 353–9. London: Sage.

Counteragent. 2009. "Good Fourth Walls Make Good Neighbors." *Supernaturalart*, September 1, 2010. Accessed October 22, 2015. http://supernaturalart.livejournal .com/1796967.html.

Craven, Gerald, and Richard Moseley. 1972. "Actors on a Canvas Stage: The Dramatic Conventions of Professional Wrestling." *Journal of Popular Culture* 6 (2): 326–36.

Crenshaw, Kimberle. 1991. "Mapping the Margins: Intersectionality, Identity Politics, and Violence against Women of Color." *Stanford Law Review* 43 (6): 1241–99.

Cronin, Kate. 2004. "Rockin' around the World to See Rod." *The Bolton News*, February 4.

Daily Post (author unattributed). 2006. "Anne Delighted after Sir Tom Gets the Knighthood She Fought for." *Daily Post* (North Wales), January 3.

Dare-Edwards, Helena Louise. 2014a. "'Shipping Bullshit': Twitter Rumors, Fan/Celebrity Interaction and Questions of Authenticity." *Celebrity Studies* 5 (4): 521–4.

Dare-Edwards, Helena Louise. 2014b. "One Direction Tweet: Social Media, Real Person Slash (RPS) and the Erosion of the Fourth Wall." Paper presented at the 35th Annual South West Popular/American Culture Association Conference, Albuquerque, February 19–22, 2014.

Davies, Dave. 2012. "Steven Moffat: The Man Who Revitalized 'Doctor Who' and 'Sherlock.'" Fresh Air. *NPR*, May 3. Accessed October 18, 2015. http://www.npr.org/templates/transcript/transcript.php?storyId=151938002.

Davies, Madeleine. 2014. "Women in China Are Really into Gay Sherlock Fan Fiction." *Jezebel*, January 15. Accessed March 17, 2015. http://jezebel.com/women-in-china-are-really-into-gay-sherlock-fan-fiction-1502679156.

Davies, Russell T., and Benjamin Cook. 2010. *Doctor Who: The Writer's Tale*. London: Random House.

de Groot, Jerome. 2009. *Consuming History: Historians and Heritage in Contemporary Popular Culture*. London: Routledge.

De Kosnik, Abigail. 2009. "Should Fan Fiction Be Free?" *Cinema Journal* 48 (4): 118–24. doi:10.1353/cj.0.0144.

De Kosnik, Abigail. 2012. "Fandom as Free Labor." In *Digital Labor: The Internet as Playground and Factory*, edited by Trebor Sholz, 98–111. New York: Routledge.

de Moraes, Lisa. 2014. "'Sherlock' Season 3 Premiere Draws 4 Million Viewers On PBS." *Deadline Hollywood*, January 20. Accessed October 18, 2015. http://deadline.com/2014/01/tca-sherlock-move-pays-ratings-dividends-to-pbs-4-million-tune-in-668164/.

Dell, Chad. 2006. *The Revenge of Hatpin Mary: Women, Professional Wrestling, and Fan Culture in the 1950s*. New York: Peter Lang.

Deller, Ruth A. 2014. "A Decade in the Lives of Online Fan Communities." In *The Ashgate Research Companion to Fan Cultures*, edited by Linda Duits, Koos Zwaan, and Stijn Reijnders, 237–49. Farnham: Ashgate.

Dennis, Anthony. 1993. "Will Success Spoil Ray Martin?" *Sunday Age*, March 28.

Diaz Dennis, Alicia. 2013. "'Larry Stylinson' Fan Fiction Writers Finally Have Their Moment in 'Crazy About One Direction.'" *Zimbio*, August 9. Accessed February 21, 2015. http://www.zimbio.com/Pop+Gossip/articles/L_7X-eV09X0/Larry+Stylinson+Fan+Fiction+Writers+Finally.

Diffrient, David Scott. 2010. "The Cult Imaginary: Fringe Religions and Fan Cultures on American Television." *Historical Journal of Film, Radio and Television* 30 (4): 463–85.

Dixon, Kevin. 2013. *Consuming Football in Late Modern Life*. Farnham: Ashgate.

Dockterman, Eliana. 2014. "Comic-Con Women Protest Sexual Harassment." *Time Magazine*, July 28. Accessed October 12, 2015. http://time.com/3045797/women-comic-con-sexual-harrassment-petition/.

Doty, Alexander. 1993. *Making Things Perfectly Queer*. Minneapolis: University of Minnesota Press.

Dowell, Ben. 2013. "Introducing Curly Fu and Peanut—Better Known as Sherlock's Benedict Cumberbatch and Martin Freeman." *Radio Times*, December 9. Accessed March 17, 2015. http://www.radiotimes.com/news/2013-12-09/introducing-curly-fu-and-peanut–better-known-as-sherlocks-benedict-cumberbatch-and-martin-freeman.

Driscoll, Catherine. 2006. "One True Pairing: The Romance of Pornography and the Pornography of Romance." In *Fan Fiction and Fan Communities in the Age of the Internet: New Essays*, edited by Karen Hellekson and Kristina Busse, 79–96. Jefferson, NC: McFarland.

Duffett, Mark. 2013. *Understanding Fandom: An Introduction to the Study of Media Fan Culture*. New York: Bloomsbury.

Dunham, Jess. 2014. "Chinese Fans Give Sherlock and Watson Bizarre Nicknames and Hail Benedict Cumberbatch as Erotic Icon." *The Independent*, January 3. Accessed March 17, 2015. http://www.independent.co.uk/arts-entertainment/tv/news/chinese -fans-give-sherlock-and-watson-bizarre-nicknames-and-hail-benedict-cumberbatch -as-erotic-icon-9037055.html.

Dyer, Richard. 1997. *White*. London: Routledge.

"Dylan O'Brien and Tyler Hoechlin: Vote for Teen Wolf on Teen Choice Awards!" 2012. *YouTube*. https://www.youtube.com/watch?v=cKTQPWbxQZk.

Ebert, Teresa L. 1980. "The Convergence of Postmodern Innovative Fiction and Science Fiction: An Encounter with Samuel R. Delany's Technotopia." *Poetics Today* 1 (4): 91–104.

Editor, Associate. 2014. "Gay Sherlock Holmes Fan Fiction Irks China's Media Regulator." *LGBT Weekly*, April 17. Accessed March 17, 2015. http://lgbtweekly.com/2014/04/17/ gay-sherlock-holmes-fan-fiction-irks-china%E2%80%99s-media-regulator/.

Ehrenreich, Barbara, Elizabeth Hess, and Gloria Jacobs. 1992. "Beatlemania: Girls Just Want to Have Fun." In *The Adoring Audience: Fan Culture and Popular Media*, edited by Lisa A. Lewis, 84–106. London: Routledge.

Everett, Anna. 2005. "Serious Play: Playing with Race in Contemporary Gaming Culture." *Handbook of Computer Game Studies*, edited by J. Raessens and J. Goldstein, 312–25. Cambridge: MIT Press.

Fahy, Colette, and Lucy Crossley. 2015. "Hysterical One Direction Fans Spark Self-Harming Fears as Disturbing Hashtag Trends on Twitter after Malik Quits." *MailOnline*, March 25. Accessed April 19, 2015. http://www.dailymail.co.uk/tvshowbiz/ article-3011449/Hysterical-One-Direction-fans-spark-concerns-self-harming -disturbing-hashtag-trends-Twitter-Malik-quits-chart-topping-boyband.html.

Fathallah, Judith May. 2010. "Becky Is My Hero: The Power of Laughter and Disruption in 'Supernatural.'" *Transformative Works and Cultures* 5. doi:10.3983/twc.2010.0220.

Felschow, Laura. 2010. "'Hey, Check It Out, There's Actually Fans': (Dis)empowerment and (Mis)representation of Cult Fandom in 'Supernatural.'" *Transformative Works and Cultures* 4. doi:http://dx.doi.org/10.3983/twc.2010.0134.

Ferguson, Roderick A. 2003. *Aberrations in Black: Toward a Queer of Color Critique*. Minneapolis: University of Minnesota Press.

Fernández, Maria. 1999. "Postcolonial Media Theory." *Art Journal* 58 (3): 58–73.

Ferris, Kerry, and Scott Harris. 2011. *Stargazing: Celebrity, Fame and Social Interaction*. New York: Routledge.

Fishzon, Anna. 2013. *Fandom, Authenticity, and Opera: Mad Acts and Letter Scenes in Fin-de-Siecle Russia*. Basingstoke: Palgrave Macmillan.

Fiske, John. 1992. "The Cultural Economy of Fandom." In *The Adoring Audience: Fan Culture and Popular Media*, edited by Lisa A. Lewis, 30–49. London: Routledge.

Flair, Ric, with Keith Elliot Greenberg. 2004. *To Be the Man*. New York: Pocket Books.

Floyd, Kevin. 2009. *The Reification of Desire: Toward a Queer Marxism*. Minneapolis: University of Minnesota Press.

Foley, Mick. 2001. *Foley Is Good… and the Real World Is Faker than Wrestling*. New York: Reagan Books.

Ford, Sam. 2007. "Pinning Down Fan Involvement: An Examination of Multiple Modes of Engagement for Professional Wrestling Fans." *MITOpenCourseWare*, http://ocw.mit.edu/courses/comparative-media-studies-writing/cms-997-topics-in-comparative-media-american-pro-wrestling-spring-2007/readings/ford_role_playing.pdf.

Ford, Sam. 2014. "Fan Studies: Grappling with an 'Undisciplined' Discipline." *Journal of Fandom Studies* 2 (1): 53–71.

Forman, Murray. 2012. "'How We Feel the Music': Popular Music by Elders and for Elders." *Popular Music* 31 (2): 245–60.

Foucault, Michel. 1975. *Discipline and Punish: The Birth of the Prison*. New York: Pantheon Books.

Foucault, Michel. 1980. "Truth and Power." In *Power/Knowledge: Selected Interviews and Other Writings* (1972–1977), edited by Colin Gordon, 109–33. New York: Pantheon.

Frankenberg, Ruth. 1993. *White Women, Race Matters: The Social Construction of Whiteness*. Minneapolis: University of Minnesota Press.

Franklin, M. I. 2004. *Postcolonial Politics, the Internet, and Everyday Life: Pacific Traversals Online*. London: Routledge.

Freedman, Des. 2014. *The Contradictions of Media Power*. New York: Bloomsbury.

Fu, Ting. 2014. "China Falls in Love with Sherlock Holmes." *The Associated Press—The Big Story*, January 19. Accessed March 17, 2015. http://bigstory.ap.org/article/china-falls-love-sherlock-holmes.

Fulton, Eileen, with Desmond Atholl, and Michael Cherkinian. 1995. *As My World Still Turns: The Uncensored Memoirs of America's Soap Opera Queen*. New York: Birch Lane Press.

Funk, Terry, with Scott E. Williams. 2005. *Terry Funk: More than Just Hardcore*. Champaign, IL: Sports Publishing.

Galbraith, Patrick W. 2012. *Otaku Spaces*. Seattle, WA: Chin Music Press.

Gamson, Joshua. 1998. *Freaks Talk Back: Tabloid Talk Shows and Sexual Nonconformity*. Chicago, IL: University of Chicago Press.

Garde-Hansen, Joanne, and Hannah Grist. 2014. *Remembering Dennis Potter Through Fans, Extras and Archives*. Basingstoke: Palgrave.

Garland-Thompson, Rosemary. 1996. *Freakery: Cultural Spectacles of the Extraordinary Body*. New York: New York University Press.

Garrison, Lindsay. 2010. "Crying for Justin Bieber and Negotiating Affective Fan Performance." *In Media Res*. Accessed March 1, 2015. http://mediacommons.futureofthebook.org/imr/2010/06/14/crying-justin-bieber-and-negotiating-affective-fan-performance.

Gee, James, P. 2001. "Reading as Situated Language: A Sociocognitive Perspective." *Journal of Adolescent and Adult Literacy* 44: 714–25. http://www.jstor.org/stable/40018744.

Geraghty, Lincoln. 2007. *Living with Star Trek: American Culture and the Star Trek Universe*. London: IB Tauris.

Geraghty, Lincoln. 2014. *Cult Collectors: Nostalgia, Fandom and Collecting Popular Culture*. London: Routledge.

Gilbert, Anne. 2015. "What We Talk about When We Talk about Bronies." *Transformative Works and Cultures* 20. http://dx.doi.org/10.3983/twc.2015.0666.

Gold, Tanya. 2008. "Barry's Barmy Army: Meet the Most Fearsome Fan Club of All… the Fanilows." *MailOnline*, December 9. Accessed June 2015. http://www.dailymail.co.uk/femail/article-1093010/Barrys-barmy-army-Meet-fearsome-fan-club-Fanilows.html.

Gold, Tanya. 2010. "How Cliff Tipped Me over the Edge." *Daily Telegraph*, October 14.

GQ. 2013. "The Most Terrifying Responses to Our One Direction Covers." *GQ*, July 30. Accessed April 18, 2015. http://www.gq-magazine.co.uk/entertainment/articles/2013-07/30/one-direction-gq-covers-most-terrifying-responses.

Grant, Drew. 2014. "TV Writers and Showrunners Increasingly 'Mute' the Fans." *Observer*, November 20. Accessed October 18, 2015. http://observer.com/2014/11/tv-writers-and-showrunners-increasingly-mute-the-fans/.

Gray, Jonathan. 2003. "New Audiences, New Textualities: Anti-Fans and Non-Fans." *International Journal of Cultural Studies* 6 (1): 64–81.

Gray, Jonathan. 2005. "Antifandom and the Moral Text: Television without Pity and Textual Dislike." *American Behavioral Scientist* 48 (7): 840–58. doi:10.1177/0002764204273171.

Gray, Jonathan. 2010. "On Anti-Fans and Paratexts: An Interview with Jonathan Gray." *Futures of Entertainment*, March 25. Accessed March 25, 2015. http://www.convergenceculture.org/weblog/2010/03/on_anti-fans_and_paratexts_an.php.

Gray, Jonathan, Cornel Sandvoss, and C. Lee Harrington. 2007. "Introduction: Why Study Fans." In *Fandom: Identities and Communities in a Mediated World*, edited by Jonathan Gray, Cornel Sandvoss, and C. Lee Harrington, 1–18. New York: New York University Press.

Gray, Melissa. 2010. "From Canon to Fanon and Back Again: The Epic Journey of *Supernatural* and Its Fans." *Transformative Works and Cultures* 4. http://dx.doi.org/10.3983/twc.2010.0146.

Guiffre, Liz. 2014. "Music for (Something Other than) Pleasure: Anti-Fans and the Other Side of Popular Music Appeal." In *The Ashgate Research Companion to Fan Cultures*, edited by Linda Duits, Koos Zwan, and Stijn Reijnders, 49–62. Farnham: Ashgate.

Guo, Martin. 2013. "David Cameron Flooded by 'Tough' Questions on Weibo." *Kantar—China Insights*, December 9. Accessed March 20, 2015. http://cn-en.kantar.com/media/social/david-cameron-flooded-by-%E2%80%98tough-questions%E2%80%99-on-weibo/.

Hadas, Leora, and Limor Shifman. 2013. "Keeping the Elite Powerless: Fan-Producer Relations in the 'Nu Who' (and New You) Era." *Critical Studies in Media Communication* 30 (4): 274–91.

Haggard, Dan. 2010. "Twilight, the Anti-Fan, and the Culture Wars." *Reviews in Depth*, March 23. Accessed November 30, 2014. http://reviewsindepth.com/2010/03/twilight-the-anti-fan-and-the-culture-wars/.

Hale News Roundup. 2009. "Rose Retires from Teaching." *Halesowen News*, July 19.

Hall, Stuart. 1980. "Encoding/decoding." In *Culture, Media, Language: Working Papers in Cultural Studies, 1972–79*, edited by Stuart Hall, Dorothy Hobson, Andrew Lowe, and Paul Willis, 128–38. London: Hutchinson.

Halskov, Andreas. 2015. *TV Peaks: Twin Peaks and Modern Television Drama*. Odense: University Press of Southern Denmark.

Hansen, Miriam. 1986. "Pleasure, Ambivalence, Identification: Valentino and Female Spectatorship." *Cinema Journal* 25 (4): 6–32.

Hara, Tomoko. 1996. *Honkon Chūdoku: Muteki No Den'ei Myōjōmeitachi* (Hong Kong addicted: peerless films and stars). Tōkyō: Japan Times.

Hardt, Michael, and Antonio Negri. 2000. *Empire*. Cambridge, MA: Harvard University Press.

Hardwood, Judas. 2012. "Telling Wrestling Fans That Wrestling Isn't Real." *Vice*, April 19. Accessed October 20, 2015. https://www.vice.com/en_uk/read/vox-pops-in-the-queue-at-wwe-raw-at-the-o2-in-london.

Harman, Sarah, and Bethan Jones. 2013. "Fifty Shades of Ghey: Snark Fandom and the Figure of the Anti-Fan." *Sexualities* 16 (8): 951–68.

Harrington, C. Lee, and Denise D. Bielby. 1995. *Soap Fans: Pursuing Pleasure and Making Meaning in Everyday Life.* Philadelphia, PA: Temple University Press.

Harrington, C. Lee, and Denise D. Bielby. 2010. "A Life Course Perspective on Fandom." *International Journal of Cultural Studies* 13 (5): 429–50.

Harris, Cheryl. 1998. "Theorizing Fandom: Fans, Subculture and Identity." In *Theorizing Fandom: Fans, Subculture and Identity*, edited by Cheryl Harris and Alison Alexander, 3–8. Cresskill, NJ: Hampton Press.

Harris, Neil. 1973. *Humbug: The Art of P.T. Barnum.* Boston, MA: Little, Brown and Company.

Hart, Jimmy. 2004. *The Mouth of the South: The Jimmy Hart Story.* Toronto: ECW Press.

"Hathor." 1997. *Stargate SG-1*, 1.14. Directed by Brad Turner. Beverly Hills, CA: MGM Worldwide, October 24.

Hayashi, Kaori, and Eun-jeung Lee. 2007. "The Potential of Fandom and the Limits of Soft Power: Media Representations on the Popularity of a Korean Melodrama in Japan." *Social Science Japan Journal* 10 (2): 197–216.

Heaf, Jonathan. 2013. "This One Direction Interview Got Us Death Threats." *GQ*, July 29. Accessed April 18, 2015. http://www.gq-magazine.co.uk/entertainment/articles/2013-07/29/one-direction-gq-covers-interview/page/1.

Heenan, Bobby, with Steve Anderson. 2002. *Bobby the Brain: Wrestling's Bad Boy Tells All.* Chicago, IL: Triumph.

Hellekson, Karen, and Kristina Busse, eds. 2006. *Fan Fiction and Fan Communities in the Age of the Internet.* Jefferson, NC: McFarland.

Hellekson, Karen, and Kristina Busse, eds. 2015. *The Fan Fiction Studies Reader.* Iowa City: University of Iowa Press.

Hernandez, Kimberley. 2013. "alksjdf;lksfd: The Language of Tumblr." *OxfordWords*, May 27. Accessed April 27, 2015. http://blog.oxforddictionaries.com/2013/05/language-of-tumblr/.

Heyman, Stephen. 2014. "A Conversation with Steven Moffat, a 'Sherlock' Co-Creator." *New York Times*, January 17. Accessed October 18, 2015. http://artsbeat.blogs.nytimes.com/2014/01/17/a-conversation-with-steven-moffat-a-sherlock-co-creator/?_r=5.

Hill, Mike. 1997. "Vipers in Shangri-La: Whiteness, Writing, and Other Ordinary Terrors." In *Whiteness: A Critical Reader*, edited by Mike Hill, 1–18. New York: New York University Press.

Hills, Logan. 2007. "The Vidder." *New York Magazine*, November 12. Accessed October 20, 2015. http://nymag.com/movies/features/videos/40622/.

Hills, Matt. 2002a. *Fan Cultures.* London: Routledge.

Hills, Matt. 2002b. "Transcultural 'Otaku': Japanese Representations of Fandom and Representations of Japan in Anime/Manga Fan Cultures." *Proceedings of MiT2*, Massachusetts Institute of Technology, Cambridge, MA, May 10–12, 2002.

Hills, Matt. 2003. "Recognition in the Eyes of the Relevant Beholder: Representing 'Subcultural Celebrity' and Cult TV Fan Cultures." *Mediactive* 2 (2): 59–73.

Hills, Matt. 2006. "'Not Just Another 'Powerless Elite'? When Fans Become Subcultural Celebrities." In *Framing Celebrity: New Directions in Celebrity Culture*, edited by Su Holmes and Sean Redmond, 101–18. London: Routledge.

Hills, Matt. 2007. "Michael Jackson Fans on Trial? 'Documenting' Emotivism and Fandom in *Wacko About Jacko*." *Social Semiotics* 17 (4): 459–77.

Hills, Matt. 2010. *Triumph of a Time Lord: Regenerating Doctor Who in the Twenty-First Century.* London: IB Tauris.

Hills, Matt. 2012a. "Psychoanalysis and Digital Fandom: Theorizing Spoilers and Fans' Self Narratives." In *Produsing Theory in a Digital World: The Intersection of Audiences and Production in Contemporary Theory*, edited by Rebecca Ann Lind, 105–22. New York: Peter Lang Publishing.

Hills, Matt. 2012b. "Sherlock's Epistemological Economy and the Value of 'Fan' Knowledge: How Producer-Fans Play the (Great) Game of Fandom." In *Sherlock and Transmedia Fandom*, edited by Louisa E. Stein and Kristina Busse, 27–40, Jefferson, NC: McFarland.

Hills, Matt. 2012c. "'Twilight' Fans Represented in Commercial Paratexts and Inter-Fandoms: Resisting and Repurposing Negative Fan Stereotypes." In *Genre, Reception, and Adaptation in the "Twilight" Series*, edited by Anne More, 113–31. Farnham: Ashgate.

Hinck, Ashley. 2012. "Theorizing a Public Engagement Keystone: Seeing Fandom's Integral Connection to Civic Engagement through the Case of the Harry Potter Alliance." *Transformative Works and Cultures* 10. doi:10.3983/twc.2012.0311.

Hipple, Dave. 2006. "Stargate SG-1: Self-Possessed Science Fiction." In *Reading Stargate SG-1*, edited by Stan Beeler and Lisa Dickson, 27–47. London: IB Tauris.

Hitchcock, Lori D. 2002. "Transnational Film and the Politics of Becoming: Negotiating East Asian Identity in Hong Kong Night Club and Moonlight Express." *Asian Cinema* 13 (1): 67–86.

Hitt, Carolyn. 2009. "It's Not Unusual for a Bloke Aged 68 to Look a Little Old." *The Western Mail*, May 18.

Hodkinson, Paul. 2011. "Ageing in a Spectacular 'Youth Culture': Continuity, Change and Community amongst Older Goths." *The British Journal of Sociology* 62 (2): 262–82.

Holden, Anthony. 2003. "Music Releases: Classical." *The Observer*, July 27.

Honey, Kim. 2001. "Diamond Is Forever." *The Globe and Mail* (Canada), June 2.

Hunter, Colin. 2007. "Today's Music Sharing is Convenient, but Thrill Is Gone." *The Record (Kitchener/Waterloo)*, February 12.

Ignatiev, N. 1996. *How the Irish Became White*. London: Routledge.

Ito, Mitsuki, Daisuke Oikabe, and Izumi Tsuji. 2012. *Fandom Unbound: Otaku Culture in a Connected World*. New Haven, CT: Yale University Press.

Ittner, Phil. 2014. "Interview: Sherlock Creators Give Clues to Holmes' Enduring Appeal." *Aljazeera America*, January 19. Accessed October 18, 2015. http://america.aljazeera.com/articles/2014/1/19/interview-sherlockcreatorsgivecluestoholmesdurability0.html.

Iwabuchi, Koichi. 2002. *Recentering Globalization: Popular Culture and Japanese Transnationalism*. Durham, NC: Duke University Press.

Jamison, Anne, ed. 2013a. *Fic: Why Fanfiction Is Taking Over the World*. Dallas, TX: Smart Pop Books.

Jamison, Anne. 2013b. "The Theory of Narrative Causality." In *Fic: Why Fanfiction Is Taking Over the World*, edited by Anne Jamison, 3–16. Dallas, TX: Smart Pop Books.

Jancovich, Mark, and James Lyons. 2003. "Introduction." In *Quality Popular Television*, edited by Mark Jancovich and James Lyons, 1–8. London: BFI.

Jenkins, Henry. 1992. *Textual Poachers: Television Fans and Participatory Culture*. New York: Routledge.

Jenkins, Henry. 1997. "Television Fans, Poachers, Nomads." In *The Subcultures Reader*, edited by Ken Gelder and Sarah Thornton, 506–22. London: Routledge.

Jenkins, Henry. 2005. "Afterword, Part I: Wrestling with Theory, Grappling with Politics." In *Steel Chair to the Head: The Pleasure and Pain of Professional Wrestling*, edited by Nicholas Sammond, 295–316. Durham, NC: Duke University Press.

Jenkins, Henry. 2006a. *Convergence Culture: Where Old and New Media Collide.* New York: New York University Press.

Jenkins, Henry. 2006b. *Fans, Bloggers, and Gamers: Exploring Participatory Culture.* New York: New York University Press.

Jenkins, Henry. 2007a. "Afterword: The Future of Fandom." In *Fandom: Identities and Communities in a Mediated World*, edited by Jonathan Gray, Cornel Sandvoss, and C. Lee Harrington, 357–64. New York: New York University Press.

Jenkins, Henry. 2007b. "Vidder Luminosity Profiled in New York Magazine." *Confessions of an Aca-Fan*, November 20. Accessed October 20, 2015. http://henryjenkins .org/2007/11/vidder_luminosity_profiled_in.html.

Jenkins, Henry. 2012a. "'Cultural Acupuncture': Fan Activism and the Harry Potter Alliance." *Transformative Works and Cultures* 10. doi:10.3983/twc.2012.0305.

Jenkins, Henry. 2012b. "The Guiding Spirit and the Powers That Be: A Response to Suzanne Scott." In *The Participatory Cultures Handbook*, edited by Aaron Delwiche and Jennifer Jacobs Henderson, 53–58. New York: Routledge.

Jenkins, Henry. 2012c. "Performing Our 'Collective Dreams': The Many Worlds of San Diego's Comic-Con." *Confessions of an Aca-Fan*, July 15. Accessed October 17, 2015. http://henryjenkins.org/2012/07/performing_our_collective_drea.html.

Jenkins, Henry. 2012d. *Textual Poachers: Television Fans and Participatory Culture.* Updated Twentieth Anniversary Edition. New York: Routledge.

Jenkins, Henry, Sam Ford, and Joshua Green. 2013. *Spreadable Media.* New York: New York University Press.

Jensen, Joli. 1992. "Fandom as Pathology: The Consequences of a Characterization." In *The Adoring Audience*, edited by Lisa Lewis, 9–29. New York: Routledge.

Jhally, Sut, and Jackson Katz. 2002. *Wrestling with Manhood: Boys, Bullying, and Battering.* Northampton, MA: Media Education Foundation Film.

Johnson, Derek. 2007. "Fan-tagonism: Factions, Institutions, and Constitutive Hegemonies of Fandom." In *Fandom: Identities and Communities in a Mediated World*, edited by Jonathan Gray, Cornel Sandvoss, and C. Lee Harrington, 285–300. New York: New York University Press.

Jones, Bethan. 2014. "Johnlocked: Sherlock, Slash Fiction and the Shaming of Female Fans." *New Left Project*, February 18. Accessed March 17, 2015. http://www .newleftproject.org/index.php/site/article_comments/johnlocked_sherlock_slash _fiction_and_the_shaming_of_female_fans.

Jones, Bethan. 2015. "My Little Pony, Tolerance Is Magic: Gender Policing and Brony Anti-Fandom." *The Journal of Popular Television* 3 (1): 119–25.

Jones, Gerard, and Will Jacobs. 1997. *The Comic Book Heroes.* Roseville, CA: Prima Publishing.

Jones, Paul. 2014. "Steven Moffat: 'Tumblr Seems to Be a Place Where People Who Really Want to Kill Me Gather.'" *Radio Times*, January 9. Accessed October 18, 2015. http:// www.radiotimes.com/news/2014-01-09/sherlock-writer-steven-moffat-we-dont-get -our-plotlines-from-tumblr.

Jones, Sara Gwenllian. 2000. "Histories, Fictions, and Xena: Warrior Princess." *Television and New Media* 1 (4): 403–18.

Jung, Sun, and Doobo Shim. 2014. "Social Distribution: K-pop Fan Practices in Indonesia and the 'Gangnam Style' Phenomenon." *International Journal of Cultural Studies* 17 (5): 485–501.

Kaltenbach, Chris. 1994. "Wrestling Legends Muscle Their Way into Hall of Fame: Monsters of the Mat." *Baltimore Sun*, June 8. Accessed October 20, 2015. http://articles.baltimoresun.com/1994-06-08/features/1994159112_1_regis-philbin-blassie-wrestling-legends.

Kearney, Mary Celeste. 2006. *Girls Make Media*. New York: Routledge.

Kelsky, Karen. 2001. *Women on the Verge: Japanese Women, Western Dreams*. Durham, NC: Duke University Press.

Kermode, Mark. 2014. "*Pulp: A Film About Life, Death & Supermarkets* Review – Fans' Fond Farewell to Jarvis and Co." *The Guardian Online*, June 8. Accessed August 24, 2015. http://www.theguardian.com/film/2014/jun/08/pulp-film-life-death-supermarkets-review-fans-farewell-jarvis.

Kerrick, George E. 1980. "Miscellany: The Jargon of Professional Wrestling." *American Speech* 55 (2): 142–5.

Kick-Ass. Dir. Matthew Vaughn. Los Angeles, CA: Universal Pictures. 2010.

Kinsella, Sharon. 1998. "Japanese Subculture in the 1990s: Otaku and the Amateur Manga Movement." *Journal of Japanese Studies* 24 (4): 289–316.

Klose, Stephanie. 2013. "Jay Bushman, Cocreator of *Welcome to Sanditon*." *Library Journal* 15, June: 50.

Kobayashi, Chiek. July 1996. "*Honkon mūbī netsuai sengen*" (A declaration of love for Hong Kong movies), Cosmopolitan (Japan), 14–31.

Kohnen, Melanie. 2014. "'The Power of Geek': Fandom as Gendered Commodity at Comic-Con." *Creative Industries Journal* 7 (1): 75–8.

Kustritz, Anne. 2003. "Slashing the Romance Narrative." *Journal of American Culture* 26 (3): 371–84.

Kustritz, Anne. 2015a. "Exploiting Surplus Labours of Love: Narrating Ownership and Theft in Crowdfunding Controversies." In *Crowdfunding the Future: Media Industries, Ethics & Digital Society*, edited by Lucy Bennett, Bertha Chin, and Bethan Jones, 47–63. New York: Peter Lang.

Kustritz, Anne. 2015b. "Transnationalism, Localization, and Translation in European Fandom: Fan Studies as Global Media and Audience Studies [Editorial]." *Transformative Works and Cultures* 19. doi:10.3983/twc.2015.0682.

Kusz, Kyle W. 2001. "'I Want to Be the Minority': The Politics of Youthful White Masculinities in Sport and Popular Culture in 1990s America." *Journal of Sport and Social Issues* 25 (4): 390–416.

Lackner, Eden, Barbara L. Lucas, and Robin A. Reid. 2006. "Cunning Linguists: The Bisexual Erotics of *Words/Silence/Flesh*." In *Fan Fiction and Fan Communities in the Age of the Internet: New Essays*, edited by Karen Hellekson and Kristina Busse, 189–206. Jefferson, NC: McFarland.

Lamb, Patricia Frazer, and Diane Veith. 1986. "Romantic Myth, Transcendence, and *Star Trek* Zines." In *Erotic Universe: Sexuality and Fantastic Literature*, edited by Donald Palumbo, 236–55. Westport, CT: Greenwood Press.

Lamerichs, Nicolle. 2013. "The Cultural Dynamic of Doujinshi and Cosplay: Local Anime Fandom in Japan, USA and Europe." *Participations* 10 (1): 154–76.

Larbalestier, Justine. 2002. "Buffy's Mary Sue Is Jonathan: Buffy Acknowledges the Fans." In *Fighting the Forces: What's at Stake in Buffy the Vampire Slayer*, edited by Rhonda Wilcox and David Lavery, 227–39. Lanham, MD: Rowman & Littlefield Publishers.

Lee, Kevin. 2008. "The Little State Department: Hollywood and the MPAA's Influence on USA Trade Relations." *Northwestern Journal of International Law and Business* 28 (2): 371–98.

Lee, Soojin, David Scott, and Kim Hyounggon. 2008. "Celebrity Fan Involvement in Destination Perceptions." *Annals of Tourism Research* 35 (3): 809–32.

Lee-Wright, Peter. 2010. *The Documentary Handbook*. London: Routledge.

Leonard, David. 2003. "'Live in Your World, Play in Ours': Race, Video Games, and Consuming the Other." *Studies in Media & Information Literacy Education* 3 (4): 1–9.

Leveugle, Lucy. 2005 *Wacko About Jacko*. London: Channel 4.

Lewis, Lisa A. 1992a. "Introduction." In *The Adoring Audience: Fan Culture and Popular Media*, edited by Lisa A. Lewis, 1–6. London: Routledge.

Lewis, Lisa A. 1992b. "'Something More than Love': Fan Stories on Film." In *The Adoring Audience: Fan Culture and Popular Media*, edited by Lisa A. Lewis, 135–59. London: Routledge.

Littlejohn, Georgina. 2012. "Sherlock Fans Take to the Internet to Share Theories on How Holmes Faked His Own Death." *Daily Mail*, January 18. Accessed October 18, 2015. http://www.dailymail.co.uk/tvshowbiz/article-2087814/Sherlock-fans-internet-share -theories-Holmes-faked-death.html.

Löbert, Anja. 2012. "Fandom as a Religious Form: Cliff Richard Fans in Liverpool." *Popular Music* 3 (2): 125–41.

Locke, Simon. 2012. "'Fanboy' as Revolutionary Category." *Participations: Journal of Audience and Reception Studies* 9 (2): 835–54. http://www.participations.org/ Volume%209/Issue%202/Locke.pdf.

Lopez, Lori Kido. 2012. "Fan Activists and the Politics of Race in *The Last Airbender*." *International Journal of Cultural Studies* 15 (5): 431–45.

Lothian, Alexis, Kristina Busse, and Robin A. Reid. 2007. "Yearning Void and Infinite Potential: Online Slash Fandom as Queer Female Space." *English Language Notes* 45 (2): 103–11.

Lotz, Amanda D. 2007. "Must-See TV: NBC's Dominant Decades." In *NBC: America's Network*, edited by Michele Hilmes, 261–74. Berkeley: University of California Press.

Lovell, Nicholas. 2014. *The Curve: Turning Followers into Superfans*. London: Penguin.

Lyan, Irina, and Alon Levkowitz. 2015. "From Holy Land to 'Hallyu Land': The Symbolic Journey Following the Korean Wave in Israel." *Journal of Fandom Studies* 3 (1): 7–21.

Madrid-Morales, Dani, and Bruno Lovric. 2015. "Transatlantic Connection': K-pop and K-drama Fandom in Spain and Latin America." *Journal of Fandom Studies* 3 (1): 23–41.

Makarechi, Kim. 2013. "Checking in with the GQ Editor Dragged by One Direction Fans over British GQ's Cover." *Huffington Post*, July 31. Accessed April 18, 2015. www .huffingtonpost.com/2013/07/31/gq-editor-one-direction-fans_n_3684282.html.

Malyon, ed. 2013. "One Direction Fans Send Gabby Agbonlahor Death Threats after Injuring Louis Tomlinson in Charity Game." *The Mirror*, September 8. Accessed April 18, 2015. http://www.mirror.co.uk/sport/football/news/gabriel-agbonlahor-tackles -louis-tomlinson-2260599.

Marwick, Alice E., and danah boyd. 2010a. "I Tweet Honestly, I Tweet Passionately: Twitter Users, Context Collapse, and the Imagined Audience." *New Media & Society* 13 (1): 114–33.

Marwick, Alice, and danah boyd. 2010b. "To See and Be Seen: Celebrity Practice on Twitter." *Convergence* 17 (2): 139–58.

Mathijs, Ernest, and Xavier Mendik. 2004. "Introduction: Making Sense of Extreme Confusion: European Exploitation Cinema and Underground Cinema." In *Alternative Europe: Eurotrash and Exploitation Cinema Since 1945*, edited by E. Mathijs and X. Mendik, 1–18. London: Wallflower Press.

Mazer, Sharon. 1998. *Professional Wrestling: Sport and Spectacle*. Jackson: University Press of Mississippi.

McArthur, J. A. 2009. "Digital Subculture: A Geek Meaning of Style." *Journal of Communication Enquiry* 33 (1): 58–70.

McBride, Lawrence B., and S. Elizabeth Bird. 2007. "From Smart Fan to Backyard Wrestler: Performance, Context, and Aesthetic Violence." In *Fandom: Identities and Communities in a Mediated World*, edited by Jonathan Gray, Cornell Sandvoss, and C. Lee Harrington, 165–76. New York: New York University Press.

McElroy, Ruth, and Rebecca Williams. 2011. "Remembering Ourselves, Viewing the Others: Historical Reality Television and Celebrity in the Small Nation." *Television and New Media* 12 (3): 187–206.

McLelland, Mark. 2001. "Local Meanings in Global Space: A Case Study of Women's 'Boy Love' Web Sites in Japanese and English." *Mots Pluriels* 19. http://motspluriels.arts.uwa.edu.au/MP1901mcl.html.

Melannen. 2010. "Science Y'all!" *Dreamwidth*, January 16, 2010. Accessed October 20, 2015. http://melannen.dreamwidth.org/77558.html.

Meltzer, Dave. 2004. "Freddie Blassie." In *Tributes II: Remembering More of the World's Greatest Professional Wrestlers,*" 14–27. Champaign, IL: Sports Publishing.

Merrin, William. 2014. *Media Studies 2.0*. London: Routledge.

Miller, Frank. 1986. *Batman: The Dark Knight Returns*. New York: DC Comics.

Miller, Laura. 2008. "Korean TV Dramas and the Japan-Style Korean Wave." *PostScript* 27 (3): 17–24.

Milton, Dermot. 2010. "I've Got 600 Pics of My Idol Daniel." *The Sun* (Ireland edition), September 24.

Mirna, Cicione. 1998. "Male Pair-Bonds and Female Desire in Fan Slash Writing." In *Theorizing Fandoms: Fans, Subculture, and Identity*, edited by Cheryl Harris and Alison Alexander, 153–77. Cresskill, NJ: Hampton Press.

Mittell, Jason. 2010. *Television and American Culture*. New York: Oxford University Press.

Moffat, Steven. 2014. In "Fans, Villains and Speculations." BBC, UK: *Sherlock* series 3 BluRay.

"The Monster at the End of This Book." *Television without Pity* forums. 2009.04.02. (Archived; forum no longer online).

Monti, Adrian. 2007. "Your Life: Obsessed!" *The Mirror*, November 13.

Morley, David. 1992. *Television, Audiences & Cultural Studies*. London: Routledge.

Morris, Errol. 2002. *Interview in Vice Magazine*. London: Vice.

Morrison, Grant, et al. 2014–2015. *The Multiversity*. New York: DC Comics.

Morton, Gerald W., and George M. O'Brien. 1985. *Wrestling to Rasslin': Ancient Sport to American Spectacle*. Bowling Green, OH: Bowling Green State University Popular Press.

Mukherjee, Roopali. 2011. "Diamonds (Are from Sierra Leone): Bling and the Promise of Consumer Citizenship." In *Commodity Activism: Cultural Resistance in Neoliberal Times*, edited by Roopali Mukherjee and Sara Banet-Weiser, 114–33. New York: New York University Press.

Murray, Jim. 1985. "Wrestling Fans—Why Tell 'Em?" *The Los Angeles Times*, March 19. Accessed October 20, 2015. http://articles.latimes.com/1985-03-19/sports/sp-1800_1 _pro-wrestling.

Nagel, Joane. 2003. *Race, Ethnicity, and Sexuality: Intimate Intersections, Forbidden Frontiers*. New York: Oxford University Press.

Nash, Kate. 2010. "Exploring Power and Trust in Documentary: A Study of Tom Zubrycki's Molly and Mobarak." *Studies in Documentary Film* 4 (1): 21–33.

Nash, Melanie, and Martti Lahti. 1999. "Almost Ashamed to Say I Am One of Those Girls: Titanic, Leonardo DiCaprio, and the Paradox of Girls' Fandom." In *Titanic: Anatomy of a Blockbuster*, edited by Kevin S. Sandler and Gaylyn Studlar, 64–88. Piscataway, NJ: Rutgers University Press.

Nayar, Promod K. 2008. "New Media, Digitexuality, and Public Space: Reading 'Cybermohalla.'" *Postcolonial Text* 4 (1). http://postcolonial.org/index.php/pct/article/ viewArticle/786.

Ndalianis, Angela. 2010. "Stargate SG-1." In *The Essential Cult TV Reader*, edited by David Lavery, 237–42. Lexington: University Press of Kentucky.

Neojaponism. 2008. "Otaku Research #1: 'This City Is Full of Otaku'" (Translated without Express Permission by Matt Alt). *Neojaponism*. http://neojaponisme.com/2008/04/02/ what-kind-of-otaku-are-you/

"The New World of Who." 2006. *Doctor Who Confidential*. Cardiff: BBC: Wales.

Newitz, Annalee, and Matt Wray. 1997a. "Introduction." In *White Trash: Race and Class in America*, edited by Annalee Newitz and Matt Wray, 1–12. New York: Routledge.

Newitz, Annalee, and Matt Wray. 1997b. "What Is 'White Trash'?: Stereotypes and Economic Conditions of Poor Whites in the United States." In *Whiteness: A Critical Reader*, edited by Mike Hill, 168–84. New York: New York University Press.

Nichols, Bill. 2010. *Introduction to Documentary*. Bloomington: Indiana University Press.

No author. 2014. "VIDEO: Pulp at Sheffield DocFest Premiere." *The Star*, June 9. Accessed June 10, 2014. http://www.thestar.co.uk/what-s-on/cinema/video-pulp-at-sheffield -docfest-premiere-1-6661073.

Nolan, Steve. 2013. "'I Expected More People': Daniel O'Donnell Superfan, 67, Queued for More than Two Days Outside Theatre to Get tickets to See Idol." *MailOnline*, May 11. Accessed June 2015. http://www.dailymail.co.uk/news/article-2322938/I-expected -people-Daniel-ODonnell-superfan-67-queued-days-outside-theatre-tickets-idol.html.

Noppe, Nele. 2011. "Why We Should Talk about Commodifying Fan Work." *Transformative Works and Cultures* 8. doi:10.3983/twc.2011.0369.

Noppe, Nele. 2014. "Social Networking Services as Platforms for Transcultural Fannish Interactions: DeviantART and Pixiv." In *Manga's Cultural Crossroads*, edited by Jaqueline Berndt and Bettina Kümmerling-Meibauer, 143–59. London: Routledge.

Norris, Craig. 2012. "Perfect Blue and the Negative Representations of Fans." *Journal of Japanese and Korean Cinema* 4 (1): 69–86.

Nussbaum, Emily. 2014. "Fan Friction: Sherlock and Its Audiences." *The New Yorker*, January 27. Accessed October 18, 2015. http://www.newyorker.com/ magazine/2014/01/27/fan-friction.

Nye, Joseph. 1990. "Soft Power." *Foreign Policy* 80: 153–71.

O'Connell, Margaret. 2009. "Sympathy for the Devil - 5.01 Episode Discussion." *Winchester Radio*, September 12. Accessed October 8, 2010. http://www.blogtalkradio .com/winchester_radio/2009/09/12/sympathy-for-the-devil-501-episode-discussion.

O'Donoghue, Dan. 2014. "Singer Daniel O'Donnell Records Personal 100th Birthday Message for Great Harwood Fan." *Accrington Observer*, January 9.

O'Guinn, Thomas C. 1991. "Touching Greatness: The Central Midwest Barry Manilow Fan Club." In *SV - Highways and Buyways: Naturalistic Research from the Consumer Behavior Odyssey*, edited by Russell Belk, 102–11. Provo, UT: Association for Consumer Research.

O'Kelly, Michael. 1995. "Fans Dye Willingly as Rod Sails by." *The Irish Times*, July 22.

Orgad, Shani. 2009. "How Can Researchers Make Sense of the Issues Involved in Collecting and Interpreting Online and Offline Data." In *Internet Inquiry: Conversations about Method*, edited by Annette N. Markham and Nancy K. Baym, 1–21. London: Sage.

"The Other Guys." 2002. *Stargate SG-1*, 6.08. Directed by Martin Wood. Beverly Hills, CA: MGM Worldwide, August 2.

Palys, Ted. 2008. "Purposive Sampling." In *The SAGE Encyclopedia of Qualitative Research Methods*, edited by Lisa M. Given, 698–9. Thousand Oaks, CA: Sage.

Pantozzi, Jill. 2014. "Several Women Arrested for Writing Fanfic in China." *The Mary Sue*, April 21. Accessed March 17, 2015. http://www.themarysue.com/fanfic-writers -arrested-in-china/.

Papacharissi, Zizi. 2012. "Without You, I'm Nothing: Performances of the Self on Twitter." *International Journal of Communication* 6: 1989–2006.

Papacharissi, Zizi. 2015. *Affective Publics: Sentiment, Technology, and Politics*. Oxford: Oxford University Press.

Passion Distribution. 2013. "Crazy About One Direction." Accessed November 2, 2014. http://www.passiondistribution.com/programmes/crazy-about-one-direction/.

"Patton Oswalt and Robert Siegel: Serious Funny Men." 2010. *Fresh Air with Terry Gross*. NPR. http://www.npr.org/templates/story/story.php?storyId=122335831.

Pauley, Nigel. 2013. "One Direction Fans Dream of Gay Marriage between Harry Styles & Louis Tomlinson." *Daily Star*, August 10. Accessed January 4, 2015, http://www .dailystar.co.uk/showbiz/331588/One-Direction-fans-dream-of-gay-marriage-between -Harry-Styles-Louis-Tomlinson.

Pearce, Gail. 2007. *Truth or Dare: Art and Documentary*. Bristol: Intellect.

Pearson, Roberta E. 2004. "'Bright Particular Star': Patrick Stewart, Jean-Luc Picard, and Cult Television." In *Cult Television*, edited by Sara Gwenllian-Jones and Roberta E. Pearson, 61–80. Minneapolis: University of Minnesota Press.

Pearson, Roberta E. 2007. "Bachies, Bards, Trekkies, and Sherlockians." In *Fandom: Identities and Communities in a Mediated World*, edited by Jonathan Gray, Cornel Sandvoss, and C. Lee Harrington, 98–109. New York: New York University Press.

Penley, Constance. 1986. "Brownian Motion: Women, Tactics, and Technology." In *Technoculture*, edited by Constance Penley and Andrew Ross, 135–61. Minneapolis: University of Minnesota Press.

Pflieger, Pat. 2001. "Too Good to Be True: 150 Years of Mary Sue." Accessed September 15, 2015. http://www.merrycoz.org/papers/MARYSUE.xhtml.

Phillips, Tom. 2015. "Wrestling with Grief: Fan Negotiation of Professional/Private Personas in Responses to the Chris Benoit Double Murder-Suicide." *Celebrity Studies* 6 (1): 69–84.

Phillips, Whitney. 2015. *This Is Why We Can't Have Nice Things: Mapping the Relationship between Online Trolling and Mainstream Culture*. Cambridge: MIT Press.

Pinkowitz, Jacqueline M. 2011. "'The Rabid Fans That Take [*Twilight*] Much Too Seriously': The Construction and Rejection of Excess in Twilight Antifandom." *Transformative Works and Cultures* 7. doi:10.3983/twc.2011.0247.

Piotrowska, Agnieszka. 2013. *Psychoanalysis and Ethics in Documentary Film*. London: Routledge.

"Point of No Return." 2000. *Stargate SG-1*, 4.11. Directed by William Gereghty. Beverly Hills, CA: MGM Worldwide, September 8.

Pointon, Ann, and Chris Davies, eds. 1997. *Framed: Interrogating Disability in the Media*. London: British Film Institute.

Pope, Stacey, and John Williams. 2011. "'White Shoes to a Football Match!': Female Experiences of Football's Golden Age in England." *Transformative Works and Cultures* 6. doi:10.3983/twc.2011.0230.

Porzucki, Nina. 2014. "Why Is China Obsessed with Sherlock?" *Public Radio International*, January 2. Accessed March 17, 2015. http://www.pri.org/stories/2014-01-02/why -china-obsessed-sherlock.

Powell, David. 2009. "Visit My Shrine to Tom Jones… for Pounds 2 Donation." *Daily Post*, March 31.

PR Script Managers. 2014. "Janet Silverthorne Obituary." *North Somerset Times*, July 9.

Pulp The Film. 2014. Accessed August 25, 2015. http://www.pulpthefilm.com/.

Punathambekar, Aswin. 2007. "Between Rowdies and Rasikas: Rethinking Fan Activity in Indian Film Culture." In *Fandom: Identities and Communities in a Mediated World*, edited by Jonathan Gray, Cornel Sandvoss, and C. Lee Harrington, 198–209. New York: New York University Press.

Radford, Eleanor. 2010. "Even a Bomb Won't Budge Daniel's Fans." *Plymouth Herald*, November 12.

Rand, Erica. 1995. *Barbie's Queer Accessories*. Durham, NC: Duke University Press.

Reagle, Joseph M. 2015. *Reading the Comments: Likers, Haters and Manipulators at the Bottom of the Web*. Cambridge: MIT Press.

Redhead, Steve. 2014. "'We're Not Racist, We Only Hate Mancs': Post-Subculture and Football Fandom." In *The Ashgate Research Companion to Fan Cultures*, edited by Linda Duits, Koos Zwan and Stijn Reijnders, 289–302. Surrey: Ashgate.

Reid, Robin Anne. 2010. "The Rhetorics of Color-Blind Racism in Racefail 09." http://hdl .handle.net/1969.1/92354.

Richardson, Niall. 2010. *Transgressive Bodies: Representations in Film and Popular Culture*. Surrey: Ashgate.

Ridley, Sarah. 2013. "Wee Dan Fans Wait 3 Nights for Tickets." *The Sun* (Ireland edition), April 17.

Riessman, Catherine Kohler. 2008. *Narrative Methods for the Human Sciences*. Thousand Oaks, CA: Sage.

rivkat. 2010. "Climbing the Walls." Accessed 31 January 2016. http://rivkat.dreamwidth. org/256743.html?thread=3097575&style=light.

Roberts, Joe. 1998. "Sarah, 89, Keen to See Daniel Wed." *The Mirror*, November 2.

Robertson, Jennifer. 1998. *Takarazuka: Sexual Politics and Popular Culture in Modern Japan*. Berkeley: University of California Press.

Robertson, Roland. 1992. *Globalization: Social Theory and Global Culture*. London: Sage.

Robinson, Peter. 2013. "One Direction Fans Have Turned Their Anger on GQ—But It Is the Magazine That's Behaved Really Badly?" *The Guardian*, August 1. Accessed April 19, 2015. http://www.theguardian.com/lifeandstyle/lostinshowbiz/2013/aug/01/one -direction-fans-gq-abusive-tweets.

Rodino-Colocino, Michelle. 2012. "Geek Jeremiads: Speaking the Crisis of Job Loss by Opposing Offshored and H-1B Labor." *Communication and Critical/Cultural Studies* 9 (1): 22–46.

Roediger, David R. 1991. *The Wages of Whiteness: Race and the Making of the American Working Class*. London: Verso.

Romano, Aja. 2013a. "One Direction Fans Are Right to Be Outraged by GQ." *Daily Dot*, July 31. Accessed April 27, 2015. http://www.dailydot.com/opinion/one-direction -fans-gq-outrage-is-valid/.

Romano, Aja. 2013b. "'Sherlock' Fans Lash Out over Sunken JohnLock Ship." *The Daily Dot*, April 26. Accessed October 18, 2015. http://www.dailydot.com/fandom/sherlock -fandom-johnlock-ship/.

Romano, Aja. 2014. "Chinese Authorities Are Arresting Writers of Slash Fanfiction." *The Daily Dot*, April 18. Accessed March 17, 2015. http://www.dailydot.com/geek/in-china -20-people-women-arrested-for-writing-slash/.

Roney, Tyler. 2014. "China's Latest Porn Purge Underway." *The Diplomat*, April 18. Accessed March 17, 2015. http://thediplomat.com/2014/04/chinas-latest-porn-purge -underway/.

Ross, Karen. 2001. "All Ears: Radio, Reception and Discourses of Disability." *Media, Culture & Society* 23 (4): 419–37.

Ross, Karen. 2006. "Open Source? Hearing Voices in the Local Press." In *Local Journalism and Local Media*, 2nd ed., edited by Bob Franklin, 232–44. London: Routledge.

Ross, Sharon Marie. 2008. *Beyond the Box: Television and the Internet*. Malden, MA: Blackwell Publishing.

Rubin, Gayle S. 1993. "Thinking Sex: Notes for a Radical Theory of the Politics of Sexuality." In *The Lesbian and Gay Studies Reader*, edited by Henry Abelove, Michèle Aina Barale, and M. David Halperin, 3–44. New York: Routledge.

Ruehl, Peter. 2003. "Time's Up, Gotta Earn Your Six—Pack." *Australian Financial Review*, September 16.

Russ, Joanna. 1985. "Pornography by Women, for Women, with Love." In *Magic Mommas, Trembling Sisters, Puritans and Perverts: Feminist Essays*, 79–99. Trumansburg: The Crossing Press.

Russo, Julie Levin. Summer 2009. "User-Penetrated Content: Fan Video in the Age of Convergence." *Cinema Journal* 48 (4): 125–30. doi: 10.1353/cj.0.0147.

Sabal, Robert. 1992. "Television Executives Speak about Fan Letters to the Networks." In *The Adoring Audience: Fan Culture and Popular Media*, edited by Lisa A. Lewis, 185–90. London: Routledge.

Sabin, Roger. 1993. *Adult Comics: An Introduction*. London: Routledge.

Saler, Michael. 2012. *As If: Modern Enchantment and the Literary Prehistory of Virtual Reality*. Oxford: Oxford University Press.

Salmon, Catherine, and Don Symons. 2001. *Warrior Lovers: Erotic Fiction, Evolution and Female Sexuality*. London: Orion.

Sammond, Nicholas. 2005. "Squaring the Family Circle: WWF *Smackdown* Assaults the Social Body." In *Steel Chair to the Head: The Pleasure and Pain of Pro Wrestling*, edited by Nicholas Sammond, 132–66. Durham, NC: Duke University Press.

San Martín, Nancy. 2003. "'Must See TV': Programming Identity on NBC Thursdays." In *Quality Popular Television*, edited by Mark Jancovich and James Lyons, 32–47. London: BFI.

Sandell, Jillian. 1997. "Telling Stories of 'Queer White Trash': Race, Class, and Sexuality in the Work of Dorothy Allison." In *White Trash: Race and Class in America*, edited by Annalee Newitz and Matt Wray, 211–30. New York: Routledge.

Sanderson, Jimmy. 2010. "Weighing in on the Coaching Decision: Discussing Sports and Race Online." *Journal of Language and Social Psychology* 29 (3): 301–20.

Sandler, Kevin S. 2007. "Life without *Friends*: NBC's Programming Strategies in an Age of Media Clutter, Media Conglomeration, and TiVo." In *NBC: America's Network*, edited by Michele Hilmes, 291–307. Berkeley: University of California Press.

Sandvoss, Cornel. 2005. *Fans: The Mirror of Consumption*. Cambridge: Polity Press.

Sanghani, Radhika. 2015. "Zayn Malik: The Dark Truth about the #Cut4Zayn Trend." *The Telegraph*, March 26. Accessed April 19, 2015. http://www.telegraph.co.uk/women/womens-life/11496335/Zayn-Malik-leaves-One-Direction-Dark-truth-about-the-Cut4Zayn-trend.html.

Sardar, Ziauddin. 2000. "ALT.CIVILIZATION.FAQ: Cyberspace as the Darker Side of the West." In *The Cybercultures Reader*, edited by David Bell and Barbara M. Kennedy, 733–52. New York: Routledge.

Satō, Tadao. 1970. *Nihon Eiga Shisōshi* (The intellectual history of Japanese film). Tōkyō: Sanichi shobō.

Savage, Christina. 2014. "*Chuck* versus the Ratings: Savvy Fans and 'Save Our Show' Campaigns." *Transformative Works and Cultures* 15. http://dx.doi.org/10.3983/twc.2014.0497.

Savran, David. 1998. *Taking It Like a Man: White Masculinity, Masochism, and Contemporary American Culture*. Princeton, NJ: Princeton University Press.

Schmidt, Lisa. 2010. "Monstrous Melodrama: Expanding the Scope of Melodramatic Identification to Interpret Negative Fan Responses to *Supernatural*." *Transformative Works and Cultures* 4. http://dx.doi.org/10.3983/twc.2010.0152.

Scodari, Christine. 2007. "Yoko in Cyberspace with Beatles Fans: Gender and the Re-Creation of Popular Mythology." In *Fandom: Identities and Communities in a Mediated World*, edited by Jonathan Gray, Cornel Sandvoss, and C. Lee Harrington, 48–59. New York: New York University Press.

Scodari, Christine, and J.L. Felder. 2000. "Creating a Pocket Universe: 'Shippers,' Fan Fiction, and *The X-Files* Online." *Communication Studies* 51 (3): 238–57.

Scott, Suzanne. 2008. "Ethnographies of Obsession: Documenting and Pathologizing Fandom." Presented at the Getting Obsessive: Culture and Excess symposium, University of Southern California.

Scott, Suzanne. 2009. "Repackaging Fan Culture: The Regifting Economy of Ancillary Content Models." *Transformative Works and Cultures* 3. http://dx.doi.org/10.3983/twc.2009.0150.

Scott, Suzanne. 2010. "The Trouble with Transmediation: Fandom's Negotiation of Transmedia Storytelling Systems." *Spectator* 30 (1): 30–4.

Scott, Suzanne. 2012a. "Textual Poachers, Twenty Years Later: A Conversation between Henry Jenkins and Suzanne Scott." In *Textual Poachers: Television Fans and Participatory Culture*, 2nd ed., edited by Henry Jenkins, vii–l. New York: Routledge.

Scott, Suzanne. 2012b. "Who's Steering the Mothership?: The Role of the Fanboy Auteur in Transmedia Storytelling." In *The Routledge Handbook on Participatory Cultures*, edited by Aaron Delwiche and Jennifer Henderson, 43–52. New York: Routledge.

Scott, Suzanne. 2013a. "Dawn of the Undead Author: Fanboy Auteurism and Zack Snyder's 'Vision.'" In *A Companion to Media Authorship*, edited by Jonathan Gray and Derek Johnson, 440–62. Malden, MA: Wiley Blackwell.

Scott, Suzanne. 2013b. "Fangirls in Refrigerators: The Politics of (In)visibility in Comic Book Culture." In "Appropriating, Interpreting, and Transforming Comic Books." *Transformative Works and Cultures* 13. doi:10.3983/twc.2013.0460.

Scott, Suzanne. 2015. "The Moral Economy of Crowdfunding and the Transformative Capacity of Fan-ancing." *New Media and Society* 17 (2): 167–82.

Seabrook, John. 2015. *The Song Machine: Inside the Hit Factory*. London: Jonathan Cape.

SecondSync. 2013. "One Direction Doc Generates Tweet High for Channel 4." August 16. Accessed March 13, 2015. http://secondsync.tumblr.com/post/58416604307/one -direction-doc-generates-tweet-high-for-channel.

Select Committee on Soft Power and the UK's Influence. 2014. "UK Parliament Website." *Persuasion and Power in the Modern World*, March 11. Accessed March 17, 2015. http://www.publications.parliament.uk/pa/ld201314/ldselect/ldsoftpower/150/15002 .htm.

Seymour, Jessica, Jenny Ross, and Monica Flegel. 2015. "*The Lizzie Bennet Diaries*: Fan-Creator Interactions and New Online Storytelling." *Australasian Journal of Popular Culture* 4 (2–3): 99–114.

Shaw, Tony. 2002. "Martyrs, Miracles, and Martians: Religion and Cold War Cinematic Propaganda in the 1950s." *Journal of Cold War Studies* 4 (2): 3–22.

Shelley, Jim. 2013. "'I Would Kill for One Direction': Jim Shelley on the Fanatical Fans Who Would Stalk, Slay and Even Give Their Right Hand, Literally, for One Minute Alone with Their Idols." *Mail Online*, August 17. Accessed April 19, 2015. http://www .dailymail.co.uk/tvshowbiz/article-2395582/I-kill-One-Direction-Jim-Shelley-fanatical -fans-stalk-slay-right-hand-literally-minute-idols.html.

Shinohara, Hiroko. 1998. *Shinema Tokkan Musume* (Rushing cinema girl). Tokyo: Fusō-sha.

Shoard, Catherine. 2015. "Star Wars and 007 Are Coming—Beware the Fanboy Clones." *The Guardian*, "Comment Is Free," October 21. Accessed October 21, 2015. http:// www.theguardian.com/commentisfree/2015/oct/21/star-wars-007-fanboy -clones-film.

Shohat, Ella, and Robert Stam. 1996. "From the Imperial Family to the Transnational Imaginary: Media Spectatorship in the Age of Globalization." In *Global/Local: Cultural Production and the Transnational Imaginary*, edited by Rob Wilson and Wimal Dissanayake, 145–71. Durham, NC: Duke University Press.

Silverstone, Roger. 1999. *Why Study the Media?* London: Sage.

Silverstone, Roger. 2007. *Media and Morality: On the Rise of the Mediapolis*. Cambridge: Polity.

Simmons, Carol. 2005. "And They Called It Puppy Love… Centerville Woman Not Alone Keeping Interest Alive in '70s Pop Icon Donny Osmond." *Dayton Daily News*, May 14.

Simpson, Mark. 2013. "Polymorphous Perversity & One Direction Fandom." *Mark Simpson*, August 23. Accessed February 22, 2015. http://www.marksimpson.com/ blog/2013/08/23/polymorphous-perversity-one-direction-fandom/.

Sotonoff, Jamie, and Joel Reese. 2004. "He's the Manilow: To the People Who Follow Barry Manilow, There's Nothing Funny (or Uncool) about Their Obsession with the Often-Ridiculed Star." *Chicago Daily Herald*, October 1.

Spivak, G. C. 1990. *The Post-Colonial Critic*, edited by Sarah Harasym. New York: Routledge.

Staff, BBC. 2014. "Gay Love Theory as Fans Relish Sherlock in China." *BBC*, January 2. Accessed March 17, 2015. http://www.bbc.com/news/blogs-china-blog-25550426.

Staff, Metro. 2014. "The Chinese Have Fallen in." *The Metro*, January 19. Accessed March 17, 2015. http://metro.co.uk/2014/01/19/the-chinese-have-fallen-in-love-with -sherlock-and-benedict-cumberbatch-whom-they-call-curly-fu-4268744/.

Stanfill, Mel. 2013. "'They're Losers, but I Know Better': Intra-Fandom Stereotyping and the Normalization of the Fan Subject." *Critical Studies in Media Communication* 30 (2): 117–34.

Stanfill, Mel, and Megan Condis. 2014. "Fandom and/as Labor." *Transformative Works and Cultures 15.* http://dx.doi.org/10.3983/twc.2014.0593.

Statham, Nick. 2014. "Ordsall Great-Grandmother Dances Her Way to 100." *Manchester Evening News,* December 10.

Stein, Louisa. 2002. "Subject: 'Off Topic: Oh My God Terrorism': *Roswell* Fans Respond to 11 September." *European Journal of Cultural Studies* 5 (4): 471–91.

Stein, Louisa. 2015. *Millennial Fandom.* Iowa City: University of Iowa Press.

Steinberg, Marc. 2012. *Anime's Media Mix: Franchising Toys and Characters in Japan.* Minneapolis: University of Minnesota Press.

Stever, Gayle. 2013. "Mediated vs. Parasocial Relationships: An Attachment Perspective." *Journal of Media Psychology* 17 (3): 1–31.

Stone, Gregory P., and Ramon A. Oldenberg. 1967. "Wrestling." In *Motivations in Play, Games and Sports,* edited by Ralph Slovenko and James A. Knight, 503–32. Springfield, IL: C.C. Thomas.

Storm, Jo. 2005. *Approaching the Possible: The World of "Stargate SG-1."* Toronto, CA: ECW Press.

Strudwick, Patrick. 2013. "Sherlock Holmes: Boy Story Bromance." *The Independent,* December 17. Accessed October 12, 2015. http://www.independent.co.uk/arts -entertainment/tv/features/sherlock-holmes-boy-story-bromance-9008969.html.

Sturdy, Mark. 2003. *Truth & Beauty: The Story of Pulp.* London: Omnibus Press.

Suler, John. 2004. "The Online Disinhibition Effect." *CyberPsychology and Behavior* 7 (3): 321–6.

Sumner, Darren. 2006. "SCI FI Opens Annual 'Get in the Gate' Contest." *Gateworld,* July 14. Accessed October 20, 2015. http://www.gateworld.net/news/2006/07/sci_fi_opens _annual_get_in_the_g.shtml.

Super. Dir. James Gunn. New York: IFC Films. 2010.

Szalai, Georg. 2014. "'Sherlock' Draws Show's Biggest-Ever U.K. Audience in BBC Return." *Hollywood Reporter,* January 2. Accessed October 18, 2015. http://www .hollywoodreporter.com/news/sherlock-draws-shows-biggest-ever-668188.

Tamagawa, Hiroaki. 2012. "Comiket Market as Space for Self-Expression in Otaku Culture." In *Fandom Unbound: Otaku Culture in a Connected World,* edited by Mitsuki Ito, Daisuke Oikabe, and Izumi Tsuji, 107–31. New Haven, CT: Yale University Press.

Tang, Kevin. 2014. "Inside China's Insane Witch Hunt for Slash Fiction Writers." *Buzzfeed,* April 22. Accessed March 17, 2015. http://www.buzzfeed.com/kevintang/inside -chinas-insane-witch-hunt-for-slash-fiction-writers#.iiZBoDWr6.

Telotte, J. P. 2014. *Science Fiction TV.* New York: Routledge.

The Onion. 2010. "Wrestling Fan's Comments Alternate between Admitting It's Fake, Forgetting It's Fake." March 6. Accessed October 20, 2015. http://www.theonion.com/ articles/wrestling-fans-comments-alternate-between-admittin,16916/.

Theodoropoulou, Vivi. 2007. "The Anti-Fan within the Fan: Awe and Envy in Sports Fandom." In *Fandom: Identities and Communities in a Mediated World,* edited by Jonathan Gray, Cornel Sandvoss, and C. Lee Harrington, 316–27. New York: New York University Press.

Thomas, Bronwen. 2014. "Fans Behaving Badly? Real Person Fic and the Blurring of the Boundaries between the Public and the Private." In *Real Lives, Celebrity Stories: Narratives of Ordinary and Extraordinary People across Media*, edited by Bronwen Thomas and Julia Round, 171–85. London: Bloomsbury.

Thomas, Katie. 2014. "Informative or Exploitative." *York Vision*, February. Accessed October 12, 2015. http://www.yorkvision.co.uk/scene/informative-or -exploitative/04/02/2014.

Thornton, Sarah. 1995. *Club Cultures: Music, Media and Subcultural Capital.* Cambridge: Polity Press.

Toepfer, Shane. 2011. "The Playful Audience: Professional Wrestling, Media Fandom, and the Omnipresence of Media Smarks." PhD diss., Georgia State University.

Tosenberger, Catherine. 2010a. "Love! Valor! *Supernatural!*" *Transformative Works and Cultures* 4. http://dx.doi.org/10.3983/twc.2010.0212.

Tosenberger, Catherine. 2010b. "Saving People, Hunting Things." *Transformative Works and Cultures* 4. http://journal.transformativeworks.org/index.php/twc/issue/view/05.

Trujillo, Nick, Paul Cruz, Georgine Hodgkinson, Heather Hundley, Ahna Ligtenberg Heller, Rebecca Livingston, and Daren Obenaus. 2000. "A Night with the Narcissist and the Nasty Boys: Interpreting the World Wrestling Federation." *Qualitative Inquiry* 6 (4): 526–45.

Tsuji, Izumi. 2012. "Why Study Train Otaku? A Social History of Imagination." In *Fandom Unbound: Otaku Culture in a Connected World*, edited by Mitsuki Ito, Daisuke Oikabe, and Izumi Tsuji, 3–30. New Haven, CT: Yale University Press.

Tulloch, John. 1995. "'We're Only a Speck in the Ocean': The Fans as a Powerless Elite." In *Science Fiction Audiences: Watching "Doctor Who" and "Star Trek,"* edited by John Tulloch and Henry Jenkins, 144–72. New York: Routledge.

Turner, Graeme. 2016. *Re-inventing the Media.* London: Routledge.

Turner, Kate. 2009. "Burnley Woman, 85, Overjoyed To Meet Singing Hero in Blackpool." *Lancashire Evening Telegraph*, September 30.

Twain, Mark, (1876) 1986. *The Adventures of Tom Sawyer.* London: Penguin Books.

Van den Bulck, Hilde, and Jasmijn Van Gorp. 2011. "Eternal Fandom: Elderly Fans, the Media, and the Staged Divorce of a Schlager Singer." *Popular Communication: The International Journal of Media and Culture* 9 (3): 212–26.

Vanderhoef, John. 2013. "Casual Threats: The Feminization of Casual Video Games." *Ada: A Journal of Gender, New Media, and Technology* 2. http://adanewmedia.org/2013/06/ issue2-vanderhoef/.

Ventura, Jesse. 1999. *I Ain't Got Time to Bleed: Reworking the Body Politic from the Bottom Up.* New York: Villard.

Verity, William. 2004. "Salvation Army Salutes Its King as Ball Rolls into Town." *Illawarra Mercury*, March 20.

Vermorel, Fred and Judy Vermorel. (1985) 2011. *Starlust: The Secret Fantasies of Fans.* London: Faber & Faber.

Walker, Cynthia W. 2011. "A Conversation with Paula Smith." *Transformative Works and Cultures* 6. http://dx.doi.org/10.3983/twc.2011.0243.

Waltz, Mitzi. 2005. "Reading Case Studies of People with Autistic Spectrum Disorders: A Cultural Studies Approach to Issues of Disability Representation." *Disability & Society* 20 (4): 421–35.

Wanzo, Rebecca. 2015. "African American Acafandom and Other Strangers: New Genealogies of Fan Studies." *Transformative Works and Cultures* 20. http://dx.doi .org/10.3983/twc.2015.0699.

Ward, Mike. 2013. "*Crazy About One Direction* Was Horrible, Mean-Spirited TV Which Set Out to Humiliate." *Daily Star Sunday*, August 16. Accessed December 2, 2014. http://www.dailystar.co.uk/columnists/mike-ward/332682/Crazy-About-One -Direction-was-horrible-mean-spirited-TV-which-set-out-to-humiliate.

Ward, Susannah. 2014. *Unlocking Sherlock*. Documentary. netflix.com.

Watson, Keith. 2013. "*Crazy About One Direction* Revealed the Disconnect between Fantasy and Reality for 1D Fans." *Metro*, August 16. Accessed December 2, 2014. http://metro.co.uk/2013/08/16/crazy-about-one-direction-revealed-the-disconnect -between-fantasy-and-reality-for-1d-fans-3925446/.

Weller, Martin. 2011. *Digital Scholars: How Technology Is Transforming Scholarly Practice*. New York: Bloomsbury.

West, Candace, and Don H. Zimmerman. 1987. "Doing Gender." *Gender and Society* 1 (2): 125–51.

Westbrook, Caroline. 2012. "One Direction Fans Threaten Taylor Swift over Harry Styles 'Romance.'" *Metro*, November 19. Accessed April 18, 2015. http://metro .co.uk/2012/11/19/one-direction-fans-threaten-taylor-swift-over-harry-styles -romance-500920/.

Wiegman, Robyn. 1999. "Whiteness Studies and the Paradox of Particularity." *Boundary 2* 26 (3): 115–50.

Wilding, Josh. 2012. "Joss Whedon Describes Agent Coulson's 'Man Crush' On Captain America in *The Avengers*." *Comicbookmovie*, March 13. Accessed September 15, 2015. http://www.comicbookmovie.com/fansites/JoshWildingNewsAndReviews/ news/?a=57216.

Wilkinson, Jules. 2010. "A Box of Mirrors, a Unicorn, and a Pony." *Transformative Works and Cultures* 4. http://dx.doi.org/10.3983/twc.2010.0159.

Williams, Andrew. 2007. "60 SECONDS: Russell T Davies." *Metro*, March 28. Accessed October 18, 2015. http://metro.co.uk/2007/03/28/60-seconds-russell-t-davies-234087/.

Williams, Maren. 2014. "Chinese Same-Sex Slash Fic Targeted in Porn Crackdown." *The Comic Book Legal Defense Fund*, April 24. Accessed March 17, 2015. http://cbldf .org/2014/04/chinese-same-sex-slash-fic-targeted-in-porn-crackdown/.

Williams, Michael. 2012. *Film Stardom, Myth and Classicism: The Rise of Hollywood's Gods*. Basingstoke: Palgrave Macmillan.

Williams, Nadine. 2003. "Fans under Cliff's Spell." *The Advertiser*, February 3.

Williams, Rebecca. 2013. "'Anyone Who Calls Muse a *Twilight* Band Will Be Shot on Sight': Music, Distinction, and the 'Interloping Fan' in the *Twilight* Franchise." *Popular Music and Society* 36 (3): 327–42.

Williams, Rebecca. 2015. *Post-Object Fandom: Television, Identity and Self-Narrative*. London: Bloomsbury.

Willis, Ika. 2006. "Keeping Promises to Queer Children: Making Space (for Mary Sue) at Hogwarts." In *Fan Fiction and Fan Communities in the Age of the Internet: New Essays*, edited by Karen Hellekson and Kristina Busse, 153–70, Jefferson, NC: McFarland.

Winston, Brian, ed. 2013. *The Documentary Film Book*. London: BFI.

Wise, Sue. 1990. "Sexing Elvis." In *On Record: Rock, Pop & the Written Word*, edited by Simon Firth and Andrew Goodwin, 390–9. London: Routledge.

Woodworth, Griffin. 2002. "Hackers, Users, and Suits: Napster and Representations of Identity." *Popular Music and Society* 27 (2): 161–84.

Workman, Kimberly Lynn. 2014. "Supernatural 10.05—'Fan Fiction' Recap | Fandomania." *Fandomania*, November 14. Accessed June 1, 2015. http://fandomania.com/ supernatural-10-05-fan-fiction-recap/.

"Wormhole X-Treme!" 2001. *Stargate SG-1*, 5.12. Directed by Peter DeLuise. Beverly Hills, CA: MGM Worldwide, September 8.

Yamashita, Shinji. 2008. "Transnational Migration of Women: Changing Boundaries of Contemporary Japan." In *Multiculturalism in the New Japan: Crossing the Boundaries Within*, edited by Nelson H. H. Graburn, John Ertl, and R. Kenji Tierney, 101–16. New York: Berghahn Books.

Yang, Ling. 2009. "All for Love: The Corn Fandom, Prosumers and the Chinese Way of Creating a Superstar." *International Journal of Cultural Studies* 12 (5): 527–43.

Young, Gerard. 2005. "Yeah, She Thinks He's Sexy!" *Times Colonist*, March 27.

Young, Matthew. 2014. "My Livin' Doll: Cliff Dummy Is Gran's 'Minder.'" *Daily Star*, October 3.

Zhang. 2014. "China's New Internet Crackdown: Not about Porn." *Foreign Policy Magazine—Tea Leaf Nation*, April 16. Accessed March 20, 2015. http://foreignpolicy .com/2014/04/16/chinas-new-internet-crackdown-not-about-porn/.

Zheng, Xiqing, interview by Henry Jenkins. 2013. "The Cultural Context of Chinese Fan Culture: An Interview with Xiqing Zheng (Part One)." *Confessions of an Aca-Fan*, February 1. Accessed October 12, 2015. http://henryjenkins.org/2013/02/the-cultural -context-of-chinese-fan-culture-an-interview-with-xiqing-zheng-part-one.html.

Zhou, Egret. 2013. "Displeasure, Star Chasing and Transcultural Networking Fandom." *Participations* 10 (2): 139–67. http://www.participations.org/Volume%2010/Issue%20 2/8.pdf.

Ziering-Koffman, Amy and Kirby Dick. 2002. *Derrida*. New York: Zeitgeist.

Zubernis, Lynn, and Kathy Larsen. 2012. *Fandom at the Crossroads: Celebration, Shame and Fan/Producer Relationships*. Newcastle: Cambridge University Press.

Index

hyperfan 3, 104, 267, 272
hyperserialization 34

immersion 34–5, 79
Inspector Spacetime 95, 253
internalized shame. *See* shame,
    internalized
intersectionality 188
intra-fandom 54, 60–1, 64, 210, 268
Iron Maiden 21

Japan 164, 230, 233, 243–4, 248, 251, 255
Japanese female fans 230, 239–41, 243–4,
    246–8, 257–9
Japanese popular culture 252–3, 260–1
Japanese regional identity 230, 240, 242–3,
    256
jargon 35
Jensen, Joli 3, 97, 108, 197, 203
journalism 42, 129, 252, 259

Kripke, Eric 141, 145, 146, 148, 150, 152
    n.3

Larry shippers 5, 54, 58, 59, 60–4, 79, 80,
    85–7, 88. *See also* Larry Stylinson
Larry Stylinson 5, 54, 58, 59, 60–4, 65 n.4
literary adaptation 169–79
Lizzie Bennet Diaries, The 169–70, 171–9
local celebrity. *See* localebrity
localebrity 23, 26, 29–32, 199
lowbrow 33

manga 230, 251–60
Marvel Cinematic Universe 163, 165
Mary Sue 7, 93, 159–68, 268
masculinity 28, 67–8, 71, 117, 147, 159,
    167, 171, 181, 187–91, 194–5, 242–3,
    249
media effects 34, 42
media literacy 170, 178–9, 207
memorabilia, also merchandise 27, 59,
    96–7, 100–1, 141, 199–201, 204, 206,
    265
Merlin 166–7
meta episode 114, 134, 139–40, 148
Metallica 13, 17–21
metaphor 92, 103, 107–11, 150, 200, 237

metatext 112–14
Moffat, Steven 118, 121–5, 167, 230, 269
moral dualism 68, 76
music fandom. *See* fandom of music

neocolonialism 209–12, 216–18
neoliberalism 195, 209–10, 212, 269,
    271–2
New Adventures of Peter and Wendy, The
    169, 173, 175–7, 180
news 1, 7, 82, 115 n.2, 129, 187, 232, 270
newspaper 7, 54, 76, 197–207, 233, 240
niche audience 96, 170, 174
normativity 188–9, 190, 195

older fans/mature fans 197–207, 251, 259
One Direction 5, 24, 53–65, 67–77, 79–88,
    184, 269
Online fandom 62, 64, 72–3, 85, 87,
    119–20, 164, 166–7, 169–80, 182, 184,
    213–16
otaku 8, 243, 251–61, 272

pathologization of fandom 1, 3–4, 8, 17,
    31, 34, 61, 71, 74, 79–80, 97–8, 108–14,
    120, 130, 155, 187–8, 197–8, 229–37,
    246–8, 267–8, 271–2
performance 35–43, 53–65, 69–77, 79–83,
    88, 99–100, 154, 170, 176, 178, 210,
    229–30, 268–9
performance studies 39, 42
performativity 34, 39, 54, 60–5, 70, 83, 166
Perkins, Emily 6, 141, 147, 153–6
place 25, 31, 57, 72, 156, 210, 255, 258
pop music 13, 21, 53, 54, 68, 80, 198, 241,
    269
postcolonialism 210, 212, 216–18
postcolonialism, digital 216–17
Presley, Elvis 54, 74–5, 156, 202
privilege 7, 15, 20, 24, 57, 128, 147, 187–8,
    191, 195, 210, 214, 216
privilege, white 187, 188, 191
professional wrestling 9 n.1, 33–43
pseuicide 85
Pulp 23–32

queer identity 79–80, 86, 149, 161–2, 169,
    195, 210, 213, 230, 235, 258

Made in the USA
Columbia, SC
09 March 2018